For the past forty years, Dr Denis Hayes has ministered in a lay capacity to numerous churches and chapels, largely in the English Midlands and the South-West of England. In addition to writing and speaking, Denis's interests include singing, running a church-based choral group, writing poetry, guitar, and puppet presentations for children.

Denis taught at five schools before training teachers and researching education themes. He has authored nineteen books. Denis is married with two adult children and is a member of an independent evangelical church.

For all my friends and fellow believers whose encouragement, insights and advice have helped to sharpen my thinking and shape my understanding over many years.

Denis Hayes

TOTALLY CHRISTIAN

AUSTIN MACAULEY PUBLISHERS™

LONDON * CAMBRIDGE * NEW YORK * SHARJAH

A CIP catalogue record for this title is available from the British Library.

ISBN 9781035854912 (Paperback)
ISBN 9781035854929 (ePub e-book)

www.austinmacauley.com

First Published 2024
Austin Macauley Publishers Ltd®
1 Canada Square
Canary Wharf
London
E14 5AA

Table of Contents

Foreword

The aim of *Totally Christian* is to demonstrate the uniqueness and wonder of the life, teaching and mission of Jesus Christ, who was 'fully God and fully human', together with the ramifications of his ministry for our lives and eternal futures.

The content is scripturally grounded (i.e., using the Bible as the major source material) and written in plain language. Assumptions are carefully examined, uncertainty acknowledged, and alternative viewpoints presented transparently. Bible quotations are mainly taken from the New Living Translation (NLT) and the New International Version UK (NIVUK). Other translations used include the King James' Version (KJV); the New King James' Version (NKJV); the New Revised Standard Version (NRSV); the Easy-to-Read Version (ERV); the Contemporary English Version (CEV) and the Amplified Bible (AMB).

Readers don't need to be Bible scholars to enjoy and benefit from *Totally Christian*. Rather, the following pages will appeal to anyone who is sincerely interested in the teaching, work, witness and impact of this extraordinary man, Jesus of Nazareth, and wish to draw closer to the one who, among his numerous other titles, is referred to as 'the Man of Calvary' where he offered his life as a ransom for the sins of the world.

Book Structure

Totally Christian is divided into six sections, each consisting of two chapters.

Part 1 (Chapters 1 and 2) introduces the person of Jesus and exposes some of the misconceptions about him.

Part 2 (Chapters 3 and 4) focuses on the key issue of sin and its devastating impact on humankind, notably our relationship with God, behaviour, life priorities and eternal future. Chapter 4 exposes the devastating effect that sin has unleashed on the world.

Part 3 (Chapters 5 and 6) provides a biblical perspective on God's answer to the destructive nature of sin and the way in which Jesus Christ's redemptive act by dying on the Cross of Calvary is central to finding forgiveness from sin's consequences and a restored life through being 'born again' of the Spirit of God. Chapter 6 explores the various demands and opportunities facing the church, a theme that is expanded in Chapter 10.

Part 4 (Chapters 7 and 8) looks at the many blessings and challenges attached to following the 'narrow way' that Jesus invites every person to take, stressing that discipleship is not an easy option, but involves sacrifice, as well as considerable blessings, all of which are rooted in our willingness to abide in Christ.

Part 5 (Chapters 9 and 10) underlines the need for wholehearted commitment to Christ and develops a number of key themes from the previous chapters, including the difficult subject of suffering for Christ's sake. Chapter 10 explores the privilege and obstacles faced by Christians in sharing the good news of the Gospel.

Part 6 (Chapters 11 and 12) covers the ways in which every believer can and should seek to emulate Jesus and enrich their daily walk with him, emphasising the importance of endurance in 'running the race of life' to its conclusion. Chapter 12 draws together many of the threads from the book to demonstrate the significance attached to becoming more like Jesus, especially in the light of his return to close world history, referred to as the Second Coming or Second Advent. The reality of eternal life in Heaven for believers is presented as a joyful prospect that they should eagerly anticipate.

Challenges

If you decide to engage diligently with the content of the book, expect to enlarge your understanding of what Jesus accomplished by delving into the fascinating elements of his life and being confronted by his powerful, radical teaching and the challenges that face those who take seriously his ministry on earth and its implications for godly living.

The book's purpose is not only intended to reinforce familiar truths but also to provoke and prompt each person to decide where he or she stands on the issues raised. I pray that everyone will find something of value to deepen faith and fortify trust in our unfailing God, encourage a diligent search of the Scriptures, pray more fervently, provoke discussion, and inspire a stronger desire to serve the One who described himself as the Way, the Truth and the Life; and the Light of the world.

At the end of each chapter, questions or statements to ponder and stimulate thought are listed for discussion and prayer, together with *Insight* boxes at intervals throughout the book containing relevant information and helpful background details.

Referencing and Nomenclature

To minimise the use of capitals, I have employed small case letters when referring to Jesus (thus: he, him and his) and large case when referring to God (thus: He, Him and His). When referring to New Testament writers, I have normally used their regular names: Matthew, Mark, Luke, John, Peter, Paul and Jude. For Bible references, I condense the chapter and verse of the letter or book; for example, John 3:16 refers to the Gospel of John chapter three, verse sixteen; 2 Peter 3:13 refers to the Apostle Peter's second letter, chapter three, verse thirteen. Similarly, 1 Samuel 16:7 refers to the first Book of Samuel, chapter sixteen, verse seven. The 2nd and third letters of John and the Letter of Jude both consist of a single chapter, so only the verse number is referenced; for example, 2 John 7 refers to the second letter of John, verse 7; Jude 18 refers to the letter of Jude, verse eighteen.

I use 'apostle' on numerous occasions throughout the book. The word is derived from the Greek word *apostolos* meaning 'one who is sent or commissioned'; thus, an apostle is a messenger sent to spread the news of salvation found in Christ. The same description is also applied to Jesus, who was 'sent by God': 'Therefore, holy brothers and sisters, who share in the heavenly calling, fix your thoughts on Jesus, whom we acknowledge as our Apostle and High Priest' (Hebrews 3:1, NIVUK). Although an apostle was the appellation initially given to the twelve disciples, it was later also given to Saul, usually referred to by his Roman name, Paul, as he had an in-person encounter with Jesus on his way to Damascus.

Reference will be made to a number of *Old Testament prophets* who lived before Jesus was born on earth and were used as sacred human messengers by God. Prophets fulfilled a dual role:

1. To declare God's message to the people living at that time, notably to the Jews.
2. To give warning of future events and consequences of sinful actions.
   The prophecies of Isaiah, Jeremiah, Ezekiel, Daniel, Joel, Amos, Hosea and Micah are particularly relevant. Other Old Testament books cited include Psalms and Proverbs, both of which consist of divinely inspired poetry, wise advice about human behaviour, expressions of praise to the Lord, warnings about the consequences of opposition to the will and purpose of God, and insights into His nature and relationship with people and nations.

Confidence in the Revealed Word of God

Exploring the person and influence of Jesus Christ is a daunting task, not only because he was a unique character in history but also because we rely on written testimonies in the New Testament of the Bible for most of the information about his life, conduct, mission and status. Interpreting the evidence about Jesus therefore invites careful examination of the Bible text. The key to discovering the truth is to accept the contents as unembellished and trustworthy, and a faithful record of eyewitness accounts and divine revelation given to the writers. Any attempt to override the veracity of the Scriptures using intellectual arguments, imposing contemporary social norms or basing textual analysis on humanistic, ungodly philosophy is doomed to fail and invites confusion rather than enlightenment.

Jesus promised that God the Holy Spirit will reveal all truth to us, as John records in his Gospel account: 'But I will send you the Advocate, the Spirit of truth. He will come to you from the Father and will testify all about me' (15:26, NLT). So when unsure or 'limping between two opinions'—as Joshua in the Old Testament expressed the unsatisfactory nature of people dithering about whether or not to follow God; see also Jesus's severe response to people who are half-hearted in their commitment to Him (Revelation 3:16)—we should turn to the One who knows all things, rather than swinging from one earthly narrative to another in a desperate search for certainty. Factual knowledge about Bible content is useful, but heavenly wisdom and Holy Spirit-inspired discernment that brings enlightenment are essential requirements for those who genuinely aspire to live a life that is 'Totally Christian'.

Insight

The place of Jesus's execution is referred to as Calvary or Golgotha.

Both words refer to the 'place of the skull' or 'bald head', owing to the skull-shaped topography of the hill in Jerusalem where Jesus forfeited his life. The word Calvary is derived from Latin, whereas Golgotha is derived from Aramaic, though most of the New Testament was written in 'common' (not classical) Greek, so as to be accessible by ordinary people. However, Calvary and Golgotha are one and the same place. The word Calvary will be used throughout the book to denote the location of Jesus's death on the cross.

Part 1
Discovering Jesus

John 1:1–5, 14

In the beginning was the Word and the Word was with God and the Word was God. He was with God in the beginning. Through him all things were made; without him nothing was made that has been made. In him was life and that life was the light of men. The light shines in the darkness and the darkness has not overcome it… The Word became flesh and made his dwelling among us. We have seen his glory, the glory of the One and only, who came from the Father, full of grace and truth (NLT).

1 Corinthians 1:15–20

Christ is the image of the invisible God, the firstborn over all creation. For by him all things were created: things in heaven and on earth, visible and invisible, whether thrones or powers or rulers or authorities; all things were created by him and for him. He is before all things, and in him all things hold together. And he is the head of the body, the church; he is the beginning and the firstborn from among the dead, so that in everything he might have the supremacy. For God was pleased to have all his fullness dwell in him, and through him to reconcile to himself all things, whether things on earth or things in heaven, by making peace through his blood, shed on the cross (NIVUK).

2 Corinthians 4:3–7

If the Good News we preach is hidden behind a veil, it is hidden only from people who are perishing. Satan, who is the god of this world, has blinded the minds of those who don't believe. They are unable to see the glorious light of the Good News. They don't understand this message about the glory of Christ, who is the exact likeness of God.

You see we don't go around preaching about ourselves. We preach that Jesus Christ is Lord and we ourselves are your servants for Jesus's sake. For God who said, "Let there be light in the darkness," has made this light shine in our hearts, so we could know the glory of God that is seen in the face of Jesus Christ. We now have this light shining in our hearts, but we ourselves are like fragile clay jars containing this great treasure ['like treasure in clay jars']. This makes it clear that our great power is from God, not from ourselves (NLT).

Preface to Part 1

The desire to explore our ancestry and discover something about our family roots has seen a surge in popularity over recent years. A number of televised programmes focus on helping people to find their distant relatives, reconciling broken families, and unearthing facts about historic events. These searches and investigations sometime reveal remarkable circumstances, episodes and relationships that have been buried over time. In Part 1, I attempt to 'break open' the past while exploring the life, words and deeds of Jesus, together with some of the misconceptions, about his identity and significance. In doing so, I reveal him to be the one he claimed to be: both God and man, who gave his life on a cross to save people from their sins.

Chapter 1
Truth and Myth About Jesus

Introduction

In this opening chapter, I establish a number of issues that will be developed and expanded in later sections of the book concerning Jesus's appearance, the reason he came to earth to live as a man, his role as teacher and Saviour, and the way in which his actions confirmed that he is truly the Light of the World who provides the light of life to all his followers (John 8:12). His words and actions point the way and provide the supreme model for every person who sincerely seeks to live as God intends.

Outward Appearance

Most of us have had the experience of meeting someone who obviously knows us, but despite recognising the person's face, we simply cannot recall his or her name or when we have previously met. Occasionally, we may not have the slightest idea who the person is, in which case we make stuttering attempts to gain a clue through casual conversation that will help us discover the stranger's identity.

Lookalike and counterfeit

Over recent years, it has been quite fashionable to hold lookalike competitions in which the contestants have to dress up or change their appearance to resemble a celebrity or a member of the Royal Family or a political leader. Some of the disguises are very convincing and there are even a few people who can truly claim to possess a likeness to the individual concerned without altering their features unduly. The counterfeit individual may not only look the part but also sound convincing; even so, we know in our hearts that it isn't the real person but simply a caricature and admirable attempt at imitation. Once the pretenders remove the make-up and revert to their true appearance, speech and behaviour, the facade is exposed.

A famous example of acting under false pretences is in the film *Singing in the Rain* (released in 1952) in which 'talking pictures' are replacing silent movies. An unknown singer/actress has to substitute for the real silent movie actress, who has a squeaky voice, so is wholly unsuitable for a speaking role (so-called 'dubbing'). The substitute remains out of sight while speaking and singing, while the up-front performer merely mimes and receives the accolades that rightly belong to the lady behind the scenes. As the plot unravels, we find that the audience, though initially fooled by the deceit, eventually discovers the truth. The genuine performer then enjoys the acclaim, while the pretender is dismissed in disgrace.

Social conventions

It is undeniably true that everybody adjusts his or her appearance and behaviour under different social conditions. Contrast the merry conversation at a birthday party with the sobriety when giving evidence in a court of law. Similarly, the same person who wears informal clothing at a barbecue will be formally attired when attending a job interview. Even allowing for such variations across different social circumstances, it is true that based on their outward appearance, speech and behaviour, people are not always whom they appear to be. Even in church and other Christian meetings, a degree of 'disguise' can exist. Thus, the gracious and friendly person in church meetings can behave in a markedly less charitable way at home or at work, while the unresponsive person in church may burst into life when situated in more comfortable and familiar surroundings.

There may be, of course, a perfectly legitimate explanation for these variations in behaviour that do not involve wilful deceit. For instance, an apparently aloof and unfriendly person may be shy or lacking confidence; the person with a jolly demeanour may hide inner turmoil and unease; the reserved person may be desperate to enjoy social interaction but lack the necessary conversational skills to express her or his feelings. Nevertheless, being consistent (that is, behaving naturally) and avoiding craftiness or duplicity should be the hallmark of every follower of Jesus, who epitomises authenticity, as I explore below and in greater depth later in the book.

One of the unfortunate outcomes of using outward appearance to determine a person's character is to jump to a wrong conclusion based on dress, speech or habits. I recall a time some years ago when I was driving through the local town and noticed a man shuffling along the pavement (sidewalk) shabbily dressed and clearly unwashed. My instinctive reaction was, I now regret to admit, one of revulsion. But the Lord by His Spirit spoke into my heart with these simple but profound words: 'This is someone for whom Christ died'. That moment changed my life and attitude, hopefully for good! I was reminded of what the Lord said to the Old Testament prophet, Samuel, when choosing a king for Israel: 'Don't judge by his appearance or height, for I have rejected him. The Lord doesn't see things the way you see them. People judge by outward appearance but the Lord looks at the heart' (1 Samuel 16:7, NLT). Too often, we judge by first impressions or the views expressed by other people, and fail to allow the love of Jesus to motivate us and give us a heart for those we see and meet.

The Genuine Jesus

His coming to earth

The Christmas story is arguably one of the most celebrated, yet misrepresented events in history. The biblical account of Mary and Joseph's journey to Bethlehem and the subsequent birth of Jesus—described in great detail by Luke—has been elaborated and commercialised in such a way that it deviates considerably from the true circumstances.

While accepting the meticulous accuracy of events disclosed in the Bible narrative and dismissing the frivolous embellishment, it is reasonable to speculate that Mary and Joseph did not travel alone, especially in Mary's advanced stage of pregnancy and in consideration of the long and dangerous journey they undertook. We might also speculate that it is unlikely that she gave birth without the aid of a local midwife.

The Bible account does not make any mention of Mary riding a donkey or of an innkeeper or a stable. Bethlehem was anything but 'silent', as the famous Carol, *Silent Night*, depicts, as the Inn was full, and many Jews from across the nation would have identified the town as their place of origin. There is no evidence that the angels had wings, though perhaps the fact that they flew would indicate such. The idea presented by numerous carols that the shepherds slipped silently in and out of the place where Jesus was lying in a manger conflicts with

Luke's description of the shepherds sharing the news excitedly with the local population.

Finally, the popular Christmas card scene of a gentle maiden dressed in a blue robe and serenely nursing her baby son, while glowing from a heavenly light and attendant angels, sanitises the reality of the filthy conditions and smells associated with an animal pen that the family must have endured. There were no sterile conditions or advanced medical aids or trained doctors on hand to ensure a safe delivery. Jesus came to earth in humility; in the words of Isaiah the prophet: 'There was nothing beautiful or majestic about his appearance, nothing to attract us to him' (53:2b, NLT).

In these matters, we must try to ground the events in the information that Matthew and Luke provide, while envisaging the practicalities and circumstances of life during that time period. Despite the conjecture and uncertainty about the details of the Virgin Birth, one thing is gloriously certain, as John summarises in his Gospel account concerning Jesus's coming to earth: 'The Word became flesh and made his dwelling among us. We have seen his glory, the glory of the one and only Son, who came from the Father, full of grace and truth' (1:14, NLT).

Insight

Mary (or in Hebrew, Miriam, named after Moses' sister from the Book of Exodus) is almost certainly the most famous woman in history, as she was chosen by God to bear Jesus and nurse him through his infancy and childhood. Mary's family origin is a subject of debate, though her birthplace was probably in Nazareth. When Jesus began his formal ministry, there was a period of time when Mary and other members of the family considered him to be insane, so she was certainly subject to human failings. Mary should be admired and acknowledged as exceptional but not seen as the focus for our prayers or proclaimed as 'the Queen of Heaven'. Such unbiblical claims about Mary's status probably explain why she has little prominence in non-Catholic church life, which is regrettable, as Mary was chosen specially by God to bear the Saviour of the world, and deserves acknowledgement and respect.

Depictions of Jesus

While the facts about Jesus's birth have been prone to distortion and exaggeration by non-scriptural additions and conjecture, the same charge can be brought about depictions of the adult Jesus. There is a popular perception of Jesus that he drifted through life effortlessly, dressed in celestial clothing and resembling one of the Old Testament prophets with a long beard and shining robes. The reality was almost certainly different from this stereotypical portrayal. As a child, Jesus would have assisted his earthly father, Joseph, in his employment as a carpenter and builder, so would have developed a strong physique and large hands. Even the lyrics from the famous children's hymn by Charles Wesley, *Gentle Jesus, meek and mild*, can offer the false impression that Jesus was fragile and shy, a description which contrasts sharply with the fearlessness and moral courage he displayed during his childhood and later ministry.

In the opening section of his Gospel account, John begins to unravel the mystery of Jesus's origin, status and role. John records that Jesus became physically weary: 'Jacob's well was there, and Jesus, tired out by his journey, was sitting by the well. It was about noon' (4:6, NRSV), so he suffered from bodily fatigue and needed times of rest and recuperation (see Mark Chapter 6). Jesus was moved to tears as he considered how far the people of Jerusalem had neglected the faith of their ancestors, and wept at the death of his friend, Lazarus (John Chapter 11). Jesus walked long miles from village-to-village and town-to-town, so he must have worn travelling clothes (simple and functional), not adorned with flowing, colourful robes like the religious leaders. Unrealistic depictions of Jesus may have created unwarranted scepticism from modern prospective followers, and helped to create a mythology about him as something of a fantasy figure, thereby detracting from his origin and purpose for coming to earth as a man.

While we don't have a clear picture of Jesus's human appearance, the Gospel writers refer to an occasion when he took three of the disciples, Peter, James and John, up a mountain to be alone, as related in Mark Chapter 9. Two of the Gospel writers (Mark and Luke) describe how Jesus's appearance was transformed and his clothes became dazzling white, as he spoke with two of the Old Testament prophets, Moses and Elijah. This amazing event gave a foretaste of Jesus's heavenly glory and the life to come. Little wonder that in the final chapter of the Bible (Revelation 22) Jesus describes himself as the Morning Star. It is an exciting prospect to know that when we see Jesus face to face in Heaven, he will shine as strongly as the brightest star imaginable. In human appearance, however, Jesus was probably little different from those with whom he mingled, other than his look of serenity, due to the absence of sin in his life. I return to the importance of presenting fact not fantasy about Jesus at the beginning of Chapter 12.

Perceptions of Jesus

When people are asked about the nature, character and relevance of Jesus Christ, the question inevitably invites a wide variety of responses; but unless the respondent has a particularly cynical view of life, it is unlikely that any serious person would suggest that Jesus was an imposter. The Jesus of the Bible was wholly transparent and, whatever an individual's view of his teaching and ministry might be, Jesus's honesty and sincerity can never be in doubt when viewed objectively.

Surveying the general public about the person of Jesus is likely to elicit a range of answers; for example, that he was someone in the Bible, a baby in Bethlehem, a prophet, a mythical figure, a good man, or 'not really sure who he was'. These sorts of responses not only reveal a confusion about Jesus and the reason for his coming to live as a man on earth but also betray a lack of understanding about the seriousness of sin (broadly defined as living for 'self' and failing to give God His rightful place; see Part 2) and the length to which Jesus was prepared to go in order to save the human race from self-destruction. Jesus's claim that those who have seen him have, in fact, seen Father God must rank among the most astounding statements that have ever been uttered (John 14:9).

Although the majority of sceptics might be willing to accept Jesus's genuineness and the absence of guile in his ministry, they may question whether he was the one that he claimed to be, namely, the Jewish Messiah and the Saviour of the whole world, whose death on the cross would atone for each person's sin and open up the possibility of eternal life in the presence of God after earthly life has ended.

Accepting the historical facts that Jesus lived as a man and did amazing and exceptional things during his lifetime is staggering in its own right but his role as sin-bearer eclipses all other relevant aspects of his life and ministry. The Bible account describes Jesus as 'paying the price' to reconcile (i.e., bring back into close relationship) God and humankind that sin threatened to corrupt and destroy. The issue of sin and its impact on people is more fully explored in Chapters 3 and 4.

Imposters and charlatans

If we accept the truth as revealed in the Bible, Jesus Christ possessed wholly unique characteristics that set him apart from any person that has lived. He is supremely positioned above and beyond the synthetic 'gods' of mythology, folklore and even the most famous and adored celebrities. All the so-called 'superheroes' of fictional fame cannot heal the sick, grant sight to the blind or raise the dead! The Jesus of the Bible was God in human form; he was fully 'in the image of God', sinless and without equal. In his letter to the Christians at Colossae, Paul was explicit in his description of Jesus: 'Christ is the image of the invisible God, the firstborn over all creation' (Colossians 1:15, NLT).

Despite the incontrovertible evidence about the uniqueness of Jesus, large numbers of people have convinced themselves or attempted to convince others that they are his reincarnation, the majority of whom have met sad or tragic ends. The Apostle Matthew records that Jesus warned of such pretence: 'Don't let anyone mislead you, for many will come in my name, claiming: "I am the Messiah." They will deceive many' (24:4, NLT). A very small sample from history of the dozens of men exhibiting delusional behaviour of this kind include:

- Arnold Potter (1804–1872), who claimed that the Spirit of Jesus Christ entered into his body and he became "Potter Christ, Son of the living God." He died in an attempt to 'ascend into heaven' by jumping off a cliff.
- Jones Very (1813–1880) was an American essayist, poet and Greek tutor at Harvard, who suffered a nervous breakdown in 1837, after which he claimed to have become the Second Coming of Jesus.
- More infamously, Sun Myung Moon (1920–2012) claimed to be the Messiah and the Second Coming of Christ, thereby fulfilling Jesus's unfinished mission. Former 'Moonie' members have alleged that they were brainwashed and had goods and property stolen. Its leader was jailed in 1984 for tax evasion; two of his sons met untimely deaths.
- Wayne Bent (born 1941), also known as Michael Travesser, claimed that he was the embodiment of God, a combination of humanity and divinity. He was convicted on 15th December 2008 on two counts of contributing to the delinquency of a minor.

The list of such deviants and confused individuals is extensive and fulfils precisely the warning that Jesus made about imposters. As the Apostle Paul informed the Philippian Christians (2:10–11), when the unique Jesus returns, every eye shall see him, every knee shall bow and every tongue confess that he is Lord, to the glory of God. There won't be any room for doubt or deception when the Son of God returns to judge the earth: all will be laid bare.

Jesus the Saviour

Personal trust in Jesus

It is noteworthy that on at least one occasion, Jesus asked his close disciples, known as 'The Twelve', also referred to as 'Apostles'—those who had been selected by Jesus from the larger number of his disciples to serve as principal purveyors of the Good News—"Who do people say that I am?" (Mark 8:27, NLT) The disciples replied that the people were offering a variety of suggestions, including claims that he was a reincarnated Elijah, Jeremiah or another of the prophets from what we now refer to as the Old Testament—the time prior to Jesus coming to earth as a baby. Jesus listened to the disciples' answers but then asked the searching question as to who *they* believed him to be. Peter was quickest to reply and affirmed that Jesus was indeed the promised Messiah (Saviour / Anointed One) sent from (on behalf of / in the form of) God the Father.

The fact that Jesus was given the name is significant because Joseph, his earthly guardian, would normally have called the first son after himself but was told by a heavenly messenger (an angel) to call him Jesus because he would save his people from their sins (Matthew 1:20–21). As the psalmist prophesied: 'Sing a new song to the Lord, for he has done wonderful deeds. His right hand has won a mighty victory. His holy arm has shown his saving power!' (98:1, NLT)

Insight

Moses' successor, Joshua, was originally named Hoshea but Moses changed it to Yehoshua, which means 'God is salvation'.

The name was shortened to Yeshua / Jeshua during the Babylonian Exile (roughly 700BC). When the Greek New Testament was written, the Greek name Yesous was used for Yeshua, but when Yesous was Latinized it became Jesus.

The Gospel writers recorded in detail Jesus's question to his disciples and the subsequent discourse because the question about his true identity was, and remains, vitally important. Expressing a belief in *who* Jesus is, as well as the fact of his existence, is a challenge to which each person must make his or her own response. Silence on the matter is acceptable only for as long as it takes the individual time to give serious consideration to the issue; as far as Jesus is concerned, neutrality or indifference is unacceptable. He is either the Saviour he claimed to be or an imposter, only worthy of contempt.

Our reply to the question that Jesus posed is probably the most important answer we can give to any question because our eternal destiny hinges on our belief about him and the truth of the Gospel of salvation that he declared. Such belief acknowledges the need for personal repentance—recognising past failings and a determination to follow God's way in future—and acceptance that he is Saviour and Lord, leading to forgiveness of sin and freedom to live life as God intends, together with the prospect of enjoying a glorious afterlife. Importantly, we are invited to believe *in* Jesus (i.e., responding to his invitation to be his follower and accepting him as Lord of all) and not merely *about* him (i.e., accepting the historical evidence but remaining detached from individual commitment to him). Mere acquiescence about his identity and reason for his human existence is not sufficient, as even the devil knows *about* Jesus!

Jesus from first to last

In John's record, we find the most remarkable claims about Jesus that sets him apart from, and above, every person who has ever existed or will ever exist. John explains that Jesus was present at the beginning of time—indeed, before the start of time, as we understand the concept. Jesus stated plainly: "Before Abraham was even born, I am" (8:28, NLT). In other words, Jesus pre-existed the life of Abraham, a man who was used by God to be the forerunner of faith-based believers throughout history, including followers of Jesus, originally referred to as 'followers of the Way' and later as 'Christians'.

When some members of the crowd picked up stones to kill Jesus at one point in his ministry, they justified their actions by claiming that it wasn't because of the miracles or good deeds that he had performed but because he was claiming to be God (John 19:31–33). Similarly, when Jesus referred to himself in the Temple Court as the 'I Am', some of the Jews attempted to stone him for blasphemy (John 8:58–59). It is significant that in the revelation given by God to the Apostle John, both God the Father and Jesus the Son are referred to as the 'first and the last' or the 'Alpha and Omega'; see the Book of Revelation Chapter 1 (with reference to the Father) and Chapter 22 (with reference to the Son).

There is a Bible time-line that leads from before the world's creation, through the period of the Patriarchs (Abraham and onward), and the history of Israel—entering the Promised Land (see the Book of Joshua); inviting the wrath of God through idolatry; conquest by foreign nations (notably Assyria and Babylonia); re-establishment of national identity following the return to Israel and the rebuilding of Jerusalem (see the Books of Ezra and Nehemiah)—and several hundred more years of largely unrecorded history until the birth of Jesus in Bethlehem. Details of these events and periods of history lie outside the scope of this book but the key elements include the fall into sin at the start of human history; the requirement to repent and worship the one true God, Jehovah; and the prospect of a coming Saviour (Messiah) who would die and rise again to reconcile (bring closely together in an intimate relationship) human beings and God. One of the many remarkable features of the Bible is the way in which events, prophecies and the coming of Jesus harmonise to reveal God's plan of salvation.

Insight

A lot of information about the person of Jesus is found in John's Gospel. John was from Capernaum on the north coast of the Sea of Galilee, about 20 miles from Nazareth (the childhood home of Jesus) working with his father and elder brother, James, in the family fishing business. John was a first cousin of Jesus, as his mother, Salome, the wife of Zebedee, was the sister of Jesus's mother Mary. It is therefore very likely that Jesus and John were acquainted prior to Jesus commencing his full-time ministry at age thirty.

Jesus: Word and Light

Jesus the Word

It has been estimated that there are at least fifty representations of Jesus declared in the pages of the Bible. One of the most powerful descriptions of Jesus is 'The Word' (based on the Greek word *logos*), not only because his spoken words carry great authority but also because, astonishingly, he was the one who 'spoke' the world into existence. We read in John's Gospel Chapter 1 that all things were made through Him and nothing was made without him, so he was and continues to be, the manager and gatekeeper of creation. He is the one who ensures that the world in its present form (human beings, creatures, plant life and physical composition) is sustained. Put simply, the Son of God, who was given the name Jesus while on earth, keeps the world functioning; without him, it would fall into decay (perish), which is the same term applied to people who die without accepting Christ into their lives. The writer of the Book of Hebrews— the author is likely to have been Paul or Apollos or Barnabas—graphically expresses the truth about the Son of God: 'The Son is the radiance of God's glory and the exact representation of his being, sustaining all things by his powerful word' (1:3a, NIVUK).

It is sadly the case that places on earth where Jesus is rejected or disregarded are usually characterised by lawlessness, hatred and hopelessness. Jesus brings light and life to every situation and to each individual who turns to him in faith and repentance. In words taken from the title of Noel Richards' well-loved song, there is power in the name of Jesus. It is little wonder that after the death of Jesus, frightening physical phenomena took place, including earthquakes, graves opening and representations of the dead seen in Jerusalem. It is reasonable to speculate that if Jesus had remained dead, the whole earth would have fallen into ruin within a short period of time, deprived of his sustaining power.

Jesus the light

Jesus also refers to himself as 'The Light', as John records in his Gospel (8:12) He went on to explain to his disciples that if we follow him, we will not have to walk in *spiritual* darkness—unaware of our sinfulness and need of a Saviour—because we will have the light that leads to fullness of life, as God intends and offers to all believers. The light to which Jesus referred is not physical light that can be seen in numerous natural and artificial forms but the pure Spirit-generated light that dispels the world's moral, social and relationship darkness and replaces it with hope, peace and confidence for the present and the future.

Just as Moses was inspired and addressed directly by God through the burning bush episode on Mount Sinai (Exodus Chapter 3), so the pure light of Christ fills us with fresh impetus and direction for our lives. Mark records that Jesus referred to the incident of the burning bush when responding to the trickery of religious leaders by emphasising that God is the God of the living, not of the dead (12:26–27).

A major challenge for followers of Jesus is that in addition to calling himself 'the light', he spoke of them in precisely the same way: 'You are the light of [Christ to] the world. A city set on a hill cannot be hidden' (Matthew 5:14, AMP). Such light is not a reflected one that relies on an external source, such as the dull surface of the moon reflecting the sun's rays and thereby appearing bright. The powerful light of believers is produced by the Holy Spirit's presence that radiates *from within* to touch and benefit the lives of others and thereby bring glory to God. The more that Christians submit to the will and purpose of God, the greater their brightness becomes.

The brightness of Jesus's presence is seen to a greater or lesser extent in every one of his followers, for they carry his flame of pure love within them and reveal it through every expression of kindness, good deeds and loving actions. The light of Jesus is not a burning glare that harms the eyes of the beholder; rather, it emanates purity to fill believers with peace and joy, and to bless those who experience it. In the same way that he is the Light, Jesus challenges his followers to be lights in a dark world that shine for all to see and bring glory to God. See also later in this chapter under 'Jesus's teaching'.

The testimony of all disciples of Jesus is that as they receive his light, they gradually understand more clearly the significance and meaning of life, and are better able to distinguish between the thoughts, words and actions that please God and those that offend Him. Christians express this revelation in various ways but commonly describe it using phrases such as 'once I was blind but now I see' or by invoking a powerful image, such as 'the scales fell from my eyes'.

Defender of the Poor and Needy

Old Testament teaching

The Old Testament has numerous references to the importance of assisting the poor and needy. For example: 'If anyone is poor among your fellow Israelites in any of the towns of the land that the Lord your God is giving you, do not be hard-hearted or tight-fisted towards them' (Deuteronomy 15:7, NIVUK). The writer of Proverbs uses an intriguing analogy about showing 'love in action': 'Giving help to the poor is like loaning money to the Lord. He will pay you back for your kindness' (19:17, ERV). The way in which God will 'pay back' is not revealed but to receive His favour in any shape or form should be seen as sufficient reward in itself and a matter for great thankfulness.

During their nomadic years in the desert, God spoke clearly to the Jews about the importance of helping less fortunate members of the community and nation. Later, He spoke through the prophets Isaiah and Ezekiel: 'When the poor and needy search for water and there is none and their tongues are parched from thirst, then I, the Lord, will answer them. I, the God of Israel, will never abandon them' (Isaiah 41:17, NLT). Ezekiel describes a righteous man's actions, emphasising the importance of integrity: 'He never cheats or robs anyone and always returns anything taken as security for a loan; he gives food and clothes to the poor' (Ezekiel 18:7b, CEV).

Isaiah also expresses the Lord's reassurance to the people that despite their grim circumstances in facing conquest and slavery, He had not and would not desert them: 'The Spirit of the Lord God is upon me because the Lord has anointed me to preach good tidings to the poor. He has sent me to heal the broken-hearted; to proclaim liberty to the captives and the opening of the prison to those who are bound; to proclaim the acceptable year of the Lord and the day of vengeance of our God; to comfort all who mourn' (61:1–2, NKJV). The background to this proclamation is that Israel was under threat and attack from more powerful nations that were enslaving and wreaking havoc on much of the population. These were brutal times and wholesale slaughter and destruction were not uncommon, so comforting promises from God through the prophets were vitally important to maintain morale and offer hope for the future.

It is also worth noting that there are three principal elements to Isaiah's proclamation: (1) good news; (2) comfort; and (3) release, all of which are preceded by the Lord's anointing for the task ahead. In providing power through His Spirit and describing the practical measures to follow—preaching, healing, proclaiming, freeing, comforting—it is clear that God uses people to be His agents in providing for the oppressed, downtrodden and distressed. The reference to 'me' in Isaiah's prophetic words indicates that they apply to all those who seek to serve the Lord.

Jesus's teaching

In the prophecy of Amos, God rails against those in positions of power and authority who are only honest when it suits them and quickly revert to robbing the poor and trampling the underprivileged, an issue pursued by Jesus in his disputes with religious leaders. Thus, Matthew records Jesus's clear instructions to his followers: 'Watch out! Don't do your good deeds publicly, to be admired by others, for you will lose the reward from your Father in heaven. When you give to someone in need, don't do as the hypocrites do—blowing trumpets in the synagogues and streets to call attention to their acts of charity! I tell you the truth; they have received all the reward they will ever get. But when you give to someone in need, don't let your left hand know what your right hand is doing' (Matthew 6:2, NLT). Jesus's commands that emphasise humility when showing loving kindness ('good deeds') contrast sharply with the flamboyance and publicity attending acts of generosity in so much of contemporary society.

On at least two occasions—commonly referred to as the feeding of the 5000 and the feeding of the 4000 (see Mark Chapters 6 and 8, respectively)—Jesus used ordinary means that were supernaturally blessed by God to ensure that the people would not go hungry. It must be noted that the people's bodily provision was placed alongside the spiritual 'nourishment' that Jesus provided them through his teaching. Most modern missionary endeavours recognise the value of feeding the *body* ('daily bread'), *mind* ('the mind of Christ', 1 Corinthians 2:16) and *soul* ('For what profit is it to a man if he gains the whole world and loses his own soul?' Matthew 16:26a, NKJV) The principle to extract from Jesus's example is that fortifying the three elements of body, mind and soul are essential for complete health and wellbeing.

Following on Jesus's behaviour in caring for the poor and needy, James is specific in his guidance for Christians: 'Pure and genuine religion in the sight of God the Father means caring for orphans and widows in their distress and refusing to let the world corrupt you' (1:27, NLT). James's reference to widows is significant in that the plight of widowed women in that society was often bleak unless their families protected them. In a period of time devoid of any type of welfare system, care of the impoverished was given high priority, even to the point that believers in the church at Antioch sent gifts to fellow Christians in Jerusalem (carried on their behalf by Paul and Barnabas) to assist in combatting imminent famine.

At one time, it was thought that the best way to alleviate poverty—especially in what was then referred to as the 'Third World', now more accurately called the 'Developing / Majority World'—was through providing food and resources to ensure survival and achieve the most basic standard of day-to-day survival. In more recent years, the emphasis has been on helping people to be self-sufficient through financing small business projects, teaching efficient farm management skills and providing other appropriate training. In practice, both approaches are necessary: people in hopeless situations need immediate assistance before they are in a position to take advantage of longer-term opportunities. Numerous charities, the large majority of which have a Christian foundation, are involved in a variety of activities carried out with the close involvement of local communities, many of which are highly specific in character; for example, in providing clean water to villages, training health education workers, and sponsoring orphan children.

The loving care that we show to the needy pleases God and is stored up for the day that He rewards His faithful people, as the writer of the Book of Hebrews explains: 'God is not unjust; he will not forget your work and the love you have shown him as you have helped his people and continue to help them' (6:10, NLT). Older Christians sometimes feel that their best days are over and the devil may even encourage them to believe that their lives have been rather pointless. In his darker moments, even the writer of Ecclesiastes (probably King Solomon) was distracted by such gloomy thoughts: '"Everything is meaningless," says the Teacher, completely meaningless! What do people get for all their hard work under the sun?' (1:2–3, NLT). In reality, every life is precious to God and the writer of Hebrews (quoted above) provides a strong reminder that God does not forget any of the kindness and sacrifice we have shown and continue to show to the needy and powerless.

> **Insight**
>
> Use of the term 'religion' (see the reference to James's letter in the main text) when applied to Christianity is not intended to indicate that the Christian faith is bound by a set of rules and regulations, as is common among other world creeds. Christianity is founded on faith in Jesus Christ, not on religious adherence that does not lead to godliness. Matthew records how Jesus scolded the Pharisees and teachers of religious law who were rejecting the revealed word of God for the sake of tradition (15:6b). In similar vein, Paul warns in the second letter to his protégé, Timothy: 'They will act religious but they will reject the power that could make them godly. Stay away from people like that!' (3:5, NLT)

Summary

In this opening chapter, I have presented the 'real Jesus' as someone who can be taken at his word and is worthy to receive the acclaim and worship that is his by right. In my quest to reveal the truth about Jesus, I have incorporated a selection of descriptions of him, both from his own lips and those who were eyewitnesses to his life and actions while on earth. Jesus's actions always accompanied his words. His teaching was entirely consistent with his ministry, as demonstrated through healing the sick, giving sight to the blind, caring for the weak, feeding the hungry and offering hope to those in despair.

One of the most striking characteristics of Jesus's ministry was the way in which he empowered his disciples to follow his example. There is much more that might have been included in exposing the 'real Jesus', which can only be gained by carefully searching the New Testament, especially the Gospel accounts. I shall elaborate many of the principles and their implications for Christian life and witness raised in this opening chapter throughout the remainder of the book.

What do you believe?

1. Jesus was an ordinary man chosen by God to be an example of how we should live.
2. Jesus was an ordinary man imbued with special powers from God to work miracles.
3. Jesus was a religious teacher, whose followers made exaggerated claims about his status.
4. Jesus was a member of the Godhead who was born of a virgin and later gave his life for the sins of the world.
5. Jesus is the way, the truth and the life, and the light of the world, whose influence is both present and eternal.

Only answers 4 and 5 are fully consistent with biblical revelation. Further evidence that Jesus was 'fully man and fully God' is explored in the next chapter.

Chapter 2
Knowing Jesus

Introduction

In the previous chapter, I described the attributes and character of Jesus and the impact he had and continues to have upon the lives of all those who place their trust in him as Saviour. In the present chapter, I first profile the extensive and transformative nature of Jesus's teaching, followed by reference to the prophecies concerning the coming of a Messiah and of Jesus's return to judge the world in righteousness—a theme further explored in Chapter 12. I also summarise the comprehensive evidence that confirms Jesus's status as fully God and fully human, as well as evaluating the arguments presented in opposition to this fundamental biblical truth.

Jesus the Teacher

A comprehensive description of Jesus's teaching and its implications for discipleship is beyond the remit of the present book but it would be a serious omission if I didn't make reference to the core elements of his ministry, some of which was directed towards the Twelve Disciples and some to a variety of audiences: crowds, religious leaders and individuals. All of his teaching has relevance for every generation and culture, including modern-day believers. Jesus is never out-of-date!

Holy living

In the Old Testament the word 'holy' is used over six hundred times, referring to subjects as diverse as the seventh day of creation in the Book of Genesis, a holy place, holy ground, holy bread, holy mountain, holy city, holy messenger, and to a holy God and holy people. In chronicling the life of Jesus on earth and the early church, some of these former uses are relevant but the emphasis is upon *personal* holiness and crucially, the work of the Holy Spirit. Naturally, Jesus's teaching largely reflects this emphasis, not least in what is commonly described as his 'Sermon on the Mount' (Matthew Chapter 5), which includes 'The Beatitudes' (see later in the chapter).

In Isaiah Chapter 35, the Old Testament prophet graphically describes the 'Way of Holiness', designed exclusively for those who love God and trust in His unfailing goodness. The prophet explains that 'the unclean will not journey on it; wicked fools will not go about on it… But only the redeemed will walk there and those the Lord has rescued will return' (verses 8b, 9b, NIVUK). From the time of the New Testament onwards, 'holy' not only refers to the state of someone separated from ungodly influences (i.e., those thoughts, ideas and actions of which God disapproves) and dedicated to His service, but also includes those who have elected (chosen) to be cleansed from sin by the blood of Christ that was shed on the Cross of Calvary and thereby claimed his righteousness (holiness) for their lives. It must be emphasised that holiness is a state of 'being' through the power of God and not simply from 'doing' to achieve it.

Insight

The concept of 'electing' to be cleansed from sin does not garner universal approval by scholars, some of whom argue that salvation is purely by God's grace and we do not therefore 'choose Him' but He 'chooses us', in which case the sinner's response to God's offer of salvation is the sole determinant as to whether he or she is cleansed from sin. The extreme form of this viewpoint is referred to as 'predestination', of which there are various forms. For further discussion of these important issues, please refer to the relevant sections in Chapters 3 and 5.

Use of the term 'holy' has been debased over recent years, not least by use of the derogatory expression, 'holier than thou'. The origin of 'holy' is from a German word that means 'blessed', but it is most commonly used to signify that someone or something is perfect in goodness and thereby deemed righteous. Unfortunately, those who claim that holiness necessitates isolation from the rest of the world (e.g., through a monastic life) have strongly influenced the popular understanding of being holy. Although there are rare occasions when temporary physical separation is deemed appropriate—notably when God calls us apart to speak directly to us without distraction or for prayer, such as Luke records about Jesus (Luke 5:16)—holiness is more about insulating our souls than isolating our bodies. That is, we are 'in the world' (not detached from it) but by the power of God and our own decision, we choose to remain under the authority of Christ (thus, being insulated from sin) and not succumb to ungodly ways of living.

The Sermon on the Mount, as fully described in Chapter 5 of Matthew's Gospel, includes a series of statements by Jesus about the various ways in which we can receive God's blessing through: (1) our longing for Him; (2) acknowledging our human condition; (3) a desire for justice and mercy; (4) purity of our hearts; (5) striving to achieve peace, in as much as lies within our control; (6) determining to do what is right before God, regardless of the human consequences.

Jesus goes on to describe how his disciples are to be like pure *salt* to counteract the decay in society and like beams of *light* shining from our good deeds that bring praise to God the Father. Further teaching includes the seriousness of anger (rage), ways in which we can commit adultery through our unholy thoughts, strictures concerning divorce, use of inappropriate oaths, refusing to take revenge, and demonstrating love for our enemies. Throughout his teaching, Jesus not only emphasised the need for his followers to live 'different' lives from other people but to do so from pure motives. He challenged the disciples to move beyond mere conformity ('religious practice') and, as he later underscored in much of his teaching, to live in a transparent way, filled with the Spirit and demonstrating true holiness.

The Beatitudes

It is sometimes alleged that Jesus's teaching was dominated by warnings, rebukes and negativity. While it is certainly true that Jesus addressed the frailties of the human condition and was unequivocal in his condemnation of hypocrisy, it is also the case that he extolled goodness and described the blessings that are bestowed on people who demonstrate their dependence on God and their love for Him and for people.

One comprehensive record of Jesus's teaching is commonly referred to as 'The Beatitudes', the name given to eight statements he made as part of his Sermon on the Mount (see above). The word 'beatitude' is based on the original Latin version of the Bible in which each of the eight statements begins with *beati* (thus, the Latin word *beatitudo*), translated as happy, rich, blessed or state of divine joy. The Beatitudes are set out in Matthew 5:3–10, from which the following extracts are taken (italicised quotations from NIVUK):

Blessed are the poor in spirit, for theirs is the Kingdom of Heaven. The phrase 'poor in spirit' does not refer to being depressed, but to an acknowledgement of our inadequacy when relying on self and the need to pursue the only secure way to find freedom from sin that resides in Jesus.

Blessed are those who mourn, for they will be comforted. The act of mourning may be due to sadness arising from situations or circumstances, but in the context of Jesus's teaching, it is equally likely to refer to mourning about our sinfulness and finding solace in God the Comforter (John 14:16, KJV), also translated 'Helper' or 'Advocate', who forgives sin and brings us into a right relationship with Him.

Blessed are the meek [humble], for they will inherit the earth. Jesus placed great store by a person's genuine humility, which is the opposite of haughtiness and arrogance. He stressed that those who are supercilious ('smugly superior') will be the least in the Kingdom of Heaven, while those who are willing to take the lowliest place will be the inheritors of spiritual riches. Thus, in Matthew 23:11, we read that Jesus stated emphatically:

'The greatest among you will be your servant; for those who exalt themselves will be humbled, and those who humble themselves will be exalted' (NIVUK).

Blessed are those who hunger and thirst for righteousness, for they will be filled. The blood of Jesus cleanses from all unrighteousness (impurity); the only way to be cleansed from sin and therefore made right with God is through trusting him as Saviour. Jesus also spoke of himself as the Bread of Life (John 6:33) and promised that those who come to him in sincere faith will never go spiritually hungry or thirsty.

Blessed are the merciful, for they will be shown mercy. God has shown us great mercy by coming into the world in the person of Jesus to give his life as a 'ransom for many'. Jesus told Simon Peter that forgiveness is the very essence of genuine love for those who wrong us. See also Chapter 4 under 'The power of forgiveness'.

Blessed are the pure in heart, for they will see God. Synonyms of 'pure' include virtuous, blameless and above reproach. The more we allow the Holy Spirit to lead, guide and correct us, the more we resemble Jesus in our attitude, words and behaviour. Sincerity and inner holiness opens our spiritual eyes to discern more of God's will and purpose for our lives and His priorities for mankind.

Blessed are the peacemakers, for they will be called children of God. The world to which Jesus came was riven with strife, cruelty and military dominance. When Jesus rode into Jerusalem on his way to being crucified, some people in the crowd clearly believed that he was to be the conquering hero to drive out their oppressors. The fact that he chose to ride a donkey raises an interesting paradox, as there is evidence that someone making claim to kingship (the highest position) would ride a donkey or an ass (the lowliest beast). When the angels celebrated Jesus's birth, they sang of peace on earth and goodwill to men; one of Jesus's titles is the Prince of Peace. Those who trust Christ are reconciled to God, filled with a desire for peace, and become one of His children.

Blessed are those who are persecuted because of righteousness, for theirs is the Kingdom of Heaven. Jesus made it clear that to suffer for obeying God was not only something to be anticipated but would also be linked to eternal rewards. Christians who are persecuted and reviled for their faith in Christ align themselves with the adversity that he experienced. The suffering of believers in areas of the world where the dominant religion or philosophy rails against Christianity, daily experience harassment, derision and malevolence; they understand the import of Jesus's words far more keenly than those of us living in more liberal countries.

Prayer and Praying

Waiting on God

I have often reflected on the fact that as a younger man, I was so keen to be involved in working for the Kingdom that I neglected prayer and, somewhat to my shame, forged ahead and failed to check with the Holy Spirit that my 'being' was consistent with my 'doing'. I was so caught up in the act of serving that I lost sight of the One I was supposed to serve! Christians who struggle with the same issue need to heed the word of the psalmist: 'Rest in the Lord and wait patiently for Him' (Psalm 37:7, NKJV). Enthusiasm is a valuable asset but must be tempered and filtered through divine guidance.

By contrast with my impulsive attitude, Jesus's earthly ministry was characterised by constant prayer and responsiveness to the Father's will and purpose: for example, to thank God for revealing spiritual truth to childlike minds before he selected the Twelve from the much larger group of disciples. Matthew records Jesus's precise words: 'O Father, Lord of heaven and earth, thank you for hiding these things from those who think themselves wise and clever, and for revealing them to the childlike' (11:25, NLT).

The most serious occasion when Jesus needed time to pray and commune with the Father was in the Garden of Gethsemane prior to his arrest. (The Garden is situated just outside Jerusalem, some way down the hill called the Mount of Olives.) In his Gospel account, Mark (14:38) and Luke (22:40) record how Jesus warned his disciples that they should pray in order to avoid falling into temptation 'for the spirit is willing but the flesh is weak'.

Although impulsiveness is often counterproductive, it is also important not to use the need to pray as an excuse for delaying a decision or squandering the opportunity to trust God and step out in faith. The oft-used expression, 'We must first pray about it' is amply justified in situations where there is genuine doubt about the right way to proceed but should not be used to justify prevarication. Collaborative involvement in prayerful discussion of the options is essential when major church decisions are proposed, though in situations where decisions are based on the voting preference of members, the wisdom and discernment of more spiritually mature should normally take precedence. See Chapter 6 under 'Challenges of change'.

For those who are living in constant, intimate touch with the Spirit, most regular decisions can be taken without the need to agonise or spend a lot of time meditating on the right direction to take. Prayer may also be needed to combat evil, seek solace for unhappy souls, draw people into the Kingdom or prepare for conflict. In every case, the inalienable principle is that in guiding our footsteps, God never contradicts His revealed word as declared in the pages of Scripture, notably the teaching of Jesus and the Apostles.

The model prayer

The best-known example of prayer is when Jesus explained to the disciples the proper way to approach praying, after they requested guidance from him (see Matthew Chapter 6). First, Jesus poured scorn on the 'hypocrites who love to pray publicly and in the synagogues' and told his disciples to find a private and intimate place to commune with God. Jesus further explained that they didn't need to use long-winded sentences and endless 'prattling' because their Father knew what they needed before they asked Him (verses 5–7). Eventually, Jesus offered a structure for praying in which he emphasised God's holiness and the way that we express our desire to extend His Kingdom and be obedient to His will. After first enunciating this fundamental premise, we are then in a position to bring before Him our earthly necessities, ask His forgiveness for our sins and those who sin against us, and request protection from temptation. This model prayer is often called 'The Lord's Prayer' or 'The Family Prayer' and quoted verbatim, precisely as it is recorded in Scripture (though translations vary). Here is the full traditional version:

Our Father, who art in heaven, hallowed be thy name; thy kingdom come; thy will be done; on earth as it is in heaven. Give us this day our daily bread. And forgive us our trespasses, as we forgive those who trespass against us. And lead us not into temptation; but deliver us from evil. For Thine is the kingdom, the power and the glory, for ever and ever. Amen.

The precise wording is less important than the sentiments expressed through the prayer, which involve addressing God intimately as 'Father' (our loving protector); worshipping Him as supreme ruler and provider; confessing our sinfulness and acknowledging Him as Saviour; and trusting Him to lead us along the right path through life. The final statement celebrating the 'Kingdom, power and glory' is not included in every translation but provides a sublime exaltation to conclude the prayer.

Another way of using Jesus's model prayer is to weave into it the separate elements of praise, commitment, thankfulness, confession, protection and celebration, using our own words to make the prayer specific to our situation ('bespoke praying'). Whichever approach we deem appropriate (reciting the prayer or customising it), Jesus adds a stern warning that forgiveness for ourselves from God and our forgiveness of others must underpin everything we say or do: 'If you forgive those who sin against you, your Heavenly Father will forgive you but if you refuse to forgive others, your Father will not forgive your sins' (Matthew 6:14–15, NLT). Jesus emphasised that harmonious human relationships must precede seeking intimacy with God through prayer: 'So if you are presenting a sacrifice [gift] at the altar in the temple and you suddenly remember that someone has something against you, leave your sacrifice there at the altar. Go and be reconciled to that person. Then come and offer your sacrifice to God' (5:23–4, NLT).

It is important to distinguish between 'saying a prayer' and 'praying', the former can be recited unthinkingly; the latter necessitates a sincere love for God and for others. It is also worth taking heed of the Apostle Paul's uplifting words in his first letter to Thessalonian Christians about our prevailing attitude to prayer: 'Always be joyful. Never stop praying. Be thankful in all circumstances, for this is God's will for you who belong to Christ Jesus' (5:16–18). Constant prayer emerges from joyful and thankful hearts, as we express our trust in God and give glory to Christ.

Insight

Paul wrote to the Colossians that they should be 'overflowing with thankfulness': 'So then, just as you received Christ Jesus as Lord, continue to live your lives in him, rooted and built up in him, strengthened in the faith as you were taught, and overflowing with thankfulness' (Colossians 2:6–7, NIVUK). Believers should strive to be thankful for the common things of life: a choice of food; a range of clothing; sights and sounds; fresh air; water out of the tap; electricity by the touch of a switch; toilet facilities; loyal friends; paid employment; social benefits; books to read; freedom to worship. Making a habit of praising God for all His benefits cements our relationship with Him and brings Him honour.

Recorded prayers of Jesus

Two further examples of Jesus praying are found in John Chapter 17 and in the Garden of Gethsemane immediately prior to his arrest and crucifixion (see Matthew 26 and Mark 14). The prayer recorded in John 17 is probably only a portion of the complete prayer, as recording every word would have been impossible. Either Jesus was within earshot of someone who was able to transcribe his words or he related what he had prayed to his followers at a later date or the Holy Spirit gave a revelation to a chronicler (possibly Peter) about its content. What we can be sure about is the authenticity of the prayer, which includes the following themes:

- Glory is due to the Father and the Son.
- The way to eternal life is through God and Jesus Christ.
- God knows the names of those who belong to Him.
- Followers of Jesus are to bring him glory through their lives.
- Because Jesus has returned to the Father, his followers are empowered and protected through his name.
- Hatred from the evil one is to be expected, but God's protection is ensured.
- The truth of God leads to holiness.
- Believers can find perfect unity 'as one' with Christ.

- Believers can share the present and eternal glory of Christ.
- The Father's love for the Son is expressed through His love residing in every believer.

The above list provides an insight into the deep passion of Jesus and his utter abandonment to the Father's will and purpose. It provides a full declaration of the relationship between Father and Son, and the spiritual benefits available to every believer. Unlike the Lord's Prayer (see earlier), Jesus's prayer recorded in John Chapter 17 focuses entirely on what we would now describe as doctrinal truth. Both prayers are characterised by a complete absence of self-indulgence or desire for personal aggrandisement.

Immediacy of prayer

It is clear that Jesus was in constant touch with the Father through prayer, which establishes its importance for every believer. Ideally, followers of Jesus should reach the point where they are so closely embedded in the Father's will that it is unnecessary for them to pray specifically about an immediate issue or decision because they are walking in the light of Christ and his Spirit leads into all truth. In practice, due to our tendency to be distracted and take our eyes off Jesus, it is good to pause and listen to God before proceeding, especially when major decisions have to be made.

There will be occasions when situations arise that require an instant response, exposing our urgent need for God's wisdom. One of the most frequently quoted examples of such a time is the account of Nehemiah's spontaneous 'arrow prayer' when King Artaxerxes asked him why he was looking so miserable, which was unacceptable behaviour for the king's steward in the culture of the day (Nehemiah Chapter 2).

The event is often quoted as an example of praying without forethought. Such an interpretation does not accurately tell the story, however, as in the first chapter of the Book named after him, we find that Nehemiah had already 'mourned, fasted and prayed to the God of heaven' (verse 4). Nehemiah's seemingly 'off the cuff' prayer before responding to the king disguises the fact that Nehemiah was a man who enjoyed an intimate relationship with God of the kind that Jesus encouraged the disciples to cultivate some 450 years later. Nehemiah was able to pray 'on the spot' because he was already in regular communion with God. It's a lesson that all disciples of Jesus need to learn and root in their daily walk.

Jesus Saviour

Prophecies about Jesus

The Old Testament prophets pointed towards the coming of a Jewish Messiah (sometimes referred to as the Redeemer or Saviour), who would save his people Israel. Most notably, we find references in Isaiah Chapter 7 and in Micah Chapter 5 about Jesus's birth; in Isaiah Chapter 53 about his rejection; in Psalm 41 about his betrayal; in Psalms 22 and 34 about his execution; and in Psalm 16 about his resurrection. These Scriptures underline the essential truth that God's plan of redemption was from the beginning of time: that is, 'time' as we understand it, as God is not governed by the clock. There are numerous other Scriptures that refer to God as Saviour who would protect His people and bring them love, joy, peace and freedom (e.g., 2 Samuel 22:3, Psalm 18:46, Zephaniah 3:17). Most of these promises are conditional upon people's obedience and are suspended when they follow 'other gods' and reject the one true God.

The psalmist Asaph prays that God will not only help the nation but 'deliver us and forgive our sins for your name's sake' (Psalm 79:9, NIVUK), which clearly shows that salvation through forgiveness of sins was available before Jesus was born as a man on earth wherever God (Jehovah) was acknowledged and worshipped. It must be remembered that all the prophecies were written independent of each other and of the other oracles in the Bible that were declared centuries before Jesus was born, yet synchronise in unbroken harmony.

Equally wonderful is that the coming Saviour would not only be born, live and die for Israel but for the *whole world* (i.e., for each person in it). Paul summarises this eternal truth: 'For God was in Christ, reconciling the world to himself, no longer counting people's sins against them' (2 Corinthians 5:19, NLT). The verse has led some scholars to conclude that God will ultimately save everybody on earth from eternal destruction, an issue with which I engage later in the book (see Chapter 5).

When the baby Jesus was taken to the temple to be presented before the Lord—a highly significant event for every firstborn son—a godly man called Simeon held Jesus in his arms and praised God with these rousing words: 'Sovereign Lord, now let your servant die in peace, as you have promised. I have seen your salvation, which you have prepared for all people. He is a light to reveal God to the nations and he is the glory of your people Israel!' (Luke 2:29–32, NLT) It may be noted that Simeon refers to 'all people' and 'to the nations' (i.e., Gentiles) to emphasise that Christ died for the sins of the world, not only for Jews. Luke prefaces his record of Simeon's prophetic words by acknowledging that Simeon was a righteous man, who was 'eagerly waiting for the Messiah' (verse 25). Such yearning for the Lord's return should act as the supreme desire for every believer, as we await the Second Coming of Jesus to earth, as outlined below. A summary of indicators ('signs') about the imminent return of Christ is listed in Chapter 6.

Separation of wheat and weeds

John the Baptist (as he was popularly known) was a fiery preacher, who denounced the religious leaders that had assembled to watch him baptise people who were truly repentant of sin and wished to 'start afresh'. John accused the Pharisees and Sadducees of merely giving an appearance of being sorry about their sinfulness, while living in a way that contradicted their public declarations. Both Matthew and Luke record how the Baptist referred to the coming of Jesus as one who would separate the genuine from the false, using the analogy of a farmer dividing the wholesome wheat from the weeds of similar appearance: 'He is ready to separate the chaff from the wheat with his winnowing fork. Then he will clean up the threshing area, gathering the wheat into his barn but burning the chaff with never-ending fire' (Matthew 3:12; Luke 3:17, NLT). Jesus echoed the analogy of separating the authentic from the counterfeit throughout his ministry, notably in his parable about the segregation of those who belong to God and those who belong to the evil one at the end of the world, as described in Matthew Chapter 13.

After his ascension (a physical manifestation of his earthly departure and return to his former place with God the Father), an angel ('messenger from God') told the awestruck disciples that 'this same Jesus' would return in the way that they had seen him go (Acts 1:11). In other words, the Jesus who ascended and the Jesus who will one day return to establish a new heaven and earth is one and the same. Whether or not the angel meant that Jesus would return to exactly the same geographical location is unclear, though it seems unlikely. What is stated clearly in the Revelation given to the Apostle John (1:7) is that 'every eye will see him', including the people who were responsible for his death, which means that the return of Jesus Christ will be a supernatural event affecting people across the whole earth, past and present.

The angel's declaration to the disciples on the occasion of Jesus's ascension that Jesus would return in the same way as you have seen him go, together with the revelation to John that every eye shall see him, negates any suggestion that Jesus was merely a man who was used as God's supreme agent, for it is impossible for a 'mere man' to return to earth and be seen by everyone throughout the whole world. However, an essential difference between the Jesus who trod the earth and died upon the Cross at Calvary, and the Son of God who will one day return to this world, is that his second coming will be as judge and re-creator of the heavens and the earth (i.e., the whole of creation). He will no longer be the 'stranger of Galilee', as the old spiritual describes him, or the 'Lamb of God who takes away the sin of the world', but the King of kings and Lord of lords (Revelation 7:14).

In his second letter to the young pastor, Timothy, Paul refers to Christ Jesus as the one who will someday 'judge the living and the dead when he comes to establish his kingdom' (4:1, NLT). No one knows when that day will come but we are reminded to be constantly vigilant by living a virtuous life and eagerly anticipating his return.

It should cause everyone to have deep concern that the revelation given to John about future world events speaks of those who have rejected Jesus being so fearful that wish they will attempt to escape from him and hide beneath rocks and mountains (Revelation 6:16). The explicit description of these final days reinforces the point that a person's calculated rejection of Jesus Christ is a serious matter with profound consequences for this life and beyond.

Insight

Supernatural acts refer to the various ways in which the Holy Spirit's unseen influence is manifested through human situations in ways that defy a natural explanation; they are exhibited and administered as and when He chooses. These Spirit-determined acts should not be confused with so-called 'black magic' and other satanic counterfeits.

Disputes About Jesus

Opposition to Jesus as both God and man

Whenever an assertion is made about an individual's superior and unrivalled status (in this case, Jesus Christ as Saviour), there will always be opposition, scepticism and a range of derisory comments plus, it must be hoped, probing questions asked by genuine seekers after the truth, whose aim is to verify or dismiss the claim. Some cults and religions dispute Jesus's status as God. They argue (incorrectly) that although His disciples accepted his divine nature, Jesus never said anything specific about being God. Serious heretical beliefs arose in the early church, sponsored by a group (referred to as 'Gnostics') who, amongst other claims, believed that they possessed superior knowledge and insight and maintained that Jesus was divine but not fully human. More commonly today, Jesus is likely to be viewed as specially chosen by God, but otherwise fully human, not divine.

Insight

Gnostics believe that the material world is bad because it is under the control of evil forces. As salvation comes from 'within' each person through enlightenment or knowledge (gnosis), there is no need for a Saviour. The resurrection of Jesus is viewed as a spiritual, not a bodily event. The loss of respect for the human body and its significance has resulted in various forms of abuse, notably a casual view of the sanctity of life revealed through abortion, assisted suicide and euthanasia. Gnosticism promotes equality in every area of life (so-called egalitarianism). The philosophy of 'uniformity' has given rise to oppressive forms of political control and abuse through Marxism and other totalitarian doctrines that purport to seek equality for all, but in practice suppress creativity and promote dutiful conformity from the population.

Other distortions of the truth maintain that Jesus was human but only in the time period between his baptism and his death, and subsequently being resurrected as divine. There were a number of variations on these misrepresentations by false teachers, who could not and would not accept that Jesus was 'fully God and fully human'. Although this dispute about Jesus's divine nature continues to divide opinion today, the Bible is clear about Jesus being the one who was the manifestation of God in human form, thus: 'The Word became human [made flesh] and made his home among us. He was full of unfailing love and faithfulness [grace and truth] and we have seen his glory, the glory of the Father's one and only Son' (John 1:14, NLT; bracketed inserts from KJV).

Combatting false teaching is a theme running throughout the Bible. One of the best Old Testament examples is found in the Book of Jeremiah when he rails against the dishonourable prophets who claimed to be speaking God's Word when they were merely expressing their own thoughts and ideas. In Jeremiah 18, we read about God's severe displeasure with such unrighteous behaviour, dressed up as divine inspiration. We are reminded of Jesus's warning that not everyone who says "Lord, Lord" shall enter the Kingdom of Heaven but those who are obedient to his word (Matthew 7:21).

Of all the New Testament writers, John was singularly determined to combat false doctrine, writing three letters to church leaders to warn them of the need for vigilance in combatting the Gnostics and similar groups. His strong advice was that the best antidote to false teaching was to adhere closely to the *truth* about Jesus being God in human form from conception until the time that he was raised from the dead. Peter, as a major figure in the early church, was so incensed about those who were promoting flawed and misleading teaching to the newly formed churches that he wrote: 'They will cleverly teach destructive heresies and even deny the Master who bought them. In this way, they will bring sudden destruction on themselves' (2 Peter 2:1, NLT). Let present-day liberal-minded Bible teachers and preachers be warned!

There is abundant evidence from the biblical account, not only to counter scepticism about Jesus's status as an integral part of the Godhead, but also to show that (a) Jesus taught and demonstrated its authenticity; and (b) his followers (eventually) accepted and believed it to be true to such an extent that they were willing to publicly proclaim the fact, often at great personal cost. The following sections offer a selection of evidence to support the veracity of these claims.

Jesus's role in the Godhead

The traditional Hebrew expression of faith from Deuteronomy is emphatic in its pronouncement: 'Hear, O Israel: the Lord our God, the Lord is one. Love the Lord your God with all your heart, with all your soul and with all your strength' (6:4–5, NKJV). Interestingly, scholars inform us that the first part of this statement can equally be translated: 'Listen, O Israel! The Lord is our God, the Lord alone'. Even so, the emphasis placed on the word 'one' in the NKJV translation is important, as opponents of Christian belief have argued that if God is 'one', He cannot therefore be 'three'—Father, Son and Holy Spirit— commonly referred to as *The Trinity*.

Adherents to other monotheistic religions (i.e., having a belief in one God as the supreme creator, ruler and sustainer of life) understandably express unease about the concept of God having a son, as the idea would negate the 'oneness' of God and, so to speak, divide Him into two or more parts. It could even introduce the bizarre notion that God had been sexually active to procreate an offspring. Two points must be made about this confusion. First, God is one entity, not three separate 'gods'. Second, the Hebrew word for 'one' is a *compound* word consisting of several elements, not a singular concept. In the same way that we refer to 'a day' as meaning morning, noon, evening and night, so the expression 'one God' refers to a singular entity consisting of different parts—in this case, three.

Putting to one side the fact that God is spirit and not flesh, it is important to stress that we are dealing with a *responsibility* relationship between God the Father and God the Son, and not a birth connection. The role relationship relies on God the Father, Son and Spirit having different emphases in their respective contributions. The place of the Holy Spirit in the Trinity adds further complexity (see below) but is not the principal subject of this present explanation.

To further emphasise the relationship of the three members of the Godhead, it may be likened to a construction company in which the father supervises the building work, the son deals with contract arrangements and the other partner in the firm (in this highly imperfect analogy) liaises with clients. All three are involved in the running and smooth functioning of the company and independent in their roles but interdependent in terms of ensuring the efficiency of the overall operation.

Using another analogy, just as an egg consists of a shell, albumen and yolk, in which all three elements can be described as 'egg' but at the same time have a distinct purpose, so Father, Son and Spirit are separate persons, yet intimately bound together.

Yet another way of picturing the relationship is when the waters of different rivers (tributaries), though separate in their flow, combine to create a united and amalgamated single, unified river. None of these descriptions are entirely satisfactory and perhaps raise more issues than they solve, but they go some way towards identifying the intimate relationship within the Godhead and its 'oneness'.

Jesus went to great lengths to explain to the disciples that seeing him was equivalent to seeing God the Father because he was 'in the Father' and God the Father was 'in him'. The symbiosis that exists between Father and Son certainly lies beyond complete human understanding but should not be dismissed because the concept happens to be difficult to grasp. To use the Apostle Paul's striking phrase in his first letter to the Corinthian Christians, there are some mysteries that presently we only 'see through a glass darkly but then face to face' (13:12, KJV) or expressed in a more modern version: 'Now we see things imperfectly, like puzzling reflections in a mirror, but then we will see everything with perfect clarity' (NLT).

In all the attempts to explain the relationship between the three Persons of the Godhead, it must be admitted that it defies simple explanation or formulation. Indeed, the concept of God being described as a Person is itself mysterious. Jesus stressed that he was 'under instruction' from God, who was 'greater than' him but also that he and the Father were 'one'; that is, they were indistinguishable. The apparent contradiction in the two statements is easily explained: the *eternal* Son of God is part of the Godhead (Father, Son and Holy Spirit) and therefore 'one' with the Father; however, the Father is greater than the *earthly* Jesus because he (that is, Jesus) humbled himself in obedience to the Father and died a cruel death on a cross by submitting to His will. In Paul's letter to the Christians at Philippi, he summarises the position perfectly: 'Jesus humbled himself in obedience to God [the Father] and died a criminal's death on a cross' (2:8, NLT).

Thomas's revelation

In support of the claim that Jesus was an integral part of the Godhead, it is significant to note that after he appeared to his disciples following the resurrection, the startled Thomas exclaimed: 'My Lord and my God'. In response, Jesus not only accepted the appellation and commended Thomas as a result, but also stated that those in future generations who believed the same about him, though never having seen him, would be even more greatly blessed (John Chapter 20).

Jesus was certainly not being polite to avoid injuring Thomas's feelings when he did not refute his cry of adulation. We read about numerous occasions when Jesus corrected inaccurate, flattering or false statements without fear or favour; for example, he even refused to accept being referred to as 'good' by a religious leader (Mark Chapter 10). In the encounter with his disciples in the upper room, however, Jesus received Thomas's acclamation of praise and wonderment as a correct interpretation of his status, namely, as Lord and God. In addition, it should be noted that none of those present contradicted Thomas or tried to correct him, as would certainly have been the case if they had disagreed with the statement.

Jesus's eternal presence

Further evidence to refute the challenge to Jesus's status as both God and man is found in his promise to his followers that he would be with them always 'even to the end of the age' (Matthew 28:20), as whom but God can possibly make such a claim? It is scarcely credible to argue that Jesus was only speaking hypothetically, as in the ubiquitous 'see you later' that has become common parlance in recent years. No, the Gospels painstakingly portray Jesus as one whose word is his bond. If Jesus said that he will be with his followers to the end of the age, that's precisely what he meant! No human being could possibly achieve such a miraculous feat, as accompanying people through their whole lives is obviously impossible for mortal mankind.

Little wonder that in Chapter 22 in the Book of Revelation (the last book in the Bible which, among other intriguing content, discloses details about the future), Jesus is referred to as the 'Alpha and Omega', denoting the 'beginning and end', which is the very title and description of God Himself given in Revelation Chapter 1. The Son of God was therefore present before the start of time and will be equally present and supreme when the existing heaven and earth is dissolved and made anew. The doxology contained in Paul's letter to the Christians in Philippi (2:6–11) and the statement in Peter's second letter—'but we are looking forward to the new heavens and new earth he has promised, a world filled with God's righteousness' (3:13, NLT)—both reinforce this profound truth. Such is the confident hope that all of Christ's followers may celebrate, regardless of their present circumstances and seemingly irresolvable difficulties.

Jesus's earthly miracles

We must add to the above affirmations about Jesus's divine nature the fact that he performed a large number of miracles that included:

- Healing physical and mental illness (e.g., the insane Gadarene / Gerasene man, Matthew Chapter 8).
- Passing through a lynch mob untouched as they picked up rocks to stone him (John Chapter 8).
- Feeding thousands of people on two separate occasions, referred to as 'feeding of the 5000'—recorded by all four Gospel writers—and

'feeding of the 4000' from food intended for one person. See, for example, the detailed account in Matthew Chapter 15.

- Stilling a storm that threatened to swamp the disciples' fishing boat on the Sea of Galilee (Lake Tiberias) by speaking to it, as recorded by three of the Gospel writers (Matthew Chapter 8; Mark Chapter 4; Luke Chapter 8).
- Restoring a man's hand after it had withered away (Luke Chapter 6) and a servant's ear after Simon Peter severed it at the time of Jesus's arrest (John Chapter 18).
- Walking on water (Matthew Chapter 14 and Luke Chapter 6)
- Supernaturally influencing nature; e.g., the disciples casting their nets over the other side of their boat and hauling in a miraculous catch of fish (John Chapter 20).
- Raising at least three people from the dead: The widow's son at Nain (Luke Chapter 7); Jairus's daughter (e.g., Luke Chapter 8); and Lazarus (John Chapter 11).

It should be borne in mind that the above references are just the recorded incidents. John enthused there were many more similar events, such that if everything Jesus said and did were included, the whole world could not contain all the books written to chronicle them. While John may have used a degree of hyperbole to emphasise the extent of Jesus's ministry, he nevertheless made the point forcefully that Jesus's life and works were beyond normal human achievement or description, and without parallel.

Insight

A miracle can be defined as those acts that only God can perform or facilitate, more often than not when He chooses to set aside the Laws of Nature to do so. God often works directly through people to divinely intervene in a situation.

Weighing the arguments

A sceptic might claim that descriptions of the miracles are fictional—the result of a fertile imagination—or that people associated with Jesus were hallucinating or in a hypnotic state or simply so desperate to find evidence to confirm their fantasies that they convinced themselves and attempted to convince others about whom they claimed Jesus to be. It has also been suggested that the Gospel writers colluded to create a new religion based on the life of a man who was certainly exceptional but just one of many outstanding figures from world history.

Other doubters might accept that Jesus did amazing things but point out that Moses, Elijah and Elisha were all used by a Divine Being (God) to perform miracles. Some revered founders of other religions and movements are also credited with miraculous powers, though the alleged evidence is contained within imaginative tales that are clearly fables or concoctions and difficult to take seriously. It has even been suggested that if Jesus were to come back to earth today, he would be astounded and horrified with the way in which he is venerated and adored, seeing himself as a mere man, though specially chosen by God.

Superseding all of the above arguments and evidence, however, the greatest miracle exclusive to Jesus the Christ (Messiah, Saviour) is when He *rose from the dead* and appeared to the disciples and to hundreds of other people. Without the resurrection, Jesus's life and subsequent death on a Roman cross would be a mere footnote in human history. Jesus's rising from the dead and ascension (returning to God the Father's side) ushered in a totally new and unique dimension to the salvation story, for it provides each one of us with a hope that is, to use a phrase from Wendy Churchill's much loved hymn, *Jesus is King*, both 'steadfast and certain'. The importance of accepting by faith the biblical revelations about Jesus Christ cannot be overestimated; Jesus stated that those who believe in him without seeing him are truly blessed (John 20:29).

Evidence for the resurrection contained in the different accounts compiled by the Gospel writers is unassailable, as so many people on different occasions witnessed Jesus's living presence. Frank Morison's classic book (his real name was Albert Henry Ross) *Who Moved the Stone?* is particularly significant in supporting the truth about the physical resurrection of Jesus because Morison began writing the book as an atheist and became a believer after he had sifted and analysed the biblical evidence. Any objective reading of the New Testament must draw the same conclusion: Jesus Christ was a genuine figure in history, whose life has been accurately recorded, who died on the Cross of Calvary, rose from the dead and ascended into heaven.

Despite concerted efforts to discredit or diminish the written evidence about Jesus, an open-minded reading of the Gospel accounts, which are presented in an unadulterated fashion and without a hint of fabrication or exaggeration, instantly establishes their veracity. It is not an overstatement to insist that the works of Old Testament prophets and every other senior religious figure throughout world history are dwarfed by comparison with the words, works and miracles attributed to Jesus over a mere two or three years of ministry. By any objective measure, it is more reasonable to accept the truth about Jesus as 'God made flesh' than to argue desperately that Jesus's claims about himself and those made by the New Testament writers were at best, fanciful, and at worst, fictional and delusory.

Transformed lives

It is a powerful confirmation of Jesus's supernatural powers that people from every generation who have acknowledged and accepted him as Saviour testify to the remarkable transformation that takes place in their lives when they do so. While it is undeniably the case that many people in a variety of secular situations experience a life-changing episode when circumstances or a crisis provides the impetus for them to follow a new path or behave differently or accept priorities that were hitherto regarded as insignificant or irrelevant, the act of being 'born anew/born again/born from above' (as Jesus described the life-changing process for those who trust in him, John 3:3,7) is supremely powerful. Peter confirms this fundamental truth: 'For you have been born again, but not to a life that will quickly end. Your new life will last forever because it comes from the eternal, living word of God' (I Peter 1:23, NLT).

Insight

Jesus described being born again in terms of two sources: water and spirit, both of which come 'from above'. The use of water and spirit makes the translation 'born from above' more relevant than the more frequently used expression, 'born again', as God is the source of all power, be it the natural elements, such as wind and rain, or spiritual transformation.

Importantly, the convert's experience of believing *about* Jesus must always be followed by believing *in* him. That is, not only accepting intellectually that Christ died for our sins according to the Old Testament Scriptures but also claiming for ourselves the liberating truth that he died for 'me' as an individual sinner. In doing so, we inherit the righteousness of Christ, such that God no longer looks upon our sinful lives but upon the perfect life of His Son (2 Corinthians 5:21). As Paul explained to the Christians in Philippi: 'I could not make myself acceptable to God by obeying the law of Moses. God accepted me simply because of my faith in Christ' (3:9, CEV). I explore in depth the fundamental issue of sin and sinfulness in Part 2.

Surviving a near-death experience or recovering from a normally fatal disease or being wholly convinced by a powerful argument can revolutionise a person's priorities and usher in a change of direction. Nevertheless, as profound these experiences may be, the transformation wrought by the Holy Spirit in convicting of sin and providing the means for every person to receive the righteousness of Christ, is far more significant. It demands an acceptance of the truth of the Gospel message about Jesus's sacrificial death on the cross, leading to personal repentance and henceforth determining to walk in step with him, as the Spirit guides and leads. Once established on the Holy Spirit's path of righteousness, new believers testify that the meaning and purpose of their existence becomes far clearer and life has a renewed impetus, hope and joy. As Paul urged the Christians in Rome: 'Don't copy the behaviour and customs of this world, but let God transform you into a new person by changing the way you think. Then you will learn to know God's will for you, which is good and pleasing and perfect' (12:2, NLT).

The importance of allowing God to use our minds (the way we think) is of great significance in transforming us and discerning His will and purpose for our lives. To state the position simply, transformation begins inwardly and becomes evident outwardly, not the reverse. Secular groups are keenly aware of the need to influence people's thoughts and (often subconsciously) to absorb their beliefs and ideologies by using advertisements, slogans and repeated assertions to achieve their aim. By contrast, the Holy Spirit has no need for such devious devices. He waits for us to respond in faith to the claims of Christ and gradually provides insight, wisdom and understanding that were previously obscured or absent.

The transformed life that Jesus offers cannot be dismissed as a whim, a short-lived burst of religious fervour or an act of fearful submission. Rather, it is a process that begins by acknowledging that we fall well short of God's perfect standard and can only be truly free from the burden and consequences of sin by trusting in the sacrifice of Jesus on the Cross, which provides the only sure means of escape from God's fateful judgement. John recorded Jesus's dire warning about the consequences of rejecting him: 'There is no judgement against anyone who believes in him [Jesus Christ] but anyone who does not believe in him has already been judged for not believing in God's one and only Son and the judgement is based on this fact: God's light came into the world, but people loved the darkness more than the light, for their actions were evil' (3:18–19, NLT).

With reference to Jesus's warning about evil actions, it is worth noting there is a strong school of secular belief that the concept of good and evil is a false dichotomy. They argue that our behaviour is solely determined by our environment, whereby social norms, family influences, wealth, poverty and education impinge on the way in which people define the concepts. The prophet Isaiah rails against those who manipulate God's expressed truth about right and wrong: 'What sorrow for those who say that evil is good and good is evil, that dark is light and light is dark, that bitter is sweet and sweet is bitter' (5:20, NLT). An example of such contrariness is in the accusation by secular thinkers that God's commandments are damaging because they make people behave in a way that is contrary to their nature and therefore induces stress in them. Such a philosophy that promotes the idea of a bespoke morality ('do it if it feels right') has created chaos and confusion about acceptable and unacceptable forms of conduct. In reality, the commandments are to provide necessary boundaries for behaviour that are entirely beneficial if we are led by the Spirit, rather than a mechanical form of slavish adherence.

The importance of faith over feeling is central to belief in Jesus Christ as the Saviour and the one who is supremely able to meet every need in accordance with the Father's will. A powerful example of exercising faith in Jesus is related in Matthew Chapter 15, where a Gentile woman begs him to heal her daughter. At first, rather strangely, Jesus ignores the woman then, as she continues to plead, explains that he has come first and foremost to help the children of Israel (i.e., the Jews). There follows an exchange between Jesus and the woman in which he tests her faith to the limit and after receiving a wisdom-filled reply, grants her request and the daughter is instantly healed. Jesus states emphatically: 'Your faith is great. Your request is granted' (verse 28, NLT). There are many lessons to be drawn from this episode, not least the importance of persistent prayer and absolute trust in the Saviour to intervene and bless, regardless of background, culture or nationality.

Jesus not only referred to evil and good behaviour in general terms but also made it clear that each person has the power to choose whether to behave in a godly or ungodly way. Despite Jesus's unequivocal condemnation of degenerate behaviour, he must have astounded his hearers when he told them to respond to spiteful acts with loving kindness, not resentfully or seeking retribution. Gospel writers Matthew and Luke both record Jesus's words that reveal the way in which the transformed life is shown to be genuine. Thus, in Matthew Chapter 5, Jesus reverses what seems to be natural justice when responding to an evildoer: 'But I say, do not resist an evil person! If someone slaps you on the right cheek, offer the other cheek also. If you are sued in court and your shirt is taken from you, give your coat, too. If a soldier demands that you carry his gear for a mile, carry it two miles' (39–41, NLT).

The reference to a soldier (which is not specified in every Bible translation) is that Jews, as the subjugated people, were obliged to carry military equipment for up to one mile if commanded to do so. Naturally, this requirement generated a great deal of resentment among the indigenous population. Jesus's words about submitting to this humiliating practice must have seemed almost treasonous to his listeners, most of whom resented being subject to their Roman conquerors. It is clear that Jesus was not suggesting that we are passive in resisting evil but rather that we do not seek revenge or allow resentment to dominate our thoughts and actions.

Many Christians have described their initial conversion in terms of 'seeing the light' or similar metaphors to indicate how they were once 'blind' to spiritual truth but now can see (i.e., understand and embrace the reality of sin, repentance and faith in Jesus as Saviour). Our conversion process continues as we learn more of God through reading the Bible, meditating on its message, praying, and listening to the Scriptures being faithfully presented and explained. The way in which this revelation is brought about can be debated; what cannot be denied is that countless millions have been liberated by its positive impact on their lives.

Conclusion

In the first two chapters, I have endeavoured to reveal and extol the person of Jesus by reference to his work and ministry, as described in various Gospel accounts but principally the one written by the Apostle John. I also quoted from epistles ('letters') by other Apostles to fledgling churches and their leaders, confirming the truth about Jesus and the implications for Christian living. I explored some of the issues surrounding Jesus as 'God and Man' and his place in the Godhead (Father, Son and Holy Spirit) and answered criticisms about his status. The fact that that Jesus Christ gave his life to free the world from the consequences of rebellion against God and reconcile ('bring together in an intimate, unspoiled relationship') God and people on earth has undergirded all other considerations.

The revelation that Jesus Christ was fully human from conception to the resurrection, yet also fully God from before the beginning of time, has engendered controversy but is a foundational belief that separates biblical Christianity from every other religion or religious affiliation. To cement this argument, I presented proof from the Bible to refute sceptics and to justify the claim that Jesus was the one he claimed to be: fully God and fully human ('God made flesh'), and the Saviour of the world.

While the Bible is unequivocal in its claim that Jesus is the sin-bearer sent from God, there are other genuinely challenging areas of uncertainty ('we see through a glass dimly', I Corinthians 13:12, NKJV) that are likely to remain a mystery until the end of time when much that perturbs and puzzles us will be made clear.

In identifying Jesus's earthly characteristics and the way in which believers can be transformed into his likeness, I have emphasised the essential role played by the Holy Spirit, a recurring theme throughout the book. For further details about the process and implications of becoming more like Jesus, see Part 6 (Chapter 11 and 12).

Where do you stand?

1. I know that Jesus claimed to be the Saviour of the world but I have troubling doubts about whether it is true for everyone.
2. I am happy to be part of a worshipping community but I am unsure about my personal standing with Christ.
3. I know plenty of things about Jesus but I'm not sure that I can claim to know him personally or even understand what it means in practice.
4. I am confident that Jesus Christ is the way, the truth and the life, and that he died for me.
5. I feel that I know Jesus more and more as time passes.
6. I have every confidence that I know Jesus as Lord and he knows me as his friend.

If any of the first three statements apply to you, please reread Chapter 2 and ask the Lord to reveal His truth afresh.

Part 2
The Sin Pandemic

Isaiah 24: 5–7

The earth suffers for the sins of its people, for they have twisted God's instructions, violate his laws and broken his everlasting covenant. Therefore, a curse consumes the earth. Its people must pay the price for their sin. They are destroyed by fire and only a few are left alive. The grapevines waste away and there is no new wine. All the merrymakers sigh and mourn (NLT).

Deuteronomy 30:19–20a

This day I call the heavens and the earth as witnesses against you that I have set before you life and death, blessings and curses. Now choose life, so that you and your children may live and that you may love the Lord your God, listen to his voice, and hold fast to him (NIVUK).

Romans 8: 5–8

Those who are dominated by the sinful nature think about sinful things but those who are controlled by the Holy Spirit think about things that please the Spirit. So letting your sinful nature control your mind leads to death but letting the Spirit control your mind leads to life and peace. For the sinful nature is always hostile to God. It never did obey God's laws and it never will. That's why those who are still under the control of their sinful nature can never please God (NLT).

Preface to Part 2

Over recent years, the threat from serious viruses has affected almost every place on earth, resulting in large numbers of deaths and inflicting terrible suffering. Thankfully, the development of drugs to combat the tide of destruction brought about by the infections has ameliorated the impact to a large extent, particularly in the more developed nations. Poorer societies have been less able to benefit from these modern advances. There has also been significant resistance among certain religious and secular groups against being inoculated, which has further complicated the situation and created considerable acrimony. In parts of the world blighted by conflict, together with the effect of death-inducing viruses, the population has also suffered from the devastations of corruption, poverty and violence.

In the following two chapters, I refer to sin as a pandemic because it affects every person on the planet and has a life-threatening impact on individuals and societies as a whole. I focus specifically on the different ways in which sin manifests itself and the negative effect on the human condition and people's behaviour.

Chapter 3
Sin and Sinfulness

Introduction

In this chapter, I address a variety of key issues attached to sin and sinful behaviour (described loosely as 'sin in action'). In doing so, I shall examine the various manifestations of sin with particular reference to ways in which God has provided each person with an internal mechanism to combat temptation and avoid the damage that sin causes in our lives and those around us. The primary focus in this chapter is on *the meaning and implications of sin* with which Christ came to deal by living as a man on earth and freely giving his life on the Cross of Calvary. In Chapter 4, I shall be concentrating on God's answer to the sin problem.

Damage Caused by Sin

"What can I do you for?" was the catchphrase of one of the old-time comediennes. It was a clever device, reversing two of the words of the original expression: "What can I do for you?" to create a wholly different meaning. Sometimes, one hears the irritable question from disgruntled people: "What have you ever done for me?" though the phrase, 'have you' might be replaced by 'has he, she or they'. Some churches have placed a poster on their notice boards with words posing the searching question: *What has God ever done for me?* as its centrepiece, with a picture of Christ upon the Cross of Calvary in the background. The intention is to emphasise that the greatest act of God on behalf of humankind was to send His Son in the form of Jesus to give his life for the sins of the world.

The human condition

It is sometimes alleged that far from being willing to give freely without expectation of reward ('something for nothing'), as witnessed by Jesus's life and death on the Cross, many people in the world only accept 'something for something', as denoted by expressions such as: "You scratch my back and I'll scratch yours!" and "One good turn deserves another." Whatever the validity of the assertion, it is undoubtedly the case that there lies within each person an understandable desire for self-improvement and for protection of those considered to be our 'nearest and dearest'. One can point to numerous examples of courage in safeguarding loved ones when they are threatened, thereby confirming the maxim that 'blood is thicker than water'. Occasionally, however, instances of bravery are reported when a complete stranger risks his life to save another person—such events usually make headline news. The ongoing tension between concern for self (thus, selfishness) and acts of *selflessness* (concern for others that overrides one's own welfare) characterises the human condition. On the one hand, people can prove to be sacrificially devoted to others, while on other occasions, the same people are capable of being unkind and egotistical.

At its root, sin is about putting our desires and wishes ahead of God's instruction and purpose, thereby depriving Him of His rightful place to guide and empower us. The Bible is unequivocal in its reference to the awfulness of our sinful condition, by which we mean our tendency, as even the Apostle Paul admitted in his letter to the church in Rome, to do those things that we should not do and fail to do the things that we ought to do. Paul admits to being a 'wretched man' (KJV) or as expressed in the NLT, 'Oh, what a miserable person I am! Who will free me from this life that is dominated by sin and death?' (Romans 7:25, NLT)

Another definition of sin is found in the notion of falling short of the target—'the target' being defined as the righteousness or holiness of God to which we are called (see next section). Such a failing not only affects individuals but can also damage a church fellowship when it adopts a lukewarm attitude towards its responsibility to glorify the Lord in every way. Christ views such a self-centred attitude very seriously, as shown by His scolding of the church in Laodicea: 'You say, "I am rich. I have everything I want. I don't need a thing!" And you don't realise that you are wretched and miserable and poor and blind and naked' (Revelation 3:14–19, NLT). The essence of the admonishment focuses on the fellowship's boastful pride that they have prospered through their *own* efforts, without acknowledging the power and guidance from the Holy Spirit in the process. Such a conceited attitude deprives God of the credit, glorifies human achievement and leads to a diminution of the church's influence and effectiveness.

Regardless of our noble deeds and effort to live a good life—both of which are commended by Jesus—we all need a surrogate to achieve righteousness on our behalf. Jesus Christ, as the only sinless person to have walked the earth, fulfils that role through his absolute obedience to the Father's will at the expense of his own welfare and reputation (see Chapter 1). In his letter to the Philippian Church, the Apostle Paul speaks of Jesus's humility: '[Jesus] made himself of no reputation and took upon him the form of a servant and was made in the likeness of men' (2:7, KJV). Peter provides a fuller explanation of Jesus's supreme sacrifice and what it accomplished: 'Christ suffered [died] for our sins once for all time. He never sinned, but he died for sinners to bring you safely home to God. He suffered physical death, but he was raised to life in the Spirit' (I Peter 3:18, NLT).

Jesus's example of servanthood is perfectly demonstrated when he washed the disciples' feet as they gathered to celebrate the Feast of Pentecost, as described in John Chapter 13. More significantly, Jesus showed his willingness to become a servant—in some translations, 'slave'—when he freely gave his life by dying for the sins of the world. For an exploration of the details and significance of the foot-washing episode, see Chapter 12.

Jesus made it clear that sin (sometimes referred to as 'wickedness') resides first of all in our *minds*, such that wrong thoughts and words—not merely our deeds—are also sinful, though being tempted is not sinful in itself, as even Jesus was tempted by Satan (Matthew Chapter 4). Later in his letter to the church in Rome, Paul contrasts the stark difference between allowing the Spirit of God to control us by submitting our minds to Him and allowing sin to control us by submitting to Satan: 'Letting your sinful nature control your mind leads to death but letting the Spirit control your mind leads to life and peace' (Romans 8:6, NLT). If we allow sinful thoughts to saturate our thinking, our lives become 'dead' because we are unable to live them as God intends, receive His blessing or find deep contentment. By contrast, the Spirit offers a peace that is beyond human comprehension and constantly refreshes and renews us.

The ugliness of sin

Regardless of background, the majority of people are peace-loving and wish to get on with their lives with minimum agitation and maximum contentment. Sadly, we don't have to look far to see that the world is also blighted by cruel and aggressive acts of abuse and violence that are contrary to the life and peace that Jesus Christ offers. Every day, distressing instances of brutality make headline news that creates shock and disquiet. Such barbarous behaviour is the result of sin that the individuals concerned have allowed to penetrate their thinking and actions, such that they have become unwitting agents for, and collaborators with, the evil one, Satan.

Insight

Satan (the devil, Lucifer, Beelzebub) is in temporary control of the world around us (I John 5:19) as far as God permits him to have this authority, but he does not have control of our minds unless we allow it to happen. To suggest that God and Satan are 'at war' for supremacy is to misrepresent the facts. God is the Supreme Ruler. Satan seeks to usurp His power but his authority is limited, though it has devastating effects when unrestrained. Jesus put matters into perspective after the disciples reported that demons were obeying them: 'Yes, he told them, I saw Satan fall from heaven like lightning!' (John 10:18, NLT) Satan's eradication is graphically described in the Book of Revelation: 'And the devil, who deceived them, was thrown into the lake of burning sulphur, where the beast and the false prophet had been thrown. They will be tormented day and night for ever and ever' (20:10, NIVUK).

Paul warns that Satan is 'blinding the eyes' of those who reject the truth: 'But even if our Gospel is veiled, it is veiled to those who are perishing, whose minds the god of this age has blinded, who do not believe, lest the light of the Gospel of the glory of Christ, who is the image of God, should shine on them' (2 Corinthians 4:3–4, NKJV). The use of the word 'perishing' is significant, indicating both the moral and physical disintegration of those who place themselves outside God's protective mantle. The separation of those who believe and are safe in Christ, and those who do not believe and are therefore controlled by the evil one, is both stark and chilling.

Though largely unreported in the general media, believers in many parts of the world—especially in authoritarian and ultra-religious countries—live in constant fear of attacks, reprisals and injustice, as their allegiance to Christ is placed under severe pressure from family, neighbours and officialdom. Demonic forces inevitably concentrate their assaults on Christians in an attempt to disable, discourage and disarm them. The situation for the Old Testament character King Jehoshaphat is relevant in understanding the intervening power of God to protect His people, for as invaders were gathering to wage war against Judah and the King was faced with potential disaster, he expressed his confidence in God through prayer: 'For we have no power to face this vast army that is attacking us. We do not know what to do, but our eyes are on you' (2 Chronicles 20:12).

Jehoshaphat strategically organised his fighting men but also, curiously, sent a line of singers in front of the troops to sing praises to the Lord. The strategy of praise brought about a supernatural victory, as Judah's enemies were thrown into confusion and fought one another to the point of extinction. The event is a reminder of the importance of praising God; the writer of Hebrews describes it as a form of oblation: 'Our sacrifice is to keep offering praise to God in the name of Jesus' (Hebrews 13:15, NIVUK). Jehoshaphat sets a commendable example of placing trust in God ahead of our fear of enemies. See Chapter 5 for details of what might be entailed in suffering for Christ.

By contrast with the extreme challenges faced by believers living under tyrannical regimes, most people living in the comparative security of the 'Free World' have concerns that are rooted in more pedestrian matters, such as job security, having sufficient money to pay bills and, perhaps, alarm over moral deterioration in society. The intrusiveness of godless attitudes and rejection of long established ethical parameters by small but influential secular groups, together with liberal political decisions, have created unease and indignation from within the Christian community. Sin is gradually crippling the lives of ordinary folk by blurring moral boundaries, tearing families apart and sexualising children from a young age through advertising, salacious images and targeted pornography.

During the first century, believers did not have to deal with technological corruption or a plethora of powerful single-issue groups that lobbied officials, but inducements to behave in an ungodly manner, exhibited through drunkenness, debauchery and dishonest gain were as prevalent then as they are today. The Apostles Paul and Peter both include sombre warnings about the need to avoid accepting or imitating such godless, lewd behaviour. Additionally, in occupied towns such as Philippi—a Roman colony—Christians were at risk from the occupying Roman army and zealous Jewish authorities in much the same way as contemporary believers are from religious fanatics and godless regimes.

Even under the challenging circumstances in which they found themselves, Paul describes in his letter to the Christians at Philippi how believers should respond to God's wonderful offer of contentment to be found uniquely in Christ: 'Don't worry about anything; instead, pray about everything. Tell God what you need and thank him for all he has done. Then you will experience God's peace, which exceeds anything we can understand. His peace will guard your hearts and minds as you live in Christ Jesus' (Philippians 4:6–7, NLT). What a life-transforming message to encourage every follower of Jesus Christ who is determined to live in God's way and not be conformed to the world's corrupt practices.

Intentional and Unintentional Sinning

Inclination to sin

The inclination to sin that is present in every person has given rise to the objection that it is unfair for God to blame people for doing wrong, due to the fact that the 'original sin' was caused by Adam and Eve's failure (their 'Fall') over which people who have lived since that time have no control. In other words, the question is asked as to why someone in the present time is being unjustly condemned for the first humans' failure at the time of the Creation.

As a way of responding to the alleged injustice, it is fair to acknowledge that although original sin is not the fault of succeeding generations, it may be judiciously separated from the *decisions* that we all make to sin or to resist sinning in our present lives. In the words of Robert Robinson's old hymn, *Come, Thou Fount of Every Blessing*, even the most dedicated believer is 'prone to wander, Lord, I feel it; prone to leave the God I love'. The issue of making decisions about our behaviour and priorities is fundamentally important in grasping why God is not being unreasonable or unjust in making each person accountable for his or her own sin.

While it is true that we are all impacted by sin, it is also the case that some people sin more than others based on their predisposition or freewill choice or the influences exerted on them by others or by a combination of these factors. The influence of *intentionality* is highly significant, as it is not only the existence of original sin that results in sinful behaviour but one that is borne of human desire, impulse and choice.

While the absence of original sin would negate the possibility of sinning (because sin would not exist), it would also create a situation in which the decision as to whether we serve and obey God or go our own way would be irrelevant. Adam and Eve were not compelled to rebel against God—they did so of their own free will—and each of us is faced with similar choices throughout our lives. In essence, we allow the Holy Spirit to guide and determine the direction of our behaviour and decisions or we disregard His influence and follow our inclinations. We are saved by our faith and trust in the work of Christ upon the Cross of Calvary and his glorious resurrection from the dead, but evidence of a genuine change of heart is found in our willingness to obey him, confess our sin daily and enjoy intimacy with our God and Maker. As Paul exhorts the Christians in Corinth: 'Because we have these promises, dear friends, [namely, that God is our loving Father] let us cleanse ourselves from everything that can defile our body or spirit. And let us work towards complete holiness because we fear God' (2 Corinthians 7:1, NLT).

Illuminating the darkness

The use of the word 'conscience' is often employed as a shorthand way of expressing our unease when we sense that an action is wrong or we know that it is wrong but proceed regardless (i.e., we choose to sin). For the vast majority of people, guilt accompanies the sin or follows soon afterwards. However, the light of Jesus Christ revealed through the internal power and influence of the Holy Spirit is a more sensitive indicator of the appropriateness of a thought, word or deed than a mere spark of conscience, for it reveals dark corners of the mind that need submitting fully to God.

As the Old Testament prophet, Jeremiah, declared: 'You test those who are righteous and you examine the deepest thoughts and secrets' (20:12, NLT). It is significant that the *righteous* people are subject to God's scrutiny, as He desires that they are cleansed from every stain. By contrast, Paul explained in his first letter to the Christians in Corinth concerning *unbelievers* who are exposed to godly prophetic preaching: 'As they listen, their secret thoughts will be exposed and they will fall to their knees and worship God, declaring: God is truly here among you' (14:25, NLT). In this case, those who have hitherto resisted the need for repentance and turning to God will be so alarmed when their secret thoughts are disclosed that they acknowledge His existence. Similarly, Matthew describes how, when the disciples were experiencing threats from godless people, Jesus reassured them that one day everything their adversaries thought, said and did would be revealed (10:26; see also Luke 12:2–4). Details about the place of conscience and guilt in avoiding and addressing sinful behaviour are explored in detail in Chapter 4.

When Christians repent of their ungodly behaviour, they receive immediate and total forgiveness and cleansing. Writing from Ephesus, in his first letter to churches in Asia Minor (modern-day Turkey), John emphasised the importance of living according to Holy Spirit guidance and His intention for our lives: 'But if we walk in the light, as he is in the light, we have fellowship with one another and the blood of Jesus, his Son, purifies us from all sin' (1:7, NIVUK). For believers, anything that creates spiritual darkness—whether it is due to their own foolishness or the impact of circumstances—should instantly cause them to seek the light and purity of Christ's presence.

Jesus told his followers that just as he is the light of the world, so they, too, are to be the light of the world (Matthew 5:14). A glowing countenance and faith-driven approach to life should be a hallmark of every true disciple, reflecting the love and radiance of Christ, even under the most challenging circumstances. The supreme example of such Spirit-filled joy is found in the trial and subsequent martyrdom of Stephen: 'At this point everyone in the high council stared at Stephen because his face became as bright as an angel's [face]' (Acts 6:15, NLT). Stephen's courage and radiant features in the face of imminent death sets a high water mark of faith and trust in God for every believer.

Contrasting two Adams

Original sin has its inception (origin) in the decision made by Adam and Eve to disobey God in the Garden of Eden—a place designed by God to provide for every human need—which introduced deception and selfish desires into the human condition and incurred His anger. Original sin is innate, embedded, installed and inborn from the moment of conception to our final breath.

The process by which this entry of sin into every human took place is not easily understood or explained but it has been clearly apparent in people's behaviour from that time onwards. As a result of the presence of sin in their lives, everyone has the potential to neglect, rebel and disobey God (sometimes, all three elements are involved) but also, as I explain later in the chapter, the capacity to resist sin and turn to God for help and forgiveness.

As through the first Adam, sin and death entered the world, so life comes through the 'Second Adam' (Jesus), a situation summarised by Paul: 'Adam's one sin brings condemnation for everyone but Christ's one act of righteousness brings a right relationship with God and new life for everyone' (Romans 5:18, NLT). Note the inclusion of the word 'everyone'. Jesus died to counteract the original sin of Adam, which is thereby dealt with ('covered') completely. However, those individuals who are capable of understanding right and wrong *also* need to repent of their ongoing sinfulness, express faith and trust in God and be 'born again/ anew/ afresh/ from above' by the Spirit of God (as Jesus taught the Pharisee, Nicodemus; see John Chapter 3), thereby qualifying them to enter the Kingdom of Heaven. As the Apostle Peter explains: 'For you have been born again [that is, reborn from above—spiritually transformed, renewed and set apart for His purpose] not of seed which is perishable but [from that which is] imperishable and immortal, that is, through the living and everlasting word of God' (I Peter 1:23, AMP).

Death was introduced through the first Adam and new life is found through the Second Adam. Paul explains in his first letter to members of the Corinthian Church that being born again creates in a believer 'heaven-likeness': 'What comes first is the natural body then the spiritual body comes later. Adam, the first man, was made from the dust of the earth, while Christ, the second man, came from heaven. Earthly people are like the earthly man [Adam], and heavenly people are like the heavenly man [Jesus]' (15:46–48, NLT). Paul introduces the wonderful revelation that Christians are citizens of heaven while still alive on earth! It's a truth that should thrill every believer.

Insight

If, as secularists claim, the world and life came into being through a cosmic 'accident' or due to a combination of chemical processes and complex physical phenomena, the story of God creating Adam and Eve is a fiction. This being the case, the Genesis account of sin infecting the human condition is mythical. The outcome of rejecting the Bible's Creation account is that the concept of 'original sin' (through the first Adam) is imaginary, so there is no need for a Saviour (the Second Adam) to be a sacrifice for the sins of the world. The sobering conclusion from this analysis is that a failure to accept the written truth of God's Word is to undermine God's saving grace and nullify the work of Christ at Calvary.

Immaturity and culpability

On the subject of *wilful sin*, it is necessary to address the issue about the responsibility of those who do not possess the ability or intellectual capacity to repent of sin, find forgiveness, become a follower of Jesus and determine to live a godly life. Setting aside the point about those who never hear the Gospel—an issue too complex to be covered adequately in the present discourse, though see the résumé under *Broad or Narrow Way* later in this chapter—I want to offer an interpretation to help clarify the position about those who, owing to premature death or mental incapacity, have never had opportunity to place their trust in Jesus.

The Apostle Paul urges in his letter to the church in Rome: 'Therefore do not let sin reign in your mortal body so that you obey its evil desires' (6:12, NIVUK) which is sound advice to those with clear minds. It is fair to ask where this command leaves stillborn or aborted babies; children who die in infancy; and severely brain damaged people. To put the matter bluntly: Are some souls eternally lost because they were unable to make appropriate decisions about their lives because they are incapable of understanding the Gospel? I shall attempt to address the key issues openly, while recognising that there are some imponderables attached to this sensitive topic that we must leave in God's hands.

First, it is a biblical precept (fundamental principle) that everyone from conception to the grave is a sinner, who needs the forgiveness that Christ offers. Second, Jesus died for the sins of each person in the world, not just for the sins of people who survive to adulthood and are blessed by a sound upbringing and a clear mind. Third, it has been shown down the centuries that even young children can grasp the basic truth of the Gospel, though it has to be admitted that the majority of them appear to belong to Bible-believing families who encourage their offspring to make a personal commitment. Fourth, Jesus had a close affinity with children and insisted that to enter the Kingdom of Heaven, we must all become 'as little children'; that is, we need to have a trusting attitude and uncomplicated faith in him.

Jesus emphasised the need for a childlike faith (not to be confused with 'childish'), as all three Synoptic Gospel writers, Matthew, Mark and Luke (*Synoptic* means 'similar in content') place on record. For example, in Matthew: 'I tell you the truth, unless you turn from your sins and become like little children, you will never get into the Kingdom of Heaven' (18:3, NLT). In similar vein, Mark wrote: 'I tell you the truth, anyone who doesn't receive the Kingdom of God like a child will never enter it' (10:15, NLT). It is noteworthy that Jesus emphasised the importance of gaining access to the Kingdom of Heaven by describing it as a precious pearl of immense value to be gained at all cost (Matthew Chapter 13). Academic achievement, talent, success and fame do not begin to compare with the spiritual potency of having a childlike trust in Jesus with its eternal reward.

Some Bible scholars suggest that as God knows all things, past and present, He therefore knows the names of those who *would* have put their trust in Jesus had they had opportunity or capacity to do so. A similar argument is proposed to cover the multi-millions who have never heard of Jesus Christ, let alone made a decision whether to trust him for their salvation. The justification for holding such a position is rooted in Bible texts that broadly express the fact that 'God knows those who belong to Him' (e.g., Numbers 16:5 and 2 Timothy 2:19a). Our attitude to this particular argument will influence the way that we approach evangelism: if we believe that people can only be saved by hearing the word, confessing their sins and unequivocally declaring their trust in Jesus, it lends urgency to sharing the Gospel. If we believe that God saves through other means or even that He has predetermined who will and who will not be saved, the need for such persistent evangelism is greatly diminished. It is essential for each of us to know where we stand on this issue. See Chapter 10 for further discussion about sharing the Gospel.

Consequences of intentional sin

Intentional sin means that we deliberately go against God's laws in full knowledge of doing so. Some sinful actions are relatively easy to identify (e.g., tax evasion); others may be less obvious, such as slipping off from work a few minutes early or using our time inappropriately. It is undeniably true that the majority of intentional sins start by allowing ungodly thoughts to embed themselves in our minds and as a result give rise to unseemly behaviour, lust, anger or resentment. As Paul urges Timothy in his second letter: 'Hold on to the pattern of wholesome teaching you learned from me—a pattern shaped by the faith and love that you have in Christ Jesus' (1:13, NLT). The concept of 'wholesomeness' (purity) is fundamental when seeking to lead a godly life and avoiding even minor transgressions that serve to blunt our witness and blemish our right standing with God.

Perhaps the most chilling examples of deliberate human failure is found in a decision made by one of the original Twelve Disciples, Judas Iscariot. In his Gospel account, Luke refers to the awful moment that Judas decided to betray Jesus: 'Then Satan entered into the heart of Judas Iscariot, who was one of the twelve apostles [disciples]' (22:3, CEV). It is worth noting that although the phrase 'Satan entered' is employed, he (that is, Satan, the devil) requires our permission or at least our passive submission to take control of our thoughts, words and deeds. We are not helpless beings, unable to refuse Satan entry or resist his deceitful overtures, thereby placing ourselves at his disposal—quite the opposite!

Insight

Although we are appalled at Judas's actions, they remind us that down through the ages, including the present time, Jesus's followers are capable of betraying him; not directly, as Judas did, but through their half-hearted commitment, casual approach to Kingdom work and failure to reflect his loving kindness in word and deed.

The Apostle James writes that we should first humble ourselves before God and come close to Him with the assurance that He will provide the strength and authority to resist the devil, who will then flee from us (James 4:7). The order of these events is important: (1) humility (2) closeness to God (3) victory over temptation by the power of the Spirit. It is not a case of gritting our teeth and uttering hollow rebukes to Satan, akin to a religious incantation. On the contrary, it is acknowledging that of ourselves we can do nothing (John 15:5), though our willing cooperation is required if the Holy Spirit is to have His unhindered way. Furthermore, Christians have access to the 'spiritual armour of God', as Paul describes it in his letter to the Christians in Ephesus. See the next chapter for details.

Lack of intentionality

In light of the significance of intentionality, the position of the unborn, infants, young children and the mentally deficient (see earlier) now becomes clearer. Although none of them are able to respond to Christ's offer of salvation, they are free from the curse of 'original sin' because of Christ's all-sufficient death and subsequent resurrection. Their undeveloped minds make them incapable of wilful sinning; consequently, God will not judge them on that basis. Those who die before maturity or are mentally incapacitated are free from condemnation based on their *deliberate* sin because they do not possess the capacity or have the maturity to sin intentionally, repent and exercise saving faith in Christ, constantly bearing in mind the fundamental truth that the 'original sin' element was dealt with by Christ at Calvary and therefore does not count against them.

By contrast, while those who are sufficiently mature and of sound mind have their 'original sin' covered by Jesus's death on the Cross of Calvary—he gave his life for sins of the *world*—they must bear the consequences of their decisions to neglect God and sin during their lifetimes. An intentional rejection of God's offer of freedom from sin through Christ leaves the people so disposed open to judgement and condemnation.

I leave the reader to humbly consider before God the scriptural validity for the explanation I have offered about these weighty issues. Whatever our position on these matters, the eternal fate of countless millions who are unable to speak for themselves is an issue about which believers and sceptics rightly demand clarification. Thankfully, we can be assured that Jesus Christ's overwhelming desire is to seek and save those who are lost—that is, those who are living lives independent of God's abiding influence—and not seeking to find the smallest fault as a justification to condemn them. Even so, dismissing or ignoring God and wilfully rejecting Jesus Christ has serious consequences for the vast majority of people who possess the capacity to think, exercise believing faith and make rational decisions.

Only the narrow way leads to life (Matthew 7:13–14) and Christ is both the gateway and doorkeeper. As Jesus declared to Thomas, one of the Twelve Disciples: 'I am the way, the truth and the life. No one comes to the Father except through me' (John 14:6). Nothing could be clearer, though the process by which it happens will vary according to individual circumstances and the abundant grace of God, as described above.

Analysing Sin

Sinful impulses

The Bible is full of instances where key figures, apparently devoted to God, committed serious offences that violated His moral law and fell well short of the standards He demanded. Among their number were leaders such as Moses (who murdered a slave-driver, though it could be argued that in doing so, he saved a fellow Israelite's life), King David (who stole another man's wife after sending him on a suicide mission) and Simon Peter, whose denial of Jesus prior to the crucifixion was a painful reminder of human vulnerability during times of temptation, stress and opposition.

The redeeming feature in the aforementioned examples is that they all repented of their sin (i.e., admitted their guilt) and sought to serve God faithfully henceforth, though not after painful consequences as a result of the original failure. Thus, Moses spent years in the wilderness; David and his mistress, Bathsheba, lost a precious son, and his family life became chaotic; Peter had to live with the shame until Jesus personally forgave him. Offences committed by these and other major figures were not only morally wrong (against the stated law of God) but were also failing to give God first place in their lives and decisions. They acted impulsively or focused on what they perceived as personal benefits or unwisely took the advice of friends and advisers, rather than turning to God for help and guidance.

Sin and choice

Although human advice is often the channel that the Holy Spirit uses to communicate His will to us, the advice will be of limited value unless the adviser is a godly person who is 'walking in step with the Spirit', as the Apostle Paul urged Christians in Galatia (5:25). For example, King Rehoboam (a son of King Solomon) chose to take advice from his inexperienced and, we must presume, ungodly young friends and dismissed the counsel of the older and wiser men, which almost resulted in Civil War and cleaved Israel into two sections (the Northern Kingdom called Samaria under Jeroboam; the Southern Kingdom called Judah under Rehoboam).

The principle to draw from this tragic example is not that older people are necessarily wiser than those who are younger, but that it is essential to take immense care when choosing whose advice to heed and whose advice to disregard, always making sure that we submit our plans to God before proceeding, and not doing it as an afterthought. Thus, we read that 'the plans of the godly are just [but] the advice of the wicked is treacherous' (Proverbs 12:5, NIVUK); similarly: 'Commit your actions to the Lord and your plans will succeed' (Proverbs 16:3, NLT). In Psalm 38, the psalmist provides an affirmation of God's desire to ensure the best for us in making our life choices: 'The Lord will work out his plans for my life; for your faithful love, O Lord, endures forever' (38:8, NLT).

Furthermore, when we are in a position to offer advice to people, it is important to avoid imposing our own thoughts and feelings on them, rather than helping them to clarify the position for themselves. Other than in an emergency when immediate action is required, it is helpful to preface what we say with, 'Is it worth considering…' or 'I wonder whether an alternative way of proceeding might be…' in preference to an abrupt 'I think you should…' that takes responsibility away from the individual and elevates the adviser to a morally superior position.

Whatever procedure has been undertaken in reaching a provisional decision, ensuring that the proposed course of action has been laid before the Lord in prayer must always be a priority, as He will provide confirmation and grant peace of mind if the course of action is right.

Seriousness of transgressions

We can be thankful that blatant acts of wickedness and foolishness are confined to a tiny percentage of the population; if it were not so, we would all be convicted criminals! Nevertheless, no one can afford the luxury of being smug or believing that 'little sins' are insignificant, as I explore below.

The Apostle John states in his first letter to Christians scattered across Asia Minor that 'all wicked actions are sin but not every sin leads to death' (5:17). In other words, God judges sin with respect to their seriousness; some 'wicked actions' are so dreadful that they result in death. John does not specify what sort of death he means but the implication is *eternal* death. Other sins are relatively mild 'wicked actions' whose consequences are more immediate in affecting what happens in this life but will be less consequential in the final judgement. Nevertheless, whether sin is supremely wicked or relatively trivial or lies somewhere between the two extremes, every aspect of sinning necessitates repentance on the part of the transgressor to receive forgiveness through Christ. It must be emphasised that trusting in the finished work of Jesus Christ on the Cross must *precede* confession of individual sins; his sacrificial death cannot be relegated to an afterthought.

For the vast majority of people, sinning against God is not through appalling behaviour; rather, it takes a more subtle form through the use of unkind words, gossip, cheating, cynicism and selfish deceit. The advance of technology has been a blessing to most people and societies in many and various ways but has also resulted in an expansion of opportunities for reprobates to insult, accuse and gratify sexual impulses at the expense of their victims' wellbeing. The oft-quoted maxim that 'sticks and stones may break my bones but words can never hurt me' must be counted amongst the most absurd and inaccurate statements ever made! We can add the use of corrupt images and release of embarrassing personal details into the public arena to the list of sinful acts that have become embedded in contemporary society.

Forms of deceits

Peter states emphatically that a key characteristic of Jesus was that 'he did no sin, neither was guile found in his mouth' (I Peter 2:22, KJV). The word guile means cunning or deceptive. By contrast to Jesus's example, deceitfulness is endemic in society and takes a variety of forms, some of which are extremely harmful.

It is necessary to distinguish 'selfish deceit'—which is for personal gain— from 'compassionate deceit', which is a strategy that is used to protect a person from emotional harm or distress and can therefore be justified. For instance, a parent may not disclose to a child or vulnerable adult the full details of a relationship problem, health issue or a particularly unpleasant event that might disturb or create mental anguish for the individual concerned. Sometimes, compassion and care outweighs accuracy.

An example of compassionate deceit is found in Jeremiah Chapter 38 when the King implores the prophet not to disclose the content of their conversation but to say (falsely) that he was reassuring Jeremiah that he would not be sent back to prison. The King was anxious that his own life might be in danger, together with the prospect of rebellion, if his officials believed that he was in cahoots with the 'troublesome' prophet. As Jeremiah left the king's chamber, the courtiers demanded to know what they had been discussing. Jeremiah repeated what he had agreed with the king to say and thereby deceived the assembled group. Although Jeremiah was not telling the truth, his actions almost certainly prevented mutiny and likely assassination, so arguably his actions were vindicated.

A second example of compassionate deceit is found in Joshua Chapter 9. The Israelites were slowly conquering each godless tribe and taking possession of the land that God had promised to them. When the Gibeonites heard of how other tribes were being annihilated, their leaders sent a delegation to Joshua, pretending to be from a far land and suing for peace. The Gibeonite representatives succeeded in convincing the Israelites of their distant lineage and Joshua made an oath that their people would be spared. Subsequently, it was discovered that the Gibeonites were near neighbours, but owing to the recently ratified treaty, the tribe were left unharmed (though made servants). When

Joshua demanded to know why the delegation had deceived them, the Gibeonite leaders explained that it was the only way to ensure that the Israelite army would not destroy them, as they had done so ruthlessly to other groups.

Insight

It is a moot point as to whether the prophet Jeremiah and the Gibeonites in the two examples quoted above were justified in maintaining the deceptions ('lies') or whether the truth should always be spoken, regardless of the likely consequences. In this regard, it is significant that the Gibeonite ruse was successful in fooling the Israelites because the leaders 'did not enquire of the Lord' before making the pledge (Joshua 9:14, NIVUK)—an important factor that everyone should heed in making decisions about what is disclosed and concealed.

Hierarchy of sin

It is important to take account of the fact that Jesus condemned relatively minor transgressions almost as strongly as he did the blatantly wicked acts. For example, he scolded the disciples for discussing who would be greatest in the Kingdom and sternly rebuked their lack of faith. On numerous occasions, Jesus also expressed disappointment at his followers' low level of commitment and failure to trust God in times of pressure and uncertainty.

Jesus's blanket condemnation of all types and graveness of sin has given rise to the assertion that there isn't a grading of sin according to its seriousness but that all transgressions are equally abhorrent to a holy and righteous God. However attractive this assertion might sound—and while it is true that every sin offends God—it has to be weighed against a raft of Scriptures that warn about the fate of those who persistently indulge in blatant forms of sinning to such an extent that it becomes engrained in their character and they take little heed as to the consequences.

An example of how sin can become deep-rooted is found in Jeremiah Chapter 9, where the Lord expresses His anger because the people of Judah have abandoned His instructions and stubbornly followed their own desires to such an extent that they actively refused to obey Him, thereby inviting disaster, which came in the form of being conquered and taken into captivity.

Jesus highlighted specific sins that invite God's wrath if indulged in as a direct form of opposition to His stated will and purpose, including lack of forgiveness, worshipping idols (graven images, celebrities, worldly pleasures and even family members), abuse of children and using positions of power to oppress the poor and needy. Matthew records Jesus's powerful warning about the time when he (Jesus) returns to judge the world: 'This is how it will be at the end of the age. The angels will come and separate the wicked from the righteous and throw them into the blazing furnace, where there will be weeping and gnashing of teeth' (13:49–50, NIVUK). In similar vein, the writer of Hebrews solemnly states that it is 'a terrible [fearful] thing to fall into the hands of the living God' (10:31, NKJV). The fact that Jesus distinguishes between 'righteous' and 'wicked' is further evidence that each person falls into one category or another; there are no in-betweens.

Sin is like a pernicious weed: once it takes root and is allowed to grow, it strangles righteousness and substitutes it with depravity of thought, word and deeds. Sinfulness begins by taking our eyes off Jesus and allowing the seed of sin to be implanted in our minds. Thus, Paul emphasises the importance of a spiritually 'renewed mind' to properly discern God's good, pleasing and perfect will (Romans 12:2).

Continuing to sin

Scripture does not support the concept of universal forgiveness from sin without repentance—a philosophy sometimes referred to as 'Universalism', see below. Jesus was explicit about the separation of good from evil at the end of the present world when the final resurrection takes place: 'Those who have done good will rise to experience eternal life and those who have continued in evil will rise to experience judgement' (John 5:29, NLT). When Paul was on trial before the governor, Felix, he boldly stated that there would be a resurrection of both the righteous and the wicked (Acts 24:15b).

The inclusion of the phrase 'continued in evil' in Jesus's statement is important, as there is always opportunity for people who have sinned, whether through minor misdemeanours or serious offences, to repent sincerely, turn away from their ungodly behaviour and put their trust in Christ as Saviour. It is *continuing* to sin wilfully that is the determining factor that not only leading to serious consequences in this life (being deprived of God's forgiveness, guidance and fellowship) but also after we die and have to face judgement without Christ as our advocate to plead our cause.

In his first letter, the Apostle John offers this reassurance about the grace of God towards those who have placed their trust in Christ: 'My dear children, I am writing this to you so that you will not sin. But if anyone does sin, we have an advocate who pleads our case before the Father. He is Jesus Christ, the one who is truly righteous' (2:1, NLT). The kindness of God does not, however, act as a 'free pass' to repeatedly indulge in sin, whether by thought, word or deed, in the mistaken belief that a simple prayer of confession after each occasion clears the way for further wrong behaviour. It does not! For further insights into the advocacy role of the Son and Spirit, see Chapter 7.

Rewards for righteous living

No one has the right to expect or demand rewards from God for placing Him at the centre of life, striving to do His will and forfeiting worldly benefits to promote Kingdom values. Nevertheless, Jesus used a number of parables to explain the allocation of different honours for wholehearted obedience and faithful service. In Matthew Chapter 25, we read that he used the *Parable of the Ten Bridesmaids (Virgins)* to emphasise the importance of being well prepared for the Master's return and not being idle as we wait. In the same chapter, Jesus explains the importance of using our time and talents effectively in the *Parable of the Three Servants* where two servants are commended for their wise use of resources and one is roundly scolded. Lethargy and a slothful attitude to life sit uneasily with the Master's call to serve him by serving others and to be ready for his imminent return by being spiritually alert and obedient.

The rewards for faithful service therefore contrast sharply with the ignominy attached to indolence and a lack of involvement in Kingdom work. Throughout the Bible there are various references to degrees of honour for the righteous based on the way that they demonstrated integrity, godly wisdom, leadership, loving kindness and generosity towards others, without any expectation of recompense or remuneration. The Prayer of St Ignatius of Loyola is instructive in this regard: *Teach us, good Lord, to serve you as you deserve, to give and not to count the cost, to fight and not to heed the wounds, to toil and not to seek for rest, to labour and not to ask for any reward, save that of knowing that we do your will.*

Crucially, the ultimate test for the distribution of heavenly rewards is not only the extent to which the fruit of the Spirit is shown in our lives (Galatians Chapter 5; see also Chapter 11 in this book) but, crucially, the *degree of faith* exercised as an expression of trust in God displayed by an individual or group or church. The exercising of faith will, for a tiny percentage of believers, lead to martyrdom, as followers of Jesus have borne testimony down the centuries. In Revelation 2:10, Jesus has these words of comfort for Christians facing extreme suffering: 'But if you remain faithful even when facing death, I will give you the crown of life' (NLT). We can only speculate what Jesus meant by 'crown of life' but it is undoubtedly something glorious.

Ignorance of the Gospel

The fate of the unenlightened

I went to some lengths earlier in the chapter to acknowledge that God's view of sin is clear with respect to those who die prematurely or have serious developmental retardation. More problematic is to understand the position for people who have never been exposed to the Gospel, owing to their immersion in an alien culture or language difficulties or living under a repressive regime that suppresses access to Bible truth. In light of this perplexing issue, the question arises as to whether those who do not have opportunity to hear about Jesus are eternally lost, to which a variety of responses have been offered, as follows:

1. The bluntest response is to state that as Christ is the only way to God, those who have not positively accepted him as Saviour, whatever the circumstances, are unrepentant sinners destined for Hell.
2. A milder response is that God will judge such people on the basis of the insights they have received through other means. For example, intrigue about the origin of beauty in nature, as David expresses: 'The heavens proclaim the glory of God. The skies display his craftsmanship. Day

after day they continue to speak; night after night they make him known' (Psalm 19:1–2, NLT).

3. The gentlest response is that God, who knows all things, will judge on the basis of the response that they *would* have made if they had been told about Jesus and his love for them.

4. A more controversial view is that there will be a 'second chance' following death to which deceased souls are invited to respond.

5. The final position is to argue that as God is love, He will ultimately forgive everyone ('Universalism').

In prayerfully considering these and associated alternatives, three fundamental scriptural truths must be acknowledged: (a) Jesus is the only way to God the Father. (b) Jesus said that the way to Heaven is narrow and few find it. (c) There is no scriptural evidence to suggest that everyone will eventually be permitted to enter God's eternal presence and inherit the new earth.

In respect of point 1 in the list above, Matthew records Jesus's warning in his Gospel account: 'You can enter God's Kingdom only through the narrow gate. The highway to hell is broad and its gate is wide for the many who choose that way' (7:13, NLT). It is instructive to note that Jesus referred to the significance of *choice*—our eternal destiny is not predetermined or, as some religions argue, a case of good deeds outweighing bad ones, but of deciding whether to take the 'narrow way' found through believing in the Son of God as Saviour or to follow the crowd along the 'wide road' of unbelief that leads to destruction ('eternal death'). See Chapter 7 for a fuller exposition of this important doctrine.

In respect of point 2, a single verse in the opening chapter of Paul's letter to Christians in Rome is frequently quoted to justify this position: 'For since the creation of the world His invisible attributes are clearly seen, being understood by the things that are made, even His eternal power and Godhead, so that they are without excuse' (1:20, NKJV). It should be noted that Paul is directing his comments towards those who are 'godless and wicked' and 'suppress the truth'. As always in Scripture, context is important.

I deal succinctly with point 3 in Chapter 5, acknowledging that there are certain imponderable issues that we must leave in the hands of our gracious Heavenly Father. We can, however, find a clue to God's intention in Paul's letter to the Romans where he explains the position: 'For God knew his people in advance, and he chose them to become like his Son, so that his Son would be the firstborn [supreme] among many brothers and sisters. And having chosen them, he called them to come to him. And having called them, he gave them right standing with himself. And having given them right standing, he gave them his glory' (8:29–30, NLT). The NIVUK translation uses more standard terms, including the enigmatic word, 'predestined'; thus: 'And we know that in all things God works for the good of those who love him, who have been called according to his purpose. For those God foreknew he also predestined to be conformed to the image of his Son, that he might be the firstborn among many brothers and sisters. And those he predestined, he also called; those he called, he also justified; those he justified, he also glorified'.

These verses have been debated at considerable length down the centuries, some scholars arguing that they reinforce the sovereignty of God in determining in advance those who are going to be saved, others pointing out that these words are directed towards those who love God and are called according to His purpose (8:28), so cannot be generalised. The first argument minimises the role of human responsibility; the latter argument emphasises the significance of personal choice, a theme that I promote throughout this book.

In respect of points 4 and 5, it should be emphasised to those who argue that Jesus's death has exonerated every person on earth—thereby freeing everyone from taking responsibility for their actions while alive—that Jesus spoke of both Heaven and Hell as real places and alternative locations of eternal destiny for souls. Jesus also underlined the fact that everyone is given a choice in selecting which path to take during this life, whether for good or for ill, along the narrow or broad way.

Those who argue that Jesus preached to those in Hell during the period between his death and resurrection to offer them a 'second chance' base their belief on Peter's words that Jesus 'also went and preached to the spirits now in prison, who once were disobedient, when the great patience of God was waiting in the days of Noah' (I Peter 3:19–20a, AMP). The problem lies in the reference to 'the days of Noah'. The argument that Jesus preached solely to the people of Noah's generation is puzzling, but also casts serious doubt on the event being universally applicable across all time. It seems more likely that Peter was encouraging the Gentile Christian readers to emulate Noah by standing firm in the face of derision and persecution, and continue to witness in the power of the Spirit. Those that refused to listen in Noah's day were already 'in prison'—the prison of unbelief—just as people of every generation who resist the need to repent and trust in God are imprisoned by sin. See Chapter 12 under 'Heaven's whereabouts' for another perspective on this crucial issue of a 'second chance'.

> **Insight**
> In seeking a correct interpretation, it is important to avoid using a single statement from Scripture to create a doctrine that is not validated elsewhere in the Bible; in this case, the issue is the claim that there will be a second chance to repent, which is referred to only once (by Peter).

Christ the final arbiter

A useful but imperfect analogy to describe the fate of those who die with and without Christ as Saviour is to imagine innumerable 'tributaries'—each one representing a deceased soul—flowing into the main tide of water that rushes towards a magnificent sluice gate, beyond which lies the Holy City of God, as described in the Book of Revelation. On reaching the gate, angel guardians are present to determine who is allowed into the city and who is caught at the gate like driftwood, removed from the river and subsequently destroyed or stacked unceremoniously in a far corner to slowly decompose ('perish').

Another imaginative representation of the final separation is to envisage two roads, one narrow and difficult, the other broad and smooth, running parallel towards the Heavenly City. The smaller number of souls traversing the narrow path pass through a gate into the city unhindered and with the sound of great rejoicing; the majority of souls on the wide road fall into an abyss.

How the Son of God determines who is allowed to 'pass through the gate' and who is denied entry is not for us to decide. All we *can* state with assurance from Scripture is that those who die 'in Christ' will land safely on heaven's shores and God will act justly with the rest of humankind. We can only attest that Jesus is the only way to God the Father. He is the gate and the one who seeks and saves the lost.

Summary

As part of my attempts to expose the seriousness of sinning, I have grappled with issues such as original sin, personal responsibility and the relevance of individual decision-making. Jesus's death at Calvary was to atone for human failings of every kind, whether judged by us to be serious or trivial. Nevertheless, it is valid to make a distinction between acts of extreme wickedness (committed by the few) and minor transgressions (committed by all), though there are, of course, many sinful acts that fall between the two extremes.

I have already made reference to the way in which we can gain better understanding of the difference between, and consequences arising from, blatant sins—for example, extortion and robbery—and those resulting from original sin, often committed out of ignorance or finding unchallenged acceptance within prevailing secular norms—for example, the inclination to meet force with force or take revenge or search for self-fulfilment through morally damaging forms of entertainment or failing to forgive others. I have also addressed the difficult question of how God will deal with people who, due to their immaturity or mental incapacity or ignorance of the Gospel, have never had the opportunity to repent of their sin and respond to Christ's gracious invitation to follow him.

Consider and discuss the validity of the following statements

1. All sins are equally offensive to a holy God.
2. Original sin is the root cause of every individual failing.
3. The original sin of every person has been dealt with at Calvary.
4. God will only take our wilful sins into account when passing judgement.
5. As Jesus died for the sins of the world, every person is forgiven unless he or she knowingly rejects the offer of salvation.
6. Only those sins that are specifically confessed can be forgiven.
7. God will judge alternative criteria to judge people who have not had the opportunity to hear and respond to the Gospel.
8. Every baby (born and unborn) and every child will be found a place in heaven.
9. Every mentally confused person will be found a place in heaven.
10. God will eventually forgive every person's sin, but eternal rewards depend on the way we have lived.

Chapter 4
The Impact of Sin

Introduction

Criminal offenders will sometimes argue that their crimes are 'victimless' or justified. For example, in the case of theft or fraud, a malefactor might protest that the sufferer is covered by insurance and will therefore be financially recompensed following the event, so no great harm is done. More menacingly, in the case of violent assault, the assailant might insist that the victims were merely getting what they deserved. Such attempts to justify blatantly sinful acts and deflect the blame onto others sit uneasily alongside the physical and emotional anguish that crimes generate.

In a less dramatic way, spiteful and callous accusations can have a negative and prolonged impact that far exceeds their initial hurtful purpose. Thus, a dismissive remark, derogatory comment or public rebuke not only wounds the person on the occasion it is made but also has the effect of unsettling and demoralising him or her for some considerable time afterwards.

Although obnoxious verbal behaviour is intended to injure the victim, the *offender* may also be adversely affected and suffer harmful repercussions, which take the form of a seared conscience and self-loathing. More gravely, it may cause wrongdoers to revel in having the power to wound and control others, which becomes embedded in their personality and conduct. In this chapter, I look at issues relating to the impact of sin, the centrality of forgiveness and the internal mechanisms that God has placed inside every person to combat falling into sinful behaviour and ways to make restitution after doing so. I also highlight the importance of confession as a means of restoring a harmonious relationship between sinners and God. Ultimately, each person has the choice to serve God or to serve Satan.

The Human Heart

Damage caused by sin

Sinning is not only directed against a person or persons, it is also offensive to God. Grievous injury and suffering, both physical and psychological, can be caused by thoughtless or wilful actions that create resentment and anger on the part of the victim towards the perpetrator. Bitterness and animosity are capable of damaging a person's health and wellbeing; in rare cases, it can cause considerable emotional damage, resulting in severe mental stress and self-harm, especially among young people. The prevalence of so-called 'honour killings' within certain religious groups and the horrifying increase in revenge attacks, often as a result of unrequited love or family partnership breakdown, are extreme outcomes that are directly related to uncontrolled rage and violence. As the psalmist warns: 'Stop being angry! Turn from your rage! Do not lose your temper—it only leads to harm' (Psalm 37:8, NLT). By contrast, the writer of Proverbs reminds us that 'love prospers when a fault is forgiven but dwelling on it separates [even] close friends' (17:9, NLT).

An elderly lady confided in me that when she behaved badly as a child, her mother would turn to her angrily and say coldly: "I'll never forgive you for that!" Whether or not the mother meant what she said and possessed bitterness in her heart or merely spoke unthinkingly is impossible to ascertain. The only certainty is that her scathing words were still echoing in the daughter's head some sixty years later!

Fierce and menacing actions (including the use of threatening words) give credence to the Old Testament prophet Jeremiah's assertion that 'the heart is devious above all else; it is perverse. Who can understand it?' (17:9, NRSV) Other Bible versions use stronger phrases, such as 'deceitful above all things' and 'desperately wicked'. No doubt, decent minded people, who do their best to lead lawful and upright lives will object to being included in such a dark description but experience shows that even the most passive and honourable person is capable of deeply sinful behaviour, as countless events throughout history have demonstrated. We are reminded of Paul's sobering message to the Christians in Rome that 'all have sinned and fallen short of the glory of God' (3:23, NIVUK) or using a more recent translation: 'For everyone has sinned; we all fall short of God's glorious standard' (NLT).

Our own horrified reaction when we hear about appalling behaviour is not only prompted by incredulity that such wickedness is possible but by a deeply rooted fear that we, too, might be capable of degenerate behaviour, given the right circumstances and opportunity. More commonly, we experience a shadowy sense of guilt in the knowledge that we all fail badly at one time or another. The popular retort: "Well, no one's perfect!" far from exonerating us, simply serves to confirm that in one way or another we are not even capable of meeting our own standards, let alone those of Almighty God!

Although minor unlawful acts and personal disputes may not have the same grievous impact on people as serious crimes, they can be hugely upsetting, as anyone who has had a credit card stolen or long-running boundary dispute with a neighbour will readily testify. I explore the breadth and limitations of God's forgiveness in greater depth in the next section. Suffice it to say that it is only through Jesus Christ that people find true and complete release from the burden and consequences of sin, whether serious or minor, though the practical impact of moral failing must still be faced by the individual concerned.

The place of remorse

Personal abuse or physical injury is difficult to handle, but a situation in which a miscreant has committed an offence against a close family member or friend can be even more upsetting. Supporting the victim not only involves standing alongside the aggrieved person but also ensuring that in doing so, the understandable indignation does not translate into a desire for revenge. It is perfectly possible for a lack of forgiveness to be a greater problem for the victim's supporters than for the victim. There is also a danger that the build-up of angst among friends and families prevents victims from finding release from their initial anger and desire for reprisal, owing to the vexatious atmosphere the indignation creates.

The situation is even more distressing when the perpetrator shows little remorse and appears emotionally detached from the incident and dismissive about his or her offence. The increase in aggressive verbal disputes and the spike in physical attacks has been characterised by callousness of this kind. When the individual is unrepentant about committing the offence, the sufferer, friends and family members are placed in a moral dilemma about whether to reach out and offer forgiveness, when the perpetrator adopts such a defiant attitude.

It is, of course, possible to forgive a gossip, spiteful aggressor, or lawbreaker, while insisting that appropriate justice be fully meted out. In recent years, judges have taken closer account of victims' statements concerning the impact that a crime has had on their lives in determining the length of sentence. Relatively minor misdeeds, such as cheating, deception, false accusation and gossip are not criminal but can create mental torment, which is not easily assuaged, even through the medium of forgiveness, as explored below.

The power of forgiveness

Christians may be consoled that where natural justice fails, God's justice will ultimately prevail. Luke records some vitally important words of Jesus, reminding us that despite human deficiencies, there are heavenly blessings awaiting those who endeavour to show loving kindness to others, even to those who act wickedly: 'But love your enemies and be good to them. Lend without expecting to be paid back. Then you will get a great reward and you will be the true children of God in heaven. He is good even to people who are unthankful and cruel' (6:35, CEV). The final phrase, 'he is kind even to people who are unthankful and cruel' is contrary to human instinct; it is also immensely reassuring, as it reminds us that although God's vengeance may be severe towards those who wilfully sin, it is also tempered by His overwhelming love for the people He has created. God's goodness is unwavering, as is His justice.

In extreme cases, failure to forgive can result in the aggrieved party seeking ways to extract revenge, resulting in distressing outcomes for everyone. The Apostle Paul deals firmly with this issue in his letter to Rome: 'Dear friends, never take revenge. Leave that to the righteous anger of God. For the Scriptures say, "I will take revenge; I will pay them back," says the Lord' (12:19, NLT). Revenge should not be confused with natural justice that takes place through legal procedures. Divine retribution is God's to make, not ours. Jesus completely reversed the old adage of 'an eye for an eye and a tooth for a tooth' (Matthew 5:38–9) by offering a new and better way of responding that reflects the grace of God, rather than the malice of mankind.

Whatever the circumstances, the abiding principle is that if someone fails to forgive another person for an offence, the injured party may suffer greater torment than the perpetrator. We do well to reflect on the fact that Jesus died on the Cross of Calvary for the sins of the whole world, including those who rejected him then and those who have refused to acknowledge him since. The next time we are tempted to be angry and contemptuous of those who do wrong, especially those whose actions harm or mistreat us or those we love, it is good to contemplate God's unconditional love towards sinners and His graciousness in forgiving our sin and constantly cleansing us from all unrighteousness, if we invite Him to do so (1 John 1:9). I cover this important issue at length in Chapter 5.

Being asked to forgive a single offence is usually manageable for the majority of people; far more challenging is to forgive repeat offences. Matthew records a seminal moment in Jesus's ministry when he responded to a probing question from his disciple, Peter: 'Then Peter came to him and asked, Lord, how often should I forgive someone [my brother] who sins against me? Seven times? No, not seven times, Jesus replied, but seventy times seven!' (18:21–22, NLT) The implications for Christians are immense, as Jesus commanded that forgiveness should cover *multiple* offences. Forgiving someone for a single instance of wrongdoing can be difficult, but to forgive the same person after repetition of the transgression is beyond the natural mode of response and can only be accomplished through a combination of divine grace and our own willingness to show mercy to others. Of the numerous requirements that Jesus demanded from his followers, the need to forgive the same person on multiple occasions must rank among the hardest.

Insight

It should be borne firmly in mind that forgiveness is a sign of moral courage, not weakness, though others may not view the act in such a positive light. Forgiveness is rarely easy—and often takes a considerable length of time to become rooted in our psyche—but the outcome is of benefit to both the perpetrator and the victim. The familiar expression: 'To err is human; to forgive, divine' is attributed to Alexander Pope. Other helpful quotations (all anonymous) include:

- 'To forgive is to set a prisoner free and discover that the prisoner was you'
- 'The stupid neither forgive nor forget; the naive forgive and forget; the wise forgive but do not forget'
- 'Forgive others, not because they deserve forgiveness, but because you deserve peace'

Resisting and Avoiding Sin

Three warning systems

It is not uncommon to hear people who have transgressed in word or deed to insist that they were unable to help themselves; or to claim that something or someone or sheer desperation drove them to do indulge in sinful behaviour (see also below under 'Personal responsibility'). While it is undoubtedly true that wrongdoing can be prompted by despair, depression, misplaced loyalty or threats from others, the argument that people cannot help themselves, either when they err on the spur of the moment or via a pre-planned intention, is countered by the fact that God has placed within the human heart three 'guidance systems' to help each person resist sin or, if the sin has been committed, to show genuine and immediate repentance.

Even people without a conscious awareness of God and His divine purposes have these internal instruments available, though it is sadly the case that they can be over-ridden by human wilfulness. In loose order—while acknowledging that it is not possible to separate out each element fully—the three systems may be classified as follows: (1) conscience (2) guilt (3) shame. Although the safeguards are interlinked, a broad definition for each of them provides a useful starting point for understanding how we are 'without excuse' in our behaviour:

Conscience is triggered when a thought, word or action generates unease, sometimes tinged with fear and concern about their probity, and the possible consequences of discovery.

Guilt occurs when conscience is disregarded and suppressed during the time the sin is committed but reactivated after the event has occurred.

Shame is triggered when a combination of conscience, guilt and regret produces self-loathing. A detailed consideration of the three safeguards follows.

Conscience

When temptation arises to think hateful or aggressive thoughts, to speak obnoxious words or to commit an unlawful or immoral act, the conscience is likely to be activated. The individual's response to the 'inner voice' will determine whether to proceed or step back, to smother the voice or submit to its warning. Sometimes, the thought, word or action has already taken place, prompting feelings of guilt (see below) and the need to repent through an apology or making amends in other ways (e.g., returning long borrowed property or making financial recompense). If the sin is undiscovered, the offender hopes that the incident can be concealed, though the fear of subsequent detection is likely to be very unsettling.

Conscience is a valuable aid in helping us to guard against sinful behaviour but with the important proviso that it is only fully functional if we are maintaining a close relationship with God. Even the Apostle Paul warns that our consciences are not always a reliable guide until we submit them to divine authority, as he admits in his first letter to the Corinthians: 'My conscience is clear but that doesn't prove I'm right. It is the Lord himself who will examine me and decide' (4:4, NLT).

God the Holy Spirit activates our consciences, so separation from Him through choice or neglect will dull or neutralise the mechanism, which in the worst excesses can lead to godless behaviour with little or no remorse. Paul warns Timothy that 'the Spirit clearly says that in later times some will abandon the faith and follow deceiving spirits and things taught by demons. Such teachings come through hypocritical liars, whose consciences have been seared as with a hot iron' (I Timothy 4:1–2, NIVUK). The NLT translates the final phrase as 'their consciences are dead', which should sound a sombre warning for anyone who is tempted to be casual about whether or not to obey God's explicit commands.

Guilt

It was noted above that the work of the Holy Spirit in a person's life is the key to retaining an active functioning conscience. If conscience is deliberately desensitised by disobedience or selfish desires and the sin is committed, or continuous sinful behaviour persists, feelings of guilt can invoke a time of intense anxiety in which the misdemeanour and its implications sear through the mind and create strong feelings of regret that affect every aspect of daily life, resulting in periods of considerable restlessness and interrupted sleep.

There have been numerous examples of people confessing to a crime that was committed many years earlier in order to ease the mind, 'get things off my chest' and usher in a much needed sense of peace. Guilt over serious offences has the potential to cause deep anguish, resulting in acute mental health problems due to the shame that accompanies it.

Referring to the most serious crime that it is possible to commit—taking an innocent life—the writer of Proverbs 28 warns that a murderer's tormented conscience will drive him into the grave (verse 17). In complete contrast to the misery caused by a tormented mind, the Old Testament prophet Isaiah describes the contentment that comes through focusing on God and doing what is right: 'You will keep him in perfect peace whose mind is stayed on You because he trusts in You' (26:3 NKJV).

Far less dramatic incidents can also result in tragedy once the conscience is reactivated and the person is emotionally tormented by the realisation that he or she has said or done something wrong. It must be emphasised, however, that persistent sinning may lead to a dulling of the senses and a carefree attitude to the action, such that it no longer causes concern. The Old Testament prophet, Jeremiah, rails against those who make light of persistent sinful behaviour: 'Are they ashamed of their disgusting actions? Not at all—they don't even know how to blush!' (6:15, NLT).

It is regrettably true that some people relish their improper behaviour and seem unmoved by the damage their actions cause. Such callousness reinforces the pressing need for everyone to submit to the Lordship of Christ and be born anew by the Spirit of God to receive forgiveness, freedom from the destructive wiles of Satan and cleansing from the corroding stain of sin. As referred to earlier, Jesus's discussion with a senior religious leader called Nicodemus is instructive: "I tell you the truth, unless you are born again [born anew, born from above], you cannot see the Kingdom of God."

"What do you mean?" exclaimed Nicodemus. "How can an old man go back into his mother's womb and be born again?"

Jesus replied, "I assure you, no one can enter the Kingdom of God without being born of water and the Spirit" (John 3:3–5, NLT).

It should be noted from Jesus's statement that the phrase 'born of water' resonates with words from another Old Testament prophet, Ezekiel: 'Then I will sprinkle clean water on you and you will be clean. Your filth will be washed away and you will no longer worship idols' (36:25, NLT). In other words, Jesus's words to Nicodemus referred to the process of being purified by the Spirit and were not referring to physical baptism which, though an important step of faith and witness, is not a requirement for salvation.

Insight

There has been extensive debate about the place of baptism in confirming salvation. While it is true that numerous verses in the New Testament affirm its importance, it is also essential to remember that we are only saved by repenting and exercising faith in the work of Jesus in redeeming the world from sin. Baptism is a subsequent witness by which we can testify that our old life has 'died' and our new life in Christ has begun. If baptism—whether by immersion or sprinkling—were a necessity for salvation, many millions of believers who, for practical reasons are unable to be baptised, would be eternally lost.

Shame

Some liberal thinkers (incorporating secularists, humanists and atheists)—broadly described as people who rely on human solutions rather than on God's revealed truth—argue that no one should ever feel shame for his or her behaviour, the caveat for such 'shame-free' acts being that the behaviour is committed out of genuine motives and no evil purpose was intended. Such a view further implies that the man or woman offending another person is merely responding to a 'natural urge', whose actions should be respected by others, even if they disapprove of them.

The irony and hypocrisy attached to those adopting such a permissive position is that while they defend the right to speak plainly without the stigma of shame, they are often the same people who accuse Christians of being 'hateful' for speaking out against unbiblical and ungodly ways of living and the insurgence of moral decadence. I further address the anti-Christian agenda and venomous behaviour by some secular organisations in Chapters 7 and 12.

A 'live and let live' philosophy infers that we should accommodate everybody else's opinions and viewpoints, however eccentric, erratic or controversial they seem, because no belief or opinion is deemed to be superior to any other and no moral choices invite a Supreme Being's retribution. After all, if there is no external monitoring of human behaviour by God and no prospect of divine judgement and wrath, why worry about the possible consequences (other than deliberate lawbreaking with the prospect of detection and punishment)? Why indeed!

Yet the Bible is clear that only those who seek to live in a way that honours God have no need to fear of being ashamed before Him. The psalmist summarises the position beautifully: 'Those who look to Him are radiant; their faces are never covered with shame' (Psalm 34:5, NIVUK).

A moment's thought will acknowledge that as a 'shame-free society' emerges, the likelihood of moral disintegration will inevitably follow. The 'no shame, no blame' approach to life is bound to have a deleterious effect on everyone's behaviour. For example, at a basic relational level, the absence of shame allows people to insist that their words or angry responses simply reflected the way they felt at the time, so should be accepted as reasonable and proportionate. Jesus views such matters more seriously, warning that the words emerging from an evil heart can have dire consequences for the user: 'A good person produces good things from the treasury of a good heart, and an evil person produces evil things from the treasury of an evil heart. And I tell you this: you must give an account on judgement day for every idle word you speak. The words you say will either acquit you or condemn you' (Matthew 12:35–7, NLT).

The phrase 'every idle word' may alarm us but Jesus was only referring to people whose hearts are evil; even so, it behoves all of us to think carefully before we speak harshly or accusingly. The writer of Proverbs 18 emphasises the benefit of employing wisdom when we speak: 'Some people make cutting remarks but the words of the wise bring healing' (verse 18, NLT). The question that all believers must ask themselves is whether their words leave the person to whom they are addressed in a better or worse state of mind.

There are a number of other moral dilemmas attached to the shame-free society that have implications for people's behaviour and societal stability. For instance, it could be argued that stealing food is justified if the person or his dependents are hungry. Again, the use of blanket protest movements to force a particular viewpoint on government or local officials or a rival gang through 'mob rule' has been justified by insisting sanctimoniously: 'This is for your own good' or 'It is all about equality' or similar statements. For Christians, achieving true fairness should always be rooted in a desire to see God's Kingdom come on earth, not airing personal grievances, promoting political ambition or exaggerating moral outrage.

It must be acknowledged that there are occasions when the finger of shame should be pointing at officialdom rather than protestors. After all, there are many examples of social change benefitting those in need that would never have taken place without forceful lobbying and widespread demonstration. It must also be accepted that there are times when illegal actions are necessary to oppose unfairness or tyranny, though such rare occurrences should not be used as a justification for reprehensible acts that violate God's laws and replace them with secular perspectives that corrupt decency and facilitate forms of behaviour that would have caused outrage a generation ago. Claims of moral superiority are often made to vindicate shameful acts and make them appear righteous.

God expresses His anger when people treat sin casually or pompously, vowing to exercise judgement on those who deliberately flout his expressed will and purpose, as Paul made powerfully clear: 'People wanted only to do evil. So God left them and let them go their sinful way. And so they became completely immoral and used their bodies in shameful ways with each other' (Romans 1:24,

ERV). God's rules and commands are for our good, not harm; they are designed to prevent us descending into increasingly corrupt and shameful practices.

Societal degeneration

Those who adopt a secular position on moral issues maintain that externally imposed requirements—such as those with an origin in biblical teaching about sexuality and relationships that require self-control and a disciplined mind—should be dismissed as being out-dated and repressive. We don't have to look far to see the societal chaos that such perverse thinking is creating, resulting in increased antisocial behaviour and heartless forms of deception and self-indulgence. The same philosophy that mocks and parodies the existence of God also rejects the commandments that form the foundation of Christian belief which, when implemented under the leading of the Spirit, provide stability and security for individuals and nations across the globe.

It is exasperatingly ironic that those who argue for accepting any and every type of behaviour, and insist on freedom and equality for all, are often the same ones who view themselves as moral guardians of truth and vilify those who object or disagree with their beliefs. So much for freedom of thought and expression! Nevertheless, every disciple of Jesus may be reassured by his words: 'God blesses you when people mock you and persecute you and lie about you and say all sorts of evil things against you because you are my followers. Be happy about it! Be very glad, for a great reward awaits you in heaven' (Matthew 5:11–12a, NLT).

Expunging shame by focusing on the alleged emotional and psychological damage that might occur to those being rightly accused is akin to switching off a smoke alarm in case the noise of the siren shocks people and makes them take evasive action. God's laws are meant to create exactly this type of effect! The writer of Proverbs 14 underscores the point that doing what is right or failing to do so has significant societal implications: 'Righteousness exalts a nation but sin is a reproach [shame, disgrace] to any people' (14:34, NKJV). When a nation replaces the law of God with secular alternatives, it leads to corruption, confusion and perverted behaviour.

Insight

'There are two freedoms—the false, where a man is free to do what he likes; the true, where he is free to do what he ought!' (Rev. Charles Kingsley, a 19th century English social reformer and writer)

Manifestations of Sin

Personal responsibility

Society tends to categorise sinful behaviour in terms of the damage it causes to people or property, the impact it has upon public order, and the extent of its physical and emotional destructive force. Small children who have behaved badly will often try to shift the responsibility onto another child or blame the circumstances; even adults are prone to employ the same types of excuses in attempting to justify their actions.

There are numerous occasions when each person must take personal responsibility for his or her behaviour and cannot point to the unwelcome influence of an external force, be it financial pressure, social trends or the prevalence of lax moral standards in society. An important passage in Jeremiah Chapter 31 (notably verses 31–34) describes how God will bless Israel but adds the proviso that each person will be responsible for his or her own sin, in which case, feigning ignorance, attempting to place the onus on someone or something else, or arguing that God's stated will and purpose is difficult to implement, are all unacceptable excuses.

Alongside human responsibility, the role that Satan (the name means 'deceiver' or 'great adversary' or 'accuser') and his angels ('demons') play in human sinfulness has been a subject of intense debate. Some people hold that evil forces are responsible for every sad and tragic event; others argue that demons are only permitted a specified degree of latitude by God and must therefore conform to His will and purpose; yet others insist that everyone must take responsibility for their actions and not attempt to absolve themselves from the responsibility by blaming extrinsic factors, including satanic ones.

The Bible is clear that Satan and those who serve him are motivated by two principal purposes in influencing Christians and opposing God's sovereign will: (1) To corrupt believers by distracting them from their principal responsibility and privilege of serving God and their neighbours. (2) To steer them into areas of life that tempt them to sin, damage their health and wellbeing, adversely affect family members and undermine their witness. In his first letter, Peter grimly warns Christians about Satan's deviousness, comparing him to a lion seeking its prey, thus: 'Stay alert! Watch out for your great enemy, the devil. He prowls around like a roaring lion, looking for someone to devour' (5:8, NLT). How encouraging that we have another lion to defend us and give us the victory, as expressed in the Book of Revelation about the end times: 'Stop weeping! Look, the Lion of the tribe of Judah, the heir to David's throne, has won the victory' (5:5, NLT). Hallelujah!

Insight

While the malevolence of demonic forces should not be underestimated, we can pray with the psalmist, King David: 'Keep me as the apple of your eye; hide me in the shadow of your wings from the wicked who are out to destroy me, from my mortal enemies who surround me' (17:8–9, NIVUK). Jesus often rebuked evil spirits and promises every disciple the authority to do the same. Although we should not be timid about using this authority, we must be careful not to overstep the mark, as 'even Michael, one of the mightiest of the angels, did not dare accuse the devil of blasphemy, but simply said, The Lord rebuke you!' (Jude 9b, NLT) As in every situation, it is the power of God in the name of Jesus that Satan fears above all else.

In addressing the issue of sin and personal responsibility, it is helpful to explore the key factors that contribute to godless attitudes and behaviour by using the following framework: *(1) Indiscipline (2) Innocent transgression (3) Wilful transgression.*

Indiscipline

Teachers of younger children claim that they can quickly identify those that are likely to be troublesome in the future, the large majority of whom are boys. Social workers are soon alerted to potential problems when they discover that the home situation is chaotic, parental controls are slack, and the adults are financially irresponsible. The seeds of antisocial behaviour and lack of respect for authority quickly become apparent and seem to be linked to families in which there is a notable absence of loving discipline, clean habits and regular routines. The lack of a stable father figure is often cited as a major factor in explaining children's and young people's unruly actions.

The sad transition from 'naughty child' to 'teenage tearaway' to 'adult criminal' *should* alert would-be perpetrators to the necessity of avoiding behaviour that clearly has an adverse impact on the victims and may have serious repercussions for those who choose to behave in that way. It is always to be hoped that the detrimental outcome for people who pursue a particular wrong action—for example, petty theft leading to a scarred reputation and a police record, thereby limiting future employment opportunities; violent temper resulting in injury and misery for others, often followed by acts of revenge;

vandalism leading to arrest for criminal damage—would act to restrain those who might initially be impressed and excited at the lawless behaviour.

Unfortunately, despite the likelihood of negative consequences, the tempting prospect of undetected theft resulting in the ability to purchase luxuries and enjoy expensive holidays; violent temper gaining fearful respect and subservience from peers; and drug dealing to reinforce profitable gang control, may encourage *imitation* rather than serve as a deterrent. Such is the pervasiveness and corrupt nature of sin. The high incidence of reoffending among younger people, even after serving a period of detention, is testimony to the fact that the temptation to transgress often outweighs the fear of detection and punishment. The absence of Christian influence and regular Bible teaching, together with secular attitudes in the home and media, reinforce the urgent need to reach children and young people with the Gospel before they become enamoured with worldly ways and temptations. See Chapter 6 for fuller information about appropriate strategies to assist in promoting the Good News.

God instructed the parents of the Israelites to take close and immediate regard to His words and instructions, ensuring that they were effectively taught and implemented: 'Impress them on your children. Talk about them when you sit at home and when you walk along the road, when you lie down and when you get up' (Deuteronomy 11:19, NKJV). The writer of Proverbs 13 links parental love (not vindictiveness or abuse) with correction: 'Those who spare the rod of discipline hate their children. Those who love their children care enough to discipline them' (verse 24, NLT). Unfortunately, the use of the term 'rod' has been wrongly associated with the use of a physical object (like a broom handle) rather than the correct interpretation encompassed by the phrase, 'rod of correction', which is used figuratively, not literally. King David, in his well-loved Psalm 23, writes that the rod of God 'protects and comforts me' (verse 4b); hardly a weapon for inflicting pain and distress!

In writing to Christians in Ephesus, Paul emphasises the importance of *fathers* in providing appropriate disciple: 'Fathers, do not provoke your children to anger by the way you treat them. Rather, bring them up with the discipline and instruction that comes from the Lord' (6:4, NLT). The phrase 'do not provoke your children to anger' reinforces the principle that parents need to be firm but reasonable in the way they administer disciple; that is, to explain the basis and purpose for particular rules, rather than shouting, being dismissive, rigid and generally unreasonable. When children and young people question parental authority and demand to know "Why?" it is preferable to offer an explanation, as opposed to the dismissive retort: "Because I say so!"

Despite every noble intention, every parent will agree that bringing children up in the fear and nurture of the Lord is far from straightforward and requires divine wisdom and endless patience (James 3:17). Without clear boundaries for behaviour and an understanding that all actions have consequences, people of every age are at risk of losing their way and ending up in difficulty. Clearly, all these instructions and practical approaches apply to every parent, both male and female, especially in the increasingly large number of households where one parent (usually the father) is absent.

In parallel to the human responsibility for nurturing and shaping children's lives, the writer of the Book of Hebrews makes reference to God's concern that we, as His children, remain faithful to His commands, but adds that if we stray, He is willing to rectify our mistakes: 'For the Lord disciplines those he loves and he punishes each one he accepts as his child' (12:6, NLT). The emphasis in this verse is upon 'love' but the inclusion of 'punish' cannot be ignored. Nevertheless, the writer goes on to explain that while discipline is unpleasant at the time, it yields 'a peaceful harvest of right living for those who are trained in this way' (verse 11). The closer we walk in step with the Spirit, the more sensitive we become to the occasions when we are deviating from His will for us and able to make appropriate adjustment, as the Spirit prompts or sanctions us.

Innocent transgression

From God's perspective, no person is entirely innocent, in as much as all have sinned and fallen short of the standards that He has established and are available to each one of us by complete submission to Him through Christ. Nevertheless, it is sometimes argued that certain culpable actions are justified because they are borne of a genuine desire to help others, rather than calculated wrongdoing. For example, someone might reveal confidential details to assist the resolution of a problem or withhold evidence out of a desire to help defuse a situation or give a false alibi out of loyalty to a close friend who is under investigation or forge a signature as a means of shortcutting a tiresome procedure. In the aforementioned cases, the 'innocence' likely arises from kindly intent as much as from wilful disobedience, though law enforcement officers might take a less charitable view!

Innocent transgression is more often associated with *sins of omission* rather than wilful malpractice. Such sins are committed by neglecting to do the things that ought to have been done rather than doing things that should not have been done, an issue with which even the Apostle Paul struggled, referring to himself as a 'wretched man' (Romans 7:24, NKJV).

An example of a sin of omission is hesitating to speak up on behalf of someone who needs support or encouragement, reneging on a promise to carry out a task, or simply failing to 'keep a short account' with God through regular confession, prayer and expressed faith in His sovereign power. Such errors may be due to slackness, lack of personal discipline, ignoring the Spirit's voice, fear of getting things wrong, or busyness with other matters. While sins of omission need to be confessed, a 'blanket' prayer of confession to cover them is sometimes all that is required, owing to a lack of awareness of the specific failings that have taken place. After all, if we don't know that we have sinned in a particular way, it is impossible to confess the failing!

While walking closely with the Lord ('in step with the Spirit', Galatians Chapter 5) reduces the likelihood of failing to heed warning signs that trouble our consciences, it is nevertheless incumbent on each person to remain vigilant about the many snares that await the unwary. Each person has to be self-disciplined, not only by avoiding wrong behaviour, but by positively espousing right behaviour ('righteousness'). Unless forced by evil people to act out of character, behaviour is ultimately for each person to determine. Only God has the power to sanctify (make us more like Jesus) but we all have to take the initiative and determine to live upright lives, enabled (though not compelled) by the Spirit.

Despite the fact that each circumstance in which sin is manifested is different, it is undeniably true that rebellion against the law of God, as clearly defined throughout the Bible and reinforced by the words of Jesus and the Apostles, ultimately requires the individual's consent and compliance. Earnest excuses after going wrong are no substitute for a properly ordered and disciplined lifestyle that safeguards righteousness and alerts us to the possibility of committing unintended sins.

Wilful transgression

Wilful transgression takes many and varied forms, from relatively minor offences, such as deciding to ignore someone we don't wish to acknowledge (at one extreme) through to placing an explosive device in order to kill and maim as many victims as possible (at the other end of the severity spectrum). The seriousness of a wilful sin such as theft is usually judged by the value of the item stolen—whether it was a loaf of bread or a diamond ring—and the circumstances under which the sinful behaviour was enacted; for example, was the offence committed while the person was under severe duress or was it calculatingly planned?

The seriousness of *personally targeted sin* (against an individual) or *socially damaging sin* (against a group of people, organisation or community) is morally and sometimes legally evaluated on the basis of the degree of threat involved and in recent years, whether a 'hate crime' has been committed, loosely defined as causing offence to another person or persons, using abusive language or making intimidating remarks. The interpretation of 'hate crime' is imprecise and has encouraged accusations from alleged victims, some of which are highly questionable and controversial, as many high-profile individuals and street preachers have discovered to their cost. The tension existing between the right to express opinions ('freedom of speech') and avoiding deliberate offence has divided opinion, created considerable acrimony and, in some extreme cases, sparked varying degrees of social protest and disorder.

Although the majority of people will never be involved in such entanglement, Jesus warned that idle talk, hypocrisy and a cold lack of love for others, were serious matters and should not be dismissed as trivial, even when weighed against sins such as assault and robbery with violence. Jesus was particularly severe towards people that he deemed to be hypocrites, describing them in uncompromising terms: 'You are like whitewashed tombs—beautiful on the outside but filled on the inside with dead people's bones and all sorts of impurity' (Matthew 23:27, NLT). In short, Jesus was saying that our inner thoughts, desires and attitudes could not be cloaked by fine words, slogans or eloquence; nothing is hidden from view that will not be exposed by the Saviour's piercing eye. As Jesus made clear: 'What you have said in the dark will be heard in the daylight, and what you have whispered in the ear in the inner rooms will be proclaimed from the roofs' (Luke 12:3, NIVUK). The writer of the Book of Hebrews reminds his readers that 'nothing in all creation is hidden from God's sight. Everything is uncovered and laid bare before the eyes of him to whom we must give account' (4:13, NIVUK).

It is significant that when Jesus was asked about the greatest commandments, he replied that loving God was the most important and loving others was second in priority order. The first commandment facilitates the second; in other words, love for God means that the indwelling Holy Spirit provides the impetus for loving others, even those who hate us or have harmed us (see earlier under 'Sin and forgiveness'). Luke records in Acts Chapter 26 how on the road to Damascus (in Syria), Jesus confronted Saul (usually known as Paul) from heaven and demanded to know why Saul was persecuting him. One of the lessons to learn from this encounter is that every time we are hateful towards others, especially fellow believers, we are persecuting Jesus, as well as the recipient of our aggression.

Harmful acts against others in word or deed, however minor they may appear to be, do not conform to Jesus's clear instruction to love others, and are thereby deemed sinful. These smaller transgressions should not, however, be confused with the right—indeed, the *obligation*—to speak out against injustice by people with evil intent and to defend biblical truth against ungodly attacks by liberal apologists.

Why is there so much violence? Why is so much advertising 'sexualised'? Why has abnormal behaviour become acceptable? Why are there so many security cameras? Why do shops and stores have to use metal shutters? Why is there such an increase in fraud and online theft? Why is there so much domestic violence? Why is pornography at epidemic levels among men? Why is there disregard for authority? Why do so many younger people resort to drugs? Why has the incidence of sexually transmitted infections escalated? Why are so many of the unborn destroyed through abortion? The answer to all of these questions is that people disregard the law of God through *wilful transgression*.

Serving God not Satan

Every person determines the way in which he or she will act and whether to do what is right or wrong, superintended by a deliberate decision to allow the conscience to guide and direct—leading to doing what is right in God's eyes—or to suppress its message and continue regardless, resulting in wrongdoing. It is important, however, for every follower of Jesus to acknowledge that although the conscience is generally reliable in pointing the way, the Holy Spirit must be allowed to be the ultimate arbiter and have the final word on every aspect of life and conduct. As Paul wrote to the churches in Galatia: 'So I say, let the Holy Spirit guide your lives. Then you won't be doing what your sinful nature craves' (5:16, NLT).

Insight

It is surprisingly easy for a sinful attitude to worm its way into our heads at the expense of wholesome thoughts and actions. When uncertain about what is appropriate, a useful guide is to ask three questions:

1. What does the Bible say about the matter?
2. What do mature fellow believers think about the issue?
3. How would Jesus's physical presence alongside us influence our decision?

The idea promoted by some secular thinkers that life can be free from constraints or parameters, so we must all do what comes naturally, is an illusion with damaging moral and practical consequence attached to it. Every philosophy about life's meaning and subsequent appropriate conduct must contain moral boundaries, clearly articulated and specified. The alternative is that 'anything goes', in which case relational and societal disintegration inevitably follows. People who deny the existence of right and wrong as the basis for shaping our lives must construct their identity and behaviour on other creeds, beliefs or doctrines if their lives are to be anything but chaotic, which is an all too familiar outcome for allegedly 'liberated' souls.

It is also true that every unbiblical philosophy or viewpoint attempts to absolve adherents from criticism about their words, opinions and actions. Extremists may even accept that instances of violent and intimidating behaviour are justified if it helps to achieve their goals. It has been evident over recent years that the growth of mob pressure has increased sharply, often creating with misery for its victims. In addition, the predominance of the 'culture of offence' that has invaded Western thought in recent years (see previous section) appears to operate in one direction only, namely: 'I can be affronted by what you say but you must accept what I say without question'. The notion of sinfulness and offending God is barely considered, if at all.

The battle to withstand godless philosophies that are characterised by rebellion, sexual permissiveness, corruption of the family unit, control of vocabulary, rabble coercion and reviling God's revealed word in the Scriptures, is part of the struggle that Paul describes as being 'against the rulers, against the authorities, against the powers of this dark world and against the spiritual forces of evil in the heavenly realms' (Ephesians 6:12, NIVUK). Unfortunately, some Christians have been slow to acknowledge the seriousness of what is taking place. Consequently, they have failed to 'contend for the faith once delivered to them' (Jude 1:3, KJV), dithered instead of actively praying against the powers of darkness, and compromised with the latest moral 'fad' rather than unashamedly and boldly declaring biblical truth about sin and righteousness. Followers of Christ must reject such worldly ways of thinking and behaving, and live instead in the Spirit, as Paul explains: 'When we were controlled by our old nature [in the flesh], sinful desires were at work within us, and the law aroused these evil desires that produced a harvest of sinful deeds, resulting in death. But now we have been released from the law, for we died to it and are no longer captive to its power. Now we can serve God, not in the old way of obeying the letter of the law, but in the new way of living in the Spirit' (Romans 7:5–6, NLT).

The seriousness of being controlled by forces other than the Spirit of God should not be underestimated. Paul sets out the 'downward slope' as being characterised by the following path of decline:

(1) We allow our old, pre-conversion nature (the 'old man', Romans 6:6, KJV) to exercise control over our lives.
(2) The harmful effect of this pre-conversion control stimulates sinful desires.

(3) Sinful desire leads to an abundance of sinful deeds.

(4) Sinful deeds culminate in spiritual death (i.e., a deadening of our spiritual antennae and responsiveness to the Spirit's leading).

In stark contrast to the descent into domination by sin, submission to Christ frees us from the constraints of being subject to a rigid framework of do's and do not's and offers a liberated new way of living in the Spirit; that is, allowing the Holy Spirit to guide and direct us beneficially. The secular argument that there is only a straight choice between either throwing off the shackles of constraint and determining our own way of doing things ('self-seeking behaviour') or attempting to follow a prescribed set of rules ('conforming behaviour') are both laid bare when compared with the joyous freedom to be found in Jesus. It should be borne in mind that submission to Christ leads to *willing* obedience, as we acknowledge his lordship and glory.

John quotes the words of Jesus when he explains how the Holy Spirit is active in identifying and exposing sin: 'And when He comes, He will convict the world of its sin and of God's righteousness; and of the coming judgement' (16:8, NLT). It is part of the Spirit's function to convict and judge, not as in a court of law but measured against the standard that God has set and the nature of each person's response. All those who claim to follow Christ have already been cleared of sin and righteousness, so will not face the Final Judgement ('Judgement Day') but *will* be rewarded according to the way in which they made seeking and serving in the Kingdom of God a priority in their lives (Matthew 6:33). As Paul reminds the Corinthians: 'For we must all stand before Christ to be judged. We will each receive whatever we deserve for the good or evil we have done in this earthly body' (2 Corinthians 5:10, NLT). While it is true that the number of good deeds ('good works') will not be the means of salvation from sin, as other major religions claim, they will become highly significant when Christ judges our life priorities, and used to evaluate our (undeserved) heavenly rewards that are only offered to us through God's grace. 'He gave his life to free us from every kind of sin, to cleanse us, and to make us his very own people, totally committed to doing good deeds' (Titus 2:14, NLT).

Summary

In this chapter, I have grappled with the challenging question of sin and sinfulness: its origin, manifestation, implications for daily living and each person's prospects beyond this life. I have described the many ways in which sin is revealed, from minor transgressions at one extreme to serious wickedness at the other. While explaining that each person has inbuilt 'warning systems' to guard against acting in a way that is contrary to the will of God, I have conceded that upbringing, societal pressure and the impact of a prevailing liberal philosophy that embraces every belief and behaviour will all affect the way each person views right and wrong behaviour. In this regard, I have explored at some length the place of conscience, guilt and shame as a means of resisting and, where relevant, repenting of sins already committed.

In evaluating the impact of sin, neglect of God's laws and statutes—falsely described by liberal apologists as artificially constraining people's behaviour—has resulted in a deterioration of societal cohesion, an explosion of unnatural sexual practices and a rejection of the concept of virtue.

Throughout the whole of Part 2, I have referred repeatedly to the significance of Christ's death on the Cross of Calvary as a sacrifice for sin and the essential role of God's Spirit to guide, direct us and bring glory to God. In Part 3 (Chapters 5 and 6), I shall explore these fundamental truths in greater depth.

Which of the following statements reflect your beliefs?

1. Sin is an out-dated term because there is no absolute right and wrong.
2. God regards all sins with the same degree of seriousness, whether small or large.
3. Some sins are so serious that they cannot be forgiven, however much the person repents of them.
4. God will take into account a person's upbringing and mental state when judging the seriousness of sin.
5. God will only count sins against a person if they are wilfully committed.
6. Christians should never feel guilt or shame.
7. God's grace is sufficient to cover every sin.
8. Salvation is open to all those who truly repent.

Part 3
God's Answer to the
Sin Pandemic

Romans 5: 5–11

When we were utterly helpless, Christ came at just the right time and died for us sinners. Now, most people would not be willing to die for an upright person, though someone might perhaps be willing to die for a person who is especially good. But God showed his great love for us by sending Christ to die for us while we were still sinners. And since we have been made right in God's sight by the blood of Christ, he will certainly save us from God's condemnation. For since our friendship with God was restored by the death of his Son while we were still his enemies, we will certainly be saved through the life of his Son. So now we can rejoice in our wonderful new relationship with God because our Lord Jesus Christ has made us friends of God. (NLT)

Mark 2: 5–12

Seeing their faith, Jesus said to the paralysed man, "My child, your sins are forgiven."

But some of the teachers of religious law, who were sitting there, thought to themselves: "What is he saying? This is blasphemy! Only God can forgive sins!"

Jesus knew immediately what they were thinking, so he asked them, "Why do you question this in your hearts? Is it easier to say to the paralysed man 'Your sins are forgiven,' or 'Stand up, pick up your mat, and walk'? So I will prove to you that the Son of Man has the authority on earth to forgive sins." Then Jesus turned to the paralysed man and said, "Stand up, pick up your mat, and go home!" And the man jumped up, grabbed his mat, and walked out through the stunned onlookers. They were all amazed and praised God, exclaiming, "We've never seen anything like this before!" (NLT)

Luke 15: 1–7

Tax collectors and other notorious sinners often came to listen to Jesus teach. This made the Pharisees and teachers of religious law complain that he was associating with such sinful people—even eating with them! So Jesus told them this story: "Then Jesus told them this parable: 'Suppose one of you has a hundred sheep and loses one of them. Doesn't he leave the ninety-nine in the open country and go after the lost sheep until he finds it? And when he finds it, he joyfully puts it on his shoulders and goes home. Then he calls his friends and neighbours together and says, "Rejoice with me; I have found my lost sheep." I tell you that in the same way there will be more rejoicing in heaven over one sinner who repents than over ninety-nine righteous people who do not need to repent' (NIVUK).

Preface to Part 3

In Part 2, I explored the concepts of sin and sinfulness and their impact on the human condition (the sin pandemic). In doing so, I endeavoured to confront and engage with issues relating to the many and various ways in which we are prone to sin by straying from God's commandments or deliberately choosing to disobey His stated requirements or, worst of all, refusing to accept His existence and sovereign right to rule in our lives.

In Part 3, I present in detail the truth about Jesus Christ as the Saviour of the world, whose life, death and resurrection offers freedom from the eternal consequences of sin. Peter likens our freedom to a ransom being paid, not with silver or gold 'but with the precious blood of Christ, like that of a lamb without defect or blemish' (1 Peter 1:19, NRSV). In his first letter, John encourages believers with the benefits of true faith: 'And we know that the Son of God has come and he has given us understanding, so that we can know the true God. And now we live in fellowship with the true God because we live in fellowship with his Son, Jesus Christ. He is the only true God and he is eternal life' (5:20, NLT). I shall also continue to emphasise that God the Holy Spirit is uniquely placed to empower us in resisting sinful behaviour and choosing the path to life.

The essential role of the church is to proclaim the full Gospel, both its joyful hope and its warnings. In doing so, fellowships of all types and sizes must be alert to the opportunities and potential obstacles that they face in declaring the truth in the midst of what seems to be a largely apathetic and occasionally hostile world. Spirit-led creativity in ways to communicate the Gospel and a willingness to embrace change lie at the heart of the church's mission in combatting the detrimental effects of the sin virus and replacing it with purity and eternal hope found exclusively in Christ.

Chapter 5
Christ the Saviour

Introduction

In this chapter, I explore in detail the way in which Jesus's death atones for sin and offers the hope of eternal life to each person who lays claim to the offer of salvation, making particular reference to Paul's letter to the Christians in Rome. In doing so, I shall emphasise that salvation is only available because of God's grace and mercy towards sinful humanity. The sacrifice of Jesus on the cross has not only provided forgiveness from sin but also offers a secure hope for the future and the prospect of heaven. I shall also focus on ways in which Jesus has impacted the world through his ministry on earth, and his death and resurrection. Of seminal importance is the way in which he will introduce a restored and sanctified world order in a 'new heaven and earth', as described most clearly in the final chapters of the Bible (the Revelation given to the Apostle John).

Romans Chapter 5 provides the anchorage for an exposition of fundamental biblical truths about what Christ has accomplished for us, together with the impact that transformed lives have on those who have accepted his gift of salvation, and their positive influence on others.

Christ Alone

By grace alone

When considering what Jesus Christ has done for each one of us through his sacrificial death, it is important to underline that every present and eternal benefit is by God's grace; that is, through His undeserved favour. Salvation is not something that can be earned by strenuous effort or good works, though Jesus commended those who serve sacrificially and show genuine love for others, as in doing so they are representing him (Matthew 25:40). Paul summarises the importance of grace in his letter to Christians in Ephesus: God saved you by his grace when you believed. And you can't take credit for this; it is a gift from God. Salvation is not a reward for the good things we have done, so none of us can boast about it (2:8–9, NLT). It may be noted in passing that although Paul stresses that salvation is not a reward for good deeds, he associates our good deeds (works) with rewards from God in the same letter (6:8). See Chapter 3 under 'Rewards for righteous living'.

One way to the Father

Jesus died for all people, past, present and future, as John the Baptist boldly declared: 'Behold! The Lamb of God who takes away the sin of the world!' (John 1:29, NKJV) The Bible makes it clear that Christ alone provides the key that unlocks the meaning of life and the mystery of eternity. This exclusiveness is not popular in a world that favours many routes to God, like the spokes of a wheel, all pointing towards the hub. Jesus stated openly, however, that he is the *only way* to God the Father, as well as being the *truth* (i.e., entirely reliable and trustworthy) and the *life* (i.e., the source of everything we need in our present lives and beyond, John 14:6), so either he was deluded, boastful, deceitful or genuine.

If Jesus's words are authentic—and there is no reason to doubt the fact—the practical implications of his declaration provides a straightforward choice about whether or not to accept his gracious invitation, as Matthew records: 'Come to Me, all you who labour and are heavy laden, and I will give you rest. Take my yoke upon you and learn from me, for I am gentle [meek] and lowly in heart; and you will find rest for your souls' (11:28–29, NKJV). In responding to those who argue that they can be indifferent and 'neutral' with regard to accepting or rejecting him, Jesus stated firmly that those who were not 'for' him were against him with no middle ground between the two positions: 'Anyone who isn't with me opposes me, and anyone who isn't working with me is actually working against me' (Luke 11:23, NLT).

Major religions, such as Islam, do not accept the concept of original sin, so obviously do not believe that a Saviour / Christ / Messiah / Anointed One is needed. Instead, salvation is gained through human effort and conforming to specified rituals, routines and regulations, including pilgrimages and regular times of saying prayers. Most religious beliefs outside Christianity deny the deity (God-ness) of Jesus and either dismiss his existence or argue that he didn't die on the cross at all but was transported alive into heaven, or they fabricate another explanation to cast doubt on the Gospel accounts. Such claims are, of course, in direct contrast to what we read in the Bible about Jesus being God as man and the only sacrifice for sin. In John's first letter, he addresses directly these repudiations of Jesus as the Saviour: 'And who is a liar? Anyone who says that Jesus is not the Christ. Anyone who denies the Father and the Son is an antichrist' (2:22, NLT). That is, such a person opposes God the Father, Jesus Christ and his church (i.e., Christians). It will be noted that John emphasises outright denial as a fundamental issue.

The Apostle Paul underlines the seriousness of rejecting Jesus as the Saviour: 'But you are not ruled by your sinful selves. You are ruled by the Spirit, if that Spirit of God really lives in you. But whoever does not have the Spirit of Christ does not belong to Christ' (Romans 8:9, ERV). We belong to Christ or we do not, though there are varying levels of commitment to him, as I elaborated in Chapter 4. Paul twice uses the term 'ruled'; those who argue that they wish to be free from imposed constraints on their behaviour and beliefs, and therefore reject the rule of Christ in their lives are, in reality, being ruled by sin.

Repentance and Confession

Acknowledgement of sinfulness

The Scriptures are plain in stating that without Christ's sacrificial death, we would be lost and eternally separated from the full length and breadth of God's blessing. The state of being 'lost' means that we cannot and do not enjoy an intimate relationship with God that can only be restored through confession of sin, genuine repentance and turning to Christ for forgiveness. People in a lost state are those who fail to acknowledge the harmfulness of sin and its serious implications for their present welfare and eternal destiny because according to Jesus's clear teaching, they are in danger of facing God's severe displeasure: 'For the wrath of God is revealed from heaven against all ungodliness and unrighteousness of men, who suppress the truth in unrighteousness' (Romans 1:18, NKJV). Other translations substitute the word 'anger' for 'wrath' but *wrath* conveys more powerfully the gravity of being lost and facing God without Christ as Redeemer.

In John's first letter, he stresses (a) the need for transparency in confessing our sinfulness to God and (b) the promise of God's cleansing from sin: 'If we claim we have no sin, we are only fooling ourselves and not living in the truth.

But if we confess our sins to him, he is faithful and just to forgive us our sins and to cleanse us from all wickedness [unrighteousness]' (1:9, NLT). Note that we confess to God and not to a person, though there is a place for confession to one another in the case of sickness, with the involvement of church elders: 'Therefore confess your sins to each other and pray for each other, so that you may be healed. The prayer of a righteous person is powerful and effective' (James 5:16). A person, however pure and devout, is unable to forgive the sins of a fellow human being. Jesus was the only sinless, spotless sacrificial Lamb of God who was and is able to 'pay the ransom' for sin, as explained in Peter's first letter, Chapter 1.

Sorrow and repentance

At the insistence of aggrieved parents, many disobedient or rude children have been told to say sorry and complied with the demand, as a means of avoiding punishment or further reprimands, though their mere utterance of the word may not involve genuine contrition. True *repentance* should not be confused with 'being sorry', which is used to apologise for a past wrongdoing but does not necessarily convey a determination to atone for the past error and strive to correct the behaviour in future. By contrast, an expression of repentance addresses both past mistakes and future intentions with a determination to leave behind sinful ways and henceforth seek to follow a godly pathway (Philippians 3:13–14).

In Chapter 3, I addressed the issue of how Christ's death has dealt with the 'original sin' (sin that has affected every person from the time of the first human being, Adam). For those who are able to make decisions about their relationship with Jesus Christ, the key factor is not only their willingness to believe and be born from above (that is, turning from their present direction in life and allowing God's Spirit to instruct them) but also, as those whose lives have been renewed, to confess their sins regularly to God and thereby 'keep a short account' with Him. Once the initial confession of our need of a Saviour has been made ('conversion'), the ongoing need for confession is of singular importance (see next section). If the initial confession of our need for Jesus Christ as Saviour has *not* been made, subsequent confessions of everyday sins are limited value, if any. To summarise the position:

- Those who repent and believe in Jesus Christ as Saviour are born again by the indwelling Spirit of God, whereby all sin is forgiven and they are immediately blessed with the promise of eternal life. Their original sin and their subsequent daily sins, both intentional and unintentional ('sins of omission') are all covered by his sacrifice on the cross. There is no condemnation for those who belong to Christ Jesus (Romans 8:1).

- Despite having all sin covered by Christ's sacrifice, believers need to regularly confess their sinfulness to God, whereby they are cleansed from all current unrighteousness by the blood of Christ (1 John, 1:9; though see also next bullet point and later discussion under 'Confession and salvation').

- Failure to confess intentional and unintentional sins prevents the Holy Spirit from working freely in and through our lives for God's glory but does not in any way nullify salvation, which is secure. If it were not so, we would be earning eternal life by means of our deeds and actions, which is contrary to Scripture.

- Those who do not confess and repent regularly, though cleared of the curse of original sin by the sacrifice of the 'Second Adam' (Jesus)—who gave his life for the sins of the world—will have to bear the responsibility for their subsequent sins; that is, for their thoughts, words and deeds that do not accord with the will and purpose of God. Such a failure to repent may place their eternal future in serious jeopardy.

Earnest confession

It is important to underline the fact that confession as a formality or ritual ('going through the motions') is dishonouring to God if it is not accompanied by true repentance. Acknowledgement of sin through confession, whether for the first time when we admit to our sinful condition and need of forgiveness by Christ, or subsequently when, as believers, we have sinned, must be accompanied by a desire to turn from our own way and seek to earnestly follow God's leading and guiding. In order to adjust our present course and achieve a lasting change of direction, sorrow must not only reject aspects of our lives that are out of step with the Spirit's purposes, but also demonstrate an active desire to place Christ at the centre of all we think, do and say. In short, confession without repentance and clear evidence of transformed behaviour is vacuous.

During challenging situations in their lives or when they are grappling with a difficult situation, people who are normally disinterested in anything they define as 'religious', often become more attentive to ways in which this 'mythical' Supreme Being (as they might describe Him) can assist them. Unfortunately, they soon lose interest in spiritual matters when the crisis is past, and revert to living without reference to God. If the problem persists or worsens, the same people who were eager for God to intervene are just as likely to accuse Him of being uncaring or otherwise 'non-existent'. In other words, they believe that God exists solely to service their needs when they call Him to do so. Such people are happy to accept God as a 'safety net' to rescue them in their troubles but unwilling to commit themselves if it involves admitting their need of a Saviour and entrusting their lives to him.

God may graciously respond to sincere requests, even when desperate people use Him as a 'last resort', but it is the fervent prayers of the *righteous* (cleansed by the blood of Christ and living in a way that honours him) that yields a positive, Spirit-directed outcome. As James declares: 'The effective, fervent prayer of a righteous man avails much' (5:16, NKJV); or in the NLT: 'The earnest prayer of a righteous person has great power and produces wonderful results'. As we shall explore in subsequent chapters, commitment to Jesus is a serious matter and not to be treated casually or as a stopgap measure when all else has failed.

Those who have an intimate relationship with God through Jesus Christ are willing to accept that His response to their pleas may not be what they were hoping for or anticipating, yet they still retain a strong belief and trust in Him. To use a phrase from William Cowper's hymn, true believers embrace the precept that 'God moves in a mysterious way, His wonders to perform'. Less spiritual people will confess, pray and wait for an answer; spiritual Christians will confess, pray, leave the outcome to God, and move forward with confidence and faith that He will control the circumstances to serve their best interests.

Failure to trust God is probably the most widespread sinful act that requires contrite confession. Jesus even had to scold his disciples for their lack of faith in times of difficulty (e.g., Matthew 6:30, calming a storm at sea; and 8:20, concerns about material needs).

Confession and salvation

As noted earlier, interpretation of John's first letter in which he states: 'But if we confess our sins to him, he is faithful and just to forgive us our sins and to

114

cleanse us from all wickedness' (1:9) and its implications for salvation has been the subject of considerable debate. First, it is a basic tenet that the death and resurrection of Jesus Christ pays the penalty for *all* sin for those who place their trust in him as Saviour: past, present and future. That being so, the need for further confession to 'cleanse us from all wickedness (unrighteousness)', as John declares, appears to be largely superfluous. After all, we are made righteous (without sin) in God's sight 'once and for all' by Jesus's sacrificial death, so why the need for subsequent confession to bring about cleansing?

In explaining this apparent contradiction—that is, Jesus's death paid the price for sin and his righteousness (cleansing) is transferred to every believer, yet further confession of sin is necessary to become righteous in God's sight— some scholars argue that John is referring to the moment in time that we *first* confess our need of Jesus, such that the cleansing from unrighteousness is instantaneous at that very point, as we move from the darkness of sin to the freedom of new life in Christ. Further confession is therefore only needed to ensure that we are living 'in the light of Christ' and we can therefore proceed with confidence to serve and witness in the sure knowledge that there is no lingering issue of sin to create a stumbling block to harm the work of the Spirit in our lives (Galatians 5:7).

Other scholars insist that *complete* salvation is reliant on regular confession of sin (Catholic theologians argue it is facilitated through the agency of a priest), the inevitable conclusion being that salvation is not fixed but instead depends on regular admission of wrongdoing. Accepting this interpretation of John's words would mean, in effect, that salvation is fluid—confession of sin restores it, while failure to confess negates it. Adopting this position has led to a fear among some Christians that if death were suddenly to occur at a time when sins had not been confessed, the eternal consequences would be grim, as the people in such a state die without being forgiven and their souls are therefore doomed to reside in a place of eternal darkness.

So how should we understand John's assertion? The present author's view is that a single verse extracted from the Bible should not be used to establish a doctrine that contradicts the weight of Scripture that establishes the 'once saved, always saved' principle. John's comment is more helpfully viewed as a necessary reminder to believers that there is a need for them to strive for holiness, which entails maintaining a regular check on behaviour and admitting to God where and when they have erred. Paul writes: 'But now that you have been set free from sin and have become slaves of God, the benefit you reap leads to holiness, and the result is eternal life' (Romans 6:22, NIVUK). The verse provides some reassurance that although we may fail Him, God restores our righteousness through His loving forgiveness and cleansing. It is also a further reminder that salvation is not gained through our deeds but by God's grace, found in Christ.

Peter offers further comfort that believers can have absolute trust in their salvation: 'All praise to God, the Father of our Lord Jesus Christ. It is by his great mercy that we have been born again because God raised Jesus Christ from the dead. Now we live with great expectation and we have a priceless inheritance—an inheritance that is kept in heaven for you, pure and undefiled, beyond the reach of change and decay' (I Peter 1:3–4, NIVUK). While we all fail and fall short of what God intends for our lives, we can celebrate the wonderful truth that our heavenly inheritance is 'pure and undefiled'.

The Gospel Message

God's sovereignty

It is self-evident that people can only respond to Jesus's offer of salvation if they first hear the Gospel explained to them or have access to its truth in printed form, which places a great responsibility on his followers to be messengers of the Good News, as Paul declared in his letter to the Christians in Rome: 'But how can they call on him to save them unless they believe in him? And how can they believe in him if they have never heard about him? And how can they hear about him unless someone tells them?' (10:14, NLT) The situation is less straightforward in seeking to understand the implications for the many millions who have not been given such an opportunity to hear and respond, as I discuss below.

First, it must be acknowledged that the way God determines the fate of people who have not heard the Gospel is humanly imponderable and we must allow Him to be sovereign over that decision, just as he is Lord over every other aspect of our lives if we permit Him to intercede and guide. The writer of the Book of Ecclesiastes advises against attempting to comprehend all of God's ways: 'Just as you cannot understand the path of the wind or the mystery of a tiny baby growing in its mother's womb, so you cannot understand the activity of God, who does all things' (11:5, NLT). There is much that we must accept by faith and by exercising trust in our Heavenly Father, as Job asserted: 'Though He slay me, yet will I trust Him' (13:15, NKJV).

The importance of faith cannot be overemphasised, as during the days of the Old Testament (before Jesus came to earth) God's favour and blessing were dependent on the personal faith of each individual, expressed through having confidence in Him to act justly and uphold righteousness; belief in His written and pronouncement through the prophets; and striving to please Him. Jesus also made it clear that the proof of having genuine faith in God is demonstrating the fruit of the Spirit, notably by showing kindness, selflessness and practical love for others. See later in the chapter under 'Life has a purpose'.

Our instinct is probably one of compassion and sadness for those who have not heard the Gospel or have been fed a distorted version of it, reasoning that it is unfair for God to judge people and deny them the hope of eternal life without offering them the chance to respond to the truth about salvation. A minority of scholars insist that God has already determined who will be saved, so we don't need to worry about such matters. Others declare that God is not obliged to save a single soul but has condescended to rescue a remnant because of His benevolent grace, akin to the eight persons delivered in the Great Flood, as described in Genesis Chapters 6 and 7. Yet others argue that although Christ is the only 'door/gate' to eternal life, God will use undisclosed means to save sinners who are ignorant of their plight.

In evaluating the various arguments, we can only speak of what has been revealed in Scripture; we leave the mysteries for our gracious and loving God to reveal or conceal, as He chooses. What we *do* know is that Jesus underlined the importance of sharing the need for repentance, turning from ungodly ways and trusting him for the forgiveness of sin, if we are to avoid the prospect of a dark future. It must also be underlined that Jesus made it clear that we can only come to the Father through him; there are no alternative routes or options.

Post-Pentecost

When Jesus sent out the Twelve Disciples, he had not yet died and been resurrected, so their message to the people focused on the need to turn from idols (whether worship of a person, ideology, statue; or a selfish ambition) and seek the Kingdom of God above all else (Matthew 6:33). Similarly, John the Baptist, as he was commonly known, only required the people being baptised to repent of their sin and turn to God to be forgiven, without the need at that point in time to trust in Jesus for salvation (see Mark Chapter 1). It was only after the extraordinary events of Pentecost described in Acts Chapter 2 that the disciples' ministry centred on the efficacy of Christ's sacrifice and the need not only to repent but also to believe in the Lord Jesus Christ as personal Saviour and Lord of all the earth.

Christians living today are assigned to declare the same message as those post-resurrection disciples by whatever means is at their disposal. Although we live in an entirely different age and culture from the people two millennia ago in Israel, the basic needs of people remain unchanged. At an everyday level, every person's requirements include access to regular food and a comfortable home; freedom from stress and strife; genuine friendship; and unconditional love. At a more spiritual level, basic needs include having confidence that each one of us matters to God; there is a purpose for living; we can have hope in every situation; and assurance that there is a glorious future beyond this life. The Gospel has the answers. Christians have the voice. See also under 'Witnessing and faithful prayer' later in this chapter and further details in Chapter 6.

What Christ Has Accomplished

To discover precisely what Christ's death has accomplished, Paul's letter to the Christians in Rome (with special reference to Chapter 5:5–11) provides an invaluable compilation of fundamental truths to thrill the heart of every believer and challenge the hopelessness of those who are living without the Spirit of Christ in them. The letter contains five promises:

(1) Christ has made us righteous ('made us right') in God's sight.
(2) Christ has given us access ('entrance') into the grace of God.
(3) Christ brings us hope that causes us to rejoice.
(4) Christ offers us salvation from the consequences of sin.
(5) Christ reconciles us to God (i.e., brings us together in harmony with Him).

Christ has made us righteous (verse 1)

The Bible states plainly that we have been justified (i.e., made righteous in God's sight, as if we had never sinned) by faith in Jesus Christ. The concept of 'faith' is closely associated with *hope*, which is not to be confused with the worldly idea of 'hoping for the best' (i.e., fatalism: 'whatever will be will be').

118

The writer of the New Testament Book of Hebrews describes the close relationship between faith and hope: 'Now faith is confidence in what we hope for and assurance about what we do not see' (11:1, NIVUK). The NLT translates the first part of the verse as follows: 'Faith shows the reality of what we hope for', the key word in the description being 'reality', as faith is rooted in the certainty of God's promises and the ongoing presence of the Spirit of Christ in the believer. It is not a distorted idealism akin to 'crossing your fingers' or 'touching wood' or other superstitious nonsense.

Insight

Some of God's promises are unconditional, such as promising to be with us until the end of time; other promises are conditional upon our willingness to cooperate fully and play our part in fulfilling the vision that the Spirit imparts. God's unconditional promises provide a secure foundation on which we can confidently respond by faith and practical action to the requirements attached to His conditional promises.

The closer we walk in step with the Spirit of God, the greater the reality becomes until we reach a point where doubts evaporate and are replaced by an 'unspeakable joy' to know that our lives are synchronised with His will and purpose. Peter speaks of how trusting Jesus Christ, even in his bodily absence, results in this euphoric experience: You love him, even though you have never seen him. Though you do not see him now, you trust him and you rejoice with a glorious, inexpressible joy. The reward for trusting him will be the salvation of your souls (I Peter 1:9, NLT). Faith makes Jesus and his promises wholly authentic, providing us a guaranteed hope beyond this life.

Sceptics have attempted to corrupt the Bible definition of faith and hope by referring to the latter as 'blind hope', implying that the hopeful person's attitude is equivalent to 'good luck' or being delusional. In truth, the biblical use of faith and hope does not rely solely on tangible evidence or on outcomes that satisfy our personal ambitions (e.g., obtaining a better job; passing an examination; liberated from a condition or malady). Rather, Spirit-led faith and hope is rooted in three certainties that originate from outside ourselves, yet have a positive impact on our lives:

(a) *The Person of God Himself*

He knows the end from the beginning and His promises never fail to materialise, for He is utterly trustworthy. In the words of Thomas Chisholm's famous hymn *Great is Thy Faithfulness*, 'there is no shadow of turning with Thee'. We must therefore 'hold tightly without wavering to the hope we affirm, for God can be trusted to keep his promise' (Hebrews 10:23, NLT). Even close friends and relatives can let us down; God will not and does not.

(b) *The salvation found in Jesus Christ*

It is significant that one of Jesus's descriptive names is the 'hope of the world' (Matthew 12:21). In a world riddled with hopelessness and despair, salvation from the consequences of sin found in the death and resurrection of Jesus Christ provides a limitless source of encouragement and confidence. Great leaders and morally upright people may temporarily inspire and revive expectations for a nation but only Jesus is the present and eternal hope for the whole world.

(c) *The prospect of eternal life*

Jesus promised the disciples that he would prepare a place for them in heaven where there is space for everyone who believes: 'There are many rooms in my Father's house. I would not tell you this if it were not true. I am going there to prepare a place for you' (John 14:2, ERV). Peter joyfully elaborates on the implications of Jesus's glorious promise: 'Now we live with great expectation and we have a priceless inheritance—an inheritance that is kept in heaven for you, pure and undefiled, beyond the reach of change and decay' (I Peter 1:4, NLT). Believers may not accumulate much worldly wealth but they are promised a 'priceless inheritance' in and through Christ.

Each certain hope described above is confirmed by an inner conviction, prompted and sustained by the Holy Spirit, who will counsel and teach all of Jesus's committed followers everything they need to know. Thus, Paul prays: 'May the God of hope fill you with all joy and peace as you trust in him, so that you may overflow with hope by the power of the Holy Spirit' (Romans 15:13, NIVUK). The prospect of being filled with joy, peace and hope through trusting in God is more precious than fame or fortune. The Apostle writes in the similar vein to the churches in Galatia: 'Yet we know that a person is made right with God by faith in Jesus Christ, not by obeying the law. And we have believed in Christ Jesus, so that we might be made right with God because of our faith in Christ, not because we have obeyed the law' (2:16, NLT). Faith in Christ is not a once-for-all-time decision but a continuous expression of trust through every circumstance of life, whether or not we *feel* like trusting.

Insight

Telling God out loud that we trust Him acts to reinforce our faith and can be highly beneficial, especially during those occasions where we scarcely know which way to turn or what is the right thing to do.

Being made right with God through faith in Christ differs from a judicial situation where the accused person, though guilty of the crime, might be set free if he or she is found not guilty through the persuasive argument of a clever lawyer or a legal technicality that prevents the felon from being convicted and punished. Occasionally, the defendant might be guilty but be released without punishment if the judge is lenient or if (say) someone steps in and pays the outstanding fine and clears the debt. Under such circumstances, the individual is *legally* innocent but *morally* guilty. By contrast, when we are justified by faith in Christ, though guilty of transgressing and in active rebellion against God each time we yield to unrighteousness, *it is as if we had never sinned*, as far as God is concerned, for Jesus has cleansed us by his shed blood on the Cross of Calvary, once and for all time. We cannot claim any merit of our own in this matter; we can only acknowledge what Christ has done and rejoice that our sins are forgiven.

In another section of his letter to the church in Rome, the Apostle Paul underlined the truth that our freedom is not due to our own efforts ('obeying the law') but because of faith: 'Can we boast then that we have done anything to be accepted by God? No, because our acquittal is not based on obeying the law. It is based on faith. So we are made right with God ['justified'] through faith and not by obeying the law' (3:27–28, NLT). Whether or not a lawbreaker is found innocent or culpable in a court of law, his or her wrongdoing remains. When we are justified by faith in Christ, however, no guilt remains and there isn't any stain on our record. What a wonderful, liberating truth!

Christ has given us access into the grace of God (verse 2a)

Linking mercy, love and grace

Two of God's attributes are frequently mentioned in the Bible:

1. *His mercy:* God does not treat us as our sins and neglect of Him deserve.
2. *His grace:* God treats us in a loving and compassionate way that our attitude and behaviour do not merit.

Paul describes God's attitude in his letter to the believers at Ephesus where he powerfully expressed the link between mercy, love and grace: 'But because of his great love for us, God, who is rich in mercy, made us alive with Christ even when we were dead in transgressions—it is by grace you have been saved' (2:4–5, NIVUK). God's mercy is not of the 'grovelling' kind, as we might envisage a slave being prostrate before an ancient Emperor, begging for clemency; or of a convicted prisoner pleading to be spared the gallows. No, God's mercy is available because He is rich (saturated, deeply embedded) in it. God has mercy because it is in His loving nature and He will dispense it lavishly to those who sincerely repent of sin and turn to Him through Jesus Christ for forgiveness and the new life that only he can offer. Love and mercy are freely available to all mankind because Jesus gave his life for us and we have access to eternal life because he was raised from the dead.

Redemption has also been defined as 'the great exchange' in which Christ exchanged his life for our freedom from the consequences of sin. It is important to be reminded that the Son of God did not have to become a sacrifice for sin; he could have chosen a different path. After all, he is the one who has existed for all time; the one who created the stars in space and the microscopic creatures that inhabit the deepest seas; the one who knows us by name and is the great 'I Am'. To be redeemed by Christ is not something to accept dispassionately; instead, in the words of the old spiritual, it should cause us to 'tremble' with thankfulness when we consider what he accomplished on the cross due to his mercy, love and grace.

Grace as a gift

Paul underlines the extent to which we are totally reliant on God's mercy for salvation by emphasising that it is only by His grace that we have been saved. One popular definition of the word 'grace' is using the letters of the word to form a memorable statement: *God's Redemption At Christ's Expense*. The literal meaning of the word 'redemption' is being bought back for a price. In this case, redemption means to be saved from sin by clearing the debt (wage) of eternal death, as Paul explains: 'The wages of sin is death, but the free gift of God is eternal life through Christ Jesus our Lord' (Romans 6:23, NLT). Jesus paid the price.

Grace is not a gift that God provides in the way that a doting grandfather distributes sweets to his grandchildren. God's grace is expressed most profoundly in the sacrifice of His Son to atone for the world's sins. The coming of Jesus Christ and his death at Calvary means that the Godhead was in human terms 'dissembled' and heaven was deprived of the presence and sustaining power of the holy and sinless Son. The one through whom all things were made and who inhabited eternity was compressed into a tiny, helpless embryo within the womb of an ordinary young woman (Mary).

As the adult Jesus, he carried the sins of the world in His body on the cross, where all our guilt, shame, selfishness, depravity, unkindness, greed, anger, fear and envy was heaped upon Him. Peter provides a wonderful summary of this truth: 'He [Jesus] personally carried our sins in his body on the cross, so that we can be dead to sin and live for what is right. By his wounds you are healed' (I Peter 2:24, NLT). Little wonder that the composer, Haldor Lillenas, exploded with praise when he penned the words: 'Wonderful grace of Jesus, greater than all my sin. How shall my tongue describe it? Where shall its praise begin? Taking away my burden; setting my spirit free; for the wonderful grace of Jesus reaches me'.

Acknowledging and celebrating the grace of God is not an academic exercise or a subject for detached interest. God's undeserved favour is a demonstration of His character and desire for our good, such that we are given the widest opportunity to be reconciled to the Father through the Son by the power of the Holy Spirit. Followers of Christ, too, are called to demonstrate the same grace in their attitude towards others. When Jesus was asked to name the greatest commandments, he replied that loving God comes first and loving others comes second in the list of priorities (see Matthew Chapter 22). We have the great privilege of 'God-likeness' in our conduct and influence, as we submit to His will and purpose and allow His Spirit to work through us for the blessing of other people.

Christ brings us hope that causes us to rejoice (verses 2b–5)

It has been claimed with considerable justification that hopelessness and loneliness are the two curses of the modern age. At a time when, despite setbacks and challenges, most people in democratic nations have never been as privileged and wealthy, there has been a substantial increase in the number of people requiring and seeking support for their mental health needs. Particularly distressing has been the increase in self-harm among young people. In addition, the creation, distribution and use of damaging narcotic substances ('drugs') have become a major challenge for law enforcement agencies and social services throughout most of the world.

Far from 'liberating' people, the loosening of moral ties and discarding biblical norms in areas of human behaviour has magnified levels of distress and created uncertainty about what is acceptable. Families have been dismantled: divorce rates have risen dramatically—in large measure due to the easing of the grounds on which divorce can be enacted—and the destruction of the unborn (let alone the tragic deprivation of life that it inflicts) has blighted the population to such an extent that numbers of the next generation of workers to service employment and medical needs in the Western World has sunk to a disturbingly low point.

Despite these worrying trends, appointed leaders at every level of decision-making are experiencing constant harassment from a minority of strident voices, radical organisations and sympathetic funding providers pressing for further relaxation of laws on the basis (they would argue) that such changes are necessary to end oppressive restrictions on behaviour and introduce the dubious concept of 'equality for all'. The mantra underpinning these damaging trends is that every personal conviction is acceptable, providing it conforms to an atheistic ('godless') worldview. Jesus's teaching about showing love for one another has been subverted by celebrating sexual deviancy and loosening moral constraints. His emphasis on the need for an inner change of heart has been replaced by an obsession with the imposition of externally imposed legislation to force compliance in the general population and create an inevitable sense of resentment and annoyance.

Far from curtailing the aspirations of liberal-minded radicals, the escalation of sexually transmitted infections, single-parent families, loneliness, gang violence, abortion, euthanasia and anti-authority attitudes seem merely to enflame their insatiable appetites for destabilising society as a whole. What hope can Jesus Christ bring to the turmoil, such that believers directly affected by this 'social tsunami' of permissiveness can not only feel encouraged but also be given divine assurance that strengthens their faith and trust in God? To answer this question, it helps to be reminded of three great benefits accruing from a life submitted to Christ that offer hope and certainty during tumultuous and troubling times:

1) Life has a purpose
2) We can be a blessing to others
3) We learn perseverance

Life has a purpose

First, we have to accept that without God's leading and guiding, together with our willing conforming to His will, even the most confident, entrepreneurial, independently minded person is a 'lost sheep' in need of rescuing. Jesus referred to himself as the 'Good Shepherd' who saves and releases from Satan's bondage all those who have strayed (John Chapter 10). He made it clear that by his Spirit working in our lives, the true purpose of life— lived for the glory of God and the benefit of others—is wonderfully revealed.

Worldly fame and fortune is impressive and satisfying to an extent but, as many high achievers have discovered, even dizzying heights of success can leave a curious emptiness and dissatisfaction for which possessions, glamorous lifestyles and celebrity status cannot compensate. It is noteworthy that the search for fulfilment over and beyond their achievements motivates some wealthy people to contribute large sums of money to charity or spurs them to undertake commendable deeds in a quest to satisfy their inner longing to have made a positive difference in the world. As the Apostle Mark records, Jesus asked the probing rhetorical question: 'For what will it profit a man if he gains the whole world, and loses his own soul?' (8:36, NKJV) What indeed!

One of the more remarkable examples of a turnabout in priorities is found in the life of Alfred Nobel, the Swedish scientist whose notable discoveries included safely controlling highly temperamental nitro-glycerine into a much safer form of explosive called dynamite. After the premature death of Alfred's brother, Ludvig, a newspaper erroneously published *Alfred's* obituary in which he was derided for amassing a fortune by creating a substance that resulted in so much death and injury during armed conflicts. Despite being a highly successful pioneer and linguist, Alfred feared being remembered solely as the inventor of a destructive explosive, so he established the 'Nobel Prizes' to honour men and women for outstanding achievements in physics, chemistry, medicine, literature and peace (thus, the Nobel Peace Prize) and left a vast fortune to ensure their continuation.

Like so many before and after him, Nobel had a deep desire to make his life count for something that benefitted people and to use his talents constructively, as God intends for each one of us to do. We can't be sure if Nobel's motivation for doing good lay principally in his relationship with Jesus Christ or if it was a desire rising from within his soul that the Holy Spirit prompted; either way, Nobel ended his life positively in obeying Jesus's commandment to be a blessing to others in every way possible. As Jesus forcibly stated to the wealthy young man who wanted to know how he could inherit eternal life: 'If you want to be perfect, go, sell your possessions and give to the poor, and you will have treasure in heaven. Then come, follow me' (Matthew 19:21, NIVUK). Similarly, each one of us needs to pause and consider carefully if we are placing anything—such as a desire for wealth, relationship, career aspiration or leisure activity—ahead of our devotion to Christ. If so, the 'other god' will cause an obstruction to the free flow of Holy Spirit power and blessing in this life and the loss of 'treasure in heaven'.

When we are young, with life stretching before us, we can enjoy dreaming of what might happen in the future and how we can achieve the goals to which our imagination takes us. Over time, childhood fancies and hopeful ambitions are replaced by the harsher reality that worthwhile accomplishments require commitment, hard work and determination, whether the aspirations are 'secular' or 'spiritual' in character. As we move past the teenage years, doors of opportunities open and shut; some pathways prove to be strewn with thorns, others appear to be accessible but circumstances prevent further progress. Motivation ebbs and flows, as situations prove to be encouraging or disappointing. Such are the ups and downs of life!

In the spiritual realm, Christians may have high expectations in respect of their ability to serve the Lord and contribute to Kingdom work, yet the pressure of responsibilities to family, paid employment and standing firm against godless forces in society can drain and depress enthusiasm over time. Certainly, pastors and church leaders can become exhausted and disheartened, such that a sizeable percentage of them feel unable to continue in their role and seek other avenues of service. While we must acknowledge that obedience to the Spirit's directing is essential, Jesus stressed that we need to be yoked (harnessed) with him if the endeavour is to bear fruit. Striving and perseverance are admirable qualities but a single-minded determination devoid of the Spirit's empowering is limited in what it can achieve. See also later in this chapter under 'Limitations of striving'.

Despite the challenges faced by every believer from spiritual attack, together with opposition from secular ideology and even enmity from within the Body of Christ (i.e., from other believers), the urge to find fulfilment in life and leave a positive legacy is a powerful motivating factor. The need to feel that life has *had* a purpose and still *has* purpose should grow stronger as we become older. Unfortunately, a damaging belief has crept into the church in recent years that people reach a certain age, after which they are of limited use in Kingdom work. From God's point of view, every believer can demonstrate the fruit of the Spirit (Galatians 5:22) and be available for Kingdom service, regardless of seniority or inexperience.

Insight

Paul stresses the importance of living by the Spirit to avoid gratifying the desires of our sinful nature. He contrasts this corrupt behaviour with the nine elements that comprise the 'fruit of the Spirit': love, joy, peace, forbearance (patience), kindness, goodness, faithfulness, gentleness and self-control. The fruit is not ours by right; it requires an act of the will in submitting to God. See further details in Chapter 11.

While it is the case that younger Christians have the vitality and optimism to be used by God in wonderful ways, wisdom and life experience are also of considerable importance in maintaining stability in the church—hopefully without becoming a hindrance to the Spirit's fresh anointing by resisting change. An old saying succinctly expresses the truism that real satisfaction comes from knowing that our lives are being used well in the Saviour's service: 'Only one life; it will soon be past. Only what's done for Christ will last'. The principle applies to every believer at every stage of life. See Chapter 6 under 'The benefits of youth' and 'The challenges of longevity' for further discussion of the age issue.

We can be a blessing to others

Nobel's change of direction in life, as described earlier, warms our hearts and alerts us to the importance of allowing Jesus's love to live (abide, dwell) in us, such that we view our existence as worthwhile, as measured by the extent to which it blesses others. Paul explains how the act of giving is doubly beneficial: 'This service that you perform is not only supplying the needs of the Lord's people but is also overflowing in many expressions of thanks to God' (2 Corinthians 9:12, NIVUK). We note that the two benefits referred to by Paul to the Christians in Corinth are:

(1) *Practical:* meeting people's bodily needs.
(2) *Spiritual:* eliciting joyful thanks to God.

Paul emphasised that giving finance or time or hands-on support should be done cheerfully, not reluctantly or due to external pressure, as our deeds should be motivated by a concern for others, not as a means of relieving our consciences or enhancing our status or expectation of reward. Indeed, Jesus emphasised the importance of humility in giving: 'But when you give to the needy, do not let your left hand know what your right hand is doing' (Matthew 6:3, NIVUK). In addition, Paul underlines the need for *love* as the prime motivator for every action: 'Three things will last forever—faith, hope and love—and the greatest of these is love' (I Corinthians, 13:13, NIVUK).

Acts of selfless giving, through largesse or sacrificing time or offering encouragement or showing practical care is undoubtedly a blessing to others, though a balance always has to be maintained between support and over-zealous 'smothering' by making the recipient unduly dependent on outside assistance. Nevertheless, our love and care for others has an impact that will be highly significant in pleasing God, as described by Jesus and recorded by Matthew: 'For I was hungry and you fed me. I was thirsty and you gave me a drink. I was a stranger and you invited me into your home. I was naked and you gave me clothing. I was sick and you cared for me. I was in prison and you visited me… And the King will say: I tell you the truth, when you did it to one of the least of these my brothers and sisters, you were doing it to me' (25:35–6, 40, NLT). Our compassion and practical support for those in need therefore has a twofold positive effect: (1) It blesses others (2) It brings glory to Christ.

Matthew also records that Jesus goes on to say that *failure* to show practical care for the poor and needy results in 'eternal punishment' while, by contrast, 'the righteous will go into eternal life' (verse 46). Jesus's comments about our care and compassion leading to eternal life are frequently quoted; his warning about eternal punishment for failing to show love for others is often glossed over but must be taken equally seriously.

Having the Spirit of Christ in our lives creates a desire to show a positive attitude towards those in need, rather than possessing a caring approach somehow makes us righteous. In other words, we are not made righteous by our good deeds, however commendable. By contrast, having the righteousness of Christ through salvation precedes and generates a desire in us for selfless acts of good works that will be recognised by King Jesus at the Final Judgement. As always, we make the final decision to allow or deny the Spirit freedom to work in us and through us. The Holy Spirit inspires every kind and loving action, whether or not the person is aware of the fact. One of the essential differences between acts of love performed by a Christian and a non-Christian is that the former is motivated by the opportunity to bring glory to God, whereas the latter invites and receives admiration and commendation from people. As Paul urges: 'And whatever you do or say, do it as a representative of the Lord Jesus, giving thanks through him to God the Father' (Colossians 3:17, NLT).

We learn perseverance

Following Christ's leading does not mean that our lives will be trouble free, as clearly outlined in the sequence described in verses 3 and 4 of Romans Chapter 5. In these verses, we first *rejoice in our sufferings* (i.e., problems and trials that come from being a disciple of Jesus). Second, our suffering produces *perseverance* (i.e., being steadfast and determined in pursuing what is right, regardless of the sacrifice required) that helps to form *character* (loosely defined as the way that we behave when not being observed by other people). Ultimately, a strong and upright character produces *hope*, the confident hope of our salvation.

Paul continues his explanation about hope in verse 5: 'And this hope will not lead to disappointment. For we know how dearly God loves us because he has given us the Holy Spirit to fill our hearts with his love.' In other words, godly hope—as opposed to superstitious practices and other puerile fantasies—that emerges from a time of testing, will foster encouragement, strengthen our faith and fill our hearts with love *if* we view the hardships as being part of God's refining work to develop our trust in Him. Sadly, believers who are weak in faith may view challenges as evidence that God has deserted them; or believe they have lost His blessing because of sin; or assume that He is vengeful; or at its most extreme, start to doubt His existence.

Secular philosophy and worldly ambition view personal fulfilment and the *absence* of difficulty as the principal goals in life and evidence of favour. By total contrast, Christians rejoice, not only in the pleasure of serving others, the glory of salvation and the providence of God, but also in the difficulties brought about from faithful adherence to Jesus Christ and his teaching. As Paul explained: 'For whatever was written in earlier times was written for our instruction, so that through endurance and the encouragement of the Scriptures we might have hope and overflow with confidence in His promises' (Romans 15:4, AMP).

Our unwise and wilful behaviour, culminating in problems and disappointment, are in an entirely different category from those that come as a result of faithful obedience. However, even if we fall into sinful ways (thought, words, deeds), the Holy Spirit will teach us all things if we repent, pay heed to His voice and subsequently pursue the right path.

Insight

An old man was asked by a younger man to identify the heaviest weight that he had ever borne in his life, and was startled to hear the answer: "It was when I had no burden to bear." Without in any way attempting to trivialise the pain and distress that some people have to endure in their lives, it has been conjectured that if we find that we are meeting the devil head-on, we should rejoice, as he is heading for destruction, so we must be going in the right direction towards heaven!

Perseverance in doing what is right enhances faith and develops character for the simple reason that a determination to follow God's way will inevitably produce a counter reaction from two sources, both of which need to be confronted and overcome. The first form of opposition is *our own inclination* to wander from, as Jesus described it, the narrow path that leads to life; thus: 'The gateway to life is very narrow and the road is difficult and only a few ever find it' (Matthew 7:14, NLT). The second form of opposition is found in *ungodly influences* that are promoted in many areas of the media, popular culture (the 'latest vogue'), acquaintances at work, some relatives, and in our social circle, all of which create a wave of pressure that for younger people in particular is difficult to resist and undermines trust in the Saviour. Older and more mature

Christians have a responsibility to nurture, advise, pray for and set an example of godliness for less experienced followers and seekers after the truth.

Christian armour

For Christians in stress-laden areas of the world where persecution and discrimination is rife, their love for Christ may bring considerable oppression and hardship that provides a true test of faith. Whether enduring this type of extreme onslaught or more modest oppression, godly character is enhanced by persevering to remain close by the Father's side through sustained prayer, coupled with our desire to honour God in our thoughts, words and actions, remembering that the 'full armour of God' is available to every born again believer, as the Apostle Paul described 'spiritual equipment' to the Christians in Ephesus (Ephesians Chapter 6).

By using the graphic illustration of Roman armour, Paul listed the way in which disciples of Jesus can be 'strong in the Lord and in His mighty power' (verse 10, NIVUK) and stand their ground against the devil's schemes. The list of armour consists of:

(1) The belt of truth
(2) The breastplate of righteousness
(3) Shoes fitted with the Gospel of peace
(4) The shield of faith
(5) The helmet of salvation
(6) The sword of the Spirit (which is the Word of God).

Every follower of Jesus Christ should also heed Paul's concluding words in his first letter to his protégé, Timothy: 'Pursue righteousness and a godly life, along with faith, love, perseverance and gentleness. Fight the good fight for the true faith. Hold tightly to the eternal life to which God has called you, which you have declared so well before many witnesses' (6:11–12, NLT). Key words from Paul's instructions include 'pursue', 'fight' and 'hold tightly', all of which convey a sense of urgency and determination.

It is important to grasp from Paul's illustration of God's supernatural armour that believers who are seriously committed to Christ cannot sit back and remain uninvolved in the process of being protectively clad, remaining unprepared for spiritual battle and passively expecting the Holy Spirit to compensate for their indolence. The Spirit invites and expects our active collaboration. We are also told to put on the *whole* armour. Paul encourages bold action, not least in the requirement to 'pray in the Spirit on all occasions with all kinds of prayers and requests' (verse 18, NIVUK).

There aren't any shortcuts to spiritual maturity of this kind. Christians with the greatest spiritual depth and most triumphant lives are those who have suffered and been tested, yet persevered and remained faithful to the Lord. They have 'passed the test' and are ready to move on to the next stage of development. For such adherents, Jesus promises that a great reward awaits them, not least to hear the 'well done, good and faithful servant' from the lips of the Master (Matthew 25:23).

An unshakeable hope

As noted earlier, character is closely allied to hope. The more we send our roots deep into the Word of God and discover His intentions for each individual and for the wider world, the more we have an unshakeable hope that allows us to hold firmly to the belief expressed in Horatio Spafford's famous hymn *When peace like a river*: 'Whatever my lot, you have taught me to say it is well with my soul'. It should be noted that Spafford wrote the hymn while in the deepest throes of anguish, following the drowning of his four daughters after a serious incident at sea. Smith Wigglesworth's oft-quoted statement, 'God said it, I believe it, that settles it!' while viewed by sceptics as being unduly simplistic, establishes a fundamental principle that once God's will and purpose is clear, acceptance and obedience must necessarily follow for those who trust Him fully.

It is beyond the brief of the present chapter to pursue the implications of Wigglesworth's assertion further, as I will deal more specifically with what is involved in following Jesus unreservedly in Chapter 12. Suffice it to say at this point that far from being fearful, tentative and defensive when circumstances are challenging or bewildering, believers should be firm in expressing their full confidence in God's over-ruling hand. In practice, such an attitude means that in addition to constant prayer and Spirit-directed actions, our daily conversation needs to be interspersed with faith statements about God's sovereign rule and with far fewer expressions of doubt and fearfulness. Faith-driven positivity should always triumph faithless negativity.

As we allow God to transform our lives, the act of bringing hope to those we encounter is doubly beneficial in that as well as encouraging them it also serves to bless and motivate us. However, unlike worldly hope that resides in vague concepts such as luck and karma, Christian hope is characterised by the knowledge that trusting Jesus not only provides a firm foundation for this life but is also a guarantee of eternal life. Jesus underlined the futility of relying on human effort for salvation and again stressed the necessary participation of the Holy Spirit: 'The Spirit alone gives eternal life. Human effort accomplishes nothing. And the very words I have spoken to you are spirit and life' (John 6:63, NLT).

The reason for Jesus returning to his Father in heaven was not only for the Holy Spirit to convict people of sin and righteousness but also to provide enduring comfort, support and challenge in such a way that believers are empowered to lead purposeful lives, brimming with hope and trusting in the promises of God that never fail. Jesus's earthly ministry was initially confined to Israel and neighbouring areas, but it was disseminated across the wider world through the ministry of the Apostles and personal testimony.

Insight

When most people say, "I hope so," it emanates from feelings, emotions or a deep-seated longing—almost a fantasy—that 'somehow' all will be well. But hope for the Christian is not based on wishful thinking or luck or fate or superstitious practices: it is rooted in certainty.

Christ offers salvation from the consequences of sin (verses 6–8)

The key word in the sub-title is 'offers'. All those who have the maturity and a sufficiently clear mind to grasp the nature of the divine invitation are given the choice as to whether or not they accept Jesus's offer of salvation and freedom from the consequences of sin. Earlier in the book, I addressed the issues relating to the eternal destiny of children who are aborted, die in the womb or only live for a short time, and the situation for people with severe brain damage. However, the decision for those with fully developed minds is between remaining spiritually dead in trespasses and sins or finding freedom from sin, cleansed by the shed blood of Christ on the Cross. As Paul explains with great clarity: 'God gave Jesus as a way to forgive people's sins through their faith in him. God can forgive them because the blood sacrifice of Jesus pays for their sins. God gave Jesus to show that he always does what is right and fair. He was right in the past when he was patient and did not punish people for their sins. And in our own time he still does what is right. God worked all this out in a way that allows him to judge people fairly and still make right any person who has faith in Jesus' (Romans 3:25–26, ERV). Importantly, the phrase 'through their faith in him' in Paul's declaration is a fundamental prerequisite for being made right with God.

It is important to emphasise that having faith in Christ is always personal; there isn't any communal hysteria, brainwashing or 'following the herd' mentality. Use of expressions denoting that (say) the United Kingdom or USA is a 'Christian country' may have credence in terms of societal norms and laws but does not bestow salvation upon the general population that happens to reside in that country.

God's perfect timing

Time governs all human and animal behaviour. People plan their day by using a watch, clock or electronic device or perhaps by taking account of physical phenomena, such as the rising sun or phases of the moon. Longer-term planning often refers to the annual cycle of seasons with particular attention to climate and weather conditions. In some (mainly Western) cultures, accurate timekeeping is considered to be an essential attribute and a measure of efficiency; in other parts of the world, attitudes to timekeeping are more relaxed and might even be interpreted as a sign of indolence or apathy.

People judge the passage of time with reference to a horizontal line, with the past stretching to the left of the present day and the future stretching to the right of it. God, however, is infinite and has no beginning or end, and is outside of human time in that He knows what has been and what will be. The existence of the Godhead reaches back before the creation of the earth, as John explains in the opening verses of his Gospel account, as he refers to the existence of the Son: 'He was with God in the beginning. Through him all things were made; without him nothing was made that has been made. In him was life, and that life was the light of all mankind' (1:2–4) Christ also controls the future new heaven and earth, as described in Revelation Chapter 21.

Counter-intuitively, lax timekeeping or an apparently unfortunate delay may prove to be beneficial if it saves someone from being involved in a dangerous or deadly situation. For example, a few late passengers were doubtless highly relieved to have missed RMS Titanic on its maiden voyage, which sank after hitting an iceberg in 1912; or those that failed to make it on time to catch RMS Lusitania, subsequently sunk by a German U-boat in 1915; or countless other tragic events in which poor punctuality proved to be a blessing and not a curse.

By contrast with these instances of 'near misses', Paul makes it abundantly clear in his letter to the church in Rome that Christ died for the ungodly at *exactly the right time*, such that he could cry out in triumph from the Cross of Calvary that his work on earth was completed according to God the Father's timetable. John's account of the crucifixion, in which he quotes Jesus's final words: 'It is finished [completed]', demonstrates the absolute certainty of God's perfect timing.

Insight

Christians do well to learn that God is never in a hurry and, if they trust and wait for Him to act, He will always do what is right for them. Impatience leads to hasty decisions, inappropriate actions and unsatisfactory outcomes.

At just the right time

There are three occasions in the Apostle Paul's letters in which he uses the phrase 'just the right time':

- The first refers to Christ's coming to earth as a man to die on the Cross: 'You see, at just the right time, when we were still powerless, Christ died for the ungodly [sinners]' (Romans 5:6, NKJV). Paul's goes on to make the key point that it was wholly pleasing to God the Father that Jesus should die as the sacrificial lamb.
- The second reference is contained in Paul's letter to the Ephesians in which he explains God's future purpose for the world: 'And this is the plan: At the right time he will bring everything together under the authority of Christ—everything in heaven and on earth' (1:10, NLT). Repetition of the word 'everything' is significant: the event involves every person who has ever lived and those still living. It is not confined to a single race, nation or people group.
- The third reference is to the fundamental role that Christ will play in the Heavenly Kingdom at the end of time, as Paul explains to Timothy: 'At just the right time Christ will be revealed from heaven by the blessed and only Almighty God, the King of all kings and Lord of all lords' (I Timothy 6:15, NLT). On this occasion, the present creation will be dissolved and replaced by a new heaven and earth.

As we stand amazed at the perfection of God's timing in sending His Son to earth to live and die for humanity, and the promise of his reappearing at a future date (known only to Father God) to have complete authority in heaven and on earth, it is important that we take careful account of Paul's warning later in the letter to Christians in Rome that 'The night is nearly over; the day is almost here. So let us put aside the deeds of darkness and put on the armour of light' (13:11–12, NIVUK) or more abruptly in the NLT: 'time is running out'.

Similarly, in his second letter to the church in Corinth, Paul urges that 'the right time is now; today is the day of salvation' (6:2, NLT). In repenting and turning to Christ, no one can afford to be negligent or delay, as extended time for us in this life is not guaranteed. There is an urgency attached to each day to ensure that we take hold of salvation and then allow God to make effective use of our gifts, talents and opportunities, and perhaps to empower us with new abilities to serve His purposes on earth. Using a line from Rudyard Kipling's famous poem: 'If you can fill the unforgiving minute with sixty seconds' worth of distance run, yours is the Earth and everything that's in it and, which is more, you'll be a man, my son!' A phrase that believers should never employ is 'I am killing time'.

Christ the Redeemer

The Apostle Paul not only emphasises that Jesus came at the right time but also that he came when we were powerless ('utterly helpless') to redeem our souls from the depravity of sin. In the New Testament, redemption is used to refer both to (a) deliverance from sin and (b) freedom from captivity, both of which are based on the metaphor of 'buying back'. Jesus is referred to as the Redeemer, referring to the redemption he accomplished on the Cross of Calvary in freeing the world from the eternal consequences of sin.

There are also numerous warnings in the Bible for nations that forsake the Lord God, worship idols and pursue ungodly practices, all of which are sadly prevalent in today's world. For example, the depravity of *individuals* (Oholah and Oholibah, though they also represent Samaria, then capital of Israel; and Jerusalem, then capital of Judah) as described in Ezekiel Chapter 23, and the depravity of a *nation* (Israel) that God described through Hosea in Chapter 9 of the prophetic book.

The oft-quoted maxim, 'God helps those who help themselves', is true in a general sense of someone willingly participating in His plans for living, but is wholly inappropriate as a means of gaining redemption. People find it difficult to acknowledge the fact that they are unable to save themselves from the curse of sin and its damaging consequences, judging their success in life on the basis of having the ability to be self-sufficient and independent. While it is commendable to be determined and resourceful, salvation cannot be earned by perseverance, worldly possessions or heroic deeds. The Apostle Paul summarised the position in his letter to Titus (minister of the church in Crete): '[Jesus] saved us, not because of righteous things we had done, but because of his mercy. He saved us through the washing of rebirth and renewal by the Holy Spirit' (3:5, NIVUK).

Crisis and extreme fear may provoke an interest in God and hopeful prayers from those who would otherwise be dismissive or disinterested in Him but such desire usually evaporates when the period of stress is relieved or, if the situation persists, mutates into resentment that God has 'allowed this thing to happen'. People may look hither and thither for meaning and purpose in life, as they sample one religion or philosophy after another, dabble in the occult or use drugs or indulge in extreme forms of behaviour. Ultimately, their quest fails to find satisfactory answers about the meaning of life and they remain spiritually unfulfilled, while all the time, Jesus the Redeemer stands waiting with arms wide open to satisfy every longing need.

In his first letter to the churches of Asia Minor, John summarised succinctly the position for born again followers of Jesus: 'But if we walk in the light as He is in the light, we have fellowship with each other, and the blood of Jesus Christ His Son cleanses us from all sin' (1:7, NKJV). It may be noted that the primary requirement is to walk in God's light—living His way and not following our own desires and preferences—which results in two principal outcomes:

1. *We are cleansed from sin by the blood of Jesus.* Just as animal sacrifices were made in the past to negate the curse of sin, Jesus's blood has been shed once and for all time on the Cross of Calvary to rescue (redeem) us and bring us from death to life. Hallelujah!

2. *We have fellowship with other believers.* That is, we receive from God, the grace to love other Christians in the same way that Christ loved us by showing unconditional care, compassion and understanding, regardless of the attitude of the recipient. Such love cannot be achieved solely through human effort but relies on the Spirit of the Lord to purify us and make us channels for His blessing. The writer of Hebrews reminds us of the importance of mutual fellowship in this endeavour: 'And let us consider how we may spur one another on towards love and good deeds, not giving up meeting together, as some are in the habit of doing, but encouraging one another—and all the more as you see the Day approaching' (10:24–5, NIVUK).

Salvation and eternal life are both a gift of God—free to us but not free to Him, as it involved the sacrifice of the Son. World events, such as famine, plague, war, recessions and the like can destroy physical goods, ruin businesses and lead to untold misery for those so affected, but cannot impact on a person's eternal destiny, which is bound up with his or her relationship with God through the indwelling spirit of the Risen Lord Jesus Christ.

Insight

What Christ has done for believers (based on Romans Chapter 5)

(1) Made me righteous in God's sight.
(2) Given me access into the grace of God.
(3) Brought hope that causes me to rejoice.
(4) Offered me freedom from the consequences of sin.
(5) Reconciled me to God.

Summary

In the above account, I have explored the truth and implications of each of the original claims that are listed near the beginning of this chapter, based largely on the verses extracted from Paul's letter to the Christians in Rome. We can rejoice that because of God's redeeming grace in and through Jesus Christ, the name of all those who accept him as Saviour and Lord are written in heaven (Revelation Chapters 3, 13, 17–21). As Peter celebrated in his first letter: 'All praise to God, the Father of our Lord Jesus Christ. It is by his great mercy that we have been born again because God raised Jesus Christ from the dead. Now we live with great expectation and we have a priceless inheritance—an inheritance that is kept in heaven for you, pure and undefiled, beyond the reach of change and decay. And through your faith, God is protecting you by his power, until you receive this salvation, which is ready to be revealed on the last day for all to see' (1:3–5, NLT).

Each person who is confronted with Peter's divinely inspired words can respond in one of three ways: (a) Dismiss the claims made about Jesus as God's answer to the sin problem. (b) Treat the above account as a matter of general interest but of no personal relevance. (c) Believe the truth of the Gospel, step out in faith and accept that Jesus Christ is the world's Saviour, who died to set each of us free from the power and penalty of sin. The church is charged with the responsibility to uphold and boldly declare the third option, an issue discussed at length in the next chapter.

What do you believe the Bible teaches about salvation?

1. Only those who hear the Gospel message, repent of their sins, and trust Jesus Christ as Saviour will be saved.
2. Only those who hear the Gospel message, repent of their sin, trust Christ as Saviour and are baptised will be saved.
3. God will judge those who never hear the Gospel by using criteria other than faith in Christ.
4. Although God already knows who will be saved, He still expects Christians to evangelise and save souls.
5. God has already decided who will be saved.
6. Everyone will ultimately be saved.
7. Every person who has not had an opportunity to respond to the offer of salvation will be given a second chance after death.
8. God knows what He is doing, so we can leave the whole matter for Him to decide.

Chapter 6
Challenges and Opportunities
for the Church

Introduction

Promises are easy to make but not always easy to fulfil. Most children have an implicit trust in adults and believe everything they tell them. It comes as a shock when they become aware of deception and barefaced falsehood. Thankfully, no such alarms are in store for Christians from God, as Jesus made everything clear concerning our lives, conduct and future. In 1886, Russell Carter wrote a hymn expresses the absolute trust that every believer can have in what God has revealed: *Standing on the Promises of Christ, my King*, the first verse of which reads: 'Standing on the promises of Christ, my King. Through eternal ages let his praises ring. Glory in the highest, I will shout and sing: Standing on the promises of God!' In this chapter, I explore the various ways in which God deals with the sin virus through the medium of the church with particular reference to the prophecy of Jeremiah. In doing so, I pay close attention to the problems faced by ageing congregations and pathways to renewal. I conclude by listing the signs that indicate the imminent return of Christ and its implications for all people on earth.

Issues Confronting the Church

The world is changing in ways that were scarcely conceivable fifty years ago. Over recent decades, the growth of technology has accelerated to such an extent that it is difficult to keep pace with it, especially for older people, who sometimes feel that they are becoming detached from the present reality. Attitudes to morality, forms of social interaction and standards of integrity have become 'elastic', as even in so-called Christian countries, the 'grand narrative' of the

Bible has largely been side-lined in favour of new interpretations that are less about bringing glory to God and more about personal fulfilment and individual preference. How different these egocentric attitudes are when weighed against Jesus's priorities, as Paul reminded the Christians in Rome: 'May the God who gives endurance and encouragement give you the same attitude of mind towards each other that Christ Jesus had, so that with one mind and one voice you may glorify the God and Father of our Lord Jesus Christ' (15:5–6, NIVUK). The expression 'one mind and one voice' emphasises the importance of church unity, brought about through individual desire for holiness and the bonds of loving fellowship.

Challenges of change

In the midst of this societal and moral turbulence, it is not surprising that some church fellowships have been reluctant to embrace change, arguing that the biblical truths and principles for which their predecessors fought and struggled for so long are not negotiable. At one level, such resolve is commendable in guarding the Gospel against error and manipulation by people who believe that compromise about biblical truths (not least, the prospect of Hell and punishment for those who reject God's gracious offer of salvation) is desirable in order to remove possible 'barriers' in the quest to attract a larger number of potential adherents.

On another level, protecting Gospel truth has sometimes been linked with preserving existing ways of 'doing church' and resistance to change. The approach to church life employed by some conservative minded leaders has resulted in some cases to staleness and inflexibility, such that meetings have been doggedly preserved in much the same format as were established by previous generations, much to the detriment of their growth today.

Partly as a result of such intransigence, fellowships have not attracted younger people or seen conversions, and some congregations have aged and dwindled until only a small number of stalwarts remain, who nobly struggle to preserve a local witness. Such fellowships are forced into a 'maintenance (survival) mode' instead of being a shining beacon for the Gospel message and hope for those who are lost. The desire among the elderly members to see God at work may not have waned but their aptitude to promote the word is constrained by physical weakness and the time and energy expended in 'keeping the doors open'.

By way of contrast with the gloomy scenario painted above, there has been an acknowledgement among many church leaders that updating forms of worship (for example, by using a mixture of established and contemporary songs) and employing less direct methods of outreach (for example, by developing close ties with the community through social events) do not necessitate 'sanitising' the truth or compromising scriptural ordinances.

The Holy Spirit is always seeking to refresh the church by challenging believers to seek Him with all their hearts and opening new opportunities for service, as well as preserving inviolable truth. On the one hand, as expressed through Jeremiah: 'Stand at the crossroads and look; ask for the ancient paths; ask where the good way is and walk in it, and you will find rest for your souls' (6:16, NIVUK). On the other hand, as declared through the prophet, Isaiah: 'Now I will tell you new things, secrets you have not yet heard. They are brand-new, not things from the past, so you cannot say: We knew that all the time!' (Isaiah 48:6b–7, NLT) In other words, take the best of the past but look expectantly for God to reveal fresh paths of opportunity, and follow His leading accordingly.

An amalgam of tried-and-tested approaches underpinned by sound doctrine—in combination with the gradual introduction of innovative, Spirit-led approaches—is a worthy aspiration for every fellowship. The difficult part is putting these ideals into action against a backdrop of tradition and embedded practice that has the potential to create a sharp dividing of opinion among the fellowship. In addition, the burden of implementation too often falls on the willing few, while the majority are content to give mere assent and observe the proceedings (or criticise them) from the margins. Wise, courageous leadership in this endeavour is essential, bolstered by godly humility on the part of those who may entertain misgivings, if the endeavour is to glorify God and bring souls into the Kingdom.

Implementing Jeremiah's counsel

Jeremiah's prophecy (quoted above) makes a number of key points that have great relevance for modern church witness and decisions about the most God-honouring way to proceed as a fellowship. When a body of believers reach a 'crossroad', whereby a choice has to be made or *should* be made about the right direction to take, they are encouraged first to *stop* (i.e., pause from what has formerly been taken for granted: 'Be still and know that I am God' Psalm 46:10) so that minds are uncluttered to receive from God; then *pray* for wisdom to know which of the 'godly' established ways should be preserved and enhanced ('where the good way lies') while relegating outmoded forms of service and practice; then *travel* the redefined Spirit-led path by moving forward in *faith and trust* that God has gone ahead to prepare the way.

Taking such steps will result in 'rest for our souls', whereby we can have full confidence that we are walking in the will and purpose of the Lord, though it must be admitted that one of the challenges in the life of a church fellowship is being willing to wait for God's 'green light', as there can be a degree of impatience on the part of some members to see concrete evidence of progress (notably, increased attendance) thereby triggering an inclination to rush ahead instead of 'waiting patiently for Him' (Psalms 37:7; 40:1, NKJ). Against the tendency to be hasty, the temptation to *procrastinate* can be equally damaging, as enthusiasm wanes, nothing of substance changes and church life atrophies. Observing how God is blessing and developing other fellowships can provide helpful insights into His will and purpose but may also invite 'copycat' behaviour in an ill-fated attempt to replicate their success.

It is important to emphasise that Jeremiah urges us to pursue the *godly* ways from the past, presumably as opposed to the ungodly ways. Such a distinction is of crucial importance in ensuring that while the centrality of God's truth and commandments are maintained, they should not be used as a justification for rigidly following the 'ancient path', regardless of the Holy Spirit's 'brand-new' ways to which Isaiah refers (48:6b–7, above).

The key words extracted from Jeremiah's prophecy, as it applies to both personal development and church renewal, may be summarised as follows:

- STOP: God needs to speak to us in the stillness of our hearts. Busyness can act to convince and satisfy us that we are serving wholeheartedly but can also prevent us from hearing the Spirit's voice.

- LOOK: Evaluating our situation—notably, how we spend our time and use our resources—and the present direction of travel, necessitates an open-minded review of present practice, unhindered as far as humanly possible by personal attachment to existing priorities. It must also be conceded that such an impartial approach is more challenging for those who are comfortable with the existing ways and will require immense graciousness to accept changes that they perceive as encumbrances rather than opportunities.

- ASK: God delights to hear the prayers of His people, not least when we invite Him to speak to us, always being mindful of the need to ask according to His will, as declared in the Bible and confirmed in our spirits.

- TRUST: Some past ways continue to be relevant and some need to cease. They are not normally 'ungodly' in the sense of being false or reprehensible but rather in the sense of lacking Holy Spirit anointing for the present and future.

- TRAVEL: We move forward by faith, trusting in the certainty of God's presence and promises. The key line from John Sammis's 1887 hymn is reassuring: 'Trust and obey, for there's no other way to be happy in Jesus'.

- REST: When we are in the will and purpose of God, we find peace of mind and confidence, which provide a strong confirmation of the correctness of our decisions and empowers us to persevere.

It must be acknowledged that even after sincerely seeking the Lord's will, a fellowship of God's people will sometimes conclude that significant changes are unnecessary or should be implemented with the utmost care. However, the 'taking stock' approach described above is never wasted, as it opens our hearts and concentrates our minds in a positive way and establishes a precedent for an ongoing evaluation of personal direction and the priorities of ministry. Though the process of appraisal may cause an unsettling and shaking of the fellowship for a period of time, it is better than to accede to the severity of the Lord's 'shaking' from displeasure, strikingly described in Isaiah Chapter 2.

We are all permitted to indulge briefly in being nostalgic about the 'good old days', thanking God for past blessings and His never-failing mercy towards us—but if reminiscing becomes a barrier to receiving new direction from the Spirit, it acts as a hindrance to the fulfilment His purposes. Let Isaiah have the final word on the matter: 'Your ears shall hear a word behind you, saying: "This is the way, walk in it" whenever you turn to the right hand or whenever you turn to the left' (30:21, NKJV).

The blessings of youth

As a result of leaders and members being open to a change of emphasis in worship style and, crucially, of responding to Spirit-inspired revelation, a larger number of younger people and families have found a home in church life to receive and benefit from the liberating truth about Jesus as Saviour. The explosion of new churches that have introduced a more modern music genre, a less dogmatic but still biblically faithful presentation of the Gospel, and an emphasis on outreach (especially targeting the younger age group) has seen extraordinary numerical growth that is rarely reported in media surveys about church attendance. While being careful not to neglect the needs of older members, flourishing fellowships place considerable emphasis on working with children, young people and families, justifying such use of human and financial resources on two counts:

Youth is the time when strong opinions and moral positions are formed, creating the bedrock for future belief and commitment.

Surveys reveal that a sizeable majority of Christians committed their lives to Christ before the age of twenty-one, so the opportunity to influence this age group is clearly a priority. Despite the need to give serious attention to the salvation and discipleship of young people, it is important to avoid any hint of coercion or the imposition of adult understanding on developing minds. While teaching biblical truths is necessary, any tendency to indoctrinate will ultimately prove damaging to the Gospel and may cause resentment and resistance to genuine commitment. Nevertheless, the emphasis must be on communicating spiritual truth and not merely conveying factual information.

For younger children, telling Bible stories, followed by colouring-in pictures and small-scale craft activities will keep them occupied, but if the children are to be properly grounded in the Christian faith, these basic elements must be accompanied by gently and appropriately explaining the life implications of the related Scripture passage or event. Learning and reciting Bible verses and singing songs that embody scriptural truths form the basis for the development of understanding but need to be fully exploited by teachers through identifying how they impact decisions, priorities and behaviour. It is possible to sing heartily and score highly on Bible quizzes, yet remain detached from the need for repentance, trusting the Saviour and leading a holy life, because these things have not been emphasised as integral to faith.

The use of vocabulary appropriate to the children's age and ability, and explaining spiritual truths simply but accurately must be a prime consideration for all those who seek to win them for the Saviour. For example, even well-loved choruses such as Norman Clayton's: *When the road is rough and steep, fix your eyes upon Jesus* benefits from an explanation about the two key phrases in the first line of the song. Understanding the significance of a 'rough and steep road' is very different for a mature seventy year-old compared to a child of seven! Similarly, 'fixing our eyes upon Jesus' is a wonderful form of encouragement for an adult who needs reassurance but may perplex the average primary-age child who interprets the phrase literally.

Teenagers are understandably wary of statements of belief and assertions without firm evidence to support them, which are best presented in the shape of 'living' testimonies, ideally provided by older 'young people', as they set an example to the younger members and have opportunity to share their experiences and the ways in which being a follower of Jesus Christ is the most satisfying and enriching life to lead. Testimonies from adults are useful if the speaker is able to establish a rapport with the young people but may be deemed less relevant to the youthful listeners if they associate them with a bygone age.

While making a commitment to Christ requires a degree of urgency, pressing too forcefully may be counterproductive, as each young person—indeed, people of any age—must be fully convinced in their own minds about the truth of the Gospel before making a firm decision to follow Jesus. Paul underscores the importance of a vibrant, Spirit-empowered life in persuading others of the truth of the Gospel: 'They were convinced by the power of miraculous signs and wonders and by the power of God's Spirit' (Romans 15:19a, NLT). The enthusiasm and entertainment that characterises so much work among younger people is not sufficient to effect change—miraculous signs and wonders must be evident to accompany the stimulating environment. Every believer should be fully and prayerfully supportive of those who are called to work among children and young people, as the future spiritual prosperity of a church—perhaps its very continuation—will depend on them.

Young people have their lives stretching before them with all the potential and opportunities that they offer.

When a child is six years old, eleven year-olds seem quite mature. At age eleven, most fifteen year-olds seem grown-up. By the time we reach seventeen, thirty seems old, and so the pattern continues throughout much of life until we reach a certain age when everyone wearing a uniform looks incredibly young! Regardless of age, God can speak to and through younger people, especially when more experienced Christians are willing to patiently guide them and offer encouragement and support.

In contemplating the potential for God to use children to achieve His purposes, it is helpful to remember that when Jesus was just twelve years old, he was filled with spiritual wisdom and discernment, such that even the religious teachers were amazed at his understanding and answers to their questions (Luke 2:41–52). Paul encourages Timothy not to be defensive about being inexperienced but to be an example to everyone instead: 'Don't let anyone think less of you because you are young. Be an example to all believers in what you say, in the way you live, in your love, your faith and your purity' (I Timothy 4:12, NLT). It is fair to add that although Timothy was probably in his late teens or early twenties, he had the benefit of a godly upbringing, a privilege that many young people are denied today. Although the majority of people choose to follow Jesus when they are young, it is a sad fact that a sizeable percentage of them then fail to grow in grace and love for the Saviour as the years pass.

In recent times, there has been considerable attention given to 'progression and succession'. *Progression* refers to the spiritual development of the young person into a mature, committed disciple of Jesus. *Succession* refers to the importance of older Christians sharing and eventually handing on leadership to capable and responsible younger people, such that there is continuity of ministry. Failure to train a successor leads to the familiar scenario of an older person wishing to step back from his or her role but reluctantly continuing because there is no suitable person available to take over. The inability of churches to organise systematic, relevant and effective ongoing discipleship training for potential leaders can be a serious flaw in their programmes and leads to a vacuum when the faithful older person reluctantly withdraws after long years of dedicated service. The issue of succession is made more challenging in recent years in that the population is increasingly mobile, with the result that a carefully trained person may move away for study or work opportunities.

Challenges and opportunities of longevity

If spared into old age, surveys suggest that many people look back over their lives and wish that they had used their time more constructively; that is, they regret that they had not taken fuller advantage of their opportunities and employed their knowledge and talents more effectively. Although God does not see elderly folk as 'past their sell-by date' (a grotesque expression), many will feel that their productive years have passed and they must leave unfinished business to succeeding generations. As noted above, the challenge for many fellowships is to ensure that there are younger people in the church to whom the baton can be handed. Sadly, in all too many cases, there is no one available for the transfer to take place.

For fellowships in which the large majority of attendees are in their retirement years, high levels of discernment, fervent prayer and moral courage are needed when deciding whether to focus time and resources on the needs and preferences of the older congregation or to realign the church's priorities to embrace change (howbeit gradually) and thereby become more attractive to younger people and families.

Even a relatively minor change in the format of services can trigger a mixture of dismay (from traditionalists) and celebration (from innovators) within the congregation. For example, replacing pews with seats, substituting the pipe organ with an electronic keyboard and supporting instruments, and moving the time of the main service, are all likely to generate widely varying reactions from existing members. Leaders must chart a careful course between introducing change, while reassuring more conservative believers that church life is not about to be thrown into turmoil. In practice, a decision to reorientate and venture into less well chartered territory will require humility and selfless sacrifice from members who are orthodox in their habits and expectations.

Insight

In endeavouring to expand the appeal of church attendance and associated activities, it is a prerequisite that younger people are first and foremost attracted to the person of the Lord Jesus and not to a church institution, its facilities or the personalities fronting it.

The sobering truth for those who resist change is that it will occur anyway, due to the fact that circumstances are in a constant state of flux: people become ill or retire or leave or die or experience a major life event that affects their ability to contribute to church and community. The choice to be made is whether to allow change to happen *to* us through occurrences beyond our control; or whether *we* enact the necessary changes—internally controlled by Spirit-led decisions from the committed members, together with guidance from other trusted and mature believers. The process is likely to create some tension and disagreement but 'as iron sharpens iron, so one person sharpens another' (Proverbs 27:17, NIVUK) which eventually leads to a more decisive outcome than failing to address key issues in a bid to maintain harmony.

A useful incentive is for members to envisage the state of the church they attend in ten years' time if present trends continue and spiritually mature younger people are not on hand to share, envision and ultimately assume major responsibility for the work. If changes are not implemented, it is likely that an increasing number of more rigidly minded church fellowships will ossify or decline.

Despite the impediments created by growing older and less mobile, there are numerous examples of people from different eras and backgrounds to show that outstanding achievements may still be possible. For example:

- Michelangelo was still working at the age of 87.
- Leonid Hurwicz won the Nobel Prize for Economics, aged 90.
- George Beverly Shea sang at Billy Graham Crusades into his 90s.
- In 2020, Tom Moore, aged 100, raised over £15 million for the National Health Service in England.
- Caleb was 85 years old when he cried out to Joshua: 'Therefore, give me this mountain!' (Joshua 14:12, NKJV)

Of singular importance for every person, whether younger or older, is the day-by-day devotion to Jesus that allows his love and grace to shine from our lives and determines our spiritual effectiveness. Increasing age simply allows more time for our love for him to grow deeper and stronger, until one day we see him 'face to face'. What a wonderful prospect!

Witnessing to loved ones

There are many Christians who pray for years that their friends and family members will come to a saving knowledge of Jesus Christ, accept by faith his offer to accompany them by his Spirit throughout their lives and rejoice in the promise of an eternal home with him in heaven. Oftentimes, these prayers seem to go unanswered and witnessing to these loved ones becomes increasingly difficult as the years pass and they become established in their ways, settle into a 'groove', live comfortable and predictable lives, and fail to see any good reason for embracing a different lifestyle and changed priorities. Nevertheless, Paul encourages believers to be fervent and persistent in prayer and thanksgiving: 'Rejoice always, pray without ceasing, in everything give thanks; for this is the will of God in Christ Jesus for you' (I Thessalonians 5:16–18, NKJV). The key words are boldly declared—rejoice; pray; give thanks—all of which apply to our worship of God and our trust in His faithfulness, regardless of how He chooses to bring about His purposes.

Insight

The Bible is replete with references to the importance of praising God for who He is and what He has done. The need to praise God in all circumstances, including sad and disappointing ones, emphasises the fact that God is worthy of our adoration, regardless of the situation we are in. Paul and Silas provide us with a powerful example of praising God under the most miserable conditions: 'About midnight Paul and Silas were praying and singing hymns to God, and the other prisoners were listening to them. Suddenly there was such a violent earthquake that the foundations of the prison were shaken. At once all the prison doors flew open, and everyone's chains came loose' (Acts 16:25–26, NIVUK). Praise may or may not alter our circumstances but it releases us from the bonds of our earthly state and elevates us to heavenly places.

By the time people have past the age of forty, the chances of them radically altering their priorities and life direction fades with every birthday, though the Holy Spirit can, of course, intervene at any stage of life. In practice, there are far fewer converts to Christianity in later years compared to those in the younger age group, as discussed in the preceding section. So what is to be done to reach mature people with the Gospel? Has God lost interest in them? Is it too late for them to be saved? Are our prayers wasted? These are crucially important issues that impact on every follower of Jesus.

Jesus warned his disciples that 'a prophet is not without honour except in his own town, among his relatives and in his own home' (Mark 6:4, NIVUK) and it is broadly true to say that witnessing to relatives and close friends, especially those who are older, can prove to be more difficult than doing so to people outside our immediate age range and social mix. Underlying this problem is the fact that those closest to us are aware of our shortcomings and less likely to respond to a message about the need for a changed life in Jesus if they detect any hint of hypocrisy or a hiatus between what we proclaim and the way we live.

Consistency in the way that followers of Jesus behave provides a powerful form of testimony for those who observe us closely, without a word being spoken.

The tension that Christians feel between having a strong concern about the salvation of loved ones and yet fearing that they may be unimpressed as a result of what they observe about their speech and actions, reinforces the need for believers to ensure two things:

(a) To live a life worthy of their high calling as followers of Jesus (Hebrews 3:1).

(b) To pray earnestly and regularly about the salvation of family and friends, not least that the Lord will use other means to confront them with their need of Christ if our witness falters or seems ineffective (James 5:16).

The principle of 'persuasion through example' is foundational, as opposed to using a direct and forceful manner that may be perceived as intrusive and confrontational. Nevertheless, our 'silent witness' must invoke questions and comments from those we seek to influence and open opportunities to describe the hope and joyful expectation that trusting Jesus brings. Once our older relatives and friends have died, the sense of unease or guilt we may feel about having said too little to them while we had the chance can only be avoided if we have gently persisted in pointing them to Jesus. The way they chose to respond is beyond our ultimate control.

Impatience with God

For those of us who tend to get restless over God's apparent reluctance to intervene or respond to our prayer requests or fulfil the desires of our heart, there is an important lesson to be learned from Christ appearing at 'just the right time' (see Chapter 5). Jesus's birth and time spent as a man on earth was not arbitrary; it was pre-planned and ordained in the will and purpose of God to bring about redemption from sin. No doubt, many of the Jews began to wonder if the promised Messiah would ever make an appearance; but God works in His own time, according to His master plan and not derailed by circumstances or human frailty.

The reason for a delay in God answering our prayers could be the fact that we are not praying according to His will and purpose or we are asking from wrong motives. However, assuming that the Holy Spirit is in agreement with our prayer, we can be confident that God is never acting prematurely or being tardy in responding. Delays are merely an opportunity for God to purify our endeavour by preparing us fully for a particular task that lies ahead. Jesus reminded his listeners: 'So if you sinful people know how to give good gifts to your children, how much more will your Heavenly Father give good gifts to those who ask him' (Matthew 7:11, NLT). In the same way that the vast majority of earthly fathers seek the best for their sons and daughters, God only wants the very best for His children. He knows our hearts and motives and will only respond in a way that brings glory to His name and benefits us.

The Spirit desires to build us up spiritually and make us more completely prepared for future service, opportunities and challenges. While Jesus taught that we must be persistent in prayer (see Luke Chapter 11), we must be careful not to persistently ask from selfish or irresponsible motives, such that God 'gave them their request; but sent leanness into their soul' (Psalm 106:15, KJV). As in everything, our priority must be to glorify the Lord and contribute to His Kingdom on earth, not to elevate self.

Our impatience with God's apparent procrastination is sometimes revealed through a tendency to 'monitor' His response—making sure that He is 'on the job', as it were. This type of scrutiny is a misguided practice that indicates a lack of faith about God's ability to do what is for our good or intervening to bless the one for whom we are anxious or the situation for which have concern. Instead, the psalmist urges us to 'Rest in the Lord and wait patiently for Him' (37:7a, NKJV), especially when it appears that others who forge ahead without the Spirit's sanction or unction are thriving. The key thing to remember is that God only wants to prosper us and bless those we are seeking to influence. Delays are because of His love and not due to His disdain or disinterest.

If we tend to struggle in knowing how to bring our petitions to God in an attitude of faith and trust, we can take comfort and gain reassurance from Paul's words to the Christians in Rome: 'We do not know what we ought to pray for but the Spirit himself intercedes for us through wordless groans… in accordance with the will of God' (8:26–27, NIVUK). The final phrase 'in accordance with the will of God' is of utmost importance in comprehending more clearly why some prayers are answered and some do not appear to be or are not answered in the way we anticipate or hope for. The importance of intercession is dealt with more fully in Chapter 7 under 'Son and Spirit advocacy'.

Message of Truth and Life

Declaring the Gospel of Jesus Christ is the privilege of each member of Christ's church. The message of truth about God's design for His world and the need to trust and praise Him for all that He has accomplished should be a constant theme throughout every generation and situation. In addition to the benefits that faith in God bestows, there are also a number of implications arising from the Gospel, as outlined below.

Truth and sentiment

A person who goes through life without believing in God and accepting the sacrificial death of Christ on the Cross may be likened to a drowning man who resists offers of assistance from a lifeguard by insisting that he can manage perfectly well on his own, with the inevitable tragic outcome. Experience shows that while the majority of people entertain a brief or superficial interest in spiritual matters, they are inclined to adopt immature beliefs that reside in sentimental images of the Nativity (baby Jesus in a cosy stable) and God as a benevolent Santa Claus figure (giving us the things we desire to satisfy our every longing). Heaven is viewed as a place in which we will all be reunited with members of our family and friends in a glorious celebration with everyone we knew intimately on earth being present, recognisable and waiting to greet us. Such expectations may be borne of desperation or fear or fantasy—a 'clutching at straws' in the vain hope that everything will be all right in the end—but cannot be aligned with the ministry of Jesus and the Apostles.

While we have yet to experience the reality of heaven, it is presumptuous to claim that everyone who has lived a broadly responsible and 'respectable' life will be welcomed there. Jesus warned that not even everyone who claims to be his follower will be saved but those who do what God commands, as Matthew records in his Gospel account: 'Not everyone who calls out to me, "Lord! Lord!" will enter the Kingdom of Heaven. Only those who actually do the will of my Father in heaven will enter' (7:21, NLT). These grave words of Jesus demand our serious attention and, though God is the final arbiter of who will inhabit Heaven and walk the new earth, the Bible is unequivocal in stating that there is no place for people whose sin is not fully covered ('cleansed') by the sacrificial blood of Christ, as we seek the walk the narrow way that leads to life. See Chapter 7 for an elaboration of Jesus's invitation to trust him fully, and the end of Chapter 12 under 'The prospect of Heaven'.

Unconditional love

Each person should have the right to hear the wonderful truth that because the Son of God has always had and still retains a deep love for the world, he bore our sins when he died at Calvary. People will gladly make great sacrifices for those for whom they have a powerful affection and are precious to them; indeed, it is fair to claim that for those who are especially dear to us, we would even give our lives to save them. However, it is unlikely that we would feel the same sacrificial inclination towards our enemies or those that we consider to be unworthy of mercy.

By contrast with our fickle nature, Jesus willingly gave up his life for all mankind in living for the glory of Father God and the redemption of sinners. He died for the lovely and the unlovely, for the grateful and the ungrateful, for the caring and the careless, for responsible citizens and lawless criminals. In the words of hymn writer, George W Robinson, we are 'loved with everlasting love'. God's love that is fully disclosed in Jesus is endless and unlimited until we make the deliberate choice to reject it. Even then, His arms are opened wide for all who will turn from evil and embrace the salvation found in Christ.

Jesus even taught his disciples that they should love their enemies (Matthew 5:43), which must have astounded those who were listening to him, just as it challenges us two millennia later. In Jesus's time, as today, most people perceived an enemy as someone to be despised and destroyed; the notion of actually *loving* them was and remains incomprehensible by the majority of people. Paul summarised the situation in just a few divinely inspired words: 'God showed his great love for us by sending Christ to die for us while we were still sinners' (Romans 5:8, NLT). We note that Paul emphasises God's 'great love' in sending Christ, *despite* the fact that we are sinners who often fail to give Him the glory and praise to which He is entitled. His grace is freely available to everyone, but the response to His invitation is for each person to decide.

Limitations of striving

The world is entitled to hear loudly, clearly and without apology, the essential truth that salvation is solely due to God's grace and mercy found in and through Christ. Paul made it clear in his letter to the church in Ephesus that 'God saved you by his grace when you believed and you can't take credit for this; it is a gift from God' (2:8, NLT). The hymn writer, John G Whittier, described the situation poetically but accurately in his hymn, *Dear Lord and Father of Mankind* when he wrote: 'Drop your still dews of quietness until all our strivings cease'. All our striving includes worthy attributes such as leading generally responsible lives, earning money through committed endeavour, acquiring wealth and possessions by honest means, doing good works (good deeds) and sacrificial living. Yet even a combination of the aforementioned cannot redeem people from sin and facilitate a right relationship with God or bring contentment and peace of mind.

Only when our lives are rooted by faith in Christ's finished work of salvation and the enabling power of the Holy Spirit to sanctify ('make pure, spotless'), and to renew, prompt and guide us each day to do those things that please Him, are we able to have assurance of salvation. In the words of the psalmist: 'Except the Lord build the house, they labour in vain that build it' (Psalm 127:1, KJV). Personal striving is commendable if directed towards fulfilling the will and purpose of God; it is ultimately futile if divorced from the righteousness found in and through His Son and the perpetual guidance of His Spirit in our lives for the glory of God and the blessing of others. As John declares in his first letter: 'Let's not merely say that we love each other, let us show the truth by our actions' (3:18, NLT).

Though Jesus became as 'nothing' and took the form of a servant, our stubborn sinful nature sometimes rails against following in his footsteps, despite the fact that obedience is fundamental to victorious living and continued blessing. Living our lives in a way that pleases God and brings glory to Jesus Christ manifests itself in inner contentment that only the Spirit bestows, even in the midst of adversity and strife. In moments of anguish, we can take courage from the words of Nehemiah—leader in Jerusalem some 430 years before Jesus was born—to the people who mourned and wept after they recognised their failure to obey the Lord's commands: 'Do not grieve, for the joy of the Lord is your strength' (8:10b, NIVUK). It may never have occurred to us that God is full of joy and, if we ask Him for it, He imputes joy to us in a supernatural way that makes us spiritually strong to endure the fiercest storms, temptations and disappointments. In words penned long ago, the more we learn to trust Him, the more we find Him true; and the more we long that others may learn to trust Him, too.

Walking in righteousness

Earlier in the book, I explored issues relating to the 'sin pandemic' and the impact that *original sin* (present in every person since the 'fall' of Adam & Eve) and *wilful sin* (that each person commits through choice) have had and continue to have on individuals, society and our relationship with God. It is important to be reminded that although original sin led to an estrangement between humankind and God—not, it must be stressed, a *complete separation* from God or no one could have enjoyed any sort of relationship with Him until after Calvary and the resurrection—the sacrifice of Christ defeated the power of sin and death and gave every person the opportunity to have a full, life-transforming relationship with the Father.

Isaiah the prophet warned the people of Israel that as a result of their behaviour, sin had separated them from God's blessing and favour. Isaiah identified murder, lying, corruption, injustice and violence as evidence of their wickedness. It is little wonder that the prophet thundered the Lord's condemnation: 'Surely the arm of the Lord is not too short to save, nor his ear too dull to hear. But your iniquities have separated you from your God; your sins have hidden his face from you, so that he will not hear' (Isaiah 59:2, NIVUK). While few people are guilty of committing such grievous offences, the principle that God's blessing is withheld when we ignore or dismiss His claim to take first place in our lives and succumb to grievous sinning must be treated with the utmost gravity. Although this fundamental truth should be communicated with loving courtesy to non-believers, they are unlikely to receive it with much enthusiasm! Nevertheless, the danger of being separated from God through sin is a message that should not be withheld solely on the basis of disturbing the listener. See Chapter 10 for further details about sharing the Gospel message.

If Christians continue sinning, ignoring God's commandments and the Holy Spirit's warnings about their behaviour, their relationship with God is marred until they repent, when His fullest blessing and approval is instantly restored. While God is gracious and merciful to those who seek His approval by living according to His statutes, He is a 'consuming fire' to those who deliberately turn away, as graphically and sternly described by the Old Testament prophet, Ezekiel: 'I looked for someone who might rebuild the wall of righteousness that guards the land. I searched for someone to stand in the gap in the wall, so I wouldn't have to destroy the land, but I found no one. So now I will pour out my fury on them, consuming them with the fire of my anger. I will heap on their heads the full penalty for all their sins. I, the Sovereign Lord, have spoken!' (22:30–31, NLT) Today, we can rejoice that Jesus was the one who was worthy to 'stand in the gap' and pay the penalty for our sins.

Insight

The significance of the phrase 'rebuild the wall of righteousness' in Ezekiel Chapter 22 should not be underestimated. God promises to guard a nation on the basis of the people's moral purity; that is, on their willingness not only to accede to His ways but to demonstrate them in practice. The opposite must necessarily also be true, namely that moral decadence leaves the country exposed to evil influences and godlessness. It is not difficult to find many such examples from history and in the present day.

Reconciled to God

To reconcile means to bring together in an intimate, harmonious relationship. Paul underlines this wonderful truth in his letter to Christians in Rome: 'We also boast in God through our Lord Jesus Christ, through whom we have now received reconciliation' (5:11, NIVUK). James specifically refers to Abraham as a 'friend of God', whose belief (trust, faith) was credited to him as righteousness (James 2:23). Use of the expression 'friend of God' is more powerful than it might sound at first hearing, as true friendship with Him means that we have a relationship with the One who is the ever-present and all-knowing Creator. Furthermore, the Lord Jesus Christ is the one who makes this privileged position possible.

I have repeatedly highlighted the fact that since Christ's death and resurrection, it is deliberate sinning that mars our relationship with God; and it is through confession of sin and genuine repentance that we completely embrace the victory that Jesus gained at Calvary and the freedom from the consequences of sin it bought for us. Where our sinning once hampered the release of God's full blessing and favour, a central tenet of the Gospel is that we can all be clothed in the righteousness of Christ. As the Old Testament prophet, Isaiah, prophesied over 700 years before Jesus was born: 'I delight greatly in the Lord; my soul rejoices in my God. For he has clothed me with garments of salvation and arrayed me in a robe of his righteousness, as a bridegroom adorns his head like a priest and as a bride adorns herself with her jewels' (61:10, NIVUK). We were once far from God without assurance about our eternal destiny, but the Good Shepherd promises to prepare a place for us after our life ends and lead us to our eternal home. Hallelujah!

No condemnation

In a world where many people are quick to condemn, while equally slow to acknowledge their own shortcomings, Jesus's parable about a farmer's two sons (usually referred to as the Parable of the Prodigal Son; 'prodigal' means wasteful, profligate) is especially appropriate. In the parable, Jesus describes how the father runs to meet his repentant younger son, as the boy returns home after squandering all his wealth on worldly pleasures. Through the parable, Jesus conveys the important truth that God the Father welcomes every person who deeply regrets his or her failure to live a life that pleases Him and is willing to change direction and endeavour to pursue the right path. In like fashion, the repentant sinner trusts that Jesus has taken away the burden of sin that should have been rightly his or hers to bear, and now desires to live a life approved by God and empowered by the Holy Spirit.

Later in his letter to Roman believers, Paul offers the following assurance to those who are reconciled to God: 'So now there is no condemnation for those who belong to Christ Jesus. And because you belong to him, the power of the life-giving Spirit has freed you from the power of sin that leads to death' (8:1–2, NLT). Opponents of Christianity sometimes claim that making a decision to follow Jesus Christ is an easy option for inadequate people who cannot cope with the challenges and struggles of life. In fact, Jesus made it clear that following him frequently leads to opposition and makes us a target for the disapproval of ungodly people and the devil's wiles. Paul refers to a 'thorn in the flesh' as a result of satanic attack through a fallen angel ('messenger'). The more we seek to serve and follow Christ, the more likely we are to attract this unwelcome attention.

Reconciliation to God through Christ has serious implications for our eternal future; it is not automatically granted but rather requires a firm decision on our behalf to align our lives with Christ Jesus, who stands with arms open wide, ready to receive us and present us faultless before Father God. In the words of Charles Wesley's famous hymn *And Can It Be?* 'No condemnation now I dread; Jesus and all in him is mine. Alive in him, my living head and clothed in righteousness divine. Bold I approach the Eternal Throne and claim the crown through Christ, my own'. Condemnation by God is wholly avoidable by trusting in the one who calls us 'friend' when we obey his commands (John 15:14 and 15:15).

The Return of Jesus ('The Second Coming')

Watching and waiting

In the same way that Jesus came to live and die at an appointed time, so he will return at a time known only to the Father. In his Gospel account, Matthew records Jesus's words: 'No one knows when that day or time will be. The Son and the angels in heaven don't know when it will be. Only the Father knows' (24:36, ERV). The reason that Jesus is not privy to the date of his return is a matter that has invited considerable interest, the details of which are outside the present discussion. Throughout the Scriptures, however, there are a variety of indicators about the Son of God's imminent return (see below), though it is important that *all* of these signs need to be evident, not just a selection of them. Even then, his return will be sudden and unexpected, even by the most perceptive, devout and biblically informed saints of God.

The uncertainty about the time of Jesus's return adds additional urgency to the importance for all believers to be constantly alert and prepared to welcome him. As Peter warns, 'the day of the Lord will come as unexpectedly as a thief. Then the heavens will pass away with a terrible noise and the very elements themselves will disappear in fire, and the earth and everything on it will be found to deserve judgement [will be burned up, NKJV]' (2 Peter 3:10, NLT). Key phrases from the letter signify an event of cataclysmic proportions, thus: 'heavens will pass away', 'terrible noise', 'elements… will disappear in fire' and 'burned up'. Peter also describes how *everything* on the earth will deserve judgement, because sin corrupts both living things and inanimate objects ('the earth').

Jesus told the disciples to be watchful and stay alert because the Master could return at any time and would expect the members of his household to be ready, active and waiting (see the Parable of the Tenants in Matthew Chapter 21). It is essential to take note that there is also a warning attached to the circumstances accompanying his return in that the Son of God will come to *judge* the earth and separate the 'good' from the 'evil' (John 5:28–29). Despite this daunting prospect, the faithful follower of Jesus need never fret or worry about his return, even after life has ended, as it is always under his control and the future is clothed in glorious hope.

Indicators of Christ's return

Understandably, there is deep interest about the way in which Christ's return will be foreshadowed by different signs, a comprehensive selection of which follows—the majority based on Jesus's words. As we consider these prophecies, it is important to establish two points: (a) a single sign is not adequate proof in itself of his appearing; (b) signs are only a portent of what will follow and not pinpointing a specific date, which is known only to God. The life-giving truth to thrill the heart of every believer is that whenever the time may be, he *will* come back, as he promised! The following ten indicators are relevant.

1. *The Gospel will be preached to all nations* (Matthew 24:14). In the past, the prospect of people from every nation being exposed to the Gospel seemed impossible. With the onset of modern forms of communication, however, the logistical barriers are being overcome and information technology means that almost no group of people in the world is inaccessible. Encouragingly, the Book of Revelation reveals that representatives from every human group and ethnicity will be present in heaven, worshipping the Lamb of God: 'After this I looked, and there before me was a great multitude that no one could count, from every nation, tribe, people and language, standing before the throne and before

160

the Lamb. They were wearing white robes and were holding palm branches in their hands' (7:9, NIVUK).

2. *Many false Messiahs will claim to be the 'I Am'* (Luke 21:8). In Chapter 1, I described how many men down the ages have declared themselves to be a reincarnated Jesus or a Supreme Ruler, thereby demanding total obedience and subservience from their followers. Such unwavering devotion has led to different forms of abuse and bizarre behaviour, as Satan has infiltrated the situation and sown confusion. In more recent times, the 'cult of personality' that was prevalent in the early days of history has re-emerged, whereby the authoritarian ruler has deliberately placed himself at the heart of national life to the exclusion of all competing religions or beliefs. In effect, the men have made themselves a 'god' in human form.

3. *There will be wars and insurrections* (Luke 21:9). It must be acknowledged that wars and conflicts have blighted world history since the beginning of time. However, Jesus appears to have been referring to a tendency towards an anti-authority spirit that would be exposed through civil disobedience, rioting and general unrest. Although modern media has facilitated our exposure to worldwide events in a way that was not possible a generation ago, it is beyond doubt that anti-government protests, rebellion and violence, are increasingly prevalent.

4. *There will be strange and disturbing phenomena on earth and in space* (Luke 21:25–26). Jesus uses powerful expressions to describe events, referring to 'strange signs' and 'nations in turmoil'. People will be 'perplexed' and 'terrified' at the emergence of these phenomena. The details of these occurrences will only be revealed when they actually take place and will then be plain for all to see. The pervasiveness of such events will indicate that demonic influences are intruding into every area of society, revealing the coming of the supreme antichrist before the true Christ's final return and the renewal of heaven and earth.

5. *The Jews will suffer extreme persecution but recover their God-ordained heritage* (Luke 21:24).

The most telling part of Jesus's statement about the fate of Jerusalem (which stands for Israel as a whole) is that the time of the Gentiles (i.e., non-Jews) will end after severe persecution ('trampling') and the country will subsequently be restored to full Jewish control. In Daniel Chapter 12, there is a prophecy about the end times, including the role played by the Archangel Michael in preserving godly people in Israel after a period of great hardship. Accusations towards the present State of Israel from hostile nations that refuse to accept its rightful heritage continues to create acrimony and strife. However, the Bible record is plain in authenticating the whole country as being a Jewish inheritance.

6. *There will be an increase in frenetic behaviour* (Daniel 12:4). A further indication that the end times are imminent is likely to be one of accelerated physical movement ('high speed') with the attendant pressure to finish tasks according to a strict timetable and the implementation of efficiency measures. These trends are certainly evident in the pace of life today as close attention is accorded to schedules and deadlines for the delivery of goods, work completion and the provision of information through media and technology.

7. *There will be an increase in knowledge acquisition* (Daniel 12:4). The recent 'explosion' in factual knowledge and expertise over recent decades has been unparalleled in human history, so much so that it is impossible for any individual to keep pace with it, even with the benefit of computerised data. Numerous powerful advances have accrued in medical treatments, communication and science. Although people in advanced nations are better informed and have access to unprecedented levels of information about every conceivable subject, their understanding of God and His intentions for their lives is often confused, due to superficial or inaccurate Bible teaching.

8. *There will be an increase in deceptive spirits and demonic teaching.* 'The Spirit clearly says that in the last times some will turn away from what we believe. They will obey spirits that tell lies. And they will follow the teachings of demons' (1 Timothy 4:1, ERV). The Apostle Paul's warning has been amply confirmed down the centuries, including numerous false claims from deluded individuals to be the returning Jesus, as noted in point 4 above. Perhaps more troublingly is the reference to demonic teaching that will deceive and corrupt, emphasising the need for vigilance by Christians and underlining the need for a careful study of the Scriptures, faithful Bible teaching and fervent prayer. The trend towards a liberal interpretation of Scripture,

particularly in technologically advanced nations, has afflicted the church, as misguided leaders are keener to accommodate worldly beliefs than to maintain God's inspired truth, as revealed in the Bible. At the same time, developing nations of a broadly Christian persuasion that refuse to compromise the Scriptures are subject to moral censure and political pressure from many leaders in the West.

9. *There will be an outpouring of scoffing to satisfy the ungodly desires of troublemakers* (Jude 18; 2 Peter 3:3–4).

It is significant that Jude refers to the division that these ungodly, complaining, selfish scoffers will try to create *within* the Body of Christ (the church). Peter warns that these deriders will dispute the truth of the Gospel and cast doubt on the authenticity of Jesus's promises. Once the integrity of the Bible is compromised, faith is replaced by human reason, and the rock of salvation is supplanted by shifting sand (see Jesus's teaching in Matthew Chapter 7). It is sadly evident that a number of contemporary church leaders are willing to compromise God's ordinances in order to (as they would argue) make church more attractive to the general population. As a result of these concessions, Gospel truth is increasingly viewed as being incompatible with modern-day thinking and rejected as being out of step with contemporary perspectives. The ungodly desires of troublemakers has become increasingly evident as the 21st century unfolds, reflected in the use of negative comments about Bible truth, worldly interpretations of Scripture and attempts to discredit faithful Christian leaders using legal pressure and accusations of sowing hatred.

10. *The 'man of lawlessness' (also called 'the man of sin') will rebel against God and bring destruction.*

'For that day will not come until there is a great rebellion against God and the man of lawlessness [man of sin] is revealed—the one who brings destruction [son of destruction]. He will exalt himself and defy everything that people call god and every object of worship. He will even sit in the temple of God, claiming that he himself is God' (2 Thessalonians 2:3, NLT). The precise meaning of this ghastly prospect is unclear; suffice it to say that it highlights Jesus's warning that those who are not for him are against him. On that day, there will not be any 'neutral ground'; all will be laid bare.

Summary

In this chapter, I have outlined the challenges facing fellowships with respect to their growth, witnessing and glorious hope to be found in the certainty of Jesus's return at the end of time. Christ's church on earth consists of those who have accepted God's gracious gift of salvation and been born again (anew, from above). They are also charged with the responsibility of sharing the good news. Christians are the standard bearers of his name and the conduit for his purposes.

The task of cultivating and nurturing faith in believers, especially younger ones, is of vital importance to ensure healthy succession from one generation to the next, rooted in a firm understanding and knowledge of the truth. Christians need to ensure that they are not only strong in their personal walk with Jesus but also able to articulate essential biblical doctrine and retain a keen awareness of God's intentions for the world.

As they await the coming of the Lord, all believers must learn to interpret the signs of the times and resist the rise of secularism that seeks to undermine Bible truth and relegate the Gospel to the status of legend.

Assess the validity of the following statements:

1. Christians are people who have been baptised and received into communion at a recognised church.
2. A person does not need to attend church to be a Christian.
3. Christians are those who have a personal faith in Christ as Saviour and strive to make him Lord of their lives.
4. The church's principal function is to help the poor and needy in society.
5. The church's principal function is to preach the Gospel.
6. The church's principal function is to make Christ knows by every possible means, including social action.
7. The church has got to modernise if it is to stay relevant.
8. Traditionalists are responsible for many of the problems encountered in church life and witness.
9. Focusing on Jesus's return is a distraction from the needs of the present.
10. Focusing on Jesus's return acts as a powerful incentive to live a godly life and evangelise the lost.

Part 4
Going God's Way

John 6: 53–69

So Jesus said again, "I tell you the truth, unless you eat the flesh of the Son of Man and drink his blood, you cannot have eternal life within you. But anyone who eats my flesh and drinks my blood has eternal life, and I will raise that person at the last day. For my flesh is true food, and my blood is true drink. Anyone who eats my flesh and drinks my blood remains in me, and I in him. I live because of the living Father who sent me; in the same way, anyone who feeds on me will live because of me. I am the true bread that came down from heaven. Anyone who eats this bread will not die as your ancestors did (even though they ate the manna) but will live forever." He said these things while he was teaching in the synagogue in Capernaum.

Many of his disciples said, "This is very hard to understand. How can anyone accept it?"

Jesus was aware that his disciples were complaining, so he said to them, "Does this offend you? Then what will you think if you see the Son of Man ascend to heaven again? The Spirit alone gives eternal life. Human effort accomplishes nothing. And the very words I have spoken to you are spirit and life. But some of you do not believe me." (For Jesus knew from the beginning which ones didn't believe, and he knew who would betray him.) Then he said, "That is why I said that people can't come to me unless the Father gives them to me."

At this point, many of his disciples turned away and deserted him. Then Jesus turned to the Twelve and asked, "Are you also going to leave?"

Simon Peter replied, "Lord, to whom would we go? You have the words that give eternal life. We believe, and we know you are the Holy One of God" (NLT).

Luke 5: 27–28

Later, as Jesus left the town, he saw a tax collector named Levi [Matthew in Greek] sitting at his tax collector's booth. "Follow me and be my disciple," Jesus said to him. So Levi got up, left everything, and followed him (NLT).

Preface to Part 4

In Part 1 of the book, I explored the mission, character, appearance and deeds of Jesus Christ. I emphasised the truth about his nature, words and actions that characterised his work as a man on earth, and responded to some of the objections made by his antagonists. In particular, I emphasised the wealth of evidence to support Jesus's claims to be the Son of God, who came to sacrifice his life for the sins of the world. I concluded by pointing to the great transforming power of the Gospel and its impact on every person who believes in Jesus and by faith accepts him as Lord and Saviour.

In Parts 2 and 3 (Chapters 3 to 6), I built upon some of the themes raised earlier; outlined the basic problem of the sin pandemic that has afflicted humankind; and described how the death and resurrection of God's Son provides the antidote to the virus. In doing so, I raised the central issue of how Jesus dealt with 'original sin' and stressed the importance of repentance in the forgiveness of our subsequent (wilful) sins. I emphasised both the present and eternal blessings that Christ has made available to everyone who trusts him for salvation. In Chapter 6, I gave particular attention to the challenges and opportunities for the church in declaring the Gospel of salvation and the responsibility of all born again believers to demonstrate the love of Jesus in their words and actions.

In Chapters 7 and 8, I shall focus more specifically on the responsibilities and opportunities for believers to be involved in Kingdom work and the way in which differing levels of commitment impacts the spread of the Gospel. The core of Chapter 7 is on the need to maintain and enhance personal discipleship as a means of following the narrow way that leads to eternal life by refusing to take the broad way that leads to destruction for those who dissent from accepting Jesus's offer of salvation.

Chapter 8 explores in depth the importance of abiding in Christ in a way that brings personal reassurance, and glory and honour to God. I shall stress that in the pursuit of righteousness, we need to embrace the essential requirement of feeding from the Son of God by his Spirit and thereby discovering life with a purpose and a secure future after death. Following Jesus is a high calling that demands an equivalent level of commitment from his disciples, yet as I describe in the chapter, there are some who opt for a comfortable, untroubled form of Christianity, while others are wholehearted in their allegiance to Christ, even to the point of death.

Chapter 7
Narrow and Broad Paths

Introduction

Being lost without any idea of the right way to go or which way to turn can be unnerving and scary. For young children, the fear of being separated from a parent or guardian triggers powerful negative emotions. All parents have experienced the momentary panic when losing sight of their offspring and the wave of relief when they are found.

When driving, it is not always straightforward to find the correct route in an unfamiliar area, even with the assistance of technological aids. Stories are told of drivers following satellite-navigated instructions and ending up along narrow country lanes, in a field or a dead end! Despite the availability of sophisticated navigational systems, a ship's captain may still utilise information from old charts or the position of the moon in helping to set a course. Beams from lighthouses send out warning signals for mariners to steer clear of dangerous waters or hazardous rocks.

At a spiritual level, the need to find the right direction in our lives is a fundamental issue that should occupy every follower of Jesus. We all need to make advantageous decisions and use our time, resources and abilities effectively. The psalmist celebrates the rewards accrued from following God's direction for our lives: 'You make known to me the path of life; you will fill me with joy in your presence, with eternal pleasures at your right hand' (Psalm 16:11, NIVUK).

Choices and circumstances

In the intricacy of life, the impact of social norms ('the way it is done these days'), parental expectations ('we had always hoped that you would be a doctor, not a freelance artist') and financial constraints (e.g., a paucity of funds for enrolment on a training course, coupled with the urgent need to earn money for basic necessities) sometimes has the effect of restricting choice significantly or creating the need to take a direction in life from which it becomes difficult to deviate. For instance, commitment to mortgage repayments, responsibility for a child or the burden of accumulated debt will often oblige someone to pursue a pragmatic but secure route and relegate aspirations and creative ideas to the back-burner.

For many people, mediocrity is the inevitable consequence of unfavourable circumstances, unexpected events or personal issues that block preferred avenues and orientate towards less inspiring ones. Slothful people choose to pursue an uncomplicated, ultra-cautious direction in life to avoid the need for perseverance, deep commitment or having to face demanding situations. Others are naturally more adventurous and relish the challenge presented by riskier but ultimately more fulfilling alternatives. Whatever our inclination, the writer of Proverbs stresses the importance of keeping to the most spiritually secure route in life: 'Mark out a straight path for your feet; stay on the safe path. Don't get side tracked. Keep your feet from following evil' (4:26–7, NLT).

The Holy Spirit patiently waits to show us the straight path that leads to life; it is our choice whether to follow it, such that we can be certain that our feet are planted firmly on 'solid ground', as Jesus promised to those who obey him (Matthew 7:24). Obedience is always the key to perceiving God's will and direction for our lives, as Moses reminded the Israelites after their escape from captivity: 'So be careful to do what the Lord your God has commanded you; do not turn aside to the right or to the left. Walk in obedience to all that the Lord your God has commanded you, so that you may live and prosper and prolong your days in the land that you will possess' (Deuteronomy 5:33, NLT).

Following the true Light

Committed Christians look towards and follow the Light of the World, which is one of the numerous titles given to Jesus (John 1:9 and 8:12). It is both instructive and challenging that Jesus not only spoke about himself as being the light but also used precisely the same expression when referring to his followers. Thus, in Matthew's Gospel: 'You are the light that shines for the world to see. You are like a city built on a hill that cannot be hidden' (5:14, ERV), which is a necessary reminder that every believer has the privilege and responsibility of carrying and displaying the flame of Christ in their daily walk.

Are followers of Jesus Christ subject to the same constraints, limitations and uncertainties that afflict non-believers? The answer is yes and no!

Christians are not immune from the vagaries of life that afflict everyone, everywhere. Every adult experiences joys and sorrows, ranging from the short-lived pain of disappointment at one extreme—failing to be appointed to a sort-after job or falling short of achieving an academic goal—to the intense and enduring pain of searing loss and physical affliction at the other extreme (notably, bereavement and life-threatening illnesses). Nevertheless, followers of Jesus Christ can be encouraged and comforted by the sure and certain knowledge of his undying love and their eternal security in him, regardless of circumstances.

Paul powerfully summarised the position in his letter to the Christians in Rome: 'For I am convinced that neither death nor life, neither angels nor demons, either the present nor the future, nor any powers, neither height nor depth, nor anything else in all creation, will be able to separate us from the love of God that is in Christ Jesus our Lord' (8:38–39, NIVUK). The power and authority of Paul's statement should not be viewed casually, as he emphasises that *nothing* can separate us from God's love that is found in Christ. What a wonderful promise!

Insight

Jesus made a statement that must go down as one the most remarkable in the history of the world: 'You should love your enemies… bless those who curse you, do good to those who hate you, and pray for those who spitefully use you and persecute you' (Matthew 5:43, NKJV). The love of which Jesus speaks is not, of course, romantic love; neither is it family love or purely compassionate love. It is the powerful agape love of God expressed most clearly in sending His Son to die for the sins of the world. Agape love does not occur naturally, for as Paul writes to Christians in Rome 'the love of God has been poured out in our hearts through the Holy Spirit, who has been given to us' (5:5, NLT) when we became His children. The Holy Spirit is the initiator and provider of this love.

There are many 'lights' in the world, some that radiate a dim glow and some that prove to be artificial or illuminate a path that initially seems secure but ultimately leads to disappointment and distress. Only Jesus Christ provides the light of life that ensures freedom from guilt, fulfilment of purpose and eternal security from sin. The primary duty of all believers is first to listen to what he says through his Spirit (using prayer, the Bible and godly advice) and then to be obedient in pursuing the path that is lit before them. The psalmist pictorially set out the position: 'Your word is like a lamp that guides my steps, a light that shows the path I should take. Your laws are good and fair. I have promised to obey them, and I will keep my promise' (119:105–6, ERV). Christian, do you? Will you?

Feeding from the Son

The Body of Christ

When Jesus told his followers that they needed to feed from his flesh and drink his blood in order to find eternal life (John Chapter 6), it is unsurprising that they were shocked and in some cases dismayed to the point of withdrawing their support for him. After all, human sacrifices were associated with pagan practices that were strictly forbidden by God, who spoke through the Old Testament prophet, Jeremiah, to express His condemnation of such appalling behaviour: 'They have built pagan shrines to Baal in the valley of Ben-Hinnom, and there they sacrifice their sons and daughters to Molech. I have never commanded such a horrible deed; it never even crossed my mind to command such a thing. What an incredible evil, causing Judah to sin so greatly!' (32:35, NLT) It is for every believer to decide whether the large-scale destruction of the unborn taking place today—including in specific cases up to the very point of birth—appals God as much as ancient pagan sacrifices did. I think they must do.

Insight

Every four years in the UK, around one million of the unborn are destroyed through abortion. In the USA, the figure is presently around three-quarters of a million each year.

Jesus's linking the consumption of bread and wine to his own physical body did not sit comfortably with Jews, who were committed to serving the one God (whom they referred to as Jehovah) and abhorring idol worship. Jesus was, of course, speaking figuratively about his body and blood; nevertheless, comparing his flesh to bread and his blood to wine personalised the issue in a startling way.

It is worth noting the import of Jesus's words such that we need to feed *on* him and not merely *from* him. Jesus does not throw us scraps. We need to be close to him to draw strength and empowerment from him—the result of an intimate, mutual relationship, as he described it: 'Abide [remain] in me, and I in you. As the branch cannot bear fruit of itself, unless it abides [remains] in the vine, neither can you, unless you abide in me' (John 15:4, NKJV).

Equally unsettling for traditional Jews was the way in which Jesus unfavourably contrasted the provision of manna—a food miraculously provided by God in the wilderness: 'It was white like coriander seed, and it tasted like honey wafers' (Exodus 16:31, NLT) with the 'bread' that he was offering. In common with everyone who has ever lived, all the people who ate manna died eventually, yet Jesus claimed that those who accepted his 'bread from heaven' would never die and inherit eternal life. What could Jesus possibly mean by using such provocative language?

Significance of bread and wine

First, it is important to acknowledge that bread and wine were extremely important to the Jews, not least because they were (and remain) a largely arable farming nation, growing crops such as grain, grapes and olives. Bread had a significance far exceeding its dietary value. Its use is mentioned frequently in the Old Testament and is particularly important in relation to (a) the unleavened bread used by the people during their escape from slavery in Egypt; (b) the provision of manna in the wilderness. Understandably, Jesus's words about himself as the Bread of Life had a dramatic impact on practising Jews, who celebrated the *Feast of the Passover* every Springtime with unleavened bread (baked without yeast) as a joyful commemoration of their ancestors' salvation when they were released from bondage.

The use of wine was also momentous in representing and commemorating the time that the angel of death 'passed over' the enslaved Jews who had put the blood of an animal on their doorposts as a sign that they were Israelite homes. As a result of following God's command to use blood as a covering to save them from judgement, the angel of death did not strike the Israelites, while death was visited upon the firstborn in all the other homes (see Exodus Chapter 12).

Subsequently, the Pharaoh released the Jews after more than 400 years of captivity (verse 40 specifies 430 years).

Both bread and wine were, therefore, significant for the Jews in a way that Gentiles cannot easily grasp. Jesus's use of those two emblems was the most powerful depiction of his status as a sacrificial lamb and a foreshadowing of his death on the cross, as described below.

Instituting Communion

Later in Jesus's ministry, while celebrating the Passover with his disciples shortly before going to the Cross to give his life for the sins of the world, the Gospel writer Mark records that: 'Jesus took bread and blessed and brake it and gave to them and said: Take, eat: this is my body' (14:22, KJV; some translations add 'which is broken for you'). In Paul's first letter to the Christians in Corinth, Chapter 11, he underlined the symbolism of the bread as representing the Body of Christ and the cup as symbolising his shed blood.

The practice of remembering the broken body and shed blood of Jesus is incorporated into the regular services at the large majority of churches, the celebration being referred to by various names: Eucharist, Holy Sacrament, Lord's Supper, Last Supper, Breaking of Bread and, as a blanket term, Communion. Although different denominations attach varying levels of significance and importance to the occasion, they all recognise the central tenet that the emblems represent the body and blood of Christ when he freely gave his life to bring salvation to a sinful world.

Jesus not only told his followers that they needed to feed from his body and drink of his blood but also that in doing so, they would live forever and he would raise them 'at the last day', confirming life after the end of the present world's existence. Jesus's claim that he would be responsible for giving eternal life must have astounded his listeners, as he was in effect declaring his divinity, an issue that enraged many of the religious leaders of the day and still precipitates a fierce reaction from adherents of other religious faiths.

At a later point in his letter to the Romans, Paul explains: 'If Christ is in you, your body is dead because of sin, yet your spirit is alive because of righteousness' (8:10). From this statement, we can grasp the liberating and empowering truth that despite our sinfulness and failure, Christ imputes (bestows) his purity to every believer.

There is no scriptural evidence that the act of remembering Christ's death by participation in a communion service sanctifies the adherent or ensures freedom from sin. Roman Catholics interpret Jesus's words literally about the bread representing his body and the cup representing his blood; that is, they believe that the emblems are miraculously transmuted into part of the body, blood and divinity of Jesus. Participation in Communion therefore intimately unites the worshipper with Christ and all other Catholics worldwide. While Protestant denominations place more emphasis on the 'remembrance' dimension, every mainline church accepts the scriptural injunction in I Corinthians Chapter 11 for communicants to examine their lives before receiving communion to see if they are harbouring unconfessed sin or failing to take the matter seriously. The enforcement of this principle is impossible to quantify or monitor, relying as it does on each individual's willingness to confront his or her spiritual condition, repent of ungodly ways and make appropriate confession.

It is important to emphasise that the 'bread and wine' of which we partake at the Communion service relates solely to the person of Christ, as evildoers are capable of utilising the same symbols with godless motives, as the writer of Proverbs reminds us: 'They eat the bread of wickedness and drink the wine of violence!' (4:17, NIVUK)

Personal communion ('friendship') with Jesus involves more than participating in a Communion service to remember his sacrifice at Calvary. It is allowing his Spirit to reside within us to make us fruitful in His service and a delight to His heart. As James explains using Abraham as an example, belief (trust) in God underpins the relationship: 'Abraham believed God, and it was accounted [credited] to him for righteousness. And he was called the friend of God' (2:23, NKJV).

Passing the test

Paul reminds Christians in Corinth of a powerful truth: 'Examine yourselves to see whether you are in the faith; test yourselves. Do you not realise that Christ Jesus is in you—unless, of course, you fail the test?' (2 Corinthians 13:5, NIVUK) Imagine the incredulity of early followers to hear that the Spirit of Christ would live *in* them!

Paul's warning about testing ourselves and the danger of 'failing the test' is in part a reference to the way in which we need to ensure that when challenges have to be faced in our lives, we respond in a way that accords with our declared allegiance to Christ. The reaction of Job—a godly and highly respected Old Testament character, who experienced the most immense suffering in the loss of his children, family and home—helps us to view extreme testing as an opportunity to declare our full trust in God in a way that is not possible during more settled times. Job expressed his strong faith in God after enduring unimaginable distress: 'But he knows where I am going. And when he tests me, I will come out as pure as gold. For I have stayed on God's paths. I have followed his ways and not turned aside' (23:10–11, NLT). There are three significant points take from Job's declaration:

1) God has an intimate knowledge of our lives.
2) Testing is a means of refinement ('pure gold'), not a punishment for wrongdoing.
3) We must follow God's direction steadfastly.

These are timeless truths that apply to each of us currently, as much they did in Job's day. How wonderful to know that God has a plan for each of our lives if we are willing to follow the path that He has chosen for us. It is also reassuring to understand that testing times reveal the graciousness of the Lord to refine us and—in the words of William Pearson's 1884 hymn—to 'lead us higher up the mountain where the whitest robes are seen' and make us more like Jesus, which is in essence the process of sanctification.

> **Insight**
> Christian, what is your reaction to Paul's disclosure that Christ is in you? Do you have a keen awareness of the Spirit at work in your life? The distinctive characteristic of a person born anew of the Spirit of Christ and walking in step with him is that regardless of circumstances, the love of Jesus and trust in him will shine through. By contrast, testing times for a non-believer are likely to reveal insecurity and a spiritual void.

Allegiance to Christ

Proximity to Jesus

Jesus stated that eternal life is available to everyone by means of the Holy Spirit working through the Son, authorised by God the Father (see John's Gospel Chapter 6), emphasising that people cannot attain to everlasting life by means of their own efforts but only by God's grace, as Paul confirmed repeatedly during his mission travels and correspondence; for example in his letter to Christians in Rome: 'For everyone has sinned; we all fall short of God's glorious standard. Yet God, in his grace, freely makes us right in his sight. He did this through Christ Jesus when he freed us from the penalty for our sins' (3:23–4, NLT).

"Keeping our eyes on Jesus" is a phrase frequently used to describe the act of remaining close to him and drawing from the power of his Spirit who resides within the mind of every believer. In his Gospel account, John records how Jesus explained the source of real spiritual power: 'The Spirit alone gives eternal life. Human effort accomplishes nothing. And the very words I have spoken to you are spirit and life' (6:63, NLT). Paul reinforces Jesus's words in his letter to Christians in the Galatian churches, who were in danger of reverting to a reliance on keeping the ancient law of Moses instead of their belief in Christ: 'How foolish can you be? After starting your new lives in the Spirit, why are you now trying to become perfect by your own human effort?' (3:3, NLT)

Importantly, we can only feed from Christ's spirit and receive his light if we make a decision to enjoy an intimate relationship with him through praying, meditating and 'feeding' on his words, not merely reading them—see Ezekiel 3:1–3 where the prophet eats the scroll and it tastes like honey—and listening to Bible-based faithful ministry. As we obviously cannot physically see Jesus, we must therefore keep close ('abide') by expressing our faith and trust in him through our general conversation, testimony and willing obedience. In doing so, we must make a conscious decision every day to listen closely to what God is saying and respond accordingly. John summarised the role of Jesus as the life giver: 'And so, if we have God's Son, we have this life. But if we don't have the Son, we don't have this life' (I John 5:12, CEV). Nothing could be clearer. In Chapter 8, I explore the practicalities and implications of abiding in Christ.

Our high calling

Throughout history, a small but highly influential number of men (mainly) and women (less often) possessed exceptional ability in being able to inspire and communicate so effectively that people become sufficiently impressed by what they said to embrace their particular cause or philosophy with fervour and dedication. Some of these inspiring figures were admirable, morally sound and courageous. Others were skilled orators and capable of persuasion but their true intentions were disguised by embedding their arguments in the supposed victimhood of this or that group of people (or whole populations) and high-sounding moral statements about seeking justice and equality for all, without defining these terms precisely. All believers must be careful to avoid adulation of any single leader or personality, always ensuring the Jesus remains the focal point of worship and adoration.

By contrast with secular and worldly idealists, Jesus did not use rhetoric, subtle persuasion or propaganda, nor did he promise a utopian world with fame and fortune for his followers if they obeyed him. Indeed, as described earlier in the book, Jesus's words were direct and uncompromising—he commended those who showed love for others and condemned the hypocrites and naysayers. Far from seeking fame and approval, he set the bar of commitment high for those considering whether to become one of his disciples, including the prospect of opposition and persecution.

As John notes in his Gospel, the impact of Jesus's words, though they encouraged the ordinary people to gather around him in large numbers because they were amazed at his teaching and authority, were also the reason that some of his lukewarm followers deserted and sought easier avenues for channelling their commitment to a cause. Jesus pinpointed the key issue for tentative adherents, namely that it was a lack of belief in him that prompted their scepticism. John adds a postscript: 'For Jesus had known from the beginning which of them did not believe and who would betray him' (6:64, NIVUK).

Jesus's sole concern was to please God the Father and obey Him, even to his own detriment. His message to would-be devotees was unambiguous: do not take lightly the step of becoming my disciples or make excuses to avoid wholehearted obedience or imagine that life will be straightforward if you decide to follow me. Luke records Jesus's serious warning about such matters in his Gospel account: "If you want to be my disciple, you must, by comparison, hate everyone else— your father and mother, wife and children, brothers and sisters—yes, even your own life. Otherwise, you cannot be my disciple. And if you do not carry your own cross and follow me, you cannot be my disciple. But don't begin until you count the cost. For who would begin construction of a building without first calculating the cost to see if there is enough money to finish it?" (14:25–8, NLT). The conditions that Jesus attaches to being a follower have not changed down the centuries; people in every age are faced with the same choices.

Expressing our devotion

In taking the narrow path that leads to life (Matthew 7:13–14), there are many and varied ways to express our allegiance to Jesus, principally through a willingness to set aside our own desires and personal ambitions. As described in previous chapters, the starting point is being born again of God's Spirit. Inevitably, there are people who refuse to acknowledge the supremacy of Christ and their need for a Saviour; others remain on the side-lines of faith, like observers at a sporting event; yet others are lukewarm in their commitment, preferring to opt for a comfortable, untroubled and compromised life, rather than face the challenges of wholehearted allegiance.

It is therefore undeniable that the attitude, level of commitment and behaviour of those who claim to be followers of Jesus Christ varies considerably. They may be broadly classified with reference to the intimacy of their walk with Jesus, willingness to feed from him and determination to walk in his light. The closer we cling to Jesus and form a union with him, the more we find that far from being oppressive, our alliance with him brings liberty, as he promised: 'Take my yoke upon you and learn from me, for I am gentle and humble in heart, and you will find rest for your souls. For my yoke is easy and my burden is light' (Matthew 11:30, NIVUK). It is striking that Jesus refers to the benefit of *learning* from him; that is, our intimacy with the Saviour provides insight and wisdom that is not available through purely human means.

Levels of commitment to Christ may be usefully explored using a framework of four broad categories, spanning a spectrum from *nil*—including blatant opposition and fierce scepticism—to *absolute* (total renunciation of self and abandonment to the will of God). In the present chapter, I focus on the first group of people, those I refer to as *Dissenters*. In the next chapter, I explore the other three forms of commitment that characterise people who claim allegiance to Christ, namely: Superficial followers; Intellectual followers; Wholehearted followers.

Insight

As we explore the distinctiveness of these four groups—Dissenters; Superficial followers; Intellectual followers; Wholehearted followers—it is instructive to consider where we are located; and where our friends and family are placed. It is also worth reflecting on the occasions in our lives that we have moved from one level of commitment to a different level, and the factors that caused the change.

Dissenters

Background

There are large numbers of people living in countries where, despite the fact that Christianity has had a powerful influence in shaping behaviour, priorities, laws and political decisions, they are careless or disinterested in embracing the truth about God, the Bible, the need for repentance and salvation, or other aspects of the Christian faith. It is significant that the increasing number of people in the United Kingdom (UK) who identify as having 'no religious faith' has coincided with an increase in antisocial behaviour, drug use, divorce rates, abortion and lawlessness. A similarly unhappy situation applies to most other European and 'Western' countries, including the USA. The absence of people from church or those who are spasmodic in their attendance or who prefer to stay 'invisible' (i.e., reticent about expressing their faith) exposes a great deal about their priorities and beliefs.

It is paradoxical that in Western culture, where the explosion of knowledge in recent years is unprecedented in human history (see 'Signs of the times' in Chapter 6), ignorance of Bible Scriptures is widespread, especially among younger age groups, who are generally dismissive of 'organised' religion (i.e., formal, structured meetings and systematic teaching) and rarely encouraged by parents to attend a Sunday School, Bible Class or equivalent. The dissension takes many forms, including a dismissal of Bible events as fables or folk tales, thereby nullifying the associated teaching and doctrines that undergird Christianity.

Perhaps it is unsurprising that in liberal cultures where the latest fad and philosophy are embraced greedily, without careful scrutiny about their validity and implications for life, surveys suggest that only about one-third of young people are aware of what happened on Good Friday (the day of Jesus's crucifixion) and Easter Sunday (when Jesus rose from the dead), though they are more likely to be familiar with the events of Christmas through the words of carols and Nativity performances—some of which are more about entertaining audiences than reflecting Bible truth—including spurious ones promoted by the media and commercial interests.

Such a lack of basic knowledge and, more importantly, the significance of key events and teaching for life and conduct, are sometimes referred to as 'Bible poverty'. In the midst of this rather depressing state of affairs, it is helpful to be reminded that new style churches, with an emphasis on more contemporary forms of worship and imaginative ways of 'doing church' are expanding numerically at an encouraging rate, especially among the teens and twenties age groups. See 'Issues confronting the church' in Chapter 6 for further insights into this important issue.

Son and Spirit advocacy

Being a dissenter should not be viewed as a non-contentious decision, as there are serious consequences attached to adopting such a position. In essence, such people are unwilling to dispose of their sinful impurity through repentance, confession and placing their trust in the Saviour. In due course, they have the unenviable prospect of facing Almighty God without a heavenly protector in Christ. By contrast, Jesus' true followers can rely on him to shield them from the wrath of God by advocating on their behalf.

Jesus is the one who will protect from eternal devastation created by sin, describing himself as the Good Shepherd and his people as sheep; thus: 'I am the Good Shepherd. The Good Shepherd sacrifices his life for the sheep' (John 10:11, NLT). Jesus is the spotless Lamb of God who surrendered his human life to carry the sins of the world in his body. The Spirit of Christ guides, protects and leads his followers throughout their lives and promises them eternal life in heaven and on a future restored earth. By contrast, those who deny Jesus existed, or dismiss his status as God and Saviour, exclude themselves from the blessings and benefits that he wishes to bestow upon them. In addition, without Christ, people have no guarantee of eternal life and must face the prospect of being separated from God eternally. Paul summarises the position with these strong words: 'For the message of the cross is foolishness to those who are perishing, but to us who are being saved it is the power of God' (I Corinthians 1:18, NIVUK).

John describes Jesus's vital role and its significance for sinners in terms of *advocacy*: 'But if anyone does sin, we have an advocate with the Father, Jesus Christ the Righteous One' (1 John 2:1, NIVUK). John adds that 'he is the atoning sacrifice [propitiation, appeasement] for our sins and not only for ours but also for the sins of the whole world'. The writer of the Book of Hebrews emphasises the totality of Jesus's role as both Saviour and intercessor: 'Therefore he is able, once and forever, to save [completely, forever] those who come to God through him. He lives forever to intercede with God on their behalf' (7:25, NLT). Paul summarises the position by posing a question and providing the answer: 'Who then is the one who condemns? No one. Christ Jesus who died—more than that, who was raised to life—is at the right hand of God and is also interceding for us' (Romans 8:34, NIVUK). Without Christ's intercession, dissenters stand with their sins exposed.

Insight

It is an astounding mystery that God, in His gracious mercy, encourages believers to intercede on behalf of others by presenting their petitions to Him through prayer. Such a responsibility is a stark reminder to Christians that they should not ignore or despise those who dismiss the claims of Christ upon their lives but plead for their souls before the Throne of Grace.

Significantly, John records in his Gospel account that before Jesus went to the Cross of Calvary, rose from the dead and ascended to heaven, he promised that he would send the Holy Spirit to be *another* advocate for his followers: 'If you love me, [you will] obey my commandments. And I will ask the Father, and he will give you another Advocate, who will never leave you. He is the Holy Spirit, who leads into all truth. The world cannot receive him, because it isn't looking for him and doesn't recognise him. But you know him, because he lives with you now and later will be in you' (14:15–17, NLT). Importantly, Jesus made it clear that our love for him and obedience to his commandments need to precede the gift of the Holy Spirit as advocate. God never uses unclean vessels (Isaiah 52:11, NKJV).

The role of Christ and the Holy Spirit as advocates differ in emphasis: whereas Jesus acts as advocate (protector) when we sin—and atones for the sin of the world through his sacrificial death—the Spirit acts as encourager, comforter and counsellor for Jesus's disciples in their daily lives. Importantly, Jesus specified that the Holy Spirit would live *with* the disciples before Calvary but his spirit would be *in* them following his resurrection. The two advocacy roles can be summarised as follows:

- Jesus's advocacy is represented through his sacrifice for every person's original sin and for believers' original *and* confessed sin after accepting Christ as Saviour. His offer of eternal life is for all those who accept him as the sin-bearer.
- Once we acknowledge the Lordship of Christ (i.e., his right to rule in our lives), the Holy Spirit's advocacy is represented through the transformed

lives of believers into the likeness of Christ while they live on earth, as He dwells within them and provides spiritual gifts, encouragement, guidance and necessary rebuke.

Such wonderful promises are not available to dissenters, who reject, ridicule or ignore Jesus's claims. They stand alone, without the Son of God as advocate in heaven or the Holy Spirit as advocate on earth.

Belief and paradox

Dissenters dismiss the Bible as irrelevant and consider God to be either a fantasy or such a remote entity that He has little relevance for their behaviour, priorities and decisions. Paradoxically, despite the fact that they tend to be casual about spiritual matters that invite personal commitment and allegiance to Christ, there is considerable interest in and fascination about the occult, mysticism and the widely publicised views and predictions about life and the future made by 'gurus' or celebrities.

While showing disdain for the Christian faith, a significant percentage of the general population are fascinated by the predictions contained in horoscopes ('horror scopes') or so-called 'magic crystals' or a 'lucky charm' or symbolic practices such as 'crossing fingers' or 'touching wood', as an indicator of prosperity or guarantee of security. They are unlikely to give God any thought unless they are in trouble or confronted by death, after which they may accuse Him of not caring if the outcome is tragic or disappointing. The Old Testament prophet, Jeremiah, expresses God's perspective on the people's inconsistent trust in Him that ebbs and flows with circumstances: 'They turn their backs on me but in times of trouble they cry out to me: "Come and save us!" But why not call on these gods you have made? When trouble comes, let them save you if they can!' (2:27b–28a, NLT)

Christian funerals are still in high demand, though secular attitudes have led to the introduction of alternative services, devoid of spiritual content, without hope or expectation of life after death. Yet while they may be sceptical about the reality of an afterlife, many bereaved families and friends take comfort in hearing reassuring scriptural references about the prospect of their ultimate reunion with the deceased person. It seems likely that beneath the general veneer of spiritual apathy lies a deep-seated longing for certainty about the meaning of life and eternal destiny.

Anti-Christian agenda

The prevailing view in Western democracies is that all people are entitled to believe what they want to believe, providing it doesn't harm or offend others, though harm and offence are difficult to define, as one person's offence is another person's reasoned opinion and the amount of emotional harm allegedly incurred is impossible to quantify. The predominance of a 'culture of offence', represented by a complaint to the effect: 'I have been offended by what you say, which I deem to be hateful, prejudiced and bigoted' has become engrained in sections of society.

However much these 'offence' beliefs may be sincerely held—though serious doubt must be attached to the fact—they have led to a worrying curtailment of free speech and respectful open debate. Atheist militants have used both legal means and intimidation to curb alternative viewpoints and create a 'people who shout the loudest, win' culture. Biblical teaching usually demurs from current moral trends, thereby making Christians vulnerable to spiteful accusations, derisive comments and legal challenges by their adversaries. Paul describes the situation grimly: 'For our struggle is not against flesh and blood, but against the rulers, against the authorities, against the powers of this dark world and against the spiritual forces of evil in the heavenly realms' (Ephesians 6:12, NIVUK). The list of opponents is daunting: rulers, authorities, powers, and spiritual forces of evil. Christ won the victory at Calvary but there are battles to be fought before the end of the present world.

It has become increasingly clear that many people living in secular countries (i.e., free from a dominant religious influence) don't wish to embrace any particular moral perspective, philosophy or religion, preferring to select their beliefs from any source that seems attractive at the time and rejecting others as the mood takes them—an approach referred to as *syncretism*. They are happy to incorporate some elements of Christianity in formulating their creeds and ordering their lives but selectively combine secular and religious beliefs gleaned from various sources to create a bespoke set of principles to guide them in making decisions for their lives. The influence of family traditions, friends and the media contribute significantly to these life choices. The outcome of such syncretistic fluidity commonly results in people modifying their opinions to avoid confrontation or remaining uncommitted or becoming obsessed with the latest 'moral crusade' and imperious towards those who don't subscribe to their ideology.

Supporters of a secular worldview also dismiss the Gospel message by arguing that religion has done more harm than good in the world and claiming that wars have been fought between proponents of different religious persuasions down the centuries. While there is some basis to this assertion, the truth is that the large majority of wars are over territorial or leadership disputes, not religion. Aggressive and inhumane behaviour towards those of a different religious persuasion is rightly reported through the media but, despicable though it is, such wickedness is rarely for ideological reasons alone. The attraction of gaining wealth, power and privilege is normally the prime motive underlying widespread conflict, all of which are rooted in greed. The writer of Proverbs contrasts avarice with having trust in the Lord: 'The greedy stir up conflict but those who trust in the Lord will prosper' (28:25, NIVUK). The prophet Habakkuk is more forceful in his condemnation of unjust gain: 'Wealth is treacherous and the arrogant are never at rest. They open their mouths as wide as the grave and like death, they are never satisfied. In their greed, they have gathered up many nations and swallowed many peoples' (2:5, NLT).

Opposition from antichrists

It is a well-attested fact that there are those who not only reject the claims of Jesus Christ but also delight in ridiculing the tenets of the Christian faith, the authenticity of the Bible and the faith of believers. Particularly in his first letter, John refers to such people as 'antichrists'. In his second letter, John is more specific about the charges he brings against those whom he describes as agents of Satan: 'I say this because many deceivers have gone out into the world. They deny that Jesus Christ came in a real body. Such a person is a deceiver and an antichrist' (1:7, NLT). Antichrists pour scorn on committed Christians who espouse the Gospel, condemning them as being naïve, gullible and charlatans. Little do these scoffers realise how much their behaviour offends God and exposes them to the serious possibility of eternal damnation.

One well-known atheist was the philosopher, Jean-Paul Sartre (1905–1980) who railed against Christianity in his writing and lectures. Yet as his life drew to an end, it is said that he was gripped by despair and, despite his intellectual genius, died with many unanswered questions about the meaning for his existence. Madalyn Murray O'Hair, who founded the American Atheists, used profanities and sarcasm to shout down Christians and provide what she believed to be powerful arguments to reinforce her own beliefs. She helped to get rid of prayer in American schools and was a severe critic of almost every group of people that she considered to be in opposition to her. After O'Hair mysteriously disappeared in 1995, her diaries were discovered and auctioned to help pay for taxes that she owed. The diary entries revealed an unhappy woman who trusted no one. It seems likely that she died a cruel death. Madalyn O'Hair declared of her life that she had failed in marriage, motherhood and as a politician. The lesson to be learned from this distressing case is that however capable, courageous and apparently successful a person may be, wrongly directed effort in opposition to the purposes of God invites sorrow and ultimate ruination.

Prominent figures (notably politicians and intellectuals) that vigorously oppose Christianity and promote a wholly different worldview may capture the public imagination and achieve fame or notoriety. The impact made by these high-profile secularists may be short-lived, but they plant seeds of doubt in people's minds that take root, grow and promote radical changes in belief and behaviour. Over time, the newfangled ideas spawn factions of highly motivated advocates who make it their aim to corrupt Christian values and replace them with their own ideals. While their passion is misdirected, it provides a stark contrast to Christian resolve, which is often passive by comparison.

Regardless of their zeal and persuasive powers, opponents of Christianity cannot withstand the rock-solid truth found in the ministry of Jesus and the power of Spirit-filled Christian testimony. Secular theories and malicious campaigns to discredit the Gospel ultimately crumble on the Rock that is Christ. Their eternal fate beyond this world—when they must give an account of their lives to God—is a chilling reminder that people who deliberately contradict His existence and authority, and refuse to repent of their sinfulness, must face the awful consequences of his wrath, as the Apostle Paul makes clear: 'For the wrath of God is revealed from heaven against all ungodliness and unrighteousness of men, who suppress [hold down] the truth in unrighteousness' (Romans 1:18, NKJV). Facing the wrath of God is not something to be dismissed or treated lightly; it is a deadly serious prospect to be avoided at all cost.

Passive Dissenters

Characteristics of passivity

We all have relatives, friends or associates who are not wilfully hostile towards Christianity and may even claim to be Christians. They appear comfortable when listening to any references about church life and activities, and are polite and good-natured when they decline the opportunity to attend a church meeting. Attempts to engage in a serious conversation about spiritual matters are gently brushed aside through the use of humour or an abrupt change of subject. Despite their pleasant demeanour and relaxed manner, it is nevertheless the case that passive dissenters have resisted embracing the Gospel message and making a commitment to follow Christ.

The expression 'hardness of heart' is used to describe the attitude of a person who stubbornly resists God's stated will and purpose. Paul describes the way in which the hardness is manifested: 'Their minds are in the dark, and they are stubborn and ignorant and have missed out on the life that comes from God. They no longer have any feelings about what is right' (Ephesians 4:18, CEV).

Most non-churchgoing people are not deeply immoral or corrupt; they simply do not see or will not see the relevance of Christianity for their lives. They may not reject God explicitly but prefer to give their time and attention to things of immediate importance to them, such as family, work and recreation. Passive dissenters fail to appreciate or perhaps refuse to acknowledge that the God of the Bible wishes to enjoy an intimate relationship with them that translates into a happier and more fulfilling life. The misapprehension that becoming a follower of Jesus results in a joyless existence seems to be a common factor among soft dissenters' reluctance to take seriously his claim upon their lives.

Passive dissenters may have a vague idea or hope that there is 'something or someone out there', and may get sentimental when little children sing *Away in a Manger* at the Nativity service, but otherwise continue with their lives without reference to God or prayer or interest in spiritual matters, other than becoming excited about paranormal events—things that happen or appear to happen outside human experience or defy natural explanation. For instance, claims about extra-terrestrial beings or unidentified flying objects (UFOs) often garner considerable interest, which is in marked contrast to the indifference about the supernatural work of God seen in creation and the astounding truth that God came to earth in human form.

In general, passive dissenters don't appear to spend much time worrying unduly about what happens after they die or giving serious attention to issues pertaining to eternity. Their desire is to 'live life to the full' and find pleasure and gratification through social events and various forms of entertainment. They treat death as something to be avoided as long as possible but not necessarily feared, either because they believe that it ushers in annihilation (final and absolute destruction) or because they hold a fanciful view of heaven where everyone apart from really wicked people gather in perfect harmony to enjoy a blissful existence for ever. These views contrast sharply with Jesus's references about the enormity of judgement; for example, Matthew notes the strong warning given by Jesus to unbelievers: 'Then Jesus began to denounce the towns where he had done so many of his miracles because they hadn't repented of their sins and turned to God' (11:20, NLT). The prospect of being denounced by Jesus should stir fear in every dissenter's heart.

The consequences of dissension

Hardening of heart and dismissing the prospect of God's judgement has immediate consequences, as His Spirit distances from the unbelieving individuals, leaving them exposed to destructive satanic influences during their lifetimes. Adopting a disdainful attitude towards God also has serious implications for the time following death, as Jesus warned that those who reject the message of salvation would fare even worse than the people of Sodom and Gomorrah when both towns were destroyed by fire (Matthew Chapters 10 and 11; Luke Chapter 10).

Deliberate rejection of God's gracious invitation to find eternal life through Christ is therefore a serious matter and should dispel complacency. Sadly, those who show little or no interest in trusting Christ are unlikely to be moved by such declarations about present disadvantage or future distress due to a spiritual blindness that they appear to self-impose. The prophet Isaiah, who lived some 700 years before Jesus came to earth, warned about people's hardness of heart; deaf ears; closed eyes; and refusal to turn to God for healing. Encouragingly, however, the prophet also declared that people could be free from their spiritual captivity, once their eyes were opened by God and they found freedom from sin—not due to their own righteousness—but thanks to the Lord's gracious favour (see Isaiah Chapters 58 and 60).

Because Jesus was scathing towards pretence or hypocrisy, he cautioned those who, despite claiming to have followed him but had not experienced a genuine change of heart and continued to break God's laws, that they would be refused entry into his eternal kingdom: 'On Judgement Day, many will say to me: Lord! Lord! We prophesied in your name and cast out demons in your name and performed many miracles in your name, but I will reply: I never knew you.

Get away from me, you who break God's laws' (Matthew 7:22–23, NLT). It is chilling to think that some people who prophesy, cast out demons and perform miracles may still be condemned by Christ. We can only assume that satanic power supplied the power for them to perform such amazing feats, while all the time they were careless about keeping God's commands. Whatever the explanation, Jesus's stern warning is a sharp reminder that *obedience* is the starting point for pleasing God, not performing impressive deeds, however spectacular they may be.

In the Paul's second letter to the church in Thessalonica (located in modern-day Greece), he reinforces the gravity of rejecting the Gospel by describing the day that Jesus will come again to earth as judge: 'He will punish those who do not know God and do not obey the Gospel of our Lord Jesus. They will be punished with everlasting destruction and shut out from the presence of the Lord and from the glory of his might' (1:8–9, NIVUK). The terrifying prospect of being separated from the Lord forever underscores the vital importance for each person to acknowledge God, accept the salvation that He offers and determine to live for Him.

It goes without saying that some people are more serious than others in their desire for certainty over the existence of God and clarification about spiritual matters. It is a matter of conjecture as to how much of the 'awakening' people receive is due to the Holy Spirit's prompting or to individual predilection or, perhaps, a mysterious interaction of Spirit prompting and personal decision. Whatever means God uses to awaken people from their apathy, the disturbing prophecy given to the Old Testament prophet Daniel some six hundred years before Jesus was born merits close attention: 'Many of those who lie dead in the ground will rise from death. Some of them will be given eternal life, and others will receive nothing but eternal shame and disgrace' (12:2, CEV). The clinical separation in Daniel's prophecy of those inheriting life and those condemned to disgrace mirrors Jesus's stark warning about the straightforward choice between eternal life or facing judgement. Personal trust in Christ the Redeemer is essential if 'eternal shame and everlasting disgrace' are to be avoided.

Almost persuaded

There are people who express an interest in the person of Jesus Christ as an historical figure but allow intellectual scepticism to cloud their judgement about his status as Redeemer. They adopt a *disbelieving* attitude and find reasons to argue against trusting Jesus rather than humbly accepting the truth about his saving power.

Other people are curious about Christianity, which is a useful starting point for discussing the validity of the Gospel and the need to exercise faith in Christ, but is not a satisfactory point at which to end. In other words, an initial interest in discovering the authenticity of the message must result in a decision to follow or reject Christ, or at least engender in the enquirer a greater desire to determine the veracity of what is being claimed. Experience shows that unless the person's preliminary interest is pursued, he or she will not normally make the effort to discover more. There is, however, a balance to be struck between further engagement with the enquirer and excessive zeal that borders on harassment. As always, persistent prayer and divine wisdom is required in knowing how best to proceed.

A fascinating event that took place during Paul's missionary work, as described in Acts Chapters 25 and 26, provides an excellent example of Paul using his intellectual strength, coupled with an appropriate style of exposition to engage and stimulate an audience. Following accusations against Paul by Jewish religious leaders for alleged blasphemy, led by their lawyer/orator Tertullus, the regional governor Felix and his successor, Festus, imprisoned Paul in Jerusalem (seemingly under some form of 'house-arrest'). Some two years later, the arrival of King Agrippa II, whose father had been responsible for persecuting Christians (including the execution of Jesus's half-brother, James), led to Paul having opportunity to speak directly to the King, present his own testimony and proclaim the Gospel message.

As Paul was concluding his speech, Governor Festus cried out that too much study had sent Paul insane but Paul's calm response made King Agrippa stutter that he was almost persuaded to become a Christian (Acts 26:28). The important point to glean from this event is that Paul used his intellect to present his case, fuelled by the power of God's Spirit, which clearly convicted the godless Agrippa of his need to trust Jesus as Saviour. Paul's education and training gave him the skill and ability to present the truth but his purpose was to win people for Christ and not to engage in an intellectual argument. History does not record whether Agrippa subsequently became a believer.

In 1871, the highly talented composer and evangelist, Philip Bliss, wrote a hymn based on Paul's encounter with King Agrippa titled *Almost Persuaded* in which Bliss describes how it is possible to be on the brink of commitment, yet to pull back and never make a firm decision to follow Christ. The final verse of the hymn, especially the last line, should make every serious believer shudder at contemplating the eternal fate of those who reject the Saviour: 'Almost persuaded, harvest is past. Almost persuaded, doom comes at last! Almost cannot avail. Almost is but to fail! Sad, sad that bitter wail: Almost, but lost!' See Chapter 8 under 'Intellectual followers' for further discussion about the advantages and pitfalls attached to the use of the intellect in seeking to work and witness for Christ.

The reckoning

Throughout this book, I emphasise the importance of personal choice and decision, and their significance for our present and eternal security. In the Gospel compiled by Luke, Jesus answers his disciples' question about the end of the present world by saying that on that occasion there won't be any advance warning 'signal' about his imminent arrival. Life will be proceeding in much the same way as normal with 'people going about their daily business—eating and drinking, buying and selling, farming and building' (17:28, NLT) until his sudden return brings the world to a close.

By contrast with the pick-and-mix approach to morality and behaviour prevalent in today's society, Jesus demands a wholly different set of priorities, referring to the importance of finding the 'narrow way' that leads to life and avoiding the 'broad road' that leads to eternal destruction. Matthew records Jesus's uncompromising words on the subject: 'Go in through the narrow gate. The gate to destruction is wide, and the road that leads there is easy to follow. A lot of people go through that gate' (7:13, CEV). Reference to Hell as a destination for wicked human beings is an uncomfortable topic but must be faced squarely. Dissenters, sceptics and liberal preachers should take particular note.

The Old Testament prophet, Daniel, was given insight into the background to Jesus's coming again and a glimpse of what the effect that his return would have on the people of earth: 'In my vision at night I looked and there before me was one like a son of man, coming with the clouds of heaven. He approached the Ancient of Days and was led into his presence. He was given authority, glory and sovereign power; all nations and peoples of every language worshipped him. His dominion is an everlasting dominion that will not pass away, and his kingdom is one that will never be destroyed' (7:13–14, NIVUK). The reference to 'all nations and peoples of every language' worshipping the Son of God is a thrilling prospect for all those who love and seek to serve Father God.

Although we will not have a warning light to indicate the immediacy of Christ's return, there will be signs of the times and trends in human behaviour that indicate the imminence of his return as judge of all the earth that are intended both to reassure us and provoke us to live holy lives in the light of his appearing. The only time that the 'trumpet sound' will be heard is at the very moment of his coming, when the world as we know it comes to an end and heralds God's judgement, and the creation of a new heaven and earth. In his first letter to the Corinthians, Paul describes the situation vividly: 'It will happen in a moment, in the blink of an eye, when the last trumpet is blown. For when the trumpet sounds, those who have died will be raised to live forever and we who are living will also be transformed' (15:52, NLT). See Chapter 6 under 'Jesus's return' for further interrogation and details about the 'signs of the times' associated with this supreme event.

Summary

Following Jesus is both a privilege and a responsibility. It is a *privilege* to be assured that he is the only way to God the Father and will lead us along the narrow road in life, regardless of our personal circumstances or situations. It is a *responsibility* to bear the name and message of Christ in our daily walk. As we do so, it is necessary for all believers to remind themselves constantly that they were once lost but have been found, rescued and brought back into a right relationship with God through trusting in Jesus's redeeming sacrifice. Consequently, it is of paramount importance to stay close by Jesus's side, walking in his light and feeding on him by faith.

Jesus requires us to seek the Kingdom of God and His righteousness above everything else (Matthew 6:33). Wholehearted Christians long that the love of Christ is communicated to those with whom we have contact, so they may learn to love and trust him, too. Christ is not only the Light of the World but also offers to illuminate the narrow way, as we respond to the promptings of his Spirit. Jesus calls every Christian to be a light in his or her community and respond to the 'high calling' placed upon each life by being his representatives (ambassadors) on earth.

Sadly, there are many people who dissent from following Jesus and must face the consequences of their decision, both during and beyond this life. These dissenters range from those who are quietly indifferent to the claims of Christ to those who are virulently antagonistic and fully prepared to act unwittingly as Satan's servants in opposing the Gospel. Jesus did not mince his words when he described the awful fate that awaits the antichrists that seek to corrupt the truth and deceive his followers.

With which of these statements do you agree?

1. Narrow paths are for narrow-minded people.
2. Anyone who is not a devout Christian is on the broad way leading to destruction.
3. Obedience is the key to finding the narrow path that leads to life.
4. There should not be any restrictions on who is allowed to receive communion.
5. Lack of Scripture teaching in schools is the main reason for Bible poverty.
6. Passive dissenters will be judged as severely as active dissenters.
7. All dissenters will be sent to Hell unless they repent.
8. Christians need to be influential in society by seeking local and political office.

Chapter 8
Abiding in Christ

Introduction

The concept of abiding in Christ has been likened to immersing a teabag in boiling water. On its own, the teabag cannot achieve its purpose of creating a satisfying drink. It is only when the water is added that the bag releases its full flavour. The longer the tea is allowed to brew, the stronger the resulting beverage. In this analogy, the teabag represents our spiritual potential; the hot water is the power of the Holy Spirit; the length of time spent brewing constitutes our abiding in Christ. The more we abide in him, the greater our personal assurance during the vagaries of life, and the more effective we become in declaring and demonstrating God's love.

In the latter part of the previous chapter, I presented four broad categories to describe levels of commitment to Christ and focused on the attitudes, strategies and arguments characterising people who refuse to believe in Jesus Christ as the world's Saviour ('the dissenters'). Some dissenters actively and aggressively pursue a humanistic (secular) agenda, the majority are simply passive, even nonchalant about what they perceive as having little relevance for their lives and conduct. In the present chapter, I focus on the other three categories, identified as follows:

1. Superficial followers
2. Intellectual followers
3. Wholehearted followers.

Superficial Followers

Justified invisibility

The main title 'Superficial Followers' might be viewed as an oxymoron (contradiction), as following Jesus presupposes 'visibility' not concealment. There are, however, many Christians who are obliged to be secret believers due to the pressure of circumstances. Some governments will not permit any form of Christian expression or involvement and will not allow anyone to change religion (e.g., from Islam to Christianity). In other countries, the church is targeted by state enforcement agencies or harassed by local communities. So fierce is the oppressive nature of government intervention and aggressive restrictions in certain areas of the world that the church has to remain 'underground' and is obliged to meet and worship in secret.

Recent pronouncements on behalf of the United Nations and aid agencies confirm that Christians have been and remain the most oppressed group of people on earth during the early years of the 21st century. Even in the so-called 'democratic' nations, denigration of Bible truth and restrictions on public preaching of the Gospel has become more evident in recent years, energised by a 'culture of offence' whereby complaints about another person's allegedly hateful remarks have been employed as a weapon to demonise and silence Christian witness.

It is understandable that believers who live in countries or areas of the world where there is local or national oppression and victimisation should feel that in order to be 'as wise as serpents and harmless as doves' (Matthew 10:16) they should remain anonymous and extremely careful about expressing their beliefs. The 'invisibility' of Christians who have to endure punitive restrictions and fear the consequences of openly declaring their faith and trust in Jesus Christ is understandable and justified.

The use of careful manoeuvring to avoid conflict and unpleasant repercussions by those who fear God and seek to obey His commands is not a new strategy. In 2 Kings 5, we read how Naaman, the commander of the Aramean army, came to Elisha the prophet for healing from leprosy and was wonderfully cleansed. However, Naaman had to return home to serve the pagan king of Aram and resume his professional duties, which presented him with a dilemma. On the one hand, he now acknowledged the true God; on the other hand he was duty bound to worship with the King at the temple of the idol 'god' (Rimmon). Naaman therefore devised a compromise: 'From now on, I will never again offer burnt offerings or sacrifices to any other god except the Lord. However, may the Lord pardon me in this one thing: When my master the king goes into the temple of the god Rimmon to worship there and leans on my arm, may the Lord pardon me when I bow, too' (2 Kings 5:18, NLT). Elisha commended and blessed Naaman, as the commander faced what would inevitably prove to be a delicate and possibly life-threatening situation.

What appears at first sight to be a cunning deceit was, in truth, a wise strategy to preserve Naaman's allegiance to the Lord God Jehovah, while fulfilling his secular duties. Many Christians are faced with a similar situation in remaining faithful to Christ while undertaking their paid employment or learning to exist in a hostile environment, thereby finding a way to 'give to Caesar what belongs to Caesar's and to God what belongs to God', as Jesus responded to the religious leaders' unscrupulous question about allegiance (recorded in all three Synoptic Gospels: Matthew, Mark and Luke). It goes without saying that those in whom the Spirit of Christ dwells must seek to be salt and light by showing his love and forgiveness in every situation, however grim it may be. They also need to be led by the Spirit in discerning the time to speak and the time to remain silent (Ecclesiastes 3:7b).

Nominalism

Although there are undoubtedly large numbers of people who scorn the notion of a 'Higher Deity' and reject their need of a Saviour (see previous chapter), there are many others who describe themselves as Christians, yet are reluctant to express their beliefs publicly or seek to put Jesus Christ at the centre of their lives if it means relegating their own desires and preferences. In the so-called 'free world' where governments allow and facilitate choice of religion or complete abstinence from it, there are Christians who, though trusting Christ for salvation, appear to have little appetite for openly acknowledging the fact or being involved in any form of witness. They may be referred to as 'nominal' or 'comfortable' or 'cultural' Christians or—the term that I presently employ—'cosy' Christians. These superficial followers of Jesus are rather akin to spectators at a sports event, preferring to remain on the fringes of church life, quietly applauding front-line workers but reluctant to express their faith through testimony, financial support or taking a firm stand against injustice.

Cosy Christians are those who are happy to believe in Jesus and accept his offer of salvation when little personal cost is attached. They are commonly known as fair-weather friends, who want (in the words of an old song by Tim Whipple of *The Fisherfolk*) a 'candy-coated Gospel'. While it is true that we cannot purchase salvation—it is the free gift of God to all who will receive it—our commitment and sanctification (where our lives are continually transformed into the likeness of Christ by the indwelling Holy Spirit) requires active submission to His will and purposes, which nearly always involves sacrifice, as well as resulting in great blessing. Such a view is not always popular in a world increasingly dominated by self-aggrandisement and the pursuit of pleasure.

The seriousness of being nominal is underlined by Paul: 'For although they knew God, they neither glorified him as God nor gave thanks to him, but their thinking became futile and their foolish hearts were darkened' (Romans 1:21, NIVUK). We see that Paul declares it is possible to 'know God' through knowing His Son but fail to glorify Him and thereby be afflicted by what amounts to spiritual paralysis. Paul describes the outcome awaiting people who confess Christ as Saviour, yet whose deeds fail to please God, that their works will be 'burned up', though the person will be 'saved through fire' (I Corinthians 3:15, NKJV). Imagine your thinking being futile, living in spiritual darkness, having a hard, unresponsive heart, being ignorant (foolish) and insensitive! What a miserable existence to know God but to be detached from Him in the way that Paul describes! It is a moot point as to whether such a person can truly claim to be saved from sin.

At a meeting I attended some years ago when the cost of discipleship was being described, there were one hundred or more people present at the commencement but many in the audience walked out when they objected to the level of commitment entailed in being a faithful follower of Jesus. As referred to earlier, in areas of the world where Christians are persecuted and reviled, the 'easy' option does not apply; people are either for or against Jesus Christ. In such situations, those who stand firm for him often do so at great personal cost: at best, being ostracised by the community or members of their families, and in extreme cases, being imprisoned or even forfeiting their lives. It is difficult to imagine many Christians in the 'free world' accepting such dire consequences of remaining faithful to Jesus.

In Luke's Gospel account, he quotes Jesus's stern words about the need to unashamedly declare our love for him: 'I tell you the truth, everyone who acknowledges me publicly here on earth, the Son of Man will also acknowledge in the presence of God's angels. But anyone who denies me here on earth will be denied before God's angels' (12:8–9, NIVUK). Matthew provides a slightly different record of what Jesus said but with equivalent meaning: 'If you tell others that you belong to me, I will tell my Father in heaven that you are my followers. But if you reject me, I will tell my Father in heaven that you don't belong to me' (10:32–33, CEV). While cosy Christians do not deny the truth of the Gospel, their failure to acknowledge him openly could have serious repercussions if it leads to them denying the Lordship of Christ in their lives.

Consequences of nominalism

The notion of 'keeping your head down' or remaining on the periphery loses its attractiveness when the consequences are openly considered, as to be invisible may place in mortal peril those who choose that position and propel them to face the unpalatable prospect of one day having to justify their silence before God. Without the Holy Spirit's leading and guiding, we will never become the people that He wants us to be here on earth. Adopting a position of 'lying low' instead of choosing a transparent walk and witness does not please God or bring Him glory. It is inviting present trouble and ultimate disappointment if we are casual about God's gracious invitation to trust Him for life's journey and beyond. All of those who identify as a Christian need to examine their hearts to see where they stand on the matter, always keeping in mind the solemn fact that the Lord has declared: 'I am he who searches hearts and minds, and I will repay each of you according to your deeds' (Revelation 2:23b, NIVUK).

In the same way that the angels in Sodom warned Lot's family to escape the impending disaster (Genesis Chapter 19), part of our task as followers of Jesus is to point out the seriousness of the situation to those who will listen. Some people may respond, others will choose to dismiss the message or react nonchalantly, but on the Day of Judgement they must explain the reasons for their attitude, as must every person. If Christians choose to remain silent, they will never be in a position to share with others the need to repent and escape from eternal destruction.

One of the best-known examples about not remaining silent is found in the Book of Esther where Esther is prompted by her uncle (Mordecai) to speak up on behalf of the Jewish people to save them from the evil purposes of their enemy, Haman. Thanks to Esther's courageous decision to inform the king about the plot, disaster is averted (see Esther Chapter 4). The incident is all the more compelling because the King (Xerxes) was renowned for sudden outbursts of unpredictable and violent behaviour. Esther's response to Mordecai, 'If I perish, I perish' was rooted in the high probability that appearing unheralded before the King would lead to precisely that outcome.

In his letter to the church at Philippi, the Apostle Paul reflected Esther's courageous stance by stating firmly that as far as he was concerned: 'for me to live is Christ and to die is gain' (1:21, NIVUK), which is in stark contrast to the tentative expressions of faith from cosy Christians. In his Gospel account, John records Jesus's piercing questions to Simon Peter about whether he truly loved him, forcing Peter to search his own heart when responding (Chapter 21). Believers down the ages are faced with the same question and the need to be similarly honest about how much they love the Saviour and are willing to sacrifice for his sake. The extent of our devotion to Christ will be evident through our willingness to be associated with him in his sufferings, as well as heirs of God's glory (Romans 8:17).

It is chastening to know that even fallen angels are kept securely imprisoned until the end of time because of their rebellion against God (Jude 6). While cosy Christians will not suffer such a desperate fate, a failure to be transparent about their faith and allegiance to Christ will certainly affect their eternal reward, as well as depriving others of their testimony.

Insight

A willingness to submit our lives wholeheartedly to Christ, even up to the point of death should not be compared with the martyrdom instincts that pervade extremists in other religions and secular movements. The Christian's 'dying to self' is first and foremost a willingness to allow the Holy Spirit to control our thoughts, words and behaviour, not a reckless attempt to end life prematurely in the hope of reward or visions of glory. It should also be noted that dying to self does not involve self-loathing. Jesus taught that the second most important commandment is to love others as we love ourselves, because we are all precious to God.

Enhancing visibility

A Christian who exhibits only a superficial allegiance to Christ has been compared to a snowflake that quickly melts in the heat of opposition or personal sacrifice. Jesus, however, did not disguise the fact that being His disciple (follower) involves a cost, as well as spiritual and practical benefits. During Jesus's time on earth, some would-be followers began to make excuses, including the need to complete a business deal (buying a field); the need to get married; and the urgency attached to sorting out family affairs. In responding to one man, Luke records that Jesus replied starkly: 'Foxes have holes and birds of the air have nests, but the Son of Man has no place to lay his head' (9:58, NLT; see also Matthew Chapter 8), whereby Jesus stressed the importance of wholehearted commitment to him. As in all things, the emphasis must be upon our dedication to and love for Jesus, not for a cause or a movement or our friends or a denomination or a church leader.

In his letter to the church in Rome, Paul emphasised the importance of being transparent about our faith, linking confession of Christ's lordship and glorification with salvation: 'If you openly declare that Jesus is Lord and believe in your heart that God raised him from the dead, you will be saved' (10:9, NLT). It is therefore unsurprising that numerous songs, hymns, anthems and choruses have been written down the centuries describing Christ's worthiness to receive our love and praise, and the need to demonstrate our personal devotion to him. Conversely, our lack of fidelity makes any expression of worship in word or song both hollow and sterile.

I emphasised earlier that for Christians in the 'free world' to remain timid and silent about their faith in Christ is not only regrettable but also an affront to fellow believers, who faithfully declare their beliefs while suffering at the hands of evil governments, antagonistic communities, disgruntled families and repressive laws. Declaring our faith and trust in Jesus Christ as the Saviour of the world, who died to set us free from the penalty of sin, create new life within us by his Spirit and promise a place in heaven at the end of life, does not require us to be public evangelists, street preachers or accomplished Bible teachers. There are, however, at least six straightforward ways to ensure that all Christians can enhance their visibility in the warp and woof of daily life:

1) Maintaining a close walk with God through prayer and meditating on Bible truth.
2) Having regular fellowship with believers and being seen in their company, whenever and wherever they gather.

3) Speaking freely and naturally in our everyday conversation about our church connections and activities.

4) Explaining to the best of our ability what Jesus has done, what he means to us, and what he can mean to others.

5) Offering to pray for someone, as God prompts us to do so.

6) Being a good witness through our words and deeds, so exhibiting the fruit of the Spirit in every aspect of life (For further details, see Chapter 11 under 'Modelling').

Each one who claims to be a follower of Jesus Christ should pay heed to Paul's determination to be bold for Jesus, as he expressed fearlessly: 'For I am not ashamed of the Gospel, because it is the power of God that brings salvation to everyone who believes: first to the Jew, then to the Gentile' (Romans 1:16, NIVUK). By contrast, superficiality and invisibility indicate that we are, in effect, ashamed of the Gospel and embarrassed about being associated with Christ and his church.

A question for all Christians to ask themselves is whether they are as filled to overflowing in their love and commitment to Jesus as they were when they first submitted their lives to him and were born again. If not, what has happened that caused them to stumble? As Paul asked the faltering Galatian believers: 'You were running the race so well. Who has held you back from following the truth?' (5:7, NLT). It's a question that demands an answer from those of us who become aware of our fading zeal in expressing our love for Jesus and living to glorify him. Jesus's parable ('Parable of the Sower') about some of the pure seed (representing the Word of God) being scattered on stony ground and withering under the heat of the day tells us a great deal about the danger of superficial commitment that leads to so-called 'backsliding' (i.e., gradually allowing worldly interests to overtake godly living) or stunted spiritual growth (i.e., failing to grow in grace and love for others).

Superficiality has numerous synonyms (words with similar meaning) such as peripheral, cosmetic, perfunctory, artificial and hollow, none of which are flattering! For alleged followers of the Saviour to be described in such a dismissive way is not only shameful for them but also an affront to the majesty and glory rightly belonging to him. Along with every other believer, superficial Christians must give an account of the way they lived, served and worshipped the Lord of Glory. If you are one such person, my friend, what will you say on that day?

Intellectual Followers

Background

The author, Mark Twain, memorably and amusingly described the arrogance of youth with the following satirical comment: *When I was a boy of 14, my father was so ignorant I could hardly stand to have the old man around. But when I got to be 21, I was astonished at how much the old man had learned in seven years!* Twain was astutely exposing the fact that older people are more knowledgeable than typically acknowledged by their offspring. The Bible is clear that those who walk closely with the Lord increase in wisdom and discernment over time, though the characteristics are not solely time-based, as Elihu comments when debating with a distressed Job after tragedy had struck his family: 'But it is the spirit in people, the breath from God All-Powerful, that makes them understand. Old men are not the only wise people. They are not the only ones who understand what is right' (Job 32:8–9, ERV; see also Jesus's prayer recorded in Matthew 11:25). The key to godly wisdom is having a healthy fear of the Lord, as the psalmist reminds us: 'Fear of the Lord is the foundation of true wisdom. All who obey his commandments will grow in wisdom' (111:10, NLT). I explore these issues further in Chapter 9.

Bible interpretation

There are many interesting philosophies that provide the substance for fervent academic study, accompanied by keen debate and earnest discussion. Yet it is probably fair to say that Christianity, especially the biblical text, has been scrutinised, commented on, written about and analysed as much as any other religious topic or area of human life. Countless numbers of books, articles and forums have delved into the minutiae of the historical content of the Old Testament, Jesus's teaching and early church doctrine.

As a result of these studies, denominations have been created, sects established and a forensic form of critical scrutiny ensued, which have provided valuable contextual and historical information about the background to key portions of the Bible. Conversely, scholarly interest in the Scriptures has sometimes been driven by an unhealthy moral arrogance on the part of sceptics, who seek to undermine the validity of faith-based claims presented in the biblical narrative and embraced by committed Christians.

The prevalence of academics that pontificate about different doctrinal theories with scant regard for the wonderful promise of salvation and evidence of transformed lives proves that it is possible to have an intellectual grasp of a Bible subject or issue, yet to do so in a detached manner, without imbibing the scriptural truth declared through the text or the implications for living propounded through the inspired words of chroniclers, prophets and godly men. Far from being a helpful, objective view of the Scriptures, the predominance of 'remote intellectualism' of this sort signifies an absence of dedicated faith in God.

Insight

It is surprisingly easy for Christians to fall into the trap of approaching their regular Bible reading and prayer in a perfunctory rather than expectant manner. An eager desire to hear afresh from the Holy Spirit transforms potentially mundane habits into vibrant experiences of discovering more about God's will and purpose from the Scriptures to be celebrated and implemented for His glory.

Subtlety and chicanery

In Matthew Chapter 13, we read that some of the local population were interested and fascinated by Jesus but at an academic level, rather than a faith-inspired one: 'When he taught there in the synagogue, everyone was amazed and said, Where does he get this wisdom and the power to do miracles? Then they scoffed: He's just the carpenter's son!' (54–5, NLT). The members of Jesus's audience were unable to deny his wisdom and power but were unwilling to accept that he had come down from heaven because it did not align with their rational (orderly, predetermined) view of life. After all, they reasoned: *We know his family. We have seen him assisting his father in the carpenter's shop and he eats and drinks like any other person. So why should we accept that he is different from the rest of us? His claim that he came down from heaven to earth in order to live like a man is hard to swallow! He is a person of great interest and we accept that his teaching stands out from the many other teachers and prophets that bombard us with their claims to be the mouthpiece of God. He is certainly not, however, someone in whom we can place our faith and trust as being the Messiah sent from God to redeem the world from sin!* Such forms of scepticism are still prevalent today.

On numerous occasions, teachers of the law and other religious intellectuals asked probing questions and attempted to subvert Jesus's message or trap him into making blasphemous statements. For instance, they asked him questions about who was greater: Caesar or God; they posed a hypothetical question about married life after death; they attempted flattery, veiled threats and accusations about a failure to keep the Mosaic Law. In all these situations, Jesus not only exposed their deception but also silenced their grubby connivances through his insight and spiritual alacrity, focusing the conversation on their godless behaviour and sanctimonious attitudes.

Mark records that early in Jesus's ministry, 'the people were amazed at his teaching, because he taught them as one who had authority, not as the teachers of the law' (1:22, NIVUK). Followers of Jesus are similarly equipped to speak with authority, though opposition is never far away, as described in the following section.

Responding to opponents

Every follower of Jesus must strive to lead a blameless life that does not invite criticism and scorn from those who seek to find fault. Peter stresses that as we await the second coming of Christ and the start of the new heaven and earth filled with God's righteousness, we should 'make every effort to be found living peaceful lives that are pure and blameless in his sight' (2 Peter 3:14, NLT). In a world where media scrutiny and access to personal information and viewpoints are invasive, the need for transparent godly living is of singular importance.

It is perfectly valid for genuine enquirers to interrogate the Scriptures as to whether the claims emerging from the Bible about Jesus are consistent. It is also fair for them to see if the behaviour of those who claim to be Jesus's followers conforms to what he taught and God requires from them. In addition, it is reasonable to judge the impact on society of Christian beliefs and practice, and to check that the moral framework being promoted is not riddled with hypocrisy and self-interest. As Paul wrote to Titus: 'And you yourself must be an example to them by doing good works of every kind. Let everything you do reflect the integrity and seriousness of your teaching' (2:7, NLT). In aspiring to live with integrity, we have the high benchmark for behaviour set by Jesus, who was particularly severe with hypocrites, defined as people who rebuke others for what they are deemed to be doing or failing to do, while indulging in similar or worse behaviour themselves.

Jesus was never inhibited in expressing his disdain for people who made impressive public announcements but whose actions contradicted their flowery speeches. Matthew chronicles how Jesus described a particular group of religious leaders who were guilty of such pretence: 'What sorrow awaits you teachers of religious law and you Pharisees. Hypocrites! For you are like whitewashed tombs—beautiful on the outside but filled on the inside with dead people's bones and all sorts of impurity' (23:27, NLT). Luke records a further episode in Jesus's confrontation with hypocritical religious leaders, who were more intent on their status and making a good impression than they were about displaying genuine love and compassion. They even attempted to cloak their cheating behaviour by pompously praying long prayers in public. Jesus was blunt about the severe punishment that they could expect, as a result of their brazen arrogance (20:47).

In recent years, opportunities for enemies of the Gospel to inflict damage on the cause of Christ have expanded through use of social media, political manoeuvring and arguing about the alleged damage that Christian belief causes, especially in restricting or constraining so-called personal liberty ('doing what comes naturally'). Thankfully, the greater the spiritual attack, the stronger believers become, as the Lord fights on our behalf and gives us the victory by the power of Christ's spirit, as Paul celebrates in his first letter to the Corinthians: 'But thanks be to God, who gives us the victory through our Lord Jesus Christ. Therefore, my beloved brethren, be steadfast, immovable, always abounding in the work of the Lord, knowing that your labour is not in vain in the Lord' (15:57–8, NKJV). It is worth taking the time to absorb the key words from this quotation: victory, steadfast, immovable, abounding, labour. Paul's words should be a comfort and source of encouragement to believers who are encountering opposition and feel demoralised because their efforts seem to be ineffective against a rising tide of secularism. Nothing done in the name and for the glory of Christ is ever wasted, as God declared through Isaiah: 'So shall my word be that goes forth from My mouth; It shall not return to me void, but it shall accomplish what I please. And it shall prosper in the thing for which I sent it' (Isaiah 55:11, NKJV).

Peter emphasises the need to be ready to respond to questions from seekers and sceptics but also to avoid giving them any cause to accuse or deride: 'Always be prepared to give an answer to everyone who asks you to give the reason for the hope that you have. But do this with gentleness and respect, keeping a clear conscience, so that those who speak maliciously against your good behaviour in Christ may be ashamed of their slander' (I Peter 15–16, NIVUK). It should be stressed that Peter does not suggest that the answer will necessarily satisfy the questioner but that the believer is prepared to *give* an answer. In other words, we need to have 'done our homework' by searching the Scriptures and being as clear as possible in explaining the reason for our hope.

The fact that many Christians struggle in responding to queries from outsiders is not necessarily that their faith is weak but that (a) they have been slack in clarifying their thinking about key issues; or (b) they attend churches where there is weak exposition and teaching; or (c) they have never been encouraged to give public testimony about their faith in Christ. Whereas improving in areas (a) and (c) are largely under the control of the individual, inadequate teaching is a more serious issue and less easily resolved without confronting the leaders about the matter or moving church or gaining insight through other sources, such as scholarly but accessible books and reliable online teaching.

Pursuing truth

Intellectual arguments are beneficial if they facilitate a search for, and discovery of, the truth, but illusory if they degenerate into mere 'talking shops'. A strong and alarming trend in the early years of the 21st century has been the suppression of genuine and persuasive discussion in a desire to reach either a consensus or 'agree to disagree'. In its place has emerged what has been termed a 'woke' culture, whereby opinions deemed to be casting doubt on a liberal, secular moral perspective are casually dismissed (at best) or elicit an enraged and spiteful response (at worst), often attached to accusations of racial intolerance and bigotry.

There have been many examples of Christians and others who reject the liberal stance—and in the case of Christians, stand firm on biblical principles and Christ's teaching—who have been banned ('cancelled') from speaking engagements. In a growing number of instances, a person who has refused to bow the knee to secular priorities has been banned from holding a voluntary public office, or even dismissed from a professional post. In essence, truth—however defined or carefully expressed—is becoming subservient to emotional and personal preference. The authoritative declaration: 'Thus says the Lord' is being replaced by the worldly: 'If it feels good, flaunt it!'

No such woke culture pertained during the period of Paul's missionary journeys to spread the good news about Jesus's work on earth and its implications for human life and eternity, though strong and sometimes violent reactions were sparked if his message threatened the existing cultural norms. One example of such a fierce reaction took place in Philippi when Paul, together with Silas and other believers, healed a slave girl of an evil spirit (a demon), which incurred the wrath of her masters, who relied on her supposed ability to tell fortunes for their income. The subsequent harsh treatment of Paul and his companion, Silas, is an indicator of how godly words and actions can trigger an aggressive reaction from those whose lives are under satanic influence.

Wherever they travelled, the Apostles scorned the status and significance of idols, just as Isaiah the prophet had done six hundred years before: 'What fools they are who carry around their wooden idols and pray to gods that cannot save!' (Isaiah 45:20, NLT) God made it abundantly clear to the Jewish people that idolatry should have no part in their national life. Jesus reinforced the principle that love for God and others must supersede any covetousness, desires, selfish ambition or other priorities that suppress or negate making Him the centre point of our lives and worship.

During one of his missionary travels, Paul spent time in Athens. One of his companions, Luke—who compiled the events described in Acts of the Apostles—commented on how people spent their days exchanging opinions on a variety of topics: 'All the Athenians and the foreigners who lived there spent their time doing nothing but talking about and listening to the latest ideas' (17:20, NIVUK). The key point we can take from Luke's description of the intellectual class of Athenian is not a criticism of talking and listening, which is an essential component of exploring issues, but of its casualness regarding the discovery of truth—God's truth.

Towards the end of Paul's life, while he languished in prison, Paul wrote to young Timothy and warned him of those who were always ready to align with the latest fad or ideology, however erroneous it might be, describing such malleable people as being those with 'itching ears': 'For a time is coming when people will no longer listen to sound and wholesome teaching. They will follow their own desires and will look for teachers who will tell them whatever their itching ears want to hear. They will reject the truth and chase after myths' (2

Timothy 4:3–4, NLT). It is not too farfetched to equate the situation that existed two thousand years ago with the present day where the latest obsession—be it in fashion, lifestyle, philosophy or speech—is seized upon as the 'new wisdom' to which all those who desire fulfilment must conform. Regrettably, sections of the Body of Christ (the church) sometimes get caught up in the mayhem, instead of relying on the enlightenment found in God's revealed word.

Despite the fact that no one reasons his or her way into the Kingdom of Heaven, it is clear that Paul, guided by the Holy Spirit, was able to use his intellect to convince some people to be accommodating of the Gospel message, though many others demurred. While the majority of his hearers appear to have been either sceptical or asked for more information about the 'new religion', as they referred to Paul's teaching, a small number became believers. From this modest beginning, it seems that Paul's preaching and teaching had a profound impact in the years that followed his visit, as the 'new religion' spread throughout the region.

While dedicated followers of Jesus today would be elated if large numbers of uncommitted folk became Christians as a result of their testimony and ministry, it is more likely that ones and twos will be convinced, who will influence others in turn. The angel's encouraging word to the Old Testament prophet Zechariah is pertinent: 'Do not despise these small beginnings, for the Lord rejoices to see the work begin' (4:10a, NLT). Our discouragement over apparent failure or minor successes should always be tempered by the revelation that the contribution made by the widow was commended by Jesus because it was given devotedly and not as a means of boosting her reputation or self-image (see Mark Chapter 12 and Luke Chapter 21). As Paul encouraged the Galatians: 'Let us not become weary in doing good, for at the proper time we will reap a harvest if we do not give up' (6:9, NIVUK).

Spirit-filled use of the mind

It is rightly claimed that whereas we need to discover the Word of God, it is more important to discover the God of the Word! The aim in searching the Scriptures is to know and understand more about God and His intentions for humankind, not simply for accumulating factual knowledge. We need to use our minds to study the Bible, access good quality teaching and interrogate key issues, but there is a significant difference between using our intellect to comprehend the purposes of God more fully, and merely assembling the information to widen our knowledge base. Spiritual growth is not acquired principally from academic study but from a willingness to be challenged and edified for Kingdom service by the Holy Spirit.

Insight

It is often claimed, with some justification, that people of high intellect are one of the more difficult societal groups to reach with the Gospel because they place greater value on enhancing their scholarship than on exercising faith. If intelligent men and women can be won for Christ, however, God can use their intellect to further His Kingdom work, as He did most notably through the Apostle Paul.

Historical figures of outstanding ability who were determined to use their abilities to serve God and needy people, are far too numerous to list exhaustively, but include exceptional achievers such as JS Bach (composer), Elizabeth Fry (prison reformer), William Wilberforce (politician), Michael Faraday (scientist), Francis van Alstyne (aka, Fanny Crosby: poet and hymn writer), Florence Nightingale (nursing), CS Lewis (author), Billy Graham (evangelist) and Mother Teresa of Calcutta. It has rightly been said that capable people have the skill to simplify complex matters, thereby making them easy to grasp, while less capable people manage to make simple things sound complicated. It is also true that high achievers invariably possess great determination and strength of character to forge ahead, despite meeting setbacks and disappointments. Nevertheless, it is worth reflecting on the fact that if people became followers of Jesus solely on the basis of academic ability and achievements, those of low intellect could never be saved. On the contrary, 'the teaching of your word gives light, so even the simple can understand' (Psalm 119:130, NLT).

In the Gospel accounts, there are numerous instances where crowds of 'common people' pursued Jesus and enthusiastically absorbed his message of love, hope and peace. There are also examples of very *able* people seeking and finding the truth in Jesus, including Luke the physician; Matthew the tax collector; Nicodemus the politician and member of the Jewish ruling council (the Sanhedrin); Joseph of Arimathea, a businessman and a member of the Sanhedrin; and various high-ranking military leaders (centurions). Whether Jesus's followers were from the 'working class' or the upper echelons of society, they recognised authenticity when they saw it, and they saw it shining out of Jesus.

Handling diversionary tactics

In discussing matters of eternal significance, there will always be people who are so enamoured with their own opinions that they are resistant to counter-arguments. In such cases, it may be a waste of time and effort to prolong the discussion in an attempt to persuade them about the truth of the Gospel, as in His eternal purposes, God can use different means to induce a response from them. Other people like to divert the conversation from the central issues—sin, God's holiness, the need for repentance, trusting Jesus for salvation—and set up what are colloquially referred to as 'straw men', by which they ask the Christian advocate to defend or explain or respond to an inaccurate or malicious assertion, as a means of enticing him or her to defend the skewed proposition and thereby sidestepping the main subject.

Matthew records a significant example of a diversionary technique when the religious leaders asked Jesus to explain how marriage would be settled in heaven if a man had married five times on earth. Jesus was soon able to expose his opponents' underhand scheme by explaining that there will not be marriage in heaven, so their original supposition was falsely based (i.e., a 'straw man'): 'You are completely wrong! You don't know what the Scriptures teach. And you don't know anything about the power of God. When God raises people to life, they won't marry. They will be like the angels in heaven' (22:29–30, CEV). Jesus's Spirit-filled response to the religious charlatans is the perfect example of how to deal with false assertions and establishes two important principles:

a) The need to be well versed in the Scriptures and the message they declare.
b) The need to be filled with the power of God when responding to spurious assertions or devious questions.

Both knowledge and Spirit-empowerment are necessary if we are to be adequately informed and spiritually perceptive to engage in a discussion about eternal matters and able to give appropriate answers to questions posed by people who may possess questionable motives.

Summary points in engaging with doubters and sceptics.

1. Make sure that you are wholeheartedly committed to Jesus, as he made it clear that those who are not for him are against him.
2. Bear in mind that accusations are from Satan. If someone accuses you, you can be certain of its source.
3. Be thoroughly familiar with your Bible, especially the New Testament.
4. Be ready to admit when you are not sure but find out and get back to the person with an answer.
5. Listen carefully to what the person is saying or alleging.
6. Keep a gentle smile on your face, stay polite, keep good eye contact and try not to be rattled if the person mocks or derides.
7. Avoid sounding smug but be firm about your beliefs.
8. Don't get drawn into a pointless argument about unimportant detail; instead, keep stating the essence of the Gospel: sin; the need for repentance; the efficacy of Christ's sacrifice; the transforming work of the Holy Spirit.
9. Pray for your enemies and those who oppose you. Don't hate or despise them or you will be doing the devil's work for him.
10. Gain courage from the fact that you are not alone. The Holy Spirit will operate through you, if you allow Him to do so. The battle belongs to the Lord.

Provocative questions

Some doubters change the direction of a conversation by introducing a highly challenging question, the most common of which is: "If God is a God of love, why does He allow suffering / little children to die / natural disasters to occur / abuse of women (and other tragic examples of human anguish)?" It is important on such occasions to remain prayerful and not to feel 'flustered' or intimidated by questions about imponderable mysteries that defy simple explanation. The obvious response is to state (correctly) that sin is the problem; in practice, the enquirer will simply respond: "So why did God allow sin to enter the world in the first place?"

In truth, some protagonists are unlikely to be persuaded by any explanation. 'There are none so blind as those who *will* not see' is a relevant quotation attributed to John Heywood, a 16th Century English writer, based on Jeremiah 5:21. Emphasising to them the need to trust God who will make things clear if they ask Him is nearly always the best approach, as it puts the onus back on the questioner. It is also helpful to add that God has promised that one day, all suffering, pain and distress will cease, as He renews heaven and earth. In particular, when witnessing to someone with genuine interest but serious doubts, it is certainly appropriate to encourage the person to ask God himself/herself and pledge that you will pray into the situation on his or her behalf.

Insight

When engaging with someone who is asking the question from a position of grief and confusion, it is essential to avoid responding in a way that might be construed as being dismissive, glib or unsympathetic. Showing compassion by listening and sympathising must always be given priority ahead of carefully crafted explanations or quoting Bible verses.

Challenging conversations and scepticism should act as a spur to spend more time prayerfully considering the Scriptures and asking God to reveal more of His will and purpose to us, such that we develop the 'wisdom of Solomon' and, as Paul explained, we are able to possess keen spiritual insight (I Corinthians 2:16). In all these matters, it is essential to remember that God can achieve far more through our weakness than we could ever do by using our own strength and endeavour. He can use our feeblest efforts to bring about His purposes. Just as a cracked water jar spills its contents when carried along the path but in doing so helps flowers to grow by the wayside, so our flawed attempts to glorify God in all we say and do will help to challenge and transform lives, regardless of our imperfections and stumbling efforts. See Chapter 12 for a list of challenging questions asked of Christians, and suggested responses.

Employing godly wisdom

It is understandable if some Christians are reluctant to discuss their faith with someone of superior intellect for fear they may struggle to respond adequately and thereby do more harm than good. The key principles to invoke when we are witnessing in *any* situation but especially when dealing with intellectually superior minds are fourfold:

1. Rely on the Holy Spirit to give us the words to speak.
2. Talk about the things we know and draw from our own experience of God at work in our lives.

3. Admit when we don't know the answer, as we can't know everything or we would be God! At the same time, agree to find out more about perplexing issues and later share the knowledge and insight with the person concerned.

4. Regardless of the person's attitude—smug, supercilious, engaging or sincere—continue to show the love of Christ and pray for his or her salvation. Sometimes, the most stubborn sceptic is the most vulnerable to the overwhelming power of the Spirit. It is the casual, vaguely disinterested scholarly person who provides the greatest challenge.

Although we may not have great intellect, God promises to give us *godly wisdom* that even a genius cannot possess—see, for instance, Paul's words on the subject (I Corinthians 1:26–31). Similarly, the early chapters in Proverbs provide a wealth of wisdom advice, including a key statement about its source: 'For the Lord gives wisdom; from his mouth come knowledge and understanding' (2:6, NIVUK). The Apostle James also emphasises the importance of divine wisdom: 'But the wisdom that comes from heaven is first of all pure; then peace-loving, considerate, submissive, full of mercy and good fruit, impartial and sincere. Peacemakers who sow in peace reap a harvest of righteousness' (3:17–18, NIVUK). Believers can be encouraged by the attributes of Holy Spirit wisdom that can be released into their lives: pure, peace-loving, considerate, submissive, merciful, bearing good fruit, impartial and sincere. No human intelligence, insight, perception or sagacity can compete with the wholesomeness and power of God's anointed wisdom.

Whatever the circumstances, we should only boast in the Lord (Jeremiah 9:24) and spiritually feed on Him through prayer, meditation on the Bible and worship. The most intellectual atheist or bombastic sceptic cannot overcome the humblest born again Christian if he or she has the insight and knowledge that comes from a life committed to the Saviour and filled with the indwelling power of the Holy Spirit. But even if we feel that we've been 'vanquished' after a discussion with someone possessing superior brainpower, our words, and especially our conduct and sincerity, will have left a lasting positive impression on the person concerned.

Beyond human intellect

I have highlighted the principle that no one can become a genuine disciple of Jesus based solely on embracing an intellectual argument. Even thoughtfully prepared, conviction-led preaching and testimony is not sufficient in itself to bring about repentance and convert a person. Nevertheless, while accepting that human effort will not in itself cause people to commit their lives to Christ, God the Holy Spirit uses both preaching and testimony to bring about belief and trust in Christ as Saviour. God has also graciously used unconventional means to reach groups of people who have never been exposed to established forms of evangelism or have resisted being persuaded. There are numerous well-attested examples of people turning to Christ after having dreams and visions, as well as through reading Spirit-empowered Christian literature.

It has often been pointed out that Jesus did not write a single book or, to the best of our knowledge, pay a scribe or use followers to faithfully record his spoken words (though the latter approach is likely). He did not acquire scholastic qualifications, study at the feet of a renowned teacher or seek to impress people with his superior knowledge. Despite all these apparent educational disadvantages, Jesus's comprehension of the Old Testament and its implications for living a godly life was unrivalled. For instance, as Jesus walked with two disciples on the journey from Jerusalem to Emmaus after his resurrection, Luke records that Jesus 'took them through the writings of Moses and all the prophets, explaining from all the Scriptures the things concerning himself' (24:27, NLT).

The sad fact that many people choose to ignore or reject Christ is testament to the fact that even though salvation comes through hearing and receiving the Gospel message, it is equally possible to reject or dismiss it as irrelevant or untrue. The Apostle Mark records the stark choice that Jesus sets before us: 'Anyone who believes and is baptised will be saved but anyone who refuses to believe will be condemned' (16:15, NLT). The inclusion of the word 'refuses' reveals that every mature person is faced with a choice to accept or reject what Jesus says. Refusal, however, has grim consequences; namely, carrying the burden of sin throughout life and facing an uncertain eternal destiny.

Jesus spelled out the situation with glorious candour: 'I tell you for certain that everyone who hears my message and has faith in the one who sent me has eternal life and will never be condemned. They have already gone from death to life' (John 5:24, CEV). It will be noted that Jesus refers to the fact that believers have 'already gone from death into life', which denotes that their eternal life begins here-and-now, thus confounding the suggestion that someone can subsequently lose his or her salvation, though sincerely held opinions differ on the matter.

The two most common explanations regarding people who once claimed to be followers of Jesus but subsequently rescinded their belief in him are: (a) They were never saved in the first place; (b) They are still saved but will forfeit their rewards in Heaven. Either way, the writer of Hebrews issues a stern warning about the folly of turning back: 'For it is impossible to bring back to repentance those who were once enlightened—those who have experienced the good things of heaven and shared in the Holy Spirit, who have tasted the goodness of the Word of God and the power of the age to come—and who then turn away from God. It is impossible to bring such people back to repentance. By rejecting the Son of God, they themselves are nailing him to the cross once again and holding him up to public shame.' (6:4–6, NLT). Serious words indeed!

Facts and feelings

Despite a tendency among intellectuals to dismiss the message of salvation in Christ, it is also the case that the present-day obsession with 'being offended' by someone's remark, opinion or stance on an issue has acted as an antidote to an objective presentation of the facts. The contrariness of dismissing verifiable truth in favour of a light touch approach to avoid injuring anyone's feelings has influenced the style and content of Gospel preaching, notably in moderating biblical teaching about what were once core issues about sinfulness, Heaven and Hell, satanic influences and eternal damnation. Speakers are increasingly cautious about preaching the full Gospel for fear of alarming and upsetting the hearers and inviting accusations of arrogance or inducing unnecessary alarm. Partly as a result of this tentativeness, aspects of teaching, scholarly debate and discussion about sensitive subjects have been largely avoided.

The revealed truth of the Bible may be dismissed by secularists as being too extreme if it generates inner conflict in people's minds. While deliberate attempts to cause offence will be rightly criticised, attempts to substitute the need for faith in Christ with a more palatable alternative, thereby avoiding the possibility of irritating listeners, inevitably leads to a diluting of the full Gospel message. Jesus is both a 'rock of offence' (Romans 9:33, KJV) over which people stumble and fall; or the 'rock of our salvation' (Psalm 89:26, KJV) upon which each person may boldly stand. Christians must never be afraid to proclaim the love of Christ, the need for having faith in him and the risks attached to rejecting his offer of eternal life, simply to ease consciences. Provoking interest in the truth of the Gospel, whatever the person's initial reaction, is the means by which the Holy Spirit convicts and saves.

Insight

While it is entirely appropriate not to avoid 'trampling on people's feelings' or causing intentional dismay, the integrity of Biblical truth about sin and salvation, and their implications for this life and beyond, must always be maintained.

Wholehearted Followers

Christ the Good Shepherd

There are countless numbers of people who recognise that their life is incomplete without believing in and trusting God the Father and demonstrating allegiance to His Saviour Son. These modern-day disciples are people who acknowledge that Jesus Christ is the way, the truth and the life, and the true light that came into the world to save sinners, both Jews and Gentiles (sometimes referred to as 'Greeks' in the Bible). Christians accept Jesus's words that they were like sheep that had gone astray and needed rescuing because they had wandered from the protection that comes from living close to God and were therefore vulnerable to attack from the destroyer of souls, Satan. Thus, Peter reminds his readers that 'you were like sheep going astray but have now returned to the Shepherd and Overseer of your souls' (1 Peter 2:25, NKJV).

King David first introduced the theme of God as Shepherd in his much quoted Psalm 23, *The Lord's my Shepherd*. In similar vein, Jesus is described as the *Good Shepherd*, who not only takes care of his sheep (followers, believers, disciples) in this life but also, through his sacrificial death on the Cross of Calvary, will usher them into eternal bliss in heaven at the end of time (see John Chapter 10 and descriptions earlier in this chapter).

Jesus also uses the illustration of himself as a shepherd when he speaks about the end of time when he will separate good people (sheep) and evil people (goats): 'But when the Son of Man comes in his glory and all the angels with him, then he [Jesus] will sit upon his glorious throne. All the nations [peoples] will be gathered in his presence and he will separate the people as a shepherd separates the sheep from the goats' (Matthew 25:31–32, NLT). Jesus's words are a stark reminder that trusting him as Saviour and committing our lives to serving God is an urgent matter if we are to avoid being identified as 'evil' (sinful) at the end of time rather than 'good' (free from sin, thanks to God's grace).

Life priorities

Born again believers, who accept that they were once lost in sin but have been 'found and rescued' by Christ, are not ashamed or embarrassed about confessing their faith in him and will do so openly (see under 'Sharing the Gospel' in Chapter 10). With the exception of those who, out of necessity, have to remain 'secret believers', they do not try to conceal their love for Jesus, linger on the margins of church life or hesitate to witness when the opportunity arises. On the contrary, they remain in close touch with God through every situation, trusting that He is faithful, regardless of whether circumstances are encouraging or bleak.

By God's grace and through submission to the direction of the indwelling Spirit, wholehearted followers of Jesus seek to identify with Paul's description of Christian priorities and lifestyle in his letter to the Colossians, Chapter 1, that they should:

- Please God in every way.
- Live purposefully.
- Show great endurance and patience.
- Share with Christians in need.
- Behave transparently (i.e., not shrouding areas of their lives).

By deliberately endeavouring to fulfil these aims, Christians become integrally bound into the fabric of God's eternal kingdom; they are redeemed and forgiven with hope for the present and certainty about the future. Such a positive, faith-motivated attitude contrasts sharply with the depressing condition of being without Christ in life or in offering mere assent to his teaching while showing little evidence of his transforming power.

Centrality of the Bible

The first disciples of Jesus were largely reliant on the Scriptures ('sacred writings') compiled prior to Jesus's coming to earth (i.e., the Old Testament). Jesus referred to those Scriptures on numerous occasions, both to underline his teaching and to combat erroneous claims by his opponents, including many of the Jewish religious leaders. After Jesus's resurrection and the special anointing of the Holy Spirit on their lives at Pentecost, the Apostles were the conduit for further revelation that focused on the person, work and status of Jesus and the ramifications for Christian life and witness in the context of both the local and worldwide church, as it would eventually become.

Today, Christians believe that God speaks through the recorded truth of Scripture, which collectively is referred to as 'The Word of God' or 'God's Word', an appellation ascribed to Jesus himself (John 1:14). Born again Christians are able to discern meaning in the Bible for life and conduct, as they rely on the Holy Spirit who will, as Jesus promised, show us all things that we need to know and understand in a way that is denied to those who treat Bible truth casually. The words of the psalmist that 'your word is a lamp to my feet and a light to my path' (119:105, NKJV) are frequently quoted as a fundamental declaration and promise to assist believers in life's journey.

Committed followers of Jesus Christ rely heavily on the truth of the Bible to inform, guide and shape their decisions about life's priorities, the correct course of action to take, and the way to handle problematic situations. They do not view the Bible as merely a superior reference book but one whose accuracy, pronouncements and teaching are inspired by God. The forty or more contributors to the complete Bible text were working independently, yet were all guided by the Holy Spirit to pen the words that faithfully express both the factual details of events that took place *and* their implications for living as God intends.

The Bible is not one 'religious' book among many others but stands alone as the wellspring for understanding God's involvement with the world: His priorities, promises, commandments and the necessity of obedience, as we discern right from wrong behaviour. Thus, in Paul's second letter to Timothy, he declares the supreme authority and empowering of Scripture: 'All Scripture is given by God. And all Scripture is useful for teaching and for showing people what is wrong in their lives. It is useful for correcting faults and teaching the right way to live. Using the Scriptures, those who serve God will be prepared and will have everything they need to do every good work' (3:16–17, ERV).

There are six elements to Paul's statement: (1) Scripture is from God. (2) It deals with truth. (3) It highlights wrongdoing. (4) It corrects us when we sin. (5) It teaches us what is right. (6) It prepares and equips us to do every good work. The authority invested in this divinely authored book deserves—indeed, *demands*—that we take its contents seriously and allow the Holy Spirit to breathe new life and fresh understanding through its words, including correction and rebuke where it is needed. Having said all of the above, it is essential that all Christians should reflect on how carefully and frequently they read the Bible, the extent to which they meditate on its message, and how they put the instructions and guidance into practice.

Insight

There are other useful sources of wisdom and insight apart from the Bible, found through inspired poetry, sagacious writings and memorable statements; but they must all align and reinforce the words of Scripture and never contradict them.

Essential work of the Spirit

Believers who acknowledge that although they were once lost in sin, they have now been redeemed by Christ, can express their commitment using the words of Simon Peter: 'Lord, to whom else shall we go? You have the words of eternal life. We believe and know that you are the Holy One of God' (John 6:68, NLT). They joyfully echo the words of Henry Francis Light's hymn that they are 'ransomed, healed, restored, forgiven' with the security of knowing that the Spirit of Christ will never leave or forsake them, and the promise of eternal life stretching ahead of them when their time on earth comes to an end.

Unwavering trust in God and faith that nothing is impossible for Him characterise true believers, who are also convinced that without His Spirit working in and through them, they cannot hope to live in a way that pleases Him or ultimately receive high reward in heaven. Jesus's words recorded by John should act as an incentive for every Christian: 'Look, I am coming soon, bringing my reward with me to repay all people according to their deeds. I am the Alpha and the Omega, the First and the Last, the Beginning and the End' (Revelation 22:12–13, NLT). Jesus's words in which he highlights the importance of 'deeds' in the salvation story should not be neglected. Equally wonderful is the astonishing promise that born again Christians are children of God and heirs of the Kingdom, as Paul describes: 'The Spirit Himself bears witness with our spirit that we are children of God and if children, then heirs—heirs of God and joint heirs with Christ, if indeed we suffer with Him, that we may also be glorified together' (Romans 8:16–17, NKJV).

Insight
The challenge for every redeemed person is consenting to be 'emptied of self' and filled with the Spirit in order to serve steadfastly, knowing that any hardship we experience, other than through our own foolishness, is experienced in partnership with the Lord of Eternity. What a privilege!

In his letter to the churches in Galatia, Paul contrasts the Holy Spirit's guidance with that of the sinful nature: 'For the flesh desires what is contrary to the Spirit, and the Spirit what is contrary to the flesh. They are in conflict with each other, so that you are not to do whatever you want' (5:17, NIVUK). All Christians are faced with the choice of whether to follow worldly desires that lead to emptiness and ineffectiveness; or those that result in godly fruit. As we assimilate the Spirit's characteristics into our words and actions, they become so firmly embedded in our minds that we hardly find it necessary to pray about everyday matters, as we are naturally moving 'in the Spirit's flow' and know instinctively if a decision aligns with His will.

In his advice to Christians in Ephesus, Paul warns them against being filled with wine—representing a feckless lifestyle—but rather to be filled with the Spirit: 'Singing psalms and hymns and spiritual songs among yourselves, and making music to the Lord in your hearts' (5:19). The enticements offered in a sin-wracked world have considerable appeal; but like the mythical tale of King Midas, though everything we touch may appear to 'turn to gold', the result is spiritual malnourishment and desolation.

Being filled with the Spirit is not a blessing confined to the New Testament era. We find a number of examples in the Old Testament that took place in different situations and circumstances. For example, the Pharaoh of Egypt said of Joseph: 'Can we find anyone else like this man so obviously filled with the

Spirit of God?' (Genesis 41:38, NLT). God spoke of Bezalel in Exodus 31:3: 'I have filled him with the Spirit of God, giving him great wisdom, ability and expertise in all kinds of crafts'. Note that the Spirit also empowers people for practical tasks. The prophet Micah uttered these words before condemning the behaviour of Israel's leaders: 'But as for me, I am filled with power, with the Spirit of the Lord' (3:8a, NIVUK).

A key difference between being Spirit-filled before and after the post-resurrection Pentecost (described in Acts Chapter 1) is that Old Testament filling was most often to empower an individual to fulfil a specific purpose and therefore time-limited for completion of the task. By contrast, empowerment of believers from the first Pentecost onwards is continuous, as the Spirit resides within to transform and permeate every aspect of thought, word and deed. Even so, God does not force any Christian to pursue a particular pathway; the choice always lies with the individual.

Jesus's disciples throughout the ages are charged with ensuring that they give God the glory at every point in their lives, especially when they succeed or are commended by others for their abilities or accomplishments. They gear their priorities and decisions to reflect what they believe to be God's will and purpose, viewing themselves as 'junior partners' with Christ in making His Kingdom's glory and righteousness the priority, as Jesus explained: 'Seek the Kingdom of God above all else and live righteously and he will give you everything you need' (Matthew 6:33, NLT). Such a mighty promise!

Surrendering all to Jesus

At the end of World War 2, the defeated enemy tried to strike a deal with the victorious allies such that surrender would be conditional upon allowing some negotiation to be agreed between the parties. The outcome of such an arrangement would be that a degree of compromise could be incorporated into the final settlement. The Allied commanders and politicians rejected the proposition, as they were not prepared to accept anything less than total surrender. The enemy would be completely subservient to the victors, who would not give them any guarantees about the future. It is not difficult to see something of a parallel in the life and sacrifice of Jesus, as he unconditionally surrendered to the Father's will and did not attempt to deviate from the agreed plan of salvation, despite the ominous prospect of death upon a cross. Jesus provides every Christian with the perfect role model of unquestioning obedience and trust in Father God.

In every area of life, there are those who are so determined to achieve success or personal gain that they are willing to compromise deeply held convictions and commit themselves to pursuing ungodly ends. Such determination may be directed towards wicked and selfish purposes, as Judas Iscariot demonstrated in betraying Jesus for financial gain. There are also many morally responsible people who are willing to sacrifice time, money, ambition or status to achieve laudable outcomes, to fulfil an ambition or satisfy a deeply held need. For followers of Jesus, the level of commitment is measured in terms of obedience and the extent of dedicated service to Christ and to our 'neighbours'—those we are in a position to influence and bless.

Although many Christians sing heartily about giving everything to Jesus, the stubborn reality is that many believers may be reluctant to face the price that such absolute allegiance involves. In sharp contrast to such timidity, Paul in his second letter to Timothy refers to himself as 'being poured out like a drink offering' (4:6, NIVUK) as he faced his imminent death. Absolute surrender to the plan and purpose of God is unlikely to result in physical suffering or death for most of us but always involves crucifying 'self' by allowing God to rule in our lives.

When the Old Testament prophet, Jeremiah, proclaimed God's grievous message—'For my people have done two evil things: they have abandoned me, the fountain of living water, and they have dug for themselves cracked cisterns that can hold no water at all' (2:13, NLT)—he was referring to Israel as a nation and not to individual inadequacy, though the seriousness of personal half-heartedness should not be underestimated. Every believer should be concerned about Jesus's warning to the church in Laodicea regarding the unhappy state of being lukewarm (Revelation 3:15–16).

In addition, the physician Luke records Jesus's words of warning about superficial devotion: 'So then, you cannot be my disciple unless you give away everything you own' (14:33, CEV) that represent a significant challenge for his followers in understanding the meaning of 'everything'. Jesus is not, of course, suggesting that his followers should cast aside all hopes, dreams, ambitions and possessions; but rather that all these things should be brought under the Lordship of Christ. Our reticence to allow God to use us in whatever way He chooses by placing our lives totally under His command does not mean that God cannot use 'imperfect vessels' but that our effectiveness is reduced if we fail to allow Him access into every area of our lives or insist on dedicating ourselves to any venture or ambition that detracts us from being obedient to His will. We are citizens of Heaven; the privilege and responsibility it carries should always be at the forefront of our thinking.

Every Christian is therefore faced with a serious decision about his or her determination to be a wholehearted follower of Jesus Christ. We can stay comfortably 'out of the firing line' and coast along gently through life without embracing the challenging claims of Christ; or we can yield through faithful service and glad obedience. If we choose the latter course, we have decided that Jesus's willingness to sacrifice himself for us when we were undeserving sinners demands a reciprocal response, expressed through walking in step with the Spirit, seeking His will constantly, placing ourselves fully and unconditionally under His control, and finding delight in living and labouring for the Master throughout our lives. See also Chapter 12 for an exploration of the significance and implications of going 'deeper with Jesus'.

Practical consequences

In making our decisions about how we live and determine our priorities, we should take heed of the fact that there are examples in Scripture where being careless about the will and purpose of God or seeking solutions outside His immediate control or imagining that we can make decisions without reference to Him had disastrous consequences. Notable examples include Samson (Judges 16) and King Saul (I Samuel 15); both were left in a hopeless and ultimately tragic condition because God the Holy Spirit withdrew His anointing from their lives. Samson died after being crushed under the pillars of a temple. Saul died in battle after being badly wounded and then committing suicide.

Wholehearted followers of Jesus acknowledge that their lives are imperfect but confess their sins and repent of wrong attitudes and inappropriate actions (1 John 1:9). They are slow to judge or become angry, yet fervently resist ungodly influences and deceptive narratives from those who seek to corrupt the truth and impose their own distorted interpretations of moral priorities. Steadfast followers of Jesus opt to stand resolutely behind the legitimacy of Jesus's ministry and the Apostles' teaching, rather than remaining passive or compliant when antichrists seek to undermine the veracity of the Gospel message.

It is regrettable that followers of Jesus Christ are also prone to respond to challenging situations or frightening developments in a similar fashion to non-Christians by allowing fear to dominate their thoughts and verbally expressing doubt or consternation, instead of demonstrating the quiet assurance that comes through a close daily walk with the Lord and confidence in his everlasting love for them.

Insight

Believers must respond to a fundamental question: Are we worriers (doubting God) or warriors (trusting God)? Is our first reaction to a challenging situation one of alarmed apprehension concerning the outcome or confidence in God's ability to carry us through the crisis?

The Body of Christ

Wholehearted followers of Jesus are part of the 'Body of Christ', that is, the fellowship of believers. Paul explains the position in his letter to Christians in Rome, stressing the interdependence of each believer: 'Just as our bodies have many parts and each part has a special function, so it is with Christ's body. We are many parts of one body, and we all belong to each other' (12:4–5, NLT).

Members of the Body are privileged to make a specific contribution to Kingdom work that will bless, encourage and build up other believers in their most holy faith and also attract non-believers to acknowledge their need of salvation. Believers are constituents in a local and worldwide body, who possess different gifts to be used for God's glory and not for personal gain, as Paul explains in his first letter to the Corinthians: 'All of you together are Christ's body, and each of you is a part of it. Here are some of the parts God has appointed for the church: First are apostles, second are prophets, third are teachers then those who do miracles, those who have the gift of healing, those who can help others, those who have the gift of leadership and those who speak in unknown languages' (12:28, NLT).

Not every believer will be gifted in leadership or the employment of supernatural capability, though it must be acknowledged that Paul refers to these gifts as an essential contribution to the effectiveness of church ministry. While it is unlikely that a single fellowship (especially a small one) will produce apostles, prophets, teachers, miracle-workers and healers, it may be anticipated that the ministry of helping others, leadership skills and speaking in unknown languages—often referred to as 'speaking in tongues'—will be more commonly evident. It is worth reflecting on the possibility that the absence of the more profound gifts may help to explain why a church or confederacy of churches lacks effectiveness. In his letter to Christians in Rome, Chapter 12, Paul also explores the importance of using whatever gifts we possess unstintingly, including the more standard but essential endowments: serving, encouraging, and giving time and practical care.

It should be noted that God may want to *create* a particular gift in us or, more likely, He will enhance our existing gifts. Either way, in the words of C. F. Alexander's well-known hymn: 'All good gifts around us are sent from heaven above', acknowledging that each gift that is graciously bestowed on us has a divine origin. The Apostle Paul underlines this truth: 'It is the one and only Spirit who distributes all these gifts. He alone decides which gift each person should have' (I Corinthians 12:11, NLT). God not only wishes to enhance the innate qualities and virtues that we possess but by the work of His Spirit, grant fresh abilities to enhance Kingdom work.

Whatever God determines for our lives and whatever He chooses—in fact, *delights*—to bless and sanctify, He first requires that we 'empty ourselves' by fully submitting to His will and purpose, such that He can empower us with the virtues of His Son. Faithful disciples need to recognise that whether they are given many spiritual gifts and talents or few, their lives must radiate the love of Christ to one another and to the world. Genuine love is the key to every aspect of Kingdom advancement and blessing.

Sadly, there are schisms and divisions between denominations, and sometimes within a church, though these often relate to procedural preferences or minor points of doctrine, rather than matters of great substance. Even so, Paul did not mince his words in condemning disagreements in the Corinthian Church that had escalated to a point that the disputes were being resolved in secular courts instead of being settled amicably within the fellowship (see 1 Corinthians Chapter 6). Followers of Christ have more than enough trouble dealing with attacks from worldly opponents, let alone giving Satan opportunity to create internal conflict! It is essential for all believers to acknowledge before God whether by their attitude, comments and actions, they contribute to unity and harmony in the church or foster discord and unease.

Standing firm

Those who know that they were once lost ('dead in sin') and have been redeemed through the blood of Christ ('found and made alive') are willing and eager to share their testimony of God's saving grace but endeavour to do so sensitively and unpretentiously to avoid sounding arrogant. When false accusations arise or opponents of the Gospel ridicule and mock, true followers of Jesus refuse to compromise the Gospel message; instead, they rejoice that they have been chosen to endure suffering and prejudice for Christ's sake, as Jesus explained: 'God will bless you when people insult you, mistreat you, and tell all kinds of evil lies about you because of me' (Matthew 5:11, NIVUK). Mockery is hurtful and demoralising, but those so afflicted may be encouraged in three ways:

1. As Jesus reminded his disciples, the earlier prophets—those who had unshakeable faith in God and boldly proclaimed His word—have always suffered persecution.
2. Jesus promises great blessing if we stand resolutely in defending and proclaiming the Gospel.
3. Those who oppose Christians are unwittingly being used as Satan's agents and therefore to be pitied, as well as resisted. Indeed, Jesus referred to religious leaders who scorned his message as being children of the devil: 'You belong to your father, the devil, and you want to carry out your father's desires. He was a murderer from the beginning, not holding to the truth, for there is no truth in him. When he lies, he speaks his native language, for he is a liar and the father of lies' (John 8:44, NIVUK). Jesus's words should help every Christian to understand the formidable nature of the enemy: a murderer, lacking truth and the father of lies. But Christ has won the victory!

To confound the attacks of those who mock, obstruct and oppose the Gospel message, all Christians should have Paul's words to the Christians at Philippi at the forefront of their thinking, words and actions: 'For I can do everything through Christ, who gives me strength' (4:13, NLT). The phrase '*everything* through Christ' should not be confused with '*anything* through Christ': the former referring to being obedient to his commands and finding fulfilment in the areas of service to which we are called; the latter falsely implying that we can and will flourish in every area of life, regardless of our calling. The strength to which Paul refers resides in our confident hope and trust in Jesus, the rock of our salvation.

It is inevitable that the level and seriousness of commitment varies considerably across and within different churches and, notably, in different areas of the world. The sacrifice required to be a wholehearted faithful disciple of Jesus Christ in lands where persecution is severe is markedly different from the situation in relatively 'liberal' countries where discipleship is largely unhindered. The faith of many believers in the Developing 'Majority' World contrasts starkly with the intellectualism and scepticism that seems to have penetrated every section of society elsewhere. A dark cloud on the horizon for Western Christians is the rise of ungodly organisations that are threatening the proclamation of the Gospel, principally by using new 'offence' laws to curb evangelism. See Chapters 9 and 10.

A glorious hope

As I have emphasised throughout the book, the Bible makes it abundantly clear that without trusting Jesus Christ as Saviour, people are in serious danger of being eternally separated from God. By contrast, salvation is ensured as we exercise faith in the atoning death of Jesus and the transforming power of the indwelling Spirit. Paul reassures believers that in the process of being empowered with inner strength through his Spirit, Christ makes his home in our hearts (Ephesians 3:17). A small percentage of Jesus's present-day followers are called to sacrifice their home comforts and serve him in foreign or inhospitable places, thereby denying themselves the benefits and privileges of familiar settings, close family ties and a regular income. In an even smaller number of cases, committed disciples of Jesus lay down their lives in his service, either through succumbing to disease and ill-health when living in an alien environment or from physical assault by enemies of the Gospel ('martyrdom'). It is often claimed that Stephen was the first Christian martyr, though it is probably more accurate to say that his death was the first *recorded* event of its kind. See the full account of Stephen's courageous testimony, mock trial and gruesome execution in Acts Chapters 6 and 7.

Alongside these rare and outstanding sacrifices, every true believer is called to forgo self and gladly embrace the will and purpose of God for their sanctification and the benefit of other people, as John explained in his first letter: 'By this we know love, because He laid down His life for us. And we also ought to lay down our lives for the brethren' (3:16, NKJV). Submitting to God is not to be thought of as something heroic or in the hope of heavenly reward, but in acknowledgement of what Jesus accomplished at Calvary in freely giving his life for the sins of the world.

Paul encourages believers to look beyond this world to the glory that awaits them: 'It is the same way with the resurrection of the dead. Our earthly bodies are planted in the ground when we die but they will be raised to live forever. Our bodies are buried in brokenness but they will be raised in glory. They are buried in weakness but they will be raised in strength. They are buried as natural human bodies but they will be raised as spiritual bodies. For just as there are natural bodies, there are also spiritual bodies' (I Corinthians 15:42–44, NLT). Every Christian can rejoice in the unshakeable truth that Jesus has promised to prepare a place in glory for each of us! Although death, whether through age, violence, accident or disease is always sad for those who remain, it opens the prospect of Heaven and an eternal home with Christ for the believer, which will joyously exceed anything experienced in this life.

Summary

In this chapter, I have described different types of Christian commitment, ranging from those who are tentative in their faith and prefer to remain inconspicuous, to those who are more intellectually driven than faith-inspired, to those who are wholehearted followers of Jesus. Within each of these broad descriptions, the sobering truth is that even the most dedicated Christian has times when faith wavers and love for Christ becomes tenuous. There are occasions that we choose to remain 'invisible' when we should be standing boldly for truth and righteousness; and there are times when we use rational arguments to persuade ourselves that God didn't really tell us to do something or guide us in a particular direction. Thankfully, the more we yield to God and allow Him to work in us and through us, the greater wisdom we accrue to live our lives as He desires. How wonderful to know that although we are often weak, self-serving and 'prone to wander', God is unchanging and Christ, the Great Shepherd of the sheep, leaves the ninety-nine to search for us and bring us home with much rejoicing.

How true are these statements of you?

1. I am happy to declare that I am a follower of Jesus.
2. I enjoy an intimate relationship with God.
3. I gladly use my gifts and abilities to support Kingdom work.
4. I endeavour to seek first the Kingdom of God and His righteousness.
5. I am sufficiently well informed to discuss spiritual matters with an enquirer.
6. I stand firm for the truth revealed in the Bible, even when I am mocked or ridiculed.
7. I view opposition and persecution positively.
8. I am fully surrendered to the will and purpose of God.

Part 5

Responding to the Challenge

Luke 9: 57–62

As they were walking along the road, a man said to him, 'I will follow you wherever you go.' Jesus replied, 'Foxes have dens and birds have nests, but the Son of Man has nowhere to lay his head.'

He said to another man, 'Follow me.'

But he replied, 'Lord, first let me go and bury my father.'

Jesus said to him, 'Let the dead bury their own dead, but you go and proclaim the Kingdom of God.'

Still another said, 'I will follow you, Lord; but first let me go back and say goodbye to my family.'

Jesus replied, 'No one who puts a hand to the plough and looks back is fit for service in the Kingdom of God' (NIVUK).

2 Corinthians 12: 8–10

But I must not be too proud of the wonderful things that were shown to me. So a painful problem ['thorn in the flesh'] was given to me—an angel from Satan, sent to make me suffer, so that I would not think that I am better than anyone else. I begged the Lord three times to take this problem away from me. But the Lord said, "My grace is all you need. Only when you are weak can everything be done completely by my power." So I will gladly boast about my weaknesses. Then Christ's power can stay in me. Yes, I am glad to have weaknesses if they are for Christ. I am glad to be insulted and have hard times. I am glad when I am persecuted and have problems, because it is when I am weak that I am really strong (ERV).

Preface to Part 5

In the previous two chapters, I have tried to paint an authentic and accurate picture of the benefits and challenges that discipleship provides, and the different levels of commitment characterising people who declare themselves to be Jesus's followers. I have also described and identified common features of those who choose not to accept the claims of Christ upon their lives, citing their objections and specifying their accusations. Similarly, I have analysed the attitude, disposition and actions of people who, though accepting that Christ is the Saviour, fight shy of declaring their allegiance to him publicly.

I have also endeavoured to show that even in the same country, region or church, the level of commitment to Jesus—not to a religion, a cause or a social imperative—amongst those who define themselves as being Christian, varies considerably, based on the prevailing circumstances, such as family pressure, the opinions of close friends and the lure of worldly pursuits. There are a small number of followers who, in the midst of personal crises, opposition or wavering faith, have forsaken their first love and backslidden, a state defined by John as 'a craving for physical pleasure, a craving for everything we see, and pride in our achievements and possessions' (I John 2:16, NLT). All these distractions are likely to come about when we falter in our love for Christ and our confidence in his revealed word.

In highlighting what each follower of Jesus is willing to 'lay down at his feet', I have frequently drawn attention to the many Christians in numerous areas of the world who, as a result of their expressed Christian faith, have been persecuted, intimidated and maligned. In the following two chapters, I will explore the theme of personal commitment to Christ more fully. The emphasis in Chapter 9 is on faith in action. Chapter 10 describes the practicalities involved in sharing the Gospel. Although the challenges of presenting the truth of the Gospel are considerable in a world that cherishes personal freedom of expression and is resistant to submission to a Higher Power, the God of the universe is able to accomplish more than we could ever ask or think. Just as Jesus 'emptied himself of all but love', the challenge for his followers is to do the same.

Chapter 9
Faith in Action

Introduction

Earlier in the book, I underlined the fact that the challenges faced by committed Christians in Western nations pale into insignificance, when compared with the hardships that the believers in different areas of the world experience. The opposition that they endure takes a variety of forms, including restrictions on evangelism, government agents monitoring their movements, censoring of resources and electronic communications, fining leaders for holding home meetings and the closure or destruction of churches. Some Christians have to combat false accusations of blasphemy brought by adherents to the majority religion that lead to blatant judicial injustice. Even if the accused person is found to be innocent and released, violent protests often follow, resulting in severe damage to property and injury to or murder of the unfortunate victim.

Particularly in more rural areas, believers have been ejected from their homes and denied basic resources by local activists or officials. A considerable number of adherents, pastors and church leaders have been attacked, imprisoned and even assassinated for refusing to compromise their beliefs or recant their faith in Christ. These facts are well established but rarely publicised; it seems that as far as the media is concerned, outrage is reserved for far less weighty but more sensational causes!

The challenge is therefore placed squarely before Christians in less volatile situations to examine the way in which their willingness to follow and serve Christ sacrificially compares with believers in inhospitable and dangerous parts of the world. The starting point for every follower of Jesus Christ is to evaluate the way in which he or she prioritises decisions, makes choices and is open to the Spirit's leading.

In the present Chapter, I explore some of the possible sacrifices, as well as wonderful blessings—peace, assurance, calmness of soul, hope for the future, fellowship with believers—that may be faced and embraced by faithful followers of Jesus.

Expressions of Faith

It has rightly been asserted that nothing worthwhile is achieved in life without sacrifice. The effort expended in attaining a goal has to be combined with determination and a strong sense of motivation, often to the detriment of all other desires, hopes and aspirations. History shows that the single-minded and resolute pursuing of an outcome (such as building a business empire) is often combined with being in 'the right place at the right time', which has led to a fateful reliance on 'good luck' and chance rather than acknowledging the Lord's blessing and favour.

On a more positive note, sacrificial striving often leads to inventions and new ways of working that benefit the wider population, as talented and creative people use their skills, expertise and ideas for the general good, as well as increasing their personal wealth and prestige. We have all benefitted from the endeavours of entrepreneurs, whose discoveries have greatly improved our quality of life. The majority of people in the world flick a switch, turn a tap, drive a vehicle, and use medication, with little or no thought to the years of struggle and self-sacrifice that led to these advances. Unfortunately, history is also rife with people who used their creative powers and skills to pursue immoral goals that resulted in corruption and wickedness, as they abused their abilities and powers for selfish purposes and the acquisition of power.

Godly faith

Matthew compiled a number of instances in his Gospel account in which Jesus commended an individual's depth of faith when healing people: a paralysed man; the daughter of a synagogue leader; a socially ostracised, desperate woman suffering from continuous bleeding, whom Jesus referred to as 'daughter'; two blind men; and a demon-possessed man (Matthew Chapter 9). In both the healing of a centurion's servant (Matthew 8:5–13) and the Canaanite woman's daughter (Matthew 15:21–8), the centurion and the woman were praised by Jesus for their great faith. In particular, Jesus was astonished with the soldier's absolute trust in his ability to heal the servant and declared that he had never found anyone with such great faith in the whole of Israel. It should be noted that neither of the central characters in these episodes were Jewish—the one was a local Gentile woman of humble origin; the other was a Gentile foreigner of high position. We can take comfort in the fact that God's grace extends to everyone who fully places his or her trust in him, regardless of race, background or status.

By contrast, when the disciples were unable to drive out demons from a boy suffering from epilepsy and they asked Jesus to explain the reasons for their failure, Jesus replied that they needed to exercise great faith to achieve a miraculous outcome (Matthew 17:14–21). From a rational point of view, it is reasonable to insist that casting out demons in full public view requires a considerable amount of faith. Yet Jesus went on to say that only a tiny seed of faith is necessary to achieve remarkable results (verse 20). So on the one hand, Jesus rebuked the disciples for their little faith (see also Matthew 8:26, 14:31) but also stressed that a tiny amount of faith could 'move mountains'. How are we to understand this seeming contradiction?

The apparent mismatch between Jesus's two comments is explained by the fact that faith is a *gift from God* for everyone to receive but also requires a reciprocal 'faith response' from each person. Paul refers to Abraham's life of obedience through his belief in God as the One who resurrects the dead and creates new things out of nothing: 'So the promise is received by faith. It is given as a free gift' (Romans 4:16, NLT). No one is able to exercise faith until God provides it through the Son. In the way that salvation is universally available but must be responded to individually, so the faith that God supplies must be personally implemented. Faith from God is an immense reservoir available for each believer to draw from endlessly. In highly challenging situations, it is necessary to use a full reservoir of God's 'faith water' to resolve or withstand the circumstances. On other occasions, only a cupful of the faith water is needed to bring about a supernatural outcome in the will and purpose of God.

When Jesus scolded the disciples for their weak faith, he was indicating that they were only exercising a small amount of faith (using a 'cupful') when a reservoir of water was necessary; the disciples were therefore guilty of having 'little (insufficient) faith'. By contrast, when a smaller amount of faith is required, even a cupful ('tiny seed') can achieve great things for God ('moving mountains'). The context for employing faith determines the quantity needed, always remembering that it is God's faith at work through us and not the other way around. In other words, it is not the case of Christians gritting their teeth to summon up faith but rather of allowing God to exercise His faith through them and believers responding by trusting Him to do His work. Faith and trust are contiguous terms, so whatever the situation or circumstances, we can have every confidence in our Heavenly Father and trust Him to provide the faith that we need.

Insight

Allowing the Holy Spirit to have His way, while at the same time exercising our freewill, should be the aspiration of every believer. Christians need to believe that God will endue them with sufficient faith for the task; they then reciprocate by trusting Him to work through them for His glory and their encouragement.

Faith as a weapon

Faith in God and in His Son, Jesus Christ, is an indispensable weapon in the battle against the forces of evil. An illuminating example from the Old Testament involved a wise man called Hanani, who spoke these inspired words to the Judean king, Asa, when the country was being besieged: 'The eyes of the Lord range throughout the earth to strengthen those whose hearts are fully committed to him' (2 Chronicles 16:9, NIVUK). It should be noted that Hanani then angered the King by telling him that he (Asa) had been a fool to rely on godless nations for protection instead of trusting in the Lord. Hanani courageously demonstrated his own confidence in God, while exposing the King's lack of it. Subsequently, the King punished Hanani by throwing him into prison and putting him in stocks (a form of torture). The principle to extract from this regrettable event is that receiving the Lord's strength to carry out a difficult assignment does not automatically protect us from suffering. We can be sure, however, that a great reward for obedience awaits us in Heaven.

Believers who take God's promises seriously are in a position to provide solace to anxious or oppressed people and encourage them to stand firm during times of trial. For example, Moses spoke these words to the Israelites when the Egyptians were pursuing them: 'Don't be afraid! Don't run away! Stand where you are and watch the Lord save you today. You will never see these Egyptians again. You will not have to do anything but stay calm. The Lord will do the fighting for you' (Exodus 14:13–14, ERV). Moses' implicit trust in the Lord led to a divinely inspired prophetic statement that gave hope and courage to the (understandably) frightened people. True faith is always linked with actions, not vague aspirations. For compelling evidence of this assertion, see next section under 'Champions of faith'.

Being bonded to Christ and remaining steadfast through faith in him help us to fight determinedly against the forces of evil, as the Apostle Paul wrote in his first letter to Timothy: 'Timothy, my son, here are my instructions for you, based on the prophetic words spoken about you earlier. May they help you fight well in the Lord's battles. Cling to your faith in Christ and keep your conscience clear' (1:18–19a, NLT). While in no way trivialising the suffering of persecuted believers, the knowledge that God strengthens, rescues and fights for them is a great consolation and a source of inner strength. There are always casualties in battle but whatever the personal cost may be, we can claim the final victory in Christ.

Faith is not only needed in declaring the Gospel and resisting the demonic powers that seek to undermine and destroy faithful testimony. Paul also encourages Christians in Ephesus by stressing the positive benefits of faith in granting spiritual illumination and focusing on the wonderful heritage awaiting believers: 'I pray that the eyes of your heart may be enlightened in order that you may know the hope to which he has called you, the riches of his glorious inheritance in his holy people' (1:18, NLT). It may be noted that every benefit is located in Jesus, thus: '*his* glorious inheritance' and '*his* holy people'.

Faith is not about fighting a rear-guard action but in employing the words of John Monsell's famous hymn, fighting the good fight with all our might, confident that Christ is our strength and Christ our right. As Paul explains to the Colossians, there is a wonderful mystery concerning 'Christ in you, the hope of glory. He is the one we proclaim, admonishing and teaching everyone with all wisdom, so that we may present everyone fully mature in Christ' (1:27–8, NIVUK). Paul makes it clear that we not only use our faith to address our own decisions and issues but in order to bless and mature others.

Champions of faith

Faith in God is a theme that runs throughout the Bible and is reflected in the lives of his followers. Christian pioneers working in foreign lands rightly attribute their successful ministry to the security of having faith in God and the power of the Spirit working through them, as they gladly yield to His will and purpose. The writer of Hebrews also stresses that faith is closely associated with an individual's character: 'Faith shows the reality of what we hope for; it is the evidence of things we cannot see. Through their faith, the people in days of old earned a good reputation' (11:1–2, NLT). Influencing the indigenous population for Christ in a different culture demands the mission worker's absolute integrity and faultless character if he or she is to impress and persuade people to pay serious attention to the Gospel message. The principle holds true, of course, wherever Christ is proclaimed.

The writer of Hebrews further explains that it is by faith that we understand God's creative work. Thus, Enoch pleased God because of his faith. Through faith, Noah obeyed God and built a boat to escape the flood when those around thought he was deluded. Through faith, Abraham responded to God's call and travelled to another land that God had prepared for him. Because of his faith (not hers), Abraham's wife, Sarah, became pregnant long after childbearing age. Jacob's faith meant that even as an old man, he continued to worship God. Joseph trusted God's promise that the Israelites would be released from slavery under the Egyptians and return to their homeland. Baby Moses was saved because of his mother's faith. Jericho fell to the invading army because the Israelites believed God and obeyed Him by marching around the walls seven times, despite the jeers of the defenders.

The adult Moses was one of the leading Old Testament figures to be highly commended for his faith: 'By faith Moses, when he had grown up, refused to be known as the son of Pharaoh's daughter. He chose to be ill-treated along with the people of God rather than to enjoy the fleeting pleasures of sin. He regarded disgrace for the sake of Christ as of greater value than the treasures of Egypt because he was looking ahead to his reward' (Hebrews 11:24–26, NIVUK). For details of Moses' errors, restoration, leadership, trust in God and key decisions, consult the Book of Exodus.

The impressive list of how faith has impacted the lives of countless people continues in Hebrews Chapter 11 to include notables such as Gideon, Barak, Samson, Jephthah, David, Samuel and the prophets. Exercising faith empowered them to achieve remarkable outcomes, escape death and even return from death (11:35). More disturbingly, the writer of Hebrews also refers to the suffering that faithful men and women of God have endured, including torture, whipping, imprisonment, poverty, banishment and violent deaths. Importantly, the writer emphasised that although the people living under the Old Testament were commended and rewarded for their absolute trust in Him, God's plan of salvation based on faith in Jesus Christ as Saviour had yet to be brought to its conclusion.

Throughout the numerous references to faith in Hebrews Chapter 11, a cardinal point is the link between faith and action—an issue that James underscores in his letter and the frequently quoted principle that faith without works is dead/useless (2:20). Faith is therefore an active word, not a passive feeling or an emotion or a good intention. Faith facilitates courageous pronouncement testimony and changes in lifestyle; it refutes worldly desires; it combats evil forces and reinforces a belief in the unfailing goodness of God. Faith allows us to perceive more clearly God's intentions for the world, just as Old Testament prophets were permitted to glimpse events hundreds of years in advance. In particular, faith reveals how the world is saved from the ravages and consequences of sin by the coming of the Messiah into the world and his sacrificial death.

Insight

Faith is not only essential for achieving God's purposes but also in resisting the pressure of carnal living and compromising the Gospel message, however unpopular or derided by unbelievers such a stance invites. When facing a belligerent and powerful group of clergy and statesmen at the Diet (Assembly) of Worms in 1521, Martin Luther is said to have concluded his testimony by stating boldly: 'Here I stand, I can do no other, so help me God. Amen'. Only unshakeable faith can create such a courageous pronouncement.

In the next chapter, I focus on the deep faith of the Apostle Paul during his mission trips to share the Gospel, during which his trust in God never wavered, despite undergoing the most brutal, life-threatening experiences and painful disappointments.

Worldly faith

Outstanding achievers in secular settings may also claim that faith is the single most important factor in their triumphs. The difference between godly and secular faith is rooted in non-Christians having faith in their *own abilities* rather than giving the credit to God. For example, it is claimed that the tightrope walker, Blondin, whose daredevil feats thrilled and amazed thousands, asked for volunteers to sit in a wheelbarrow that he used as a part of his balancing act in crossing the Niagara Falls. Apparently, the crowd watching from a safe distance that had shouted its enthusiasm for Blondin and expressed their confidence in his ability to accomplish such a breath-taking feat, stepped back from proving their declared beliefs when a request was made for a volunteer. Understandably, perhaps, not a single person came forward to undertake the hazardous journey. It appears that it fell to Blondin's manager to assume the unenviable role! Expressions of faith from the spectators were not linked to subsequent action, contrasting with James's insistence that for Christians, the two should be inseparable (see James Chapter 2).

An example of how enthusiastic support was followed by affirmative action was demonstrated when the explorer Ernest Shackleton was recruiting people for an expedition to the South Pole. It is claimed that Shackleton placed the following advertisement: *Men wanted for hazardous journey. Small wages, bitter cold, long months of complete darkness, constant danger; safe return unlikely. Honour and recognition in case of success.* Whether or not the advertisement is genuine, there was certainly no shortage of volunteers for the trip that went ahead with a full complement of men, unlike the Blondin event described above.

The courageous exploits of Sir Ernest Shackleton and his team draw justifiable admiration, yet the same qualities of courage, tenacity and strong belief in the cause they espouse should characterise Christian endeavour, as well as secular ones. Both the intrepid explorer and Jesus gave serious warnings about the true cost of commitment, but while Shackleton drew attention to the physical challenges involved and threat to life, he also referred to the prospect of honour and reward in this life. By contrast, Jesus made it clear that discipleship demanded wholehearted devotion and obedience, which would lead to life 'in all its fullness' (godly fulfilment) but might also result in ridicule, oppression and violence. The greatest reward for faithful followers would be to hear the Lord's commendation after life has ended. The many rugged experiences of Paul, as chronicled by Luke in the Acts of the Apostles, bear witness to the extreme suffering that faithful testimony can bring, as oppressed Christians in certain areas of the world know only too well.

Joys and Sorrows in the journey of faith

In 1994, singer-songwriter, Graham Kendrick, was inspired to write a song titled 'For this I have Jesus' (Copyright *Make Way Music*), in which the phrase 'for this I have Jesus' is used as the refrain. The opening lines convey the important truth that life does not consist of a smooth, uninterrupted journey along a silky surface; rather, it is punctuated by moments of elation and disappointment in equal measure, as reflected in the lyrics: 'for the joys and for the sorrows; the best and worst of times'. Importantly, however, Kendrick reassures us that despite the challenges and struggles we face, we have the wonderful assurance that whatever the circumstances, 'for this I have Jesus'.

Christians are not immune from suffering, as countless believers will testify. Faithful, lovely Christian people can be struck down by serious illnesses and tragedy. Horatio Spafford heard that his four daughters had drowned at sea but as a result, wrote one of the greatest hymns of all time: 'When peace like a river: it is well with my soul'. Joseph Scriven's fiancée drowned on the eve of their wedding; years later another fiancée died before they could marry. Despite the tragic circumstances, Scriven's faith prompted him to pen the words: 'What a friend we have in Jesus, all our sins and griefs to bear' that has blessed and helped heartbroken people to find hope in the midst of tragedy. Fanny Crosby went blind as a young child due to injudicious treatment from an incompetent doctor, but she wrote thousands of wonderful poems and hymns, such as 'Blessed assurance, Jesus is mine'. Frances married Mr Van Alstyne and they lost a baby daughter but Frances lived to be ninety-five and continued writing until the end of her life. Gordon Wilson lost his daughter in the Enniskillen bombing in Northern Ireland but used the tragedy to help bring about peace and reconciliation in the province.

Insight

A painting competition was held in which artists were asked to represent the theme of 'Peace'. Many participants presented rural scenes of gently rolling hills, babbling brooks, sheep with their lambs, and cottonwool clouds. The winning entry, however, showed a raging waterfall behind which a bird was sitting contentedly upon a roughly constructed nest. The artist wanted to convey the fact that true peace is most evident in the midst of adverse circumstances.

Numerous other examples could be given to demonstrate that unexpected joy and blessing can emerge from the most tragic and desperate situations. However, while Christians are as subject to the vagaries of life as anyone else, it is important to be reminded of the many positive benefits in being a faithful disciple of Christ, not least in having the promise of his Spirit living within to guide, direct and provide reassurance during times of difficulty. As Paul explained to Christians in Rome: 'Your body will always be dead because of sin, but if Christ is in you, then the Spirit gives you life, because Christ made you right with God' (8:10, ERV). The dual condition that pertains to believers of sinfulness and righteousness is easily explained, as the former is a constant human condition ('original sin'), yet believers enjoy the righteousness of Christ that covers their sin. By contrast, those who reject him are left exposed in their sin and are therefore deemed unrighteous by God: a perilous position.

Jesus did not attempt to conceal from his followers the numerous challenges that they would face if they aligned themselves with him in proclaiming the Gospel message. He did, however, promise to be with them constantly to ensure deep contentment and inner peace through the stormiest periods of life. Christ shares our burdens, and supernatural rest—beyond the scope of human devices—is promised for those who trust him (see Jesus's assurances in Matthew 11:28). The 'sharing of our burdens' does not equate with the sudden removal of a problem or trial but rather that through expressing our confidence in God's power and authority over every situation (saying it out loud provides a powerful affirmation), we have the assurance of knowing that as Paul further reminded Christians in Rome: 'God causes everything to work together for the good of those who love God and are called according to his purpose for them' (8:28, NLT).

It should be noted that 'working together for good' is conditional on two factors: (1) Our love for God; and (2) Being aligned with His purpose. In similar fashion, true rest is not the absence of deeply felt concern or avoiding active participation in resolving a situation by sitting back and trying to ignore its reality. Rather, it is refusing to fret or be overwhelmed with anxiety when the emotional or psychological demands appear unresolvable. Nothing is impossible when we place our full trust in God.

Being born again/anew/afresh/from above by the Spirit of God also means that in addition to receiving absolution from the penalty of sin, transformation of our minds and restoration of our relationship with God, Jesus promises to be with each of us to the end of the present age and into eternity (Matthew 28:20b). These benefits are so compelling that it is difficult to imagine rational people refusing to embrace them and accept that Jesus Christ is the Saviour and Redeemer. Sadly, such an optimistic hope is frequently disappointed.

Counting the cost

It is possible to be strongly influenced by the presentation of an idea or philosophy, yet start to experience doubt or lose enthusiasm due to a fear of the consequences that might arise from following that way of life and a gnawing doubt that the cost could be greater than the benefits. It is hardly surprising that Jesus cautioned enthusiastic would-be followers about rushing into a commitment to be his disciples without careful consideration about the implications of doing so. In his Gospel account, Luke records Jesus's warning: 'If you do not carry your own cross and follow me, you cannot be my disciple. But don't begin until you count the cost. For who would begin construction of a building without first calculating the cost to see if there is enough money to finish it?' (14:27–28, NLT) Following Jesus is not an impulsive, ill-considered step of faith but one that resides in having total confidence in the one who is the 'faithful one'.

Despite the benefits and attractiveness attached to Christ's offer that each person should 'come unto him' and receive freedom from sin, a new life in the Spirit and eternal security, Jesus still maintained that following him was a serious business that should not be entered into carelessly or with the hope of personal gain. Jesus's sombre warning about the cost of discipleship stands in stark contrast to the 'easy come, easy go' attitude that characterises so much Christian commitment in the affluent Western World.

One of the most striking examples about Jesus's soul-searching wisdom in discerning a person's true motives in wanting to be his disciple is recorded by Luke (Chapter 9), in which three men indicated that they wanted to follow Jesus but made excuses when it came to the point of doing so. Jesus asked the men to count the cost of discipleship but each one was unwilling or reluctant to pay the price associated with becoming his follower, as described below.

The first man in the account recorded by Luke volunteered enthusiastically without thinking sufficient thought about the practical consequences; I shall refer to him as *Hezekiah Hasty*. The second man made excuses because he appeared to lack sufficient faith and trust; I refer to him as *David Dither*. The third man tried to put off making a decision by appealing to the priority of family affairs; I refer to him as *Peter Procrastinator*. Jesus had something significant and personal to say to each man but the principles apply to all of us because there is likely to be something of those men's character weaknesses in everyone— impetuous behaviour or weak faith or the use of diversionary tactics—to avoid or dampen wholehearted commitment. Such is the importance of Jesus's encounters with and responses to the three men that they merit a close examination of the issues and practical implications attached to each of them.

Hezekiah Hasty

Hezekiah Hasty was eager and enthusiastic about following Jesus but appears to have given insufficient thought to the cost involved. It appears from Matthew's account of the incident that the man was a teacher of the law (8:19), so it is reasonable to assume that he was well educated and not prone to irrational decision-making. Indeed, he not only volunteered to be Jesus's disciple but also made the bold claim that he would follow Jesus wherever he went. It is probable that if you or I were to encounter such fervour for the cause that we espouse, we would respond warmly and positively. Counter-intuitively, Jesus warned Mr Hasty that there was a price to pay, as well as spiritual benefits to accrue from his decision. Perhaps Jesus had become all too familiar with the underhand methods that some of the Jewish teachers employed to undermine his ministry, and was determined to resist subversion by anyone seeking to gain entry to his closely knit disciple group. Perhaps, he saw into the man's heart and responded accordingly.

1st lesson from Mr Hasty: We need to discern God's plans for our lives

It soon becomes obvious in Mr Hasty's case that his enthusiasm was not rooted in his faith in God but in his human instinct to explore new areas of service which, though an admirable attribute, does not supersede the need for Holy Spirit guidance and a sober consideration of the likely cost: personal, financial, emotional and physical. We also need to take account of the possibility that Jesus was aware of his intent to deceive, but let us assume that the man was sincerely motivated.

True faith is not defined as rushing ahead in an ill-considered way without acknowledging the implications and sacrifices involved. While a person's feelings may trigger a desire to 'do something to help', God may have other plans that take precedence over an initial rush of fervour. For example, we have all responded with pity and felt acute distress when we hear about severe poverty and see images of suffering children in other parts of the world. It is likely that many of us react by offering financial help or even by an urge to travel to that area of need and provide practical assistance, which is a commendable and compassionate response. In the latter scenario (going to the area of need), careful and prayerful consideration of such a major decision would be necessary in determining whether or not it is God's will to become actively involved. He may want the individual to stay at home, providing funds and encouragement to support the work of others who have been called to serve there.

Mere impulse, however sincere and heart-felt, is not usually a good guide to taking drastic measures in the way that Mr Hasty did. The prophet Habakkuk warns against premature action, underlining the point that God has matters under control and His timing is perfect: 'This vision is for a future time. It describes the end, and it will be fulfilled. If it seems slow in coming, wait patiently, for it will surely take place. It will not be delayed' (2:3, NLT).

An alarming example of how wrongly directed enthusiasm can lead to disastrous consequences is described in Acts Chapter 19 during Paul's two-year ministry in Ephesus. After receiving a mixed reception to his preaching in the synagogue, Paul moved to a local lecture hall and continued speaking and debating. God worked miracles through Paul, such that many were healed and evil spirits were cast out. A group of Jews, including the seven sons of Sceva (a priest) were impressed and inspired by what they observed, so tried to emulate Paul by invoking the name of the Lord Jesus in their attempts to do so. Unfortunately for them, on one occasion, the man's demon answered them aggressively: 'Jesus I know, and Paul I know about, but who are you? Then the man who had the evil spirit jumped on them and overpowered them all. He gave them such a beating that they ran out of the house naked and bleeding' (15–16, NIVUK). There are many lessons to be learned from this startling event, one of which is the inadvisability of engaging in a work for God that does not have His sanction and anointing.

Insight

Here is a poem that I penned after a close friend was grappling with the dilemma of whether to serve God at home or abroad. Its title is 'Responding to the Call'.

Should I go or should I stay? Work at home or far away?

Speak the Word in places new or be content with what I do?

Is God still able now to use those who fear but don't refuse?

Those who keep the lost in sight, labouring with all their might?

Though He knows His geography, Jesus just says: 'Follow me'.

Some He'll lead to distant lands; for some He has quite different plans.

God's more interested to know whether you're prepared to go.

For everywhere there are folk to meet: in jungle, desert, park or street.

God's witnesses are needed here, as well in places dark and drear. And who knows what the Lord has planned for those who serve in their fair land?

> The One who always sees afar can give you grace just where you are.
> Can make you salt in your hometown and shine your light to all around. So there's no
> need to fret at all that you have missed His great high call; across the world or down
> the lane—God's purposes are just the same.

In a situation where someone claims to have waited upon God for guidance and is convinced that he or she should take a major step of faith and become involved in a specific form of ministry—and while such willingness to trust and obey is commendable—the scriptural guidance is to involve other believers in the decision and ensure that they are prayerfully convinced that the path ahead is good, both to them and to the Holy Spirit (Acts 15:28).

In practice, working out the will and purpose of God for a person or couple requires prayerful consideration, wise counsel and step-by-step obedience. It is true that there are instances of where people have received such a clear word from God that they are in absolutely no doubt about what they must do. Such instances are comparatively rare and there is an additional danger that enthusiastic friends, who possess limited spiritual insight and discernment, will provide ill-considered advice to proceed. As referred to in Chapter 2, the classic case of taking poor advice involved King Rehoboam of Israel, who heeded the opinions of his young friends and ignored the wise counsel of mature godly men, which ultimately separated the country into two autonomous regions (see 1 Kings Chapter 12).

2nd lesson from Mr Hasty: We need to take godly advice

Someone may experience a 'blinding light' like Saul (later referred to as the Apostle Paul) on the way to persecute Christians in the city of Damascus (Acts Chapter 9) or 'hear God speak' through reading Scripture, praying or listening to a stirring appeal. Nevertheless, the person still needs a prophetic word of wisdom from a godly person, such as Ananias in the case of Saul/Paul, or a commendation from church leaders—for example, when Barnabas and Saul embarked on their missionary journey from Syrian Antioch (see Acts Chapter 14). In the latter case, it is important to note that the leaders in Antioch were praying and fasting when the Holy Spirit spoke clearly to them; they did not act on a whim.

Insight

Fasting is defined as refraining from eating or reducing the amount and content of our intake. The practice is mentioned frequently in the Bible, principally in the Old Testament, where participants fasted for a variety of reasons, including a means of expressing repentance; seeking guidance; in conjunction with prayer; and as a means of drawing closer to God. There are contrasting views about the appropriateness and relevance of fasting for today's Christians, but whatever position we hold on the issue, the act must be motivated by a humble desire to discover more of God's will and be submissive to His purposes. Jesus recognised the need for fasting but did not make it a religious requirement, which drew criticism from some of the Jewish traditionalists. Some Christians use the six-week period leading up to Easter for fasting: a period in the church calendar known as Lent. Lent is especially important for Christians within the Anglican, Catholic and Orthodox traditions.

Spiritual discernment is borne of waiting upon God, not intellectual evaluation of a situation, though an awareness of practical considerations also necessitates godly wisdom. The leaders at Antioch could have identified a number of others to undertake the mission; instead, the Holy Spirit singled out an experienced, well-respected Christian called Barnabas, whose birth name was Joseph, described as a 'good man, full of the Holy Spirit and of faith', (Acts 11:24) and a relatively new convert (Saul/Paul). The selection of Barnabas and Paul established two principles:

(a) The value of pairing a less experienced person with someone of greater spiritual maturity.

(b) Allowing God to be in control of key decisions to ensure progress in the proclamation of the Gospel.

Paul later wrote passionately about the need for unity and single-minded purpose in the church: 'Therefore encourage one another and build each other up, just as in fact you are doing' (I Thessalonians 5:11, NIVUK). And to the Corinthians: 'Finally, brothers and sisters, rejoice! Strive for full restoration; encourage one another; be of one mind; live in peace. And the God of love and peace will be with you' (2 Corinthians 13:11, NIVUK). Both Scriptures use the phrase 'encourage one another' as the catalyst for building up believers and embedding peace, joy and love among them, while guaranteeing God's presence in doing so.

The disciple Joseph was given the sobriquet Barnabas (meaning 'son of encouragement') because of his positive disposition. His presence and attitude was clearly a delight to those who knew him, as he must have radiated the love of Jesus in his life and ministry. Barnabas should inspire every believer to be an encourager, not a cynic, critic or faultfinder.

It is also noteworthy that later in the Book of Acts, Saul (Paul) is named ahead of Barnabas and designated the chief spokesman and evangelist, reversing the original order of seniority. Barnabas's humility in respecting Paul's spiritual authority is a fine example of Christian submission and recognition of God's sovereignty. Regrettably, Paul and Barnabas separated later after having a sharp disagreement about the role of another disciple, John Mark (Acts 15:38–40), though they were later reconciled. Such events are a painful reminder of human frailty.

Nevertheless, God ensured that the Gospel message of hope and salvation in Jesus Christ was maintained and (it could be argued) enhanced, following the parting of the two men.

3rd lesson from Mr Hasty: We need to follow the Holy Spirit's directing with resolute action

It has been known for church leaders to actively pursue a policy whereby they are the only people that formulate the vision and the direction in which the fellowship as a whole is to proceed, but then leave other believers with the task of implementing the decision without his or her active engagement. Jesus did not, however, separate the vision from the practice when instructing his disciples that they must go forth, spread the good news and serve others. Thus, after washing the disciples' feet, Jesus added: 'Now that you know these things, you will be blessed if you do them' (John 13:17, NIVUK). Inspired aspirations need to translate into decisive action. The significance and application of foot-washing is explored in Chapter 12.

If we fail to fulfil Jesus's commands, we will need to give an answer to his searching question: 'So why do you keep calling me Lord, Lord when you don't do what I say?' (Luke 6:46, NLT) As he ascended into heaven, Jesus underlined the need to receive power *prior* to being actively involved in sharing the message of salvation: 'But the Holy Spirit will come upon you and give you power. Then you will tell everyone about me in Jerusalem, in all Judea, in Samaria and everywhere in the world' (Acts 1:8, CEV). Jesus therefore established the order for receiving divine guidance as follows: (a) Wait for the prompting of the Holy Spirit. (b) Receive His power for the task. (c) Move forward in faith with God's authority. (d) Become practically involved in the calling.

When Jesus used phrases in his teaching such as: 'Go and be salt and light' and 'Go and say to this people', he made it clear that the act of stepping out in faith was always prefaced by the Spirit's enabling, and invariably gave a description of the commission's scope and purpose. Thus, in the example of Jesus's command to the disciples as he ascended, they were to witness 'everywhere', not just locally; they were to be specifically 'salt and light', as well as proclaimers of truth; and they were sent with particular messages for specific groups of people ('say to *this* people'). Experience has shown that one of the key factors in ensuring the effectiveness of evangelistic endeavour is to first understand the culture of the people and, where possible, to become familiar with their customs, hopes and priorities, while demonstrating the love of Christ and setting a positive example. More direct evangelistic efforts normally have to be restrained until the Gospel workers have gained the trust of the community.

A further example of the way in which God communicates the specific challenges that await his messengers is found in the Book of Acts when the prophet Agabus came to Paul in Caesarea and employed a powerful visual illustration to support his prophetic pronouncement: 'He took Paul's belt, and with it he tied up his own hands and feet. Then he told us, "The Holy Spirit says that some of the Jewish leaders in Jerusalem will tie up the man who owns this belt. They will also hand him over to the Gentiles."' (21:11, CEV) Despite these sobering words and the pleas of his fellow believers, Paul continued to be obedient to God and courageously faced the consequences. I wonder what our response would be in a similar situation?

Every follower of Jesus needs to abide in his presence through prayer and meditation to receive confirmation—often via human agency—and to receive instruction about where to go, what to say and to whom to say it. Mere enthusiasm or a 'sudden urge' may be the Spirit's prompting or may be an instinctive reaction that necessitates His approval before proceeding; it may be a short-lived emotional response that requires waiting on the Lord until we have peace in our hearts. In the case of major decisions, endorsement from other wisdom sources is essential. Naturally, the desire to share the fundamental truth of salvation found in and through the sacrifice of Jesus and his resurrection must be at the heart of every step of obedience that we take. The ideal state of affairs is when a believer is walking so closely in step with the Spirit that receiving from Him and walking in His way becomes as natural as breathing.

As confirmation of the disciples' calling, Jesus promised that the Holy Spirit would lead, guide and empower them, so they were not alone when they followed his command and did not need to be concerned about their weaknesses, frailties or fears. It is a necessary reminder for everyone who desires to fulfil a heavenly vision that although hard work, talent and dedication are important attributes, they cannot compensate for a lack of God's divine authority for the task in hand. Anyone seeking to serve the Lord can proceed with confidence that He will not only specify the nature of the assignment, action or activity but also provide the means to achieve an outcome that extends His Kingdom and brings Him glory.

It is only fair to add that despite being consecrated by God for service, the nature of the challenges entailed are not always revealed by Him in advance. When difficulties arise, the assurance of having complete confidence in our calling acts to deepen faith and trust in Him, and strengthens the resolve to persevere, despite uncertainty and even bewilderment about why He is permitting barriers to be erected. The writer of the Book of Hebrews emphasises the need to press forward when unhelpful circumstances are putting our lives under pressure: 'You need to persevere, so that when you have done the will of God, you will receive what he has promised' (10:36, NIVUK).

In addition, as the present world draws to a close, the promise given to those who refuse to be deterred in pursuing the path laid out for them offers a confident hope for every believer who seeks to emulate Jesus and submit to doing the Father's will. A prophecy in the Book of Revelation offers further encouragement to those who 'endure patiently': 'Since you have kept my command to endure patiently, I will also keep you from the hour of trial that is going to come on the whole world to test the inhabitants of the earth' (3:10, NIVUK). The 'hour of trial' is not specified, but faithful believers can be reassured that they will be spared from its impact and consequences.

4th lesson from Mr Hasty: We need to learn absolute dependence on God

When Jesus sent the disciples to travel around the region, proclaiming the message of repentance and hope, he told them to go in pairs and take only the bare essentials with them, as they moved from place to place. As noted in the previous chapter, there were many other would-be followers who found the level of commitment to be far higher than they were willing to accept or accommodate

248

into their preconceived ideas. It is little wonder, therefore, that Jesus impressed upon the eager lawyer, Mr Hasty, that having a desire to follow Him was insufficient reason to become his disciple: the cost and implications in respect of human ambition, comfort and reputation first needed to be weighed carefully before a definite decision was reached. Although our own day-to-day decisions are less profound than the one that confronted Mr Hasty, the principle of choosing either God's narrow way with its attendant challenges or going our own, less demanding way, makes his case entirely relevant.

It seems more than likely that Mr Hasty eventually decided that the cost of following Jesus was too high. Perhaps, as a qualified lawyer of eminent societal status, he succumbed to the lure of worldly acclaim and position above the challenge of being Jesus's disciple. On the other hand, perhaps he changed his mind after careful consideration and realised that discipleship is not a 'spectator sport' to be viewed in much the same way as we might view a film (movie) from the comfort of our padded seats, so came back to Jesus and confirmed his genuine desire to follow him. For today's believers, the equivalent challenge is to recognise that attending church is not just a pleasant pastime or opportunity to socialise; following Jesus wholeheartedly is a serious (not to be confused with 'grim') commitment and should not be undertaken casually or treated as an 'optional extra'.

Regardless of whether we consider our calling to be 'high' or 'ordinary', every Christian is called to love God and demonstrate the love of Jesus in the circumstances of everyday life—family, employment, leisure and relationships. As John explains in his second letter, the central issue is that of displaying love through obedience: 'And this is love: that we walk in obedience to his commands. As you have heard from the beginning, his command is that you walk in love' (1:6, NLT). Grand exploits are admirable and rightly cause us to be enthralled at the way God uses particular individuals to further His Kingdom purposes, but it is essential to bear in mind that the Father's pleasure and our heavenly reward will be based on following His expressed will, not prestige or worldly acclaim.

David Dither

Mr Dither was invited by Jesus to follow him but hesitated too long because it appears that he lacked the conviction to put other pressing matters to one side and make serving Jesus his priority. Jesus must have recognised the man's potential and sincerity, but needed to test his faith and encourage him to search his own soul and heart to see if he was determined to serve God ahead of other considerations.

In response to Jesus's invitation, the man explained that he must first bury his father, which at first sight seems to be a perfectly reasonable request, especially as the burial service for a deceased person is an integral element of the Jewish tradition. However, scholars surmise that it may have been the case that the man's father had not yet died! Mr Dither wanted to wait until his father's death because, were he to follow Jesus and the father died while he was away, he might miss out on the proceeds of the estate or be cheated by unscrupulous relatives. We are not informed whether the death had actually taken place or was impending, but the man used the event as a reason—or perhaps as an excuse—to step back from total commitment to Jesus. One way or another, the situation was almost certainly more complex than an initial reading of the encounter might suggest.

1st lesson from Mr Dither: We need to decide where our priorities lie

While there is every reason to be critical of Mr Dither's response, it is unfair to be spiritually supercilious about his decision. After all, Jesus demanded that each person must 'count the cost' and Mr Dither appears to have decided that giving up the security of economic stability available through acquiring the inheritance was simply too much to sacrifice. Jesus was not persuaded by the man's seemingly justifiable excuse but was forthright in telling him that others were perfectly capable of performing the domestic task of administering his father's estate (as Mr Dither undoubtedly knew).

In the same way, each of us seeking to follow and serve the Saviour will be faced with innumerable decisions about our willingness to sacrifice cherished possessions, familiar habits, financial security and, perhaps, adopt a different lifestyle. The decision may be a major one, such as whether to leave a promising career to serve in a full-time capacity in Christian mission; or it may be a comparatively minor choice about whether to attend a prayer meeting or to remain at home and watch a favourite television programme. Making responsible, God-honouring judgements about such matters, whether great or small, requires that we are walking closely with Him, listening intently to the Spirit's leading and, as previously emphasised, being willing to pay the cost.

Our faith and trust in God is probably put to the test most keenly when the relinquishment of worldly wealth is a significant factor; it is therefore unsurprising that it forms the central theme in about half of Jesus's parables. Ideally, every believer would like to conform to the sentiment expressed in James Rowe's old hymn: 'Earthly pleasures vainly call me. I would be like Jesus. Nothing worldly shall enthral me. I would be like Jesus', yet we must heed Jesus's warning in Matthew's Gospel account that 'no one can serve two masters; for either he will hate the one and love the other, or else he will be loyal to the one and despise the other. You cannot serve God and mammon [riches]' (6:24, NKJV) or using a more current translation from the CEV: 'You cannot be the slave of two masters! You will like one more than the other or be more loyal to one than the other. You cannot serve both God and money'. In the same verse, the NLT employs the phrase 'enslaved to money'. The acquisition of money and using it in a prudent manner is completely different from hoarding it in the way that Jesus described in his parable about the greedy farmer who was intent on building bigger barns to store the produce, such that he could then retire and live comfortably (Luke Chapter 12). The farmer did not realise that his life would shortly end and he would not live long enough to benefit from his self-indulgence. King Solomon, though one of the richest men who ever lived, recognised the folly of 'chasing after the wind... because I must leave them [his possessions] to the one who comes after me' (Ecclesiastes 2:18).

Although the majority of us may not be materially wealthy, it is interesting to consider how Jesus would ask us to use an unexpected windfall involving a very large sum of money, were it to happen. We might also reflect on how our attitude to the use of money might be different if we had accumulated a sizeable sum through hard work, perseverance and prudent investment, rather than as a gift or legacy. It is easy to be critical of Mr Dither but the challenge is to reflect on whether our reaction would be any different from his and how it might vary according to the circumstances under which the wealth was acquired and our immediate needs or those of our loved ones.

2nd lesson from Mr Dither: We need to decide whether to put obedience or comfort first

Mr Dither had every right to take a responsible attitude to his father's welfare and the implications for his family's financial position. On the other hand, if he were placing the lure of money and comfort ahead of his obedience to God, his motives for following Jesus were questionable and unlikely to result in blessing. Being obedient always incurs a personal cost, which Mr Dither appears to have been unwilling to pay.

Away from the limelight, thousands of committed Christians have forsaken well-paid and secure careers to serve needy people across the world, share the Gospel through medical practice, education, orphanage work, caring for the poor and destitute, prison visiting, improving facilities (housing, water supplies, etc.), multi-media communication and expressing Christ's love in numerous forms of word and deed. For each of these devoted followers, the cost that they incur financially, physically, mentally and emotionally may be high, but the rewards of knowing that their labour is pleasing to God and a blessing to others more than compensates for the rewards associated with familiar, less challenging settings.

Paul expressed his thanks when he received a generous gift from Christians in Philippi: 'I have received full payment and have more than enough. I am amply supplied, now that I have received from Epaphroditus the gifts you sent. They are a fragrant offering, an acceptable sacrifice, pleasing to God' (4:18). Every time we give money to a needy cause out of a pure heart, we should recall the three parts of Paul's description: 'fragrant offering', 'acceptable sacrifice' and 'pleasing to God', and be thankful that we are so privileged. By contrast, dropping money into a bag or box out of habit instead of from a loving motive is unlikely to result in God's blessing.

Insight

There are historic instances where a person incurred considerable financial loss as a result of being wholly committed to Christ. For example, as a result of his obedience to the Lord, Anthony Norris Groves set up a lucrative dental practice in the early 19th century and sailed with his wife and young sons to serve in Baghdad and India.

Charles Studd relinquished his outstanding cricketing career and large fortune to serve as a missionary from 1885 in China, India and Africa (Belgian Congo). Studd's motto was 'If Jesus Christ is God and died for me, then no sacrifice can be too great for me to make for Him'.

It is doubtful whether any of the pioneer mission workers in centuries past could predict the hardships that lay ahead but their determination to pursue their calling meant that obstacles and sacrifices could be handled confidently (if apprehensively) in the certain knowledge that they were obeying their heavenly Master and were 'yoked with Christ' and supported by the Holy Spirit in their endeavours (Matthew 11:29–30). Today's 'soldiers of Christ' have far greater access to advice and guidance about the likely challenges and opportunities of serving in a particular capacity but must still weigh the likely costs and blessings involved. The position is particularly acute when close family members will be affected by a man's decision to forgo home comforts and be subjected to hardship and insecurity. Sacrifice has wider implications than its impact on the principal individual.

3rd lesson from Mr Dither: We need to distinguish between reasons and excuses

It is possible for Christians to hear and read about great men and women of faith with a sense of wonder, without recognising that the call of Jesus Christ upon every believer's life to trust him and follow the leading of the Holy Spirit applies universally. While it is true that some believers are given the gift of faith and respond to their calling in exceptional ways, the principle of waiting upon God, listening for His voice through prayer, receiving advice from wise fellow believers, absorbing anointed ministry and simply waiting for the 'quiet whisper' of God's Spirit (e.g., Elijah in the cave; see 1 Kings Chapter 19) is in the gift of every true follower of Jesus. Acknowledging the Spirit's leading, confirming the call through the support of mature Christians and stepping out in obedience to God's will and purpose, should form a natural part of discipleship. Admiring the faith and obedience of others can inspire and motivate us, but failure to act on our own calling by finding excuses deprives potential recipients of the blessing that would otherwise accrue.

It is important to stress that there is a difference between legitimate reasons for delaying our response (such as the urgent need to care for an elderly relative) and making excuses for following God's express command (such as citing time pressures or arguing that we don't possess the necessary qualities). Luke records that Jesus told a parable to highlight the disquieting truth that 'making excuses' could even become a pretext to delay accepting his offer of salvation (Luke Chapter 14). Examples of this refusal are seen when someone claims to be too busy or not religious or too young or too immersed in family life or work commitments to seriously consider the claims of Christ upon his or her life. While the reasons may have some legitimacy, they become a stumbling block when used as excuses.

Decisions made on the basis of discerning the call of God are often delicate and challenging ones that require earnest waiting on Him as to His will and purpose. In contrast to the timidity that leads to hesitation about serving God in a specific, Spirit-led way, it is possible to be drawn to a sphere of service that appears to offer excitement and personal fulfilment, while overlooking the work for Jesus that is immediate and pressing. To quote the words of Elsie Yale's hymn: 'There's a work for Jesus, ready at your hand, it's a task the Master just for you has planned. Haste to do His bidding, yield Him service true. There's a work for Jesus none but you can do'. Jesus famously commented that there is plenty of 'harvesting' of souls to be done but there is a shortage of workers (labourers) who will commit themselves to the task (Matthew 9:37).

In contemplating our level of commitment and how we employ our time and resources, we must be sensitive to the fact that whereas God can always find ways to circumvent our unwillingness to be obedient to the heavenly vision by using others to fulfil the mission, disobedience may have implications and consequences that extend beyond the immediate situation. For example, withholding finance might delay important medical or compassion work in needy areas; failing to pray for a specific need might have negative repercussions for those affected, who rely on prayer partners to aid their spiritual and practical challenges; reluctance to be involved in an outreach project might discourage others and result in their withdrawal from participation or the collapse of the enterprise. Mr Dither's excuses did not sabotage Jesus's ministry but they alert us to the fact that our own dithering could have serious consequences for Kingdom work, as well as our own spiritual maturing.

Peter Procrastinator

The third person mentioned in Luke's account of Jesus's encounters with three men (though they did not necessarily occur on the same occasion) is *Peter*

Procrastinator. In common with Mr Dither, his reason for hesitating to follow Jesus in order to say goodbye to his family appears to be perfectly reasonable and again raises the question as to why Jesus reacted so strongly.

To understand Jesus's seemingly unsympathetic response to the man, we have to remember that he looks beyond the outward appearance and into the heart and deepest motives (1 Samuel 16:7). All is laid bare before his searching eye. He recognises when we are 'half-hearted'. He knows that we are inclined to search for safety and security in familiar situations when he asks us to follow his guiding and leading into places that stretch our faith. It should also be noted that our motives will be a key factor when we stand before God at the end of time, as Paul reminded the Corinthian Christians: 'He will bring to light what is hidden in darkness and will expose the motives of the heart. At that time each will receive their praise from God' (I Corinthians 4:5, NIVUK). Nothing escapes His piercing eye.

1st lesson from Mr Procrastinator: Families and friends are influential

A key factor that may dissuade someone from following the Spirit's leading is when family and friends warn him or her about getting too deeply involved in an enterprise. They fear that even a true disciple of Jesus may be drawn into an unsuitable lifestyle or make a serious, irreversible decision or be indoctrinated by an influential group of enthusiasts. An example of such a tension is described in John Bunyan's *Pilgrim's Progress*, where Christian's wife rails against her husband when he seeks to faithfully follow God's leading and flee from the doomed city.

God is, of course, well aware that family members can be pivotal in persuading someone whether or not to be obedient to Him, especially if it entails great personal cost. It is understandable if relatives and friends, especially if they are unsympathetic towards the Christian message, express their disappointment and emotional anguish at the prospect of losing regular physical contact with their loved ones. In particular, parents of aspiring overseas mission workers may not see their grandchildren very often, though technological advances have made 'virtual' contact far easier. Similarly, the wife of a man considering Bible College training or full-time Christian service is naturally concerned about practical issues such as loss of finance, struggles to find suitable accommodation, disruption to the children's education and severance from close friendships. Little wonder that Paul cautioned that married life could seriously restrict mission work and distract people from their primary purpose of obeying God. With such considerations in mind, remaining unmarried had to be given serious consideration: 'So I say to those who aren't married and to widows—it's better to stay unmarried, just as I am. But if they can't control themselves, they should go ahead and marry. It's better to marry than to burn with lust' (I Corinthians 7:8–9, NLT).

It must be understood that Paul's advice was directed towards those who were considering sharing the Gospel in distant, inhospitable regions and not to regular local witness. As Luke records in his Gospel account, Jesus had already set the bar very high for his followers: 'If you want to be my disciple, you must, by comparison, hate everyone else—your father and mother, wife and children, brothers and sisters—yes, even your own life. Otherwise, you cannot be my disciple. And if you do not carry your own cross and follow me, you cannot be my disciple' (14:26–27, NLT). The key point is that our priorities should always be God-focused, even if it is at the expense of our natural inclinations and desires, including potential marriage or remarriage.

Anyone considering full-time service, whether at home or abroad, will inevitably take account of the impact that the decision has on family and friends. Nevertheless, despite the need for carefully weighing the wider implications of a major commitment in being obedient to the Holy Spirit, the sincere seeker after the Lord's plan and purpose for his or her life cannot allow the weaker faith of others—even precious family members—to be the determining factor in taking a step of faith. Such matters are emotionally sensitive, requiring wisdom and humility to discern the Lord's will and negotiate the path ahead. Although friends and family may be uneasy or positively hostile to the proposed course of action, they may also provide enthusiastic advice and support, even if tinged with sadness about the likely sacrifices entailed.

2nd lesson from Mr Procrastinator: Godly women play an important role

Mr Procrastinator asserted that he needed time to say farewell to members of his family, an excuse that Jesus refused to accept for reasons discussed above. Although the man did not specifically refer to his wife in explaining his hesitation to follow Jesus, it is timely to address the key role that women play in Kingdom work at this point. See also Chapter 4 for details about parental responsibility and children under 'Indiscipline'.

The majority of pioneers and evangelists in the early church were men because women had a great deal less freedom than they typically enjoy in the majority of nations today. During the time of the early church, widows (in particular) would be making a considerable level of sacrifice to undertake discipleship duties, as their low status in society made them open to exploitation and opposition. To ensure security and wellbeing, widows would hope that they could find practical and emotional security by remarrying or being cared for by a close relative.

The Apostles made a particular point of urging members of the early church to take care of vulnerable members; James even makes compassion for the poor the yardstick against which to evaluate genuine religious conviction: 'Pure and genuine religion in the sight of God the Father means caring for orphans and widows in their distress and refusing to let the world corrupt you' (1:27, NLT). We see that James links caring for the disadvantaged and resisting worldly corruption that places self-interest ahead of love for others. The ERV translates part of the same verse as: 'This is the kind of worship that God accepts as pure and good', thereby emphasising the point that serving others is an expression of worship. It is also noteworthy that as Jesus was dying, he made sure that his mother (presumably widowed) was taken care of by John. In an age where women were regularly treated as second-class citizens, Jesus's positive attitude towards them and the mixed composition of the early church must have been a revelation in that male-dominated society.

Insight

The fact that Jesus asked John and not Mary's son, James (Jesus's 'half-brother'), to take care of his earthly mother may indicate that James was not a believer at this point in time (see John 19:26–27), though later he became wholly committed, even to the point of death.

Women were not only the main providers of sustenance and hospitality for Jesus and the disciples, but many of them were Jesus's closest allies and faithful followers. Jesus readily commended women when they showed spiritual discernment (e.g., Mary, as recorded in John 11:26–7) and was happy to engage in discussion with them publicly (e.g., the Samaritan woman at the well in John 8:10–11). Although these instances seem unexceptional in Western society today, they were unusual at the time, especially if the man and woman were from different ethnic backgrounds. Such interactions doubtless surprised onlookers and provoked criticism from some of Jesus's contemporaries.

One of the outstanding women who featured in Luke's record of the development of the fledgling church, as chronicled in the Book of Acts, was Priscilla, the wife of Aquila. Priscilla was closely involved with mentoring Apollos while he was in Ephesus (Acts 18); and she and her husband also demonstrated hospitality and support for the Apostle Paul in his ministry. It is interesting that Paul often referred to 'Priscilla and Aquila' in that order, which suggests that Priscilla was a significant figure, perhaps viewed as spiritually more mature than her husband. Many other women played a significant role in early church life, including Lydia (businesswoman, Acts 16), Damaris (society person, Acts 17) and Phoebe (church deacon, Romans 16:1–2).

In his Gospel account of the events surrounding the crucifixion, Mark highlights the steadfast loyalty and contribution of women: 'Some women were watching from a distance. Among them was Mary Magdalene, Mary the mother of James the younger and of Joseph [Joses], and Salome. In Galilee, these women had followed him and cared for his needs. Many other women who had come up with him to Jerusalem were also there' (15:40–41, NIVUK). It is significant that Mark makes a specific point of acknowledging the role of women who had followed and cared for Jesus. He makes particular mention of the *many* other women who had come with him to Jerusalem. The early female disciples were both numerous and closely involved with Jesus's ministry, not peripheral to it.

It is a humbling fact, especially for men who mistakenly imagine that God favours them solely on the basis of their sex, that a majority of contemporary church members are female, many of whom are highly gifted and more than capable of contributing and using their talents for the glory of God. In addition, a substantial percentage of overseas mission workers consist of women, both of married and single status. While men are expected to exhibit leadership (not dominance), teach and instruct in the faith, and set an example through their love, devotion and conduct, attempts to relegate women to an inferior role is contrary to the will of God and likely to constrain the important contribution they can make. While Paul raised a number of issues about the role of women in the church that have created disagreement and conflicting opinions, Jesus set the bar high to ensure that women were honoured and immersed in the fabric of church life and witness. The sex of a believer is of less significance to God than a willing, submissive heart and obedient spirit.

3rd lesson from Mr Procrastinator: Commitment to Jesus looks forward

From our perspective, Mr Procrastinator's request was perfectly valid and we may find it puzzling that Jesus appears to have been so abrupt in his response. It is important, however, to take careful note of Jesus's exact words to the man, namely that 'no one who puts his hand to the plough and looks back is fit for service in the Kingdom of Heaven' (Luke 9:52). Jesus did not say that Mr Procrastinator would be *excluded* from the Kingdom of Heaven by turning back; rather, he emphasised that 'service' in the Kingdom involves a clear focus on the task in hand such that total, unhindered commitment is essential (see Matthew 9:62). It is probable that Jesus had in mind the events involving Abraham's nephew, Lot, and Lot's wife, as they escaped from the burning inferno of Sodom, only for Lot's unnamed wife to 'look back' and forfeit her life in doing so (Genesis 19). He could equally have made reference to the case of Orpah, a daughter-in-law of Naomi, who chose to turn back and remain in Moab rather than accompany Naomi and Ruth (her other daughter-in-law) to Bethlehem (Book of Ruth Chapter 1).

Interestingly, a serious conflict of opinion occurred in the early church when one of the disciples, John Mark (normally referred to as Mark or Marcus, KJV) turned back from following the Apostle Paul on his missionary journey (see earlier). Despite this blemish on his record, Mark wrote a vivid account of Jesus's life, death and resurrection, and was the person that Paul asked to visit him in prison. The act of 'looking back' does not spell the end of our service for God but may disqualify or hinder us until we repent and determine to live afresh for His glory.

although such a step may initially appear frightening, once we take it, our only regret will be that we didn't do it sooner!

Recognising our calling

Jesus's encounter with the three men (as described above) exposes four principles in the process of discovering God's will, serving Him with a joyful heart, and having a high level of expectancy as to what He can achieve through lives submitted to Him:

1. Commit to following Jesus unreservedly, without excuse or procrastination.
2. Receive clear guidance from the Holy Spirit about the specific sphere of service that He has designed for us, making use of the skills and talents that we presently possess, while recognising that God sometimes places us in unfamiliar areas of service to test our faith, widen our horizons and make us rely more on His enabling.
3. Share the vision that we believe God has placed in our hearts with mature Christians to gain their advice, support and prayerful encouragement.
4. Persevere and be courageous in pursuing the goal and proclaiming the Kingdom of God with hearts full of love for those we serve.

Regardless of the nature of our calling, it is incumbent on every believer to 'seek first the Kingdom of God and His righteousness' (Matthew 6:33, NKJV) through living in a way that pleases God by exhibiting loving kindness, goodness and self-control. God is reluctant to use spiritually leaking vessels, as He made clear through the Old Testament prophet, Jeremiah. Nevertheless, because of His deep, abiding love, God graciously overlooks our failings, as Christ our Advocate pleads for us in heaven. For further details about advocacy, see Chapter 7.

Summary

Counting the cost of discipleship is an ongoing process of self-examination to determine the extent of our faith in God and our willingness to endure whatever circumstances we may meet on life's journey. The demands made of Christians in democratic and relatively peaceful countries contrast sharply with the life-and-death situations that other believers have to endure. The way in which we exercise faith in God directly impacts upon our own walk and the proclamation of the Gospel. Abiding in Christ demands more than good intentions. We have already been made keenly aware from earlier descriptions of Jesus's response to the three would-be followers that each person needs to count the cost before making an unconditional commitment to him.

As we reflect upon the responses of the three men, it helps us to gain a fuller understanding about the sacrifices that may be involved in doing so. If our calling is to be little more than an emotional impulse, wise advice from godly believers and confirmation from the Holy Spirit are essential components of the process. The need to stop, wait, be still and listen to God's voice is a fundamental requirement for all believers if they truly want to know His will and translate the vision into a reality. When Jesus becomes the pivotal point of our life and supersedes status, possessions, and societal and family approval, God may direct us in surprising ways and along unexpected paths, one of which is to focus our efforts on sharing the Gospel directly, as described in the next chapter.

Which statements are true of you?

1. My whole life is lived by complete faith and trust in God's power to lead and guide.
2. I employ faith when important decisions have to be made.
3. My faith in God varies, depending on my mood and disposition.
4. I tend to be impulsive in volunteering to serve the Lord.
5. I find it easy to make excuses to avoid wholehearted commitment to Christ.
6. The needs of my family must be placed ahead of any other consideration.
7. God cannot use my sinful life for His glory because I am too prone to making mistakes.
8. I prefer to leave major steps of faith to those who are specially called by God.

Chapter 10
Sharing the Gospel Message

Introduction

Throughout the book, I have emphasised that the message of salvation through Jesus Christ demands a *personal* response. Other than in exceptional circumstances—notably the prospect of physical danger—it should not be a *private* one. All born again (born from above) believers have a testimony to share about how their lives have been transformed in a way that defies human understanding but is clearly apparent through a complete realignment of their attitudes, priorities and behaviour. The responsibility of all Christians is to share the truth of the Gospel by whatever means possible, principally by the way they live, but also by communicating God's plan of salvation through word and example, as guided by the Spirit.

Discipleship

Pioneers

Men and women have been impelled by the love of Jesus Christ to take the Gospel message to distant lands. Some of the earlier pioneers include men during the mid-1700s, such as William Carey—known as the father of modern missions—to India, and David Brainerd to Native Americans. In the early 1800s, Adoniram and Ann Judson dedicated their lives to reach the Burmese people; John Paton worked among the cannibals in Papua New Guinea. Perhaps two of the best-known missionaries from the mid-1800s are Hudson Taylor (China) and Amy Carmichael (India), both of whom spent over fifty years sacrificially serving the people of those lands.

More recently, the early 20th century missionary to Africa, Charles T. Studd was directed to release his considerable fortune before venturing into what was a largely unknown area of service in Africa (see Chapter 9). Studd later wrote that while some Christians were content with the easy life 'within the sound of church or chapel bell' he devoted himself to 'building a rescue shop within a yard of hell'. In the 1950s, Jim Elliot and four friends gave their lives in reaching the Auca Indians in Ecuador. Elliot's wife, Elisabeth, continued to live among the Aucas and share the love of Jesus with them.

Other Christian pioneers have been called by God to serve much closer to home but equally sacrificially. For example, notable figures in Britain include Robert Raikes (founder of Sunday Schools), Hannah Moore (anti-slavery), Elizabeth Fry (prison reform) and George Müller (orphans), each of whom were compelled by the love of Christ to devote themselves to serving the poor, marginalised and oppressed. Müller explained the success of his ministry as follows: *There was a day when I died, utterly died to George Müller, his opinions, preferences, tastes and will; died to the world, its approval or censure; died to the approval or blame of even my brethren and friends; and since then I have studied to show myself approved only unto God.* Müller helpfully reminds us that the mark of God's approval should be the key objective of every committed Christian. Love for the Saviour has prompted many 'ordinary' present-day believers to take giant steps of faith to fulfil their heavenly calling, often at considerable personal cost.

Dedicated discipleship

Although God does not expect the majority of people to make supreme sacrificial commitments, all Christians have to make decisions about their use of time and resources, every one of which acts as a measure of their obedience to Christ. The demands of true discipleship far exceed being regular members of a church or conforming to a lifestyle that rarely stretches faith or, in the worst case, restricts the Holy Spirit from doing His work. Wholehearted devotion to Jesus involves a willingness to lay aside personal preferences, comforts and desires. It necessitates a deliberate act of the will to follow Him who is 'The Way'.

If we are walking in close accord with the Spirit, our choices and decisions are made far more straightforward than if we have a superficial relationship with the Father and only come to Him as a last measure when we are confused about the right path to select. As the Apostle Paul urged the Christians in Galatia: 'Those who belong to Christ Jesus have crucified the flesh with its passions and desires. Since we live by the Spirit, let us keep in step with the Spirit' (5:24–5,

NIVUK) or in the New Living Translation: 'Those who belong to Christ Jesus have nailed the passions and desires of their sinful nature to his cross and crucified them there. Since we are living by the Spirit, let us follow the Spirit's leading in every part of our lives'. The phrase 'keep in step with the Spirit' should be blazoned on every believer's heart. Similarly, the final phrase in the NLT version, 'every part of our lives', signals the need to be in constant prayer and alertness to the Spirit's promptings. The dedicated disciple of Jesus does not have secret closets or closed doors. God works through the ordinary experiences of life, if we joyfully acknowledge His presence and respond to His leading.

Insight

In his challenging book, True Discipleship (Gospel Folio Press, 1982), William MacDonald (1917–2007) wrote: A disciple can be forgiven if he does not have great mental ability or physical prowess. But he cannot be excused if he does not have zeal. If his heart is not aflame with a red-hot passion for the Saviour, he stands condemned. MacDonald's words are a powerful reminder to eschew a 'take it or leave it', undemanding form of Christianity.

Perhaps church leaders, evangelists and those who 'gossip the Gospel' to friends and relatives have failed to explain adequately the demands, as well as the joys, of accepting Jesus Christ as Saviour. Outlining the theology is relatively straightforward, thus: every person is a sinner in need of forgiveness; the substitutionary death of Christ on the Cross of Calvary was to atone (make amends) for our sins; new life is promised, both presently and beyond the grave. However, the fear of alarming would-be converts makes it tempting to present a slightly skewed message in which the benefits are celebrated, while the possible suffering and hardships are scarcely mentioned, if at all. As a result, when new converts begin to face difficulties and opposition, they are likely to be shaken and dismayed. Subsequently, they wonder why God is allowing these things to happen and may begin to lose confidence. They may also worry that He is disciplining them because of their failings.

While it is counterproductive and unnecessary to over-emphasise the likely trials that await new believers, it is incumbent upon mature Christians to gently explain the cost of discipleship, as well as the present and everlasting joy of being held securely by the Heavenly Father's love. See Chapter 9 for details.

Cultural influences in presenting the Gospel

Everyone is searching for something (and possibly, someone) in their lives that will give them a sense of purpose, hope and direction. Most people in the world are seeking financial security, stable relationships and personal fulfilment, all of which are perfectly legitimate aims if kept in proportion. In addition, there exists a deep yearning to understand the essential meaning of life, summarised in the question: What am I here for and why? The writer of Ecclesiastes (probably King Solomon) gloomily reflected on what appears to be the futility of life but concluded that happiness, fellowship and obedience to God were more important than riches and possessions (all of which Solomon had in abundance).

Undemanding, organised religion, in which acceding to a list of rules, procedures and regulations are the basic requirements for adherents, has largely lost its appeal among discerning seekers after truth. Younger people, in particular, don't want a 'feather bed' Christianity, replete with unlimited optimism and the promise of happy times in store (please refer to 'Cosy Christians' in Chapter 8); neither are they persuaded by a simplistic Gospel, devoid of Jesus's challenging statements about loving the unlovely, battling evil forces in the power of the Spirit and separation from worldly ways.

Most people have an inner desire to conform and it is difficult to ask them to break the mould and reject popular culture (e.g., liberal attitudes to sexual behaviour) or the prevailing social norms ('everybody's doing it'). Children are always anxious to secure solid friendships; being excluded from the 'crowd' is among a teenager's greatest fears. The problem for those who wish to advance the cause of the Gospel is that Christianity breaks the mould of widely accepted deceit that Satan ('the Deceiver') has sown throughout society. Far from conforming to the world's behaviour and attitudes, the church of Jesus Christ must offer a unique set of priorities that are bound up in God's design for mankind.

Interacting with non-believers

True discipleship invites commitment that supersedes all other considerations. It rejects many of the desires and ambitions that the rest of the world holds dear. Identifying closely with Jesus can also bring about a feeling of isolation, which is one reason that Christians seek fellowship with other believers. A determination to avoid being polluted by worldly attitudes and habits means that Christians tend to have few non-Christians with whom they are on close and friendly terms, which makes witnessing more difficult because there are few starting points or shared interests on which to build a meaningful conversation. The balance between maintaining strong ties with fellow believers and avoiding a 'holy bubble', floating serenely apart from the rest of society, is a delicate one that requires great prudence. Jesus mingled with a wide variety of people from different classes of society because he had the confidence and authority borne of a life totally committed to the Father's will.

While it is true that presenting the Gospel of Jesus Christ requires wisdom and no small amount of discernment, the response of the recipients will in large measure reflect the way in which believers conduct themselves and show genuine concern for them. Friendships should not, of course, be developed as a deceitful method of evangelising. To speak plainly to someone, however gently, about issues relating to sin, judgement, heaven and eternal separation from God necessitates that our lives are free from any hint of hypocrisy, arrogance or condescension. Common courtesy, amiable sincerity and keeping a 'light touch with a serious intent' are all necessary attributes in helping to deflect negative reactions. As the Apostle Paul taught: 'Since God chose you to be the holy people he loves, you must clothe yourselves with tender-hearted mercy, kindness, humility, gentleness and patience' (Colossians 3:12) and 'clothe yourselves with love, which binds us all together in perfect harmony' (3:14, NLT). A relaxed smile and bright countenance transform social interactions at every level.

Ahead of each form of testimony or witness, Christians need to examine their lives and see where they stand in regard to Jesus's command to put 'self' to one side and place him at the centre of everything they think, say and do. There is no room for superciliousness in witnessing, only great humility, integrity and a sincere burden for the person's present situation and eternal destiny. Thus, as Paul wrote to the young pastor, Timothy: 'If you keep yourself pure, you will be a special utensil for honourable use. Your life will be clean and you will be ready for the Master to use you for every good work' (2 Timothy 2:21, NLT). It will be noted that Paul emphasises personal responsibility in the matter by including the phrase, 'keep yourself pure', involving a deliberate decision that nothing unsavoury or corrupt will hinder the free flow of the Spirit.

Best and worst news

News travels fast today, especially if it reports on a catastrophic or tragic event. Good news tends to be filtered through media editing—often politically biased—depending on which individual or organisation is considered to deserve the credit or blame.

Christians have two types of news to share, a mixture of the best news and worst news imaginable. The *best* news is the promise of salvation available through Jesus Christ to everybody who repents and calls upon Him to save them. The *worst* news is that God hates sin and will not abide it in His presence, so the wage we receive for unpardoned sin is a restriction on His guidance and empowering during this life and forgoing the heavenly blessings that Christ has prepared in advance for us after death.

Alongside the best and worst news divide, the over-arching *wonderful* news is that every life can be and will be transformed by God's indwelling Spirit, such that the hopeless are encouraged and the downcast experience a supernatural joy that supplants their circumstances. By contrast, a piece of *alarming* news is that Satan is at work in the world and those who do not call upon the Lord are exposed to his deceptive, evil and destructive influence.

Some *encouraging* news is that God does not want anyone to self-destruct through sin and guarantees eternal life with Him when life ends for those who truly seek him and repent of their sinful ways. Set against this joyful truth is the *sobering* news that Hell is a real place and not a figment of an overactive imagination or a comic book fantasy.

An incident recorded in 2 Samuel Chapter 4 is a solemn reminder that good news must always be interpreted with reference to the expressed purpose of God and not according to human design. A man cheerfully brought news of King Saul's death in battle to (King) David but his 'reward' was to forfeit his own life. Later, two men assassinated Saul's son and brought his head to David, thinking that they would receive praise and honour for doing so; instead, they, too, were both executed. In attempting to 'please man' instead of obeying God, the perpetrators paid the ultimate price.

In contemporary society, it is inevitable that while a moral victory will be welcomed and celebrated by one group, opponents will be disappointed and depressed by it. However, the only criterion by which an outcome may be considered a victory for Christians is whether (a) it is in line with the plan and purpose of God; (b) it promotes Kingdom values.

Boldness with sensitivity

The prospect of divine judgement and eternal separation from God for unbelievers is an important, though sometimes neglected consideration for anyone who possesses a desire to share the whole Gospel. The seriousness and implications for those who have not embraced the love of God in Christ Jesus is often described as 'going to a lost eternity' after death. Raising this sensitive issue is viewed as being unpalatable when discussing Christian beliefs, despite the fact that Jesus, the Apostles and many scriptural references made frequent reference to the possibility, and sometimes the certainty, of eternal condemnation.

While reference to being lost in sin should be raised gently and carefully, it is incumbent on every practising Christian to have a keen awareness of the mortal danger involved for someone who ignores or dismisses God's gracious invitation to be saved. While we wish to avoid causing undue alarm among hearers, the serious prospect of facing death without hope should not be downplayed in an attempt to make the Gospel more palatable. In explaining the position, however, we should avoid giving contradictory messages in declaring on the one hand that God is love, yet presenting Him as being vengeful. It is also worth being alert to the fact that whenever we engage with other people about eternal matters, wholehearted commitment to Christ in our *own* lives should be confronted.

Although the majority of secular minded people may acknowledge the existence of Hell, they tend to equate it with the fate of blatantly wicked souls (e.g., despots, child-abusers and murderers) and not as a destination for ordinary non-religious folk, as they might describe themselves. Ensuring that we are clear in our own minds about biblical truth and exercising great wisdom in explaining it are essential if our witnessing is to be both compassionate and remain true to Scripture. Above all, we must pray to have a heart of love for the unsaved person.

Communicating the Gospel message with a sole focus on how we can be transformed in this life without referring to the consequences of rejecting God and His Son after we die is likely to draw a response to the effect: 'The experience you describe about being born again is fine for you but I have an alternative method of finding fulfilment and contentment in life that does not require belief in God or accepting your message. As for the prospect of damnation, I believe that when you die, it's like blowing out a candle—a puff of smoke!'

There are many and various ways in which people choose to spend their lives aside from commitment to Christ; however, being presented with the stark choice of spending eternity in Heaven or Hell does not allow any such latitude. Confident statements about being able to enjoy a satisfying life without faith in Christ tend to evaporate when the prospect of death and its consequences enter the conversation, though a common riposte is for non-Christians to declare that death means 'total death': body, soul and spirit (i.e., annihilation).

Personal testimony

In our attempts to be influential in rescuing sinners from satanic influence through the medium of witnessing, it is the Holy Spirit who opens eyes to their lost condition and initiates the work of persuading them to repent. He lifts the blindfold of unbelief from their eyes and reveals the truth about sin and salvation, though the way that each person responds to the Spirit's revelation remains a personal decision. As God fulfils His role, followers of Jesus must play their part by responding to His prompting, as He leads and guides them to say the right thing at the right moment and in the right way. The Spirit provides the power and 'lubricant' in the exchange; witnessing disciples provide the channel for Him to touch and impact the listener.

The Holy Spirit makes divine energy available to every believer and is at the heart of personal testimony. No listener can deny a Christian's account about the 'wonderful change in my life [that] has been wrought since Jesus came into my heart', as Rufus McDaniel expressed the conversion experience in his hymn, though the concept of Jesus coming into someone's heart is likely to take some explaining to those for whom it is an unfamiliar concept. Perhaps an alternative explanation might be couched in terms of Christ becoming 'an ever-present friend' or 'taking centre stage' in our lives.

It must be acknowledged that significant life reconstruction can take place in a setting that lies outside Christian faith, whereby a dramatic change in a secular person's priorities rejects formerly accepted behaviour and embraces wholly different ones. People have been known to forgo traditional living and become embedded in isolated or hostile or eccentric forms of existence. Others have become wholly obsessed with a new hobby, activity or relationship. A very small number have rejected their biological, God-ordained sex and opted for the use of powerful drugs and bodily mutilation in an attempt to 'become' a different sex, though the term 'gender' is normally employed instead of 'sex'.

By contrast with worldly ambitions and life-changing habits and behaviour, the transforming work of the Holy Spirit invokes a spectrum of unique, positive changes:

(1) Focusing attention on God's divine nature.
(2) Embracing the truth about Jesus as Saviour.
(3) Awakening a desire to discover God's will.
(4) Bringing peace of mind and inner contentment.
(5) Repairing areas of character weakness.
(6) Increasing love for others.
(7) Restoring broken relationships.
(8) Providing hope for the future.

Individual testimony can be a powerful instrument in persuading unbelievers and sceptics about the validity of the Gospel message; it does not, of course, ensure that the listener will be sufficiently convinced to make a conscious decision to stop, consider his or her ways and accept the need for a personal encounter with Jesus Christ. Polite interest or even admiration for the transforming work of God in a Christian's life by an unbeliever should only be an initial step on the faith journey for the seeker. The seed of interest must be nurtured and developed through further conversation, together with careful teaching about the importance of godly living, always bearing in mind that the Holy Spirit is the ultimate evangelist. Christians can only play their part and leave the outcome to Him.

Christ-centred witnessing

As the Spirit's enabling and our willingness to be used by Him are fundamental requirements to ensure effective witness, it is important to be prayerfully sensitive about the best approach to use for specific situations. A 'one size fits all' approach to witnessing is unsatisfactory in the task of relating to different people under diverse circumstances. Jesus's command to share with others the need for repentance and renewal demands that careful consideration should always be given to the most appropriate way of engaging with individuals and small groups. For instance, a wholehearted (though always courteous) discussion with someone from a different religious persuasion would clearly be unsuitable when talking to an atheist or to children. Similarly, addressing a congregation in a formal church environment would require a wholly different mode of persuasion from the personal touch needed in counselling someone who is earnestly seeking the Lord. Regardless of the context in which the encounter takes place, however, five principles are relevant:

1. The Gospel of grace is for every person

Jesus interacted with a wide range of people: men and women; slaves and free; bitter and charming; rich and poor; married and single; and young and old. No one was viewed as beyond his influence or unworthy of being helped and changed, apart from duplicitous time-wasters, whom Jesus dismissed summarily. He used people from a spectrum of society to take the message of the Gospel, including fishermen, intellectuals, accountants and doctors, both single and married. Jesus didn't search for 'super-saints' or someone of a particular status or position; he simply looked and still looks for people who will follow Him obediently.

In considering the call of Jesus upon our own lives, the words attributed to Scottish preacher and evangelist James Stewart (1896–1975) are appropriate and challenging: *The concern for world evangelisation is not something tacked on to a person's personal Christianity, which he may take or leave as he chooses. It is rooted in the character of the God who has come to us in Christ Jesus. Thus, it can never be the province of a few enthusiasts, a sideline or a speciality of those who happen to have a bent that way. It is the distinctive mark of being a Christian.*

To enhance our effectiveness in carrying out the Great Commission, scholarship and diligent study of the Bible (especially the New Testament) is essential; in doing so, however, we need to take careful account of three potential pitfalls:

a) *Failing to study the Bible closely.* It is possible to read the Bible casually without having a high expectation of what the Holy Spirit is saying through the written word. It is also possible to read familiar passages in a perfunctory manner and miss fresh revelation that awaits us if we were willing to allow it to penetrate our minds and hearts.

b) *Assuming that knowledge alone is sufficient to equip us for witnessing.* We need both the Word and the Spirit. The Word gives knowledge; the Spirit sparks the knowledge into life and applies it to our thinking, actions, relationships and conversations.

c) *Making our lack of knowledge a reason to avoid witnessing.* Such timidity is often borne of fear that we will be asked a difficult question or be challenged about a controversial subject. Church leaders have an important role in developing their own understanding of Scripture, whereby they can assist believers to grasp doctrine and to examine and think through difficult issues to which seekers demand answers. We can gain confidence from Jesus's promise that we will be given the right things to say when placed in tricky situations. We don't have to feel stressed or anxious about the things that we don't know or fully understand but simply speak of what we do know with confidence and joyful hearts. See Chapter 8 for some practical suggestions about addressing these concerns and further discussion later in this chapter under 'Handling Unbelief'.

2. The Gospel is worldwide

After promising them the power of the Holy Spirit, Jesus commanded his disciples to spread the Gospel locally, then in adjacent regions and finally, into the wider world. There are five practical implications that emerge from his command:

a) *We must spread the Gospel in every place, including our own street and neighbourhood. Some years ago, I had a teenage friend who was apparently disinterested in Christianity, church and religion generally—but God had other ideas! He was wonderfully converted, went to Bible College, married a Christian lady, served overseas, became a pastor and now trains Christian leaders around the world. When he initially approached a missionary Bible College to explain that he felt called to serve overseas, he was met with this response: 'If you want to be a missionary overseas, begin with the people you know first!' Sound advice for all of us!*

b) *We should be alert to spontaneous opportunities, while being aware that so-called coincidences are often designed and ordained by God's Spirit.*

It has been surmised that coincidences are merely times when God chooses to remain anonymous. Nevertheless, God is actively involved in every situation because He is interested in each of our lives and wants to use Christians to bless others and draw them to himself. The part that we play is to walk by faith and have continuous high expectations as to how God infiltrates every encounter.

c) *We must guard against the enemy. The importance of remaining vigilant to Satan's wiles when sharing what we believe necessitates spiritual protection. Feelings of discouragement, fear and confusion emanate from demonic influence and not Spirit-led discernment. Both Paul and Peter deal directly with these issues and offer similar advice: 'So be on your guard, not asleep like the others. Stay alert and be clear-headed' (1 Thessalonians 5:6, NLT) and 'Stay alert! Watch out for your great enemy, the devil' (1 Peter 5:8, NLT). We must constantly check that we are wearing the 'whole armour of God'. See Chapter 5 under 'We learn perseverance' for details.*

d) *We must maintain a keen awareness of the imminent return of Christ. Someone has penned this shrewd maxim: 'Live as if Christ died yesterday, was raised from the dead today and is coming again tomorrow!' In other words, make the event of Christ's sacrificial death central to our existence; reflect the joy of his being alive in our daily walk; and order our lives with the vigilant expectation that he could reappear at any time.*

e) *We must ensure that we are in the right place, which applies both to our spiritual condition and to our location (serving where God has placed us). The assassination of the US President, Abraham Lincoln, is attributed in large measure to the fact that his bodyguard, John Parker, had left his post shortly before the killer, John Wilkes Booth, committed the atrocity unchallenged. Christians must never be guilty of 'abandoning their post' or being 'absent without leave'. See also point 4 below.*

3. The primary purpose is to point people to Jesus

Jesus told his disciples that they would be witnesses on his behalf in all places and circumstances. He did not tell them to highlight the attractive church facilities or the friendship or the exciting events or the great music or the free food, though all these factors act as incentives for the un-churched to come to an event and be exposed to the wondrous truth of salvation. Certainly, it is important for visitors to a church or chapel to have a positive experience and, in the purposes of God, translate their interest into genuine commitment. The attractions should not, however, be the end point of our endeavours but a way to enjoy fellowship with ordinary folk in an unthreatening and relaxed environment, such that their hearts become more receptive to the Good News. Jesus Christ should and must be the focal point of all that we think, say, plan and do, saturated in love for the lost.

People were found, blessed and healed by Jesus as they went about their regular working lives, as well as those who came to him in acute distress, and during his teaching inside the synagogue. Today, much evangelism seems to occur in familiar environments, rather than in more formal settings, though both have their place in Kingdom work. For Christians in Western societies, occasional encounters (when meeting a fellow dog-walker, say) or more structured assembling (such as a family service when parents come to watch their children perform in a pageant) or a regular church service, all provide opportunity to show the love of Jesus and demonstrate our faith in natural, unpretentious ways.

In addition, every believer needs to be alert for the 'divine encounters' that God provides unexpectedly, so that we don't miss the moment and fail to be spiritually 'primed and ready' to speak and listen. Jesus's parable about the ten bridesmaids (virgins) in Matthew Chapter 25 underlines the importance of readiness: five of the young women in the story were alert and anticipating the bridegroom's return, and five were unprepared, so were denied the blessing that could have been theirs.

I suspect that every believer has been in a position to speak about the Saviour but hesitated and then regretted missing the opportunity. Perhaps we feel embarrassed to speak of Jesus because of people's existing perceptions of him, whereby they view him as a baby in a manger, a mythical figure or a religious version of Santa Claus. Sometimes our awkwardness is because we struggle with our own distorted images of him based on countless pictures and presentations in books and films; for instance, that he had a long beard, spotless white robes and shoulder-length hair, all of which are improbable. See Chapter 1 for further details.

In reality, Jesus must have been extremely fit and healthy, weatherbeaten and, as God foretold through his prophet, there was nothing special or impressive about the way he looked (Isaiah 53:2). At the same time, Jesus would have stood out from the crowd, due to the radiance beaming from his face, reflecting the wholesome image of the invisible God (Genesis 1:27, Colossians 1:15). A shining visage is a characteristic of all those who abide in Christ, as exemplified by the appearance of the martyr, Stephen, whose face shone like an angel. See also Chapter 3 under 'Illuminating the darkness'.

It is also the case that believers may be hesitant to steer a conversation towards matters of eternal significance with an acquaintance lest the person begins to avoid them on future occasions! Some Christians, eager to share their testimony or discuss spiritual issues, may inadvertently discourage interest rather than fostering it by being over-exuberant. During non-church-based encounters, a casual mention of something we were involved with at church recently will usually open a conversation in an unthreatening and natural way.

In truth, it is much easier for us to chat about the state of the weather, the recent football match, the problems affecting the economy or our homemade recipe than about the limitations of our present existence and eternal consequences. While more general subjects are useful 'icebreakers', the conversations needs at some point to orientate towards Jesus and evoke people's interest in Him. As in all things, we need Holy Spirit wisdom and discernment to speak naturally and show serious but good-natured interest in the person's response.

Insight
When we feel guilty about missing an opportunity to speak of the Saviour, it is tempting to allow feelings of despair to fill our minds. It is far better to allow the past to rest in the Saviour's forgiving embrace than to allow negativity about our failings to interfere with future opportunities to witness.

4. Serving in the place of God's choosing

There are countless places, both at home and abroad, that have need of Gospel witness, and it is stating the obvious to say that one person cannot be everywhere at once. Deciding the 'right place' is usually determined by our present circumstances and the constraints of existing responsibilities. Wide-eyed wonderment about serving in 'faraway places with strange-sounding names' may form the substance of desires and daydreams but is more likely to be a prompt about the need to pray for those who are currently serving than to go oneself.

We noted in Chapter 9 that Mr Hezekiah Hasty was too intent on following his natural impulses, rather than reacting to the Spirit's guidance. I have met a number of dedicated Christians who were exercised about whether or not they had missed their calling or were frustrated that their yearning to serve in a particular context had been thwarted by practical considerations, such as having to care for an elderly relative or pressing financial commitments. The following poem is called *'Just where you stand'*. It offers reassurance to those who wonder if they have missed the will of God or are serving in the 'wrong place'. It is based on an old, anonymously written poem, considerably amended by the present author.

Just where you stand in the conflict; that's the place that you should be. Just where you think you are useless, lift up your head and you'll see God placed you there for a purpose, whatever that purpose may be.

Believe that he chose you especially and work for the King loyally.

Put on your armour, be faithful, whether you labour or rest

Whatever you do, never doubt Him, for God's way is always the best!

Out in the battle, with friends or alone, ever stand firm and be true For this is the work that the Master has decided that you—only you—have to do.

Paul sternly charges the young man, Timothy: 'But you, keep your head in all situations, endure hardship, do the work of an evangelist, discharge all the duties of your ministry' (2 Timothy 4:5, NIVUK). It has been pointed out by those who say they are not called to evangelise that Timothy was a pastor and therefore had a responsibility to evangelise, while they are not 'called' to do so. However, William Booth, founder of the Salvation Army and never a man to mince his words, was typically forthright about Christians who use this particular argument to excuse themselves from witnessing:

Not called, did you say? Put your ear down to the Bible and hear Him bid you go and pull sinners out of the fire of sin. Put your ear down to the burdened, agonised heart of humanity and listen to its pitiful wail for help. Go stand by the gates of hell and hear the damned entreat you to go to their father's house and bid their brothers and sisters and servants and masters not to come there. Then

276

look Christ in the face, whose mercy you have professed to obey, and tell Him whether you will join heart and soul and body and circumstances in the march to publish His mercy to the world. In our lifetime, wouldn't it be sad if we spent more time washing dishes or swatting flies or mowing the yard or watching television than praying for world missions?

5. Supernatural authority to fulfil Jesus's command

Prior to his ascension, Jesus gave his disciples a specific promise that they would receive power when the Holy Spirit came upon them, manifested in their boldness to proclaim the Gospel, influence people for Christ and withstand opposition. These significant changes in their lives should not be underestimated. They were transformed from an anxious group of men with little appetite for service into a powerful force that was described as turning the world upside down. Perhaps a more accurate interpretation of the disciples' influence is that they were turning the world the right way up!

In the same way that the early disciples were emboldened, we must recognise that devoid of God's supernatural power, our efforts to persuade someone about the truth of the Gospel and the need for repentance will be like attempting to start a vehicle with a dead battery or an empty fuel tank. Regardless of how slick the presentation, how modern the music, how impressive the preaching, how modern the technology or how hard we work, only God provides the potency to influence people's spirit and transform their lives.

In truth, it is highly tempting to imagine that a leader's personality, style of worship, compelling messages, improvisation and wholehearted commitment are sufficient of themselves to bring about changed lives. However, as Paul further wrote to Timothy, it is possible to have 'a form of godliness but deny its power' (2 Timothy 3:5, NIVUK). In fact, Paul was scathing about people who relied on contrivances to promote the Gospel and warned Timothy to steer clear of those who are 'lovers of pleasure' rather than lovers of God. The benefits of employing positive and innovative approaches to glorify Jesus Christ are evident in the way that numerous struggling church fellowships have gradually attracted larger and more youthful congregations, and elevated enthusiasm for worship. Nevertheless, the principle that genuine transformation depends on the Spirit's enabling is fundamental, without which all our efforts will have limited long-term impact, regardless of apparent success in terms of attracting larger numbers to services.

In all our dealings with unbelievers, Christians have to be wise about their priorities, such that they don't waste their time or get drawn into bad company and slip into worldly ways of thinking and behaving. A danger for those who are keen to share the Gospel with lost souls is that in trying to be accommodating and understanding of alternative, worldly perspectives, they compromise their own close relationship with God and confidence in His revealed Word.

While we may balk at the thought of lapsing into unspiritual conduct, it is possible for even responsible and dedicated believers with good intentions about contacting outsiders to be drawn into attitudes and actions that reflect godless priorities through continued association with them. Gaining insight into secular people's thinking and views of life should help us to pray more earnestly for them and thank God wholeheartedly for His mercy towards us, as sinners saved by His grace. Nonetheless, there is a difference between being informed about secular ideas, priorities and ways of viewing the world, and allowing them to penetrate our minds and adversely influence our thinking and behaviour.

Releasing power in the church

Some Christians must face the uncomfortable fact that their attitude and intransigence may contribute to people rejecting Christianity and seeking answers elsewhere in their search to explain life's mysteries and discover ways to find fulfilment. A factor in creating a perception that the church is antiquated and irrelevant might be that the supernatural dimension of the Holy Spirit's work has been relegated to the margins. A reason for leaders being cautious about allowing the Spirit to have free rein is a fear that over-exuberant zeal might dominate the worship of God and services will focus too much on personal satisfaction ('Christian entertainment') at the expense of the ministry of God's Word. Unfortunately, a number of well-publicised 'extreme' events involving excessive forms of behaviour have understandably sparked alarm among mainstream church leaders.

A second reason for the reticence to embrace the Holy Spirit's fresh anointing is a lack of confidence to depart from a tried-and-tested approach that has proved satisfactory over many years. It is easy for church life to slip into a routine of maintaining regular meetings, Bible instruction and social fellowship—all of which are good and necessary—yet to lose sight of a faith-driven expectation that God is willing and able to do more than we ask or think (Ephesians 3:20), reflected in celebratory worship, eager consumption of the

Scriptures and an earnest desire to see people yielding their lives to Christ. As a result, church life can become blandly repetitive, whereby even if the meetings are satisfying and fulfilling for the regular attendees, they fail to inspire deeper fellowship or influence seekers. Maintaining a balance between 'feeding the flock' through, notably, expositional Bible preaching, and reaching the lost by being open to a refreshing work of the Holy Spirit, is a challenge that must be confronted if church life is to sparkle into life and be a channel for the radiance of Christ to thrill the hearts of seekers.

A large number of fellowships have taken on board Jesus's command to care for those in immediate need within the fellowship but may have been less enthusiastic about allowing the Spirit to energise for evangelism or heal the sick or raise the dead or fight injustice or resist the advance of secularism. The churches that have become insular and defensive in outlook and behaviour contrast unfavourably with the early church's emphasis on preaching the Gospel fearlessly, trusting God for the seemingly impossible and displaying the Spirit's power through genuine supernatural acts.

Insight

When Moses and Aaron stood before Pharaoh to demand the release of the Israelites, God performed a miraculous act through Aaron's rod by turning it into a snake. The ungodly court magicians used their rods to 'replicate' the phenomenon. However, the Lord demonstrated His superior power and the bogus nature of the enchanters' actions when Aaron's snake consumed their imitations (see Exodus Chapter 7). The need for vigilance in distinguishing between a genuine work of the Spirit and Satan's attempts to counterfeit is one of many lessons to be drawn from this astonishing event.

In the Old Testament, we read of how God confronted the prophet Ezekiel's low expectations by showing him a pile of dry human bones and asking him whether they could become living people again (Chapter 37). Ezekiel is understandably confounded and admits that only the Lord can answer that question. God breathed life into the seemingly dead remnants and created a mighty army to illustrate in the most powerful way imaginable that He is capable of recreating even those who appear beyond redemption. The power of Almighty God has not changed between that incident and today; nothing is impossible for Him.

Every fellowship must face the tough question as to whether doubters or casual seekers would be helped in making sense of their lives and take their need of a Saviour more seriously if they attended one of its regular meetings. The majority of church services are likely to be geared towards praise, worship and teaching for believers, rather than designed to allow seekers to feel at ease and be introduced to the truth of the Gospel. Indeed, it is worth considering whether even a so-called 'seeker' service or similar event is genuinely tailored towards those outside the fellowship and if so, whether sufficient thought been given to follow-up and further engagement with anyone who attends. There are many practical issues to be addressed to ensure that 'outsiders' feel comfortable while ensuring that the gathering is not purely a social event (unless specifically designed for that purpose). Even if the occasion is devoid of any overt spiritual content, it should still exude Holy Spirit vitality and be underpinned with believing prayer.

Exercising wisdom and discernment

In their desire to reach the lost, followers of Christ must be careful to avoid imitating secular strategies, outmoded approaches or relying on their own ingenuity. God's power and free rein will do more than we can think or imagine, as He uses the resources that we submit to Him to build His church, as Jesus affirmed to Peter: 'And I tell you that you are Peter, and on this rock I will build my church, and the gates of Hades will not overcome it' (Matthew 16:18, NIVUK). Despite having Jesus's statement as a rock of assurance, it is still puzzling that so many fellowships seem tentative about relying on and drawing from the Spirit's potency. There appear to be three principal reasons for the hesitation:

1) A belief that the supernatural work of the Holy Spirit (other than bringing about conversion) was reserved exclusively for the early church and is no longer relevant. In doing so, believers lose sight of the miraculous powers that God exercises through them for healing, exercising spiritual discernment, banishing Satan, uttering words of knowledge and prophesying.

2) A belief that we should evaluate success in terms of the effort exerted rather than the results it achieves, as reflected in changed lives, increased faith and heightened prayer, praise and worship.

3) A belief that taking hold of what God offers runs the risk of being thought of as being excessive rather than exalting, and unsettling the more conservative members of the church by spontaneity and passion in worship.

It must be acknowledged that those who are filled with the Spirit, overflowing with love for Jesus, and excited about the ways in which He is refreshing worship and witness, may alarm more cautious people who become uneasy about, or even resentful towards, their fervent fellow believers. Reactions to a surge in more exuberant behaviour are bound to vary. On the one hand, those who are eager to grow in grace and the knowledge of our Lord Jesus Christ, and produce spiritual fruit, will be energised and encouraged when they observe how God is revitalising church life. On the other hand, more orthodox members may criticise, actively withdraw from involvement and, in some instances, decide to move to a different church.

Church leaders therefore need to exercise great wisdom and discernment in pursuing a God-honouring way forward without antagonising those who may be reluctant to embrace change, yet satisfying more passionate people who want to explore greater depths of Spirit-filled renewal. It is unrealistic to expect all believers in a fellowship to subscribe unreservedly to a particular vision or embrace what they may deem to be excessive zeal. Nevertheless, gradual persuasion and demonstrating the benefits of drawing more fully on the Spirit's power should convince and reassure more reticent members over time. All leaders need to remember that solid unity is preferable to division, even if it means that progress is more gradual than they anticipated or hoped for.

Evangelism has a time limit

How long before the Lord Jesus returns to bring an end to the present era? How long before bodily weakness constrains a person's witnessing? How long before each of us take our final breath? The answer to all of these questions is, of course, that none of us know! Arthur Pierson (1837–1911) was a Christian leader, pastor and writer who, it is said, preached more than 13,000 sermons and wrote over fifty books. He commented: *If missions languish, it is because the whole life of godliness is feeble. The command to go everywhere and preach to everybody is not obeyed until the will is lost by self-surrender in the will of God. Living, praying, giving and going will always be found together.*

Those who trust in Christ have full assurance of salvation and the certainty of his Spirit in them throughout this life and into eternity, so to whom else can people turn than Jesus? Who better should they follow? Whose light shines more brightly to show them the way than the one who is The Light and The Way? Who can satisfy their needs more than the One who is the Bread of Life? Jesus invites each one to share an intimate relationship with him; to enjoy a lightness of spirit; to talk with him and walk with him along life's narrow way; to learn from him and to follow faithfully until the end of our days. Once these characteristics are embedded in our daily walk, we are ready and able to communicate the Good News in a natural way, as the glow of heavenly light radiates from our faces and spiritual maturity penetrates our words and actions.

Each Christian has a part to play in sharing the message of hope. Jesus's command to spread the good news and make disciples applies to every believer, whether at home or abroad; whether old or young; whether fit or unfit; and whether talented or ordinary. The most important factor is to know that we are in the right place; trusting God for everything; constantly attentive to His voice and prompting; eager to be useful in Kingdom work; and ready to obey in whatever sphere we are empowered to occupy. God will see to the rest, as Paul reminded the Ephesian Christians: 'Now all glory to God, who is able, through his mighty power at work within us, to accomplish infinitely more than we might ask or think' (3:20, NLT).

God offers reassurance through the prophet Isaiah that He will both answer and help His people: 'This is what the Lord says: "In the time of my favour I will answer you, and in the day of salvation I will help you."' (49:8a, NIVUK) Paul uses the quotation from Isaiah and adds that the need for taking hold of salvation is an urgent one: 'I tell you, now is the time of God's favour, now is the day of salvation' (2 Corinthians 6:2b). Repetition of the word 'now' is clear evidence of the urgency attached to finding salvation. Tomorrow may be too late.

Insight

Even if we feel that our efforts have been unsuccessful in bringing someone to accept the truth about Jesus and put their trust in him, we can rely on the Holy Spirit to prompt people to reach a point where they 'seek and find' him of their own volition or via another person's testimony. Although each believer has a part to play, it is not the case that 'everything depends on me'. God is not limited by our shortcomings and will employ other means to fulfil His purposes.

Handling Scepticism

Responding to doubters

Being a disciple of Jesus Christ is likely to mean that our message will be rejected by passivity from the individual concerned, rather than hostility. Nevertheless, even mild rejection can be painful, especially if the person let it be known that he or she would prefer not to discuss spiritual matters further. When the individual is a friend or relative with whom you have regular contact, the position becomes even more delicate.

It should not come as a surprise if some number of people refer dismissively to Jesus being the equivalent of the Tooth Fairy or Bible events being on a par with a belief in the flat earth hoax. A Christian's reference to miracles, supernatural events, and to Jesus's death, resurrection and ascension, may similarly be dismissed as fables or the result of an overactive imagination. More recently, it is common for opponents of the Gospel to raise issues attached to views about sexuality and relationships that challenge biblical definitions of male and female. Regardless of people's responses, however, the words of Jesus should encourage us to remain faithful to God's revealed truth: 'We speak of what we know and testify to what we have seen' (John 3:11, NKJV), including transformed lives, hope for the present and the future, acts of love, forgiveness (even for enemies) and the abiding grace of God in our daily lives. No amount of apathy, sneering or scepticism can negate those realities.

When opponents of the Gospel rail against us, showing unconditional love for them becomes of paramount importance. Rejection of the Lord's offer of salvation may well feel like a personal insult but is principally a rejection of the message and the Saviour, not a personal slight. Even so, Christians must ensure that when witnessing, how be it gently and indirectly, they do not give the impression that they are ashamed of declaring the eternal truth by being apologetic and coy and 'moving on' swiftly to more easily digestible topics that do not invite a negative reaction.

As both sceptics and serious enquirers ask challenging questions about the Christian faith, it is essential to be clear about what we believe and what the Bible has to say about difficult issues, while recognising that we cannot search the mind of God or know His thoughts in every detail. (I addressed a number of these points in earlier chapters and also offer a selection of likely questions we may face, together with our responses, in Chapter 12). We must therefore be wise but positive about the sorts of claims that we make about God and His intentions for humankind through the eternal plan of salvation in Christ. The Apostle Paul graciously comments to the Christians in Corinth that 'anyone who claims to know all the answers doesn't really know very much' (I Corinthians 2:21, NLT). Paul's statement does not, however, absolve believers from searching the Scriptures and becoming immersed in God's Word. The Holy Spirit did not inspire over forty men to write and create a book that sits on the shelf for most of the year!

Peter summarises how we should approach witnessing and give an appropriate response to negative reactions: 'Now, who will want to harm you if you are eager to do good? But even if you suffer for doing what is right, God will reward you for it. So don't worry or be afraid of their threats. Instead, you must worship Christ as Lord of your life. And if someone asks about your hope as a believer, always be ready to explain it. But do this in a gentle and respectful way. Keep your conscience clear. Then if people speak against you, they will be ashamed when they see what a good life you live because you belong to Christ' (I Peter 3:15, NLT). It will be noted from Peter's comments that our primary motive should be to do good and worship Christ. God will reward us for obeying Him.

Peter also offers advice about the courteous way in which we should engage with people, contrasting the blessing we receive when we suffer for doing what is right against suffering for doing wrong due to our own foolishness. Genuine hunger for God supersedes earthly barriers, turns conflict into victory and strengthens faith.

Insight

Peter's advice is overflowing with foundational teaching:

- Always seek to do what is right, regardless of people's responses.
- God is aware of our sincere intentions and will reward us accordingly.
- We should be clear about what we believe.
- Our conversation must be courteous.
- Our lives must be pure.
- Those who seek to shame us will themselves be put to shame.

While every Christian should be careful to live in an upright and godly manner, it is important to remember three things when exposed to the emotionally painful experience of being ridiculed or spurned. First, although we are in a battle against evil forces that try to disrupt and create distress, Christ has won the victory over fear and death. Second, nothing in all creation can separate us from the love of God found in Jesus, the key word being 'nothing' (Romans 8:38–9). Third, scoffers and malcontents must one day have to answer to God and are therefore more to be pitied than condemned.

Paul explains the sad fact that people's resistance to receiving the truth may be because 'the god of this age has blinded the minds of unbelievers, so that they cannot see the light of the Gospel that displays the glory of Christ, who is the image of God' (2 Corinthians 4:4, NIVUK). He goes on to say that even though God's light shines in our hearts, we must not imagine that it is through our own ability but by God's power working through us. 'We have this treasure from God but we are only like clay jars that hold the treasure' (4:7a, ERV). Despite trials and tribulations, setbacks and disappointments in the Master's service during this life, the prospect of eternal glory should spur us on and give us confidence to persevere.

Standing firm

A desire to be admired and appreciated can jeopardise Christian witness because we want to avoid being thought of as 'a bit odd' or someone who holds extreme views. Similarly, a desire for eminence or the lure of possessions or the enticement of worldly status—accorded by human decision, not by God's will and purpose—can deflect from a total commitment to the cause of Christ. In making choices about how to use our knowledge, expertise and abilities, we are reminded that true discipleship demands 'unconditional surrender' to the point where we can say with Paul that 'I have been crucified with Christ and I no longer live but Christ lives in me. The life I now live in the body, I live by faith in the Son of God, who loved me and gave himself for me' (Galatians 2: 20, NIVUK). The renunciation of self to which Paul refers may be a 'once-in-a-lifetime decision or more likely, a series of decisions made during life's journey, as we become increasingly aware of the paucity of our commitment and the need for repentance, renewal and a fresh determination to live by faith, not by sight' (2 Corinthians 5:7).

While the prevailing approach among many people in the liberal-minded Western World is syncretism ('pick-and-mix' from a variety of sources and beliefs), followers of Jesus need to immerse themselves in the truth claim that he is the only way to the Father, as Jesus emphasised in his ministry and the

Apostles reinforced in their written testimonies (Gospel accounts and letters). Opposition is uncomfortable but we should welcome such interest rather than resent it or be uneasy that challenges by sceptics will cause us to falter in our witness or hinder the impact of the message. The Holy Spirit is the supreme evangelist and His influence should reassure us that whatever the apparent outcome of an interaction with a non-believer, we do not need to concern ourselves with it. Our role is to speak, pray and trust God to bring about change in the person, in line with God's will and purpose.

Summary

In Part 5, I have sought to show that discipleship involves cost, as well as accruing spiritual blessing. Potential followers of Jesus vary in the sacrifices that they are willing to endure in serving the King of kings. Committed believers are able to celebrate suffering and challenges for the sake of the Gospel and their allegiance to Christ when convinced that they are obeying him and following the narrow path that leads to life eternal.

Jesus made it clear that mere mental assent to his demand for total allegiance does not provide the necessary persistence and courage required when faced with the realities of living wholeheartedly for him in a world that is largely dismissive or passive towards the urgency for repentance, turning from sin and placing their trust in the Saviour. Jesus set the example for every believer to press on and 'run the race of faith' even when circumstances are unpromising; thus: 'We have come to share in Christ, if indeed we hold our original conviction firmly to the very end' (Hebrews 3:14, NIVUK).

The suffering endured by many fellow Christians (brothers and sisters in Christ) puts into perspective the relatively low levels of persecution in more liberal societies. Suffering for Christ is outweighed by the joy of knowing that if we are walking in step with his Spirit then by God's grace, we will receive our reward when life comes to an end and hear his commendation: 'Well done, good and faithful servant' (Matthew 5:21, NKJV). In the meantime, there is a Gospel to proclaim in word, deed and lived testimony.

What do you believe?

1. Jesus's command to go out into the world and share the Good News was a command intended solely for his disciples at the time.
2. Evangelism is the job of clergy and full-time workers.
3. God will bring the people of His choosing into the Kingdom, despite our limitations.
4. Christians who are reluctant to share their testimony are failing their Lord.
5. It is better to emphasise the good news of redemption and say as little as possible about the consequences of rejecting Christ.
6. Truth with sensitivity is the best approach to use with unbelievers.
7. Evangelism is most effective through the way our lives are in harmony with the things we say and do.
8. More people are more likely to be won for Christ through prayer and friendship than through direct evangelism.

Part 6
Becoming More Like Jesus

Philippians 2: 5–11

In your relationships with one another, have the same mind-set as Christ Jesus who, being in very nature [in the form of] God, did not consider equality with God something to be used to his own advantage; rather, he made himself nothing by taking the very nature [form of] of a servant, being made in human likeness. And being found in appearance as a man, he humbled himself by becoming obedient to death—even death on a cross! Therefore God exalted him to the highest place and gave him the name that is above every name, that at the name of Jesus every knee should bow, in heaven and on earth and under the earth, and every tongue acknowledge that Jesus Christ is Lord, to the glory of God the Father (NIVUK).

I Peter 2: 4–6

The Lord Jesus is the living stone. The people of the world decided that they did not want this stone. But he is the one God chose as one of great value. So come to him. You also are like living stones, and God is using you to build a spiritual house. You are to serve God in this house as holy priests, offering him spiritual sacrifices that he will accept because of Jesus Christ (ERV).

Preface to Part 6

There is a well-known saying that imitation is the sincerest form of flattery. It is undoubtedly true that vogues in dress, speech and behaviour have become increasingly prevalent in Western nations, as forms of communication and advertising have become more widespread and sophisticated. The urge to imitate others seems to have grown stronger over recent generations, as the standard of living has risen, reflected in the growth of consumerism and fashion. Among younger people, the need to stay relevant and conform to the latest styles and beliefs has accelerated in recent years, though older folk have not escaped being affected by these trends. Terms and identities such as 'celebrity' and 'influencer' and 'icon' have dominated the media, with close attention paid to the espoused customs and opinions expressed by public figures.

Christians are not immune from the impact of these societal currents but their chief purpose in life must be to find fulfilment in Christ-likeness, and learning to love him and those with whom we have contact more earnestly. While 'separation from the world' has implications for the way in which we speak, act and behave, there is a balance to be sought between being 'in the world' (i.e., where God has placed us at this time in our lives; Esther 4:14) but not 'of the world' (i.e., not conforming to worldly ways; Romans 12:2).

The immense human and economic damage caused by viral pandemics, together with an increasing awareness of the need to conserve natural resources and address worldwide changes in temperatures, has created a new class of celebrities. These modern-day champions include medical practitioners at the forefront of producing vaccines and pioneers of information technologies.

While thanking God for the skills and abilities that He has given to men and women, and admiring their contributions to people's wellbeing, Christians must ensure that worshipping and serving Jesus, and declaring the Gospel, constitute their focal points, howbeit alongside doing practical work to (a) earn an honest living and (b) on behalf of humanitarian causes.

Chapter 11
Emulating Christ

Introduction

In earlier chapters, I highlighted the need for Christians' lives to be transformed by the indwelling Holy Spirit, as they submit to His will and purpose. Trying hard or crudely copying what is perceived to be a likeness of Jesus or even immersion in a study of the Scriptures does not achieve genuine transformation. Rather, it is by coming to Christ and abiding in him through prayer, meditating on the Bible ('Study to show yourself approved of God', 2 Timothy 2:15, KJV) and walking in step with the Spirit. In this way, believers become his ambassadors on earth and 'the face of Jesus' to the world.

I have also emphasised that becoming more like Jesus demands more than a once-for-all decision. We are created in his likeness through *continual* submission and demonstrating our love for God and for others in practical ways (as Jesus commanded), while acknowledging that in addition to God's favour and the approval of fair-minded people, we also run the risk of opposition and scorn.

In this chapter, I follow up and expand some of the issues raised in Chapter 1, in which I distinguished between imitation and true likeness. Emulating Christ is to be submerged in his love and desire to see people saved from sin and the power of death, such that they receive the gift of eternal life and have hope in this life and beyond. Jesus fully submitted to the Father's will and exemplified the ways in which God can similarly use our lives for His glory and the promotion of Kingdom values. In all these things, the key principle is that change must occur from within a person before it can be manifested outwardly.

Transformation Not Adulation

Modelling

When we are young, it is a common wish to emulate a person we admire, such as a television celebrity, an older friend, a group leader or a relative. We may marvel at their talent or applaud their expertise or eulogise about their personality or extol their character. We may attempt to model ourselves on aspects that are particularly attractive, though in all likelihood with limited success. Even so, the urge to adopt somebody else's persona is strong, notably among children (e.g., imagining themselves to be Superheroes) and young people (adopting their idol's dress, speech and mannerisms). Over time, fantasies and flights of imagination are replaced by life's realities, whereby most of these transient fancies fade and die.

As we grow older and more mature, it becomes increasingly apparent that most of our earlier heroes were far from faultless and their lives were sometimes tainted by sinful habits and self-indulgence. We also begin to realise that much of the advice offered to us by older family members and caring friends about the folly of modelling our lives on the rich-and-famous was wiser that we had been willing to accept at the time.

While the urge to imitate other people is deeply rooted in our human condition, it has to be balanced against several factors, including a realisation of the sacrifices that they had to make to achieve their goals or status, and the private side of their characters (often far less impressive than their outward appearance). There is also the need to allow our own personalities, abilities and desires to blossom naturally without the constraints imposed by an obsession with an individual, movement, crusade or human activity.

There are a number of Old Testament Scriptures that warn against imitating godless practices, particularly idol worship. The New Testament writers focus on a more positive message of imitating their leaders' faith, goodness and way of life (e.g., Hebrews 13:7), while avoiding anything evil (3 John 11). The writer of the Book of Hebrews emphasises that imitating examples of godly lives that are lived for the glory of God requires a willing and active engagement in demonstrating love: 'We want each of you to be willing and eager to show your love like that the rest of your life. Then you will be sure to get what you hope for' (6:11). The writer also warns about the danger of slothfulness and a lack of diligence, such that they miss out on their present and eternal inheritance. By contrast, exhibiting faith and patience brings its own reward: 'We don't want you to be lazy. We want you to be like those who, because of their faith and patience, will get what God has promised' (6:12).

Regardless of state of health, age, experience or ability, every Christian should seek to display the fruit of the Spirit (Galatians Chapter 5). Our 'modelling' entails responding openly to the sort of attitude and behaviour that pleases God, so that He can produce in us the qualities that glorify Him. As Paul explained to the Galatians, 'the Holy Spirit produces this kind of fruit in our lives' (5:22–23, NLT), summarised as follows:

➢ *Love:* Not the sentimental love depicted in countless films and books, but allowing the love of Jesus to become a natural part of our lives and conduct that produces healing and blessing.

➢ *Joy:* Not a fleeting happiness, but a deep contentment that comes from having complete confidence in God to lead and guide us through life's journey.

➢ *Peace:* Not appeasement, but a desire to put into practice the words of Jesus: 'Blessed are those who work for peace, for they will be called children of God' (Matthew 5:9, NLT).

➢ *Patience:* Not a case of barely containing our frustration, but of being calm, measured and courteous, remembering that Christ died for even the most obnoxious person.

➢ *Kindness:* Not reluctantly, but from a passionate desire to speak words of encouragement and to support others, motivated by a loving heart.

➢ *Goodness:* Not merely doing what is right, but displaying a purity of spirit and wholesomeness that draws respect and admiration from others, as Jesus demanded: 'Let your light shine before others, that they may see your good deeds and glorify your Father in heaven' (Matthew 5:9, NIVUK).

➢ *Faithfulness:* Not an unthinking allegiance to a person (other than Jesus) or cause (other than the Gospel of life), but being reliable, determined, steadfast and supportive.

➢ *Gentleness:* Not being weak or feeble, but sympathetic and approachable, with a deep-rooted determination to show concern for those we meet in our words and actions.

➢ *Self-control:* Not only controlling the way we speak and behave, but allowing the Spirit to make us calm, clear-headed, decisive and restrained in our responses to every situation, even under provocation or in a time of crisis.

Insight

In allowing the Holy Spirit to transform our lives in the ways described above, it is often the case that He will help us to develop the fruit by placing us in situations that demand the need to exercise them. In other words, God doesn't simply bestow the qualities on us but provides opportunities for them to evolve in the warp and woof of everyday life.

Change from within

While seeking to emulate admirable qualities that we observe in other people is commendable, the quest for genuine and long-lasting adjustments in our outlook and behaviour involves far more than a superficial attempt to copy their conduct. Transforming change (literally, 'conversion') must be generated internally and expressed externally, rather than using outward forms of mimicry, which we then attempt to internalise and take root. After a discussion about lifestyle, character and behaviour, I recall a senior member of the church commenting to the group about one of his character weaknesses by stating: *I am as I am*, to which the wise minister replied: *Yes, but God doesn't necessarily want you to stay that way!* The centrality of the work of the Holy Spirit is woven throughout the remainder of this chapter, reinforcing the necessity that He should be integral to all of our lives and conduct on a continuous basis.

In Chapter 1, I explored issues relating to who the 'real' Jesus was and highlighted the popularity of 'lookalike' competitions or other forms of representation in which competitors attempt to convince the judges of their authenticity. It soon becomes obvious that despite their superficial appearance and accurate mannerisms, the contestants are merely doppelgangers or to use a more modern expression, 'dead ringers' and not the person they are imitating. The story is told that for a joke, the real Charlie Chaplin entered a 'Charlie Chaplin lookalike' competition and was only given third place, which only serves to illustrate the limitations of deception! By contrast, the writer of the Book of Hebrews asserts that those who wish to emulate Christ must allow his power to work within them and transform each of us into his likeness; in essence, seeking to please the Father and living for His glory.

The Apostle Paul underlined the importance of being transformed rather than attempting to imitate admirable behaviour: 'Don't copy the behaviour and customs of this world but [rather] let God transform you into a new person by changing the way you think. Then you will learn to know God's will for you, which is good and pleasing and perfect' (Romans 12:2, NLT). We note in Paul's words that he emphasises the need to change the way we *think*, as mindless conformity does not lead to life-changing attitudes and behaviour. Importantly, such regenerating work requires each person's active cooperation and is never forced upon him or her. Put simply, God is not in the business of brainwashing or coercion—a claim sometimes made by unbelievers. I address the important issue of using our minds and the way we think at greater length later in the chapter.

Drawing on the transforming power of the Holy Spirit to renew our minds facilitates godly wisdom and insight to impact our thoughts, words and deeds. Although God accepts us as cleansed from sin by trusting in His salvation, our underlying sinful nature (described in old versions of the Bible as our 'old man') necessitates constant confession and repentance, such that we are cleansed from all unrighteousness. In the next section, I rehearse some of Jesus's attributes on earth, not least how his determination to go to Calvary and carry the sins of the world in his body are highly significant for every believer desiring to emulate the Saviour.

Insight

An unknown author penned these words to summarise the believer's role in seeking to please God: 'Little self-denials, little honesties, little passing words of kindness; little victories over favourite temptations—these are the silent threads of gold which, when woven together, gleam out so brightly in the pattern of life of which God approves'. The question that every believer should be asking is: 'In what way am I denying self to honour Jesus in my life?'

Jesus as the Supreme Example

Evidence and proof

It is only possible to discover what Jesus was like in his daily life by studying the Gospel accounts compiled by Matthew, John Mark (usually known as Mark), Luke the physician (a Gentile) and John, together with insights provided by the letters written by the Apostles—defined as being men with a first-hand experience of Jesus's life and ministry or otherwise given divine insight into

God's purposes. In doing so, there is a crucial distinction to be made between *evidence* and *proof*, as the former provides the substance for the latter. In a court case, the weight of evidence has to convince the judge and jury that proof has been established. In the case of Jesus's status and mission, the evidence from eyewitness accounts and the transformed lives of his followers down the ages all testify to its validity.

While the first three Gospel writers principally focused on what Jesus said and did during his earthly ministry, John helps us to understand the *person* of Jesus, notably to prove beyond dispute that he was Christ, the Son of God, and that those who believe in him might be rescued from sin and granted eternal life. John concludes his Gospel with this summary of Jesus's ministry and its purpose: 'And truly Jesus did many other signs in the presence of His disciples, which are not written in this book; but these are written that you may believe that Jesus is the Christ [Messiah], the Son of God, and that believing you may have life in His name' (20:30–31, NKJV). The nature of these signs and their significance form a fascinating study but the critical factor centres on each person 'believing' and thereby receiving 'life in his name'. Mere acknowledgement of the things that Jesus said and did is insufficient; it must be accompanied by exercising faith and trust in him, authenticated through the way in which we think, speak and behave.

Evidence from the Synoptic Gospels and letters

The Gospel accounts compiled by Matthew, Mark and Luke—the Synoptic Gospels, derived from the Greek word *synoptikos*, which loosely translated means: 'able to be seen together'—share details of the events, messages and prophecies made by Jesus, many of which are placed in the same chronological order and with similar wording. Owing to the similarity in content across the three Gospels, it has been speculated that they either collaborated to produce as accurate a description of Jesus's life and work as possible; or they drew from a common source (sometimes referred to as 'Q') and/or other sources. We have a description about the origin of the source of the information and its fidelity in Luke's Gospel from his opening statement: 'Many have undertaken to draw up an account of the things that have been fulfilled among us, just as they were handed down to us by those who from the first were eyewitnesses and servants of the word. With this in mind, since I myself have carefully investigated everything from the beginning, I too decided to write an orderly [accurate] account for you, most excellent Theophilus, so that you may know the certainty of the things you have been taught' (1:1–4, NIVUK). Key words in Luke's statement include 'eyewitnesses', 'carefully investigated', 'orderly account' and 'certain' of the truth.

The fact that Luke emphasised the accuracy of his account, drawn from eyewitnesses (plural) and the truth of the events that he had carefully investigated, is significant because he was a well-educated man communicating with someone in high office (Theophilus), who would not be easily swayed by a contrived narrative. Luke—who also compiled the Acts of the Apostles—is noted for his attention to detail and painstaking descriptions of real-life episodes. Theophilus, to whom the Acts account was also sent, was evidently an intelligent Roman official, who would need to be convinced by the writing's authenticity before sharing it widely, as he undoubtedly did subsequently.

The Synoptic Gospel accounts, together with the writings of the Apostles— Paul (the major contributor), Simon Peter, James (half-brother of Jesus), Jude and an unknown writer of the Book of Hebrews, so-called owing to its Jewish orientation, provide a detailed compendium of Jesus's earthly life, ministry and teaching, and the implications for his followers. In addition to his letters and Gospel account, John also wrote a powerful summary of the extraordinary revelation given to him by God concerning the risen Jesus's assessment of the current state of the churches, thus: 'Write in a book everything you see, and send it to the seven churches in the cities of Ephesus, Smyrna, Pergamum, Thyatira, Sardis, Philadelphia, and Laodicea' (Revelation 1:11). The revelation also described spiritual warfare in heavenly realms, the fate of believers, the different fate of godless people, and the end of the world as it currently exists. The Book of Revelation ('the revealing') is therefore aptly named.

Insight

None of the written accounts offer the slightest hint of being contrived or exaggerated and should be taken at face value, with the proviso that only the Holy Spirit can furnish the insight needed to fully grasp all the truth contained within them and their implication for living and dying.

The humility of Jesus

In seeking to emulate Jesus, we should note in Paul's letter to Christians in the Roman barrack town of Philippi that Jesus Christ in his pre-earthly existence did not 'hold on' to His equality with the Father; rather, he proceeded to fulfil the salvation role that God the Father assigned to him (see a full description in

Philippians Chapter 2). It was an unparalleled sacrifice for the Maker of the Universe and the One who created all things to vacate his place in heaven and choose the 'narrow path that leads to life', a phrase that Jesus later used in his ministry as a means of describing a decision that we must all make about following the direction that God has set before us. The Father asked the Son to save mankind by giving up heaven's glory and being willing to undertake an unenviable course of action:

- To be born as a baby on earth.
- To grow up in humble circumstances with a young mother and adoptive father.
- To be admired by many but rejected by religious zealots and their supporters.
- To endure hate, scorn, ridicule and persecution.
- To carry the sins of the world in his body by dying a criminal's death upon a cross.
- To trust the Father to raise him from the dead.

The Son of God would have had the right to remain in glory with the Father but voluntarily agreed to become 'God incarnate' because he was the only sinless one able to bear the sins of the world in his body on the cross. No human could have accomplished the task because, as we read in Paul's letter to the Christians in Rome: 'Everyone has sinned; we all fall short of God's glorious standard' (3:23, NLT). As every person is tainted with sin and fails in many and various ways, it makes us ineligible to be the 'Lamb of God, who takes away the sin of the world', as John the Baptist declared the man Jesus to be (John 1:29, NIVUK). The Baptist's acknowledgement of Jesus's high status is evident when John accepted that despite his own popularity, he (John) must become less ('decrease') while Jesus must become greater ('increase'). For John the Baptist to make such a declaration is astounding, as he was the centre of public attention, fulfilling God's call upon his life and—a fact not to be underestimated—a close relative of Jesus.

The Son made it clear that he would be willing to submit to all the above conditions. Imagine if he had replied to the Father that the price of the sacrifices he would have to make were too great and sought an easier, less demanding alternative! Thank God that Jesus's response was—coining a phrase from

Charles Wesley's famous hymn, *And can it be*, 'empty himself of all but love' and leave the unimaginable glory of Heaven to tread this earth as a human being. Right to the end of his life, Jesus's single aim was to obey the Father and even as he faced his crucifixion, John records that Jesus prayed in the Garden of Gethsemane: 'I want your will to be done, not mine' (26:39, NLT).

Furthermore, the Son of God did not agree grudgingly to come down from his glory but completely subjugated his own will to that of the Father, taking the form of a servant in the earthly setting—born under degrading circumstances in an animal pen and becoming the adopted son of a carpenter/builder in the disreputable Galilean town of Nazareth. Jesus did not insist on residing in a palace, as the most privileged person on earth—a status to which he was fully entitled—but made plain his priority, as John records in his Gospel: 'My food is to do the will of him who sent me and to finish his work' (4:34, NIVUK).

It is significant that Jesus did not set preconditions in enacting his Father's will but 'made himself nothing'. The principle that he established for us to follow is that it is one thing to be obedient and do what is right (in Jesus's case to come to earth, live as a man and sacrifice his earthly body), it is quite another thing to become as 'nothing' in doing so. In other words, just as Jesus humbled himself and became completely submissive to the Father's plan of salvation for the world, so we should set aside our own priorities and desires, and be willing to let the Holy Spirit work in us and through us to achieve His purposes. Our response to this crucially important 'high calling' is explored later in the chapter.

Jesus the sacrificial lamb

There are more astounding truths about Jesus from which we can draw strength and inspiration. Not only was Jesus obedient; not only did he humble himself and become a servant; not only did he become as nothing; he also went willingly to the Cross of Calvary, bearing the shame, false accusations and ridicule; being despised and rejected, forsaken and completely alone, without even the comfort of the Father to support him, as his anguish was compounded by his isolation.

It is impossible for us to fully grasp what it meant for the sinless Son of God to carry the sin burdens of the whole world and allow his shed blood to be spilt in order to cleanse each person from the guilt and responsibility of the sin that has blighted humanity from the beginning of time. We can only stand amazed at Jesus's love for us. How wonderful, too, that we catch a glimpse of the Father's response to Jesus in Paul's letter to the Philippians: 'He exalted Him to the highest place and gave him the name that is above every other name' (2:9–11, NIVUK) or in the NLT translation: 'elevated him to the place of highest honour'. In the same letter, Paul goes on to say that one day, every knee shall bow to the Son of God and admit (confess) that he is Lord, which is quite a prospect, not least for people who have refused to accept God's claim upon their lives and are confronted with their spiritual nakedness, as they face judgement without the blood of Christ to cover their sins or his advocacy on their behalf.

Characteristics of Jesus's Ministry

While accepting that imitating Jesus's behaviour and priorities is subject to the extent to which we allow the Holy Spirit to penetrate our mind and will and heart, and our willingness to respond obediently, it is nevertheless instructive to identify characteristics of Jesus's ministry in setting the standard for all those who aspire to be his true disciples and 'follow in his footsteps', notably:

1. The nature of his words and the tone of his language
2. The way in which he prioritised his time
3. His response to human crises
4. His wisdom when dealing with controversial situations
5. The way in which he responded to the poor and needy

As a means of examining the above list of characteristics, it is helpful to distinguish the way in which Jesus used his mind, heart, eyes, voice, feet and hands in responding to and addressing human situations, thereby establishing the highest possible standard for believers who are fully committed to following and serving the Master.

Having the mind of Christ

Jesus knew the right decisions to make and the correct way to proceed in his ministry because his mind was fully God-orientated and not self-centred. He didn't set off to pursue His own way and then, when an important decision had to be made, start pleading with the Father to show Him what he should do. Instead, Jesus did nothing of his own volition but allowed the Holy Spirit to lead and guide him continually. John documents Jesus's words: 'I tell you the truth: the Son can do nothing by himself. He does only what he sees the Father doing.

Whatever the Father does, the Son also does. For the Father loves the Son and shows him everything he is doing' (5:19–20, NLT). Such total abandonment of his own will did not mean that Jesus was some kind of automaton but that his thoughts, words and deeds were wholly synchronised with that of the Father.

For those who seek to emulate Jesus, it is sometimes difficult to know when it is their own desire (either selfish or altruistic) that motivates them to make particular choices, or when they are being prompted and led by the Spirit. The solution lies in ascertaining whether we are *exercising faith* in the pursuit of the purposes of God (to bless, heal and create the best conditions for moral righteousness) or pursuing our own goals (status, prestige, wealth, success, indulgence, popularity). In other words, to achieve God's purposes in the world, we need the faith that He provides and we employ in the way we use our time and resources. Achieving our own purposes that are not birthed in heavenly wisdom and divine enabling, however well-intended they may be, are unlikely to have a lasting impact for Kingdom work.

Although we are too sinful to approach the Father directly for guidance in precisely the way that Jesus did, a course has been provided to overcome this handicap, as Paul explained to the Christians in Corinth: 'For who has known the mind of the Lord so as to instruct him? But we have the mind of Christ' (1 Corinthians 2:16, NIVUK, quoting from Isaiah 40:13) or as profoundly translated in the CEV: 'We understand what Christ is thinking'. The clear implication of Paul's declaration is that if we want to know the mind of God, we must first allow Christ's spirit to empower us and permit his love to possess us. The process by which this empowerment and creation of a loving heart takes place is largely beyond human comprehension but it becomes a reality when we accept its truth and step out in faith and joyful obedience.

Having the heart of Christ

In the 1960s, a popular song called *Anyone who had a heart*, written by Burt Bacharach (music) and Hal David (lyrics), included the memorable line: 'Anyone who ever loved could look at me and know that I love you'. These lyrics evoke the sense of love being so deep and sincere that it affects our physical appearance and reactions. Use of the term 'heart' indicates that a belief, emotion or desire is embedded in the deepest recesses of our human existence ('the soul'). To claim that there is no love like the love of Jesus and that his heart was pure love (i.e., akin to the Father) is not fanciful and can be stated with full confidence, as even a cursory examination of the Gospel accounts readily confirms. Jesus's love was not sentimental or transitory; rather, it was generated by a passionate desire from within his being to save sin-ravaged people by pointing them to their creator God and rescuing them from Satan's control. In short, his mission was rooted in selfless love, not judgement or vengeance or self-aggrandisement. John offers a succinct statement of this wonderful truth: 'Herein is love, not that we loved God, but that he loved us, and sent his Son to be the propitiation [atonement] for our sins' (I John 4:10, KJV).

We may be tempted to ask whether Jesus's love not only embraces generally decent people, who endeavour to live responsible lives—sinful, weak and prone to failure as they may be—but also those whose existence has been devastated by the ravages of sin and wickedness to the extreme detriment of themselves and others. To discover the answer, we need only to look towards Calvary where Jesus freely gave his life to carry the world's sin and offer hope for the hopeless and freedom for those in the depths of despair and the grip of ungodly desires. Whether those sin-stricken individuals choose to repent and turn to Christ for complete cleansing and renewal is a vital factor in the salvation process. Suffice it to state that in describing the loving heart of Jesus, we can gain reassurance and hope from the fact God does not want anyone to be lost but to repent and receive forgiveness. As the Apostle Peter explains: 'The Lord is not slow in keeping his promise, as some understand slowness. Instead he is patient with you, not wanting anyone to perish, but everyone to come to repentance' (2 Peter 3:9, NIVUK).

As we contemplate the love and passion in the heart of Jesus for the world's population—past, present and future—we do well to consider where our own motivation lies in serving others and seeking their salvation. Is it duty or habit or fear or instinct or love? In his first letter to the Christians in Corinth, Paul emphasised the need for them to check their motives to ensure that genuine love (not contrived or prideful or otherwise 'manufactured') had to be the driving force for their actions: 'What if I could speak all languages of humans and of angels? If I did not love others, I would be nothing more than a noisy gong or a clanging cymbal' (13:1, NKJV). The significance of Paul's words is that whether we like or loathe someone, Holy Spirit love should subsume all other emotions and provide the motivation for our responses and actions.

Furthermore, as James emphasised throughout his epistle, expressing our faith in God without accompanying action is hollow and meaningless. In his speech before King Agrippa (Acts Chapter 20), the Apostle Paul explained that repentance and turning to God is only shown to be genuine by a person's subsequent actions. In pursuing good deeds ('good works'), it is therefore imperative to heed Jesus's warning: 'Watch out! Don't do your good deeds publicly, to be admired by others, for you will lose the reward from your Father in heaven' (Matthew 6:1, NLT), but also to be encouraged by the promise in Revelation 14:13 that although our deeds may not be acknowledged in this life, they will have significance when we enter Heaven and God evaluates the level of our commitment to Him and service to others.

Having the eyes of Christ

Despite Jesus's clear instruction that we should not judge someone based solely on his or her outward appearance, it is a common experience to form an opinion of a person constructed purely on the way that he or she looks, speaks and conforms to societal norms (such as table manners or rough language). An important question for all those who seek to emulate Jesus is whether we see people through a lens of love or curiosity or suspicion or superiority. With few exceptions, the Gospel writers do not give any indication of the coarseness or sophistication of people's speech and dress; just their state of heart, motives, and depth of health and poverty. The only significant occasion that Jesus employed these descriptors was when he pointed out that despite their eloquent words and regalia, a group of the religious leaders were full of weasel words and hypocrisy (Matthew 23:27–8).

The Gospels give numerous examples of the way in which Jesus's eyes viewed the world in which he lived. His eyes filled with tears as he wept over the sin of the people of Jerusalem (Luke 19:41) and when Lazarus died (John Chapter 11). He was saddened when the rich young man turned away because he valued his possessions more than his desire to obey Jesus (Mark Chapter 10). He reacted with anger at the way in which those in authority and many of the religious leaders treated the poor and helpless. He lifted his eyes to heaven, as he prayed to the Father to confirm His will and purpose (John 11:41 and 17:1).

It is a challenge for every believer to see people as Jesus saw them: sheep without a shepherd, lost and helpless, and in need of a Saviour. Our eyes should be eyes that fill with tears of happiness when others are richly blessed and tears of sadness when they suffer pain or reject the claims of Christ or choose a pathway that is likely to damage their present lives and have a negative impact on those around them through destructive habits, wrong decisions or selfishness. The psalmist describes how God collects our tears in His bottle and records them in His book (56:8, KJV).

In some cultures, tears are perceived as evidence of weakness and resisted, yet who cannot weep at the thought of multitudes 'in the valley of decision' that are destined for a lost eternity, devoid of God's protecting hand and separated from Him forever. As the prophet Joel predicted: 'Multitudes, multitudes in the valley of decision. For the day of the Lord is near in the valley of decision. The sun and moon are darkened and the stars withdraw their shining' (3:14–15, NRSV). It has rightly been said that no believer should speak of Hell with dry eyes.

Insight

We can give glory to God if we ever reach the point that one exceptionally caring Christian missionary experienced when a new convert who knew very little about Christianity, came to the mission church 'asking to see Jesus'. The seeker thought the mission worker was Jesus because his life was so similar to the Jesus of the Bible about whom the new believer was hearing. The challenge is plain for all those who claim to be followers of Christ.

Having the voice of Christ

The voice is a powerful instrument and no one can fully tame the tongue. Words spoken in haste and perhaps later regretted can result in emotional pain for the recipient, as their negative impact worms its way into the person's mind. By contrast, a sincere word of kindness or encouragement can bring joy to the heart and lightness of spirit. James reminds us about the tongue's contrasting functions: '[The tongue] is restless and evil, full of deadly poison. Sometimes it praises our Lord and Father and sometimes it curses those who have been made in the image of God. And so blessing and cursing come pouring out of the same mouth. Surely, my brothers and sisters, this is not right!' (3:8–10, NLT). In similar vein, Paul urges the Christians in Colossae to be careful about the way in which they speak: 'Let your conversation be gracious and attractive ['seasoned with salt', NKJV], so that you will have the right response for everyone' (Colossians 4:6, NLT).

The voice of Jesus was encouraging, direct, personal and serious, but always Spirit-led. He spoke with authority to the wind and waves threatening to swamp the disciples' boat. He raised his voice to address thousands gathered to hear him preach on the hillside. He sternly exorcised evil spirits. He rebuked the disciples when they tried to prevent the children from coming to greet him. He criticised the religious leaders for their hypocrisy and arrogance. He gently chided Martha for giving too much attention to practical tasks at the expense of listening to his message. He reassured his fearful followers that although they would experience opposition and trouble, they could find peace in the midst of turmoil. He made a request that the disciple John would take care of his mother before gasping a final cry of victory when dying on the Cross.

Jesus used his voice in many and various ways but never in a pompous or self-opinionated manner; rather, he constantly referred to the importance of being obedient to his Heavenly Father and speaking the truth, even when his listeners were abusive towards him. There is never a hint of Jesus seeking popularity or trying to create a personality cult. On the contrary, he spoke of himself in terms of being a servant, as he freely gave his life for the sins of the world. Humility was a hallmark of Jesus's life, ministry and death.

In considering our own use of the voice, a habit worth cultivating is not only to listen to what the other person has to say but also to listen carefully to what *we* are saying, not merely the words themselves but also the tone we employ and any tendency we might have to accuse or insert a critical edge into our speech. The way in which people perceive the loving motive and earnestness of our discourse will make a considerable difference to the likelihood that they will be drawn to us and to the Saviour. On the one hand, there is a danger of being too assertive and forceful in conveying what we find it necessary to share; on the other hand, there is an equivalent challenge in ensuring that we don't miss an opportunity to speak for fear of offending the person or causing them to withdraw from the conversation.

An important principle is to ensure that whatever we say leaves the recipient feeling reassured and retaining self-respect (at all times), the only exception being the rare occasion when a firm word or rebuke is needed to combat unacceptable behaviour. The advice offered in Proverbs that 'a soft and gentle and thoughtful answer turns away wrath, but harsh and painful and careless words stir up anger' (15:1, AMP) is highly appropriate in today's society where abruptness, disparaging comments and derogatory remarks are all too frequently used to silence contrary views and belittle those who hold them. Paul was clear about the nature of our conversation: 'Do not use foul or abusive language. Let everything you say be good and helpful, so that your words will be an encouragement to those who hear them' (Ephesians 4:29, NLT). Key words in Paul's advice include 'good', 'helpful' and 'encourage'. We must not sound apologetic or pompous when speaking about God's love and redemption in Jesus Christ; nor should we seek to drown the person with 'many words' but rather be prepared to listen as much as speak and permeate all that we say with sensitivity and wisdom.

Having the feet of Christ

The feet of Jesus show us the steps we must take throughout life, for his feet took him where the Spirit directed. Jesus's actions at each location and situation were not based on a whim or personal preference but on a desire to exert his influence in a way that honoured the Father. As the psalmist reminds us: 'The Lord directs the steps of the godly; he delights in every detail of their lives' (Psalm 37:23, NLT), a necessary reminder that God is not merely a strategist who deals with the broad picture, but an intensely caring one, who is interested in the minutiae of our daily lives. It should be noted, however, that it is the steps of the *godly* that God directs.

One instructive example of the Spirit's intervention is found in Acts Chapter 16 when the Apostle Paul changed his plans after he was prompted by God to go to Macedonia: 'That night, Paul had a vision: A man from Macedonia in northern Greece was standing there, pleading with him: Come over to Macedonia and help us!' (16:9, NLT) The common factor in the decisions that Jesus and the prophets and apostles made was their determination to put their own preferences to one side and be obedient to the heavenly mission. Wandering from the narrow path that God sets before us is a hazardous and unwise venture, however tempting it may appear, as the character, Christian, in John Bunyan's *Pilgrim's Progress* quickly came to acknowledge after attempting to take a short cut through 'By-pass Meadow' and ending up imprisoned in the castle of Giant Despair.

It is important to recognise that Jesus trusted the Father on every occasion, even when the conditions were extremely grim. A common error made by Christians is to believe that hardship equates with taking the wrong direction and that apparent failure necessarily corresponds with misreading God's will or indicates a lack of true faith. While such sentiments are understandable, it is important to acknowledge Jesus's promise that if we are yoked with him, the bumpy road becomes 'straight' and the burden of responsibility becomes 'easy'. These promises are not given to us as a sop or sedative but rather as a firm foundation for proceeding confidently in knowing that 'this God is our God forever and ever' (Deuteronomy 33:27, NIVUK).

A helpful well-known adage correctly asserts that there is no failure except in the failure to keep trying. If we are endeavouring to follow the Spirit's leading, there is no defeat except that which emanates from our minds and there are no insurmountable barriers, save our own inherent weakness of purpose. The Holy Spirit is not in the business of withdrawing us from the battlefield when things get tough.

God has a pathway that He established for each of us before we were conceived and to the very end of life and beyond, so the principle of persevering until our final breath should be burnt into each of our hearts and minds. The psalmist writes that 'He will be our guide even to the end' (48:14b, NIVUK). Like Jacob who, in extreme old age, worshipped the Lord while using his staff to support his ailing body (described in Hebrews 11:21), we must finish well and not lose our passion for Kingdom work, despite physical or situational limitations or temptations and enticements offered by godless people and the enemy of souls, Satan. As John warned in his first letter: 'Do not love this world nor the things it offers you, for when you love the world, you do not have the love of the Father in you. For the world offers only a craving for physical pleasure, a craving for everything we see, and pride in our achievements and possessions. These are not from the Father, but are from this world' (2:15–16, NLT).

Feet are not for 'marching on the spot until we drop' but for 'walking in step with the Spirit' as our minds are focused on the will of God. If we want to be like Jesus, we have to be willing to follow the difficult path that he took: step-by-step and day-by-day, yet confident in his promise that he has set eternity in our hearts and that our labour for him will not be wasted: 'He has planted eternity in the human heart, but even so, people cannot see the whole scope of God's work from beginning to end' (Ecclesiastes 3:11b, NLT). Similarly, as Paul wrote to Christians in Corinth, we presently only see life through opaque glass or 'through a glass darkly' (I Corinthians 13:12, KJV) but one day, all things that presently perplex us will be made clear. In the meantime, God asks that we trust and obey and leave the consequences to Him.

Having the hands of Christ

The hands of Jesus play an essential role in an exploration of how he acted and responded during many and varied situations and circumstances. The poem, 'Touch of the Master's Hand' (author unknown) asks the question as to what made the difference in the quality of the music played on an old violin by a virtuoso violinist compared to an unskilled musician. The answer given is that it is the touch of the master's hand that creates the beautiful music but also, in a spiritual sense, to a person's life when God (the Master Musician) is invited to take control.

The words of Margaret Cropper's hymn, 'Jesus hands were kind hands, doing good to all' paints a strong image of the different ways in which Jesus employed his hands, as he cured those who were suffering from leprosy and touched blind eyes to restore sight; as he rebuked and calmed the raging waters; as he caressed the heads of children and grown-ups alike to bless and heal them; as he equipped his followers to sanctify others by laying his hands on them. We must also acknowledge, however, that Jesus used his hands to overturn tables in the temple courtyard—recorded by Matthew, Mark and Luke in their respective accounts of Jesus's ministry—as he confronted those who were turning a 'house of prayer' (as Jesus described it) into a 'den of robbers'.

It would be wholly neglectful when focusing on Jesus's hands to avoid making reference to the way in which they were pierced as he hung upon the Cross of Calvary. The hands that Graham Kendrick describes in his modern hymn, 'The Servant King', were those that 'flung stars into space', yet surrendered them to 'cruel nails'. The hands that blessed, healed, restored, guided and sanctified people were, in the words of Isaiah, 'pierced for our transgressions... crushed for our iniquities; the punishment that brought us peace was on him and by his wounds we are healed' (53:5, NIVUK).

It may seem that doing the equivalent of the Master's work is simply not feasible, owing to the fact that we are sinful and do not possess the same relationship with Father God that Jesus had. Whereas it is possible to emulate a loving touch or assist those in need by offering support in practical ways, it may be argued that using hands to heal the sick and empower someone for a specific task (often referred to as the 'laying on of hands') is outside the remit for the ordinary believer.

In discerning the truth about the extent to which it is possible that present-day believers should be a conduit for powerful spiritual actions, the following six points listed below are relevant. The first three points tend to support the proposition that miraculous deeds ('signs and wonders') ended with the death of the last Apostle, John, while points 4, 5 and 6 tend to support their continuation through every generation to the present day.

1. If miraculous deeds and events ended after the 'Apostolic Age', they are by definition, irrelevant today until the End Times when they signal the return of Christ.
2. Jesus warned that signs and wonders will sometimes be performed by 'false Messiahs and prophets' in an attempt to deceive Christians. See, for example, Mark 13:32.
3. Jesus was unimpressed with people who demanded signs and wonders before they would believe in him (John 4:48).
4. Jesus said that if the disciples believed in him, they would do 'greater works' because he was ascending to the Father and would send the Holy Spirit to dwell in every believer (John 14:12).
5. There have been a large number of well-documented miracles over recent years, notably—but not exclusively—in the Developing World where trust in God is more likely to be freely exercised.
6. God is perfectly capable of repeating His signs and wonders in any era, time or place to fulfil His purposes if He chooses to do so.

Where we stand in respect of each of the above points will also influence the way in which we use our hands to bless others. If we consider that the miraculous elements are not relevant today or will occur through the will of God without human involvement, we are more likely to be drawn towards practical tasks, such as helping to alleviate poverty or assisting the elderly. If we are convinced that the Holy Spirit still works to perform signs and wonders (as occurred in the early church), our focus is likely to be on more transcendent activities, such as healing and empowerment through prayer. Jesus demonstrated that it is perfectly possible to combine the 'practical' and 'spiritual' elements, but the evidence indicates that modern church fellowships tend towards taking one direction or another, the majority of which seem to favour practical works embedded within a prayerful context.

The Challenge of Implementation

Glorifying God in our lives

In seeking to become like Jesus, we must take account of the fact that although he gave up his reputation and 'made himself nothing', he was never willing to compromise his integrity. Jesus refused to meet godless people halfway over moral or life-centred issues in order to avoid unpopularity or to court favour. In the same way, though nearly all of us rightly feel that our reputation is important in helping us to witness effectively, we are not to *seek* people's praise, approval or adoration.

We read that some of the religious leaders in Jesus's day loved praise from their admirers and sycophants more than receiving God's commendation—see John Chapter 12. Praise accorded to us by people after a job well done or showing wisdom or acting for the good of others becomes more acceptable if we give God the glory for our accomplishments. Prayerful thanks and a publicly expressed desire to attribute recognition to the Lord will signal our genuine humility, strengthen the bond of intimacy we enjoy with Him and release His favour upon our lives.

Giving God thanks and glory is a far more serious matter than is conveyed through merely being courteous towards Him. In Luke's account of the early church, we read in Acts Chapter 12 that Herod Agrippa died after accepting the praise of the people, in which they claimed that he was a 'god', a declaration that he did not make any attempt to reject. This incident provides a warning that presenting oneself as worthy of receiving praise is a precarious business. It also teaches a vital lesson about the importance of deflecting praise away from an individual and towards God.

In complete contrast to Agrippa's presumptuous behaviour, Jesus refused to accept or affirm his own 'hero-worship' because it would have undermined his relationship with the Father by denying Him glory. Instead, he insisted that the Father is greater than all, despite he and the Father 'being one'. The apparent contradiction is easily explained: as a man, Jesus was the servant; as the Son of God, he is the creator, victor, redeemer, advocate and an equal part of the Godhead.

Maintaining focus

There are a large number of key figures in the Bible who demonstrated admirable perseverance in the midst of turmoil and challenge. For example, Noah spent one hundred years constructing a boat when rain was an unknown phenomenon. Abraham followed God's directing through many years of nomadic existence before His will became completely clear for Abraham's life and destiny. King David held fast when he was forced to escape both King Saul and later from his own son, Absalom (see below). The Apostle Paul endured the most appalling conditions and fierce opposition but continued to fulfil his Spirit-directed mission (see next section).

People in the Old Testament who trusted God during challenging periods in their lives did not know directly about Jesus but placed their hope and trust in the promised Redeemer who would come to save his people from their sins, as numerous prophecies foretold. King David's life had numerous peaks and troughs, yet it was during one of his most severe 'valley experiences', when he was forced to run away and hide in the desert after his son Absalom set out to kill him and seize the throne, that he discovered so much about God's character. Thus, in Psalm 63, David describes how God is worthy of our praise: 'Your unfailing love is better than life itself; how I praise you! I will praise you as long as I live, lifting up my hands to you in prayer… I will praise you with songs of joy' (63:3,5, NLT). In fact, the whole Psalm (as with numerous others in the Psalter) is saturated with expressions of praise and rejoicing. If David was so full of gratitude and thankfulness when he was suffering such intense emotional pain and anguish, we have so much more for which to thank God, not least, forgiveness from sin through Jesus Christ and the promise of an eternal home.

A focus on the Person of Jesus helps to turn our eyes away from the dissatisfaction or anxieties that we might be feeling in our present circumstances. We can luxuriate in the warmth of His love for us and the certainty of His promises, regardless of the situation. Certainly, such an attitude is easier to speak about than to practise, especially when there is a long term, worrying problem or condition gnawing its way through our minds and affecting our ability to function normally, but an essential element of faith is to trust and praise God through the challenging times in life, as well as in the straightforward ones. The prophet Isaiah declared God's Word on the matter: 'For I, the Lord, love justice. I hate robbery and wrongdoing. I will faithfully reward my people for their suffering and make an everlasting covenant with them' (61:8, NLT). It is interesting that robbery is singled out as being particularly odious, no doubt because it takes many forms, such as stealing property, depriving an innocent person of justice, and failing to give people credit for their achievements. Today, online 'theft' of someone's character and profile through impersonation is a growing problem, and brings considerable distress to the injured party.

Insight

If we develop the habit of thankfulness during the 'sunshine days', we will find it easier to give God thanks and praise during the tough times, as countless believers have discovered down the ages.

A significant incident recorded by Matthew (14:29–31) reinforces the need to look to Jesus as our source of hope and protection, and not to be distracted by discomforting circumstances. Shortly before dawn, Jesus walked on the water of Lake Galilee towards the disciples. In the half-light, the disciples initially thought they were seeing a ghost. After hearing Jesus's invitation to come to him, however, Simon Peter jumped into the sea and found that he was able to walk on the water towards Jesus. As soon as Peter took his eyes off Jesus and focused on the turbulence, he began to sink. Fortunately for Peter, Jesus rescued him and they both climbed into the boat, much to the amazement of the other disciples.

There are many lessons to be learned from Peter's actions, not least his initial courage and eagerness to be with his Lord and Master; but also his loss of confidence when he took his eyes off Jesus. We can also be reassured by a number of encouragements emanating from Jesus's involvement—his close, unseen presence in the darkest hour; his invitation to reach out to him in the storms of life; and his ability to rescue us when we falter. Of equal encouragement is the fact that even if our faith fluctuates when faced with challenging circumstances, the Master offers protection and restoration. We need only 'grasp his hand' by expressing our confidence in him and offering him praise and worship. He never fails to respond and draw us back to himself.

The Apostle Paul's example

In the time following Jesus's death, resurrection and ascension, the Apostle Paul is the supreme example of someone who persevered against all odds and remained faithful to his calling, despite the hardships he faced. In his second letter to the Christians in Corinth (11:23–31) Paul describes all that he had to endure:

- Received thirty-nine lashes on five occasions (an agonising form of torture)
- Beaten with rods three times
- Stoned
- Shipwrecked three times
- Spent one day and night adrift in the open sea
- Constantly on the move
- In danger from rivers, bandits, Jews and Gentiles
- In danger in the city and in the country
- In danger at sea
- In danger from false believers
- Often going without sleep
- Being hungry and thirsty, after going without food
- Being cold and naked
- Carrying a burden for the new churches and its people

Paul's ministry was characterised by misunderstanding, harassment by religious leaders, and threats to his life from individuals and mobs. Along with Silas, he was imprisoned in Philippi; and on his own in Jerusalem, Caesarea and during the journey to Rome, after he appealed directly to Caesar for justice. In addition, Paul and his companions were attacked or threatened in Thessalonica, Berea and Ephesus; in the last instance, a silversmith called Demetrius incited the aggression because he was unhappy about people turning away from idol worship (notably, of the goddess Artemis) and towards the true God and His Son, Jesus Christ (see Acts 19). Yet despite these vexatious and alarming experiences, Paul continued to trust God and preach the Gospel faithfully.

We are given further insights into the depth of Paul's devotion to Christ by means of the predictions that he shared with the elders of the Ephesian Church before he made the perilous journey to Jerusalem: 'And now I am bound by the Spirit to go to Jerusalem. I don't know what awaits me, except that the Holy Spirit tells me in city after city that jail and suffering lie ahead. But my life is worth nothing to me unless I use it for finishing the work assigned me by the Lord Jesus—the work of telling others the Good News about the wonderful grace of God' (Acts 20:22–24, NLT). Paul's trials and his remarkably calm and courageous response to them puts into sharp relief our relatively minor discomforts, such as:

- Being teased by friends for our beliefs.
- Being rejected or ridiculed by those we try to influence.
- Finding ourselves excluded because we refused to conform to worldly ways.
- Being overlooked for promotion because we insist on maintaining our integrity.
- Having few suitable marriage partners because we will only marry a committed Christian.
- Experiencing bodily and mental weariness because we expend our efforts in active Christian service.
- Focusing on the lowly and needy, rather than seeking the support and approval of influential people.

The relatively modest degree of suffering and sacrifice featuring in the above examples is not to minimise the distress and anguish they can produce. Teasing can morph into bullying; rejection can cause depression; lack of suitable promotion can lead to frustration; exclusion while seeking to live holy lives instead of pursuing worldly ways can create loneliness; weariness from serving the Lord leaves fewer resources for other interesting pursuits; associating with those in need may result in being taken advantage of and losing status. In addition, it must be acknowledged that one person's mild suffering may be the source of another person's serious distress. Nevertheless, in all these things, we can gain confidence from knowing that Jesus the Son of God understands our weaknesses, 'for he faced all the testing that we do, yet did not sin. So let us come boldly to the throne of our gracious God [in prayer]. There we will receive His mercy and find grace to help us when we need it most' (Hebrews 4:14–16, NLT).

Running the race
Author Mark Twain claimed that the two most important days in a person's life are the day you are born and the day you find out why! Christians can modify

the statement to say that apart from the day you are born, the two most important days are the day you are born from above by the Spirit of God to receive new life in Christ, and the day you find out the right direction in life for the race that God has set before you.

For genuine effectiveness, the direction in which we run the race must be inspired and controlled by the Holy Spirit, motivated by a love for Jesus Christ and a serious concern for fallen humanity that needs to know about the Saviour, who gave his life for them and promises the wonderful prospect of a blissful eternity. As featured earlier, it is possible to grind away in an area of service that does not have the Spirit's anointing and thereby render our efforts largely ineffectual. We can also be committed to what we believe we are called to do, which is commendable, but to lose sight of its principal purpose, which is to serve and glorify the Master and not to keep us usefully occupied.

Furthermore, over-commitment in Kingdom work can be and often is counterproductive, as exhaustion sets in and health suffers. Men with family commitments, who also work hard in the local church or other forms of Christian ministry, together with a demanding secular job, can quickly become overwhelmed with the intensity of balancing these responsibilities. Women with family responsibilities seem endlessly busy. Unmarried women are sometimes wrongly considered to have unlimited freedom and therefore called upon whenever there are jobs to be done or vacancies filled. Wisdom about 'doing more by doing less' is needed, especially as in church life there are too few workers and too many observers.

In Revelation 14:12, the Apostle John records God's warning that as the end of the world as we presently know it draws ever closer, the need for 'running the race' with endurance and single-mindedness becomes ever more pressing, as the writer of the Book of Hebrews explains: 'For you have need of patient endurance [to bear up under difficult circumstances without compromising], so that when you have carried out the will of God, you may receive and enjoy to the full what is promised' (10:36, AMP). God's blessing awaits us, as we run the race with determination. By persevering in the direction that God has set before us and empowered by His Spirit, we will enjoy to the full what is promised: the saving of our souls.

The Apostle Paul clearly expressed his own intentions, as he wrote to Christians in a number of the churches that he established during his missionary journeys: 'But one thing I do: Forgetting what is behind and straining towards what is ahead, I press on towards the goal to win the prize for which God has called me heavenwards in Christ Jesus' (Philippians 3:13–14, NIVUK). The writer of the Book of Hebrews echoes a similar sentiment: 'Therefore, since we are surrounded by such a huge crowd of witnesses to the life of faith, let us strip off every weight that slows us down, especially the sin that so easily trips us up. And let us run with endurance the race God has set before us' (Hebrews 12:1, NLT).

Insight

Although the idea that the huge crowd (other versions use 'cloud') mentioned in Hebrews Chapter 12 refers to thousands of saints watching from heaven is an attractive one, it lacks scriptural credibility. The crowd of witnesses are those who have set an example to us by remaining faithful to God down the centuries, even under trial, as listed in Hebrews Chapter 11. Significant statements in the Bible should always be read and interpreted in context, not in isolation.

Once we are clear about our God-given calling, waiting around for 'something to happen' is not an option; sensitivity to the Spirit's leading and showing godly patience should not be confused with procrastination. Life really is too short to neglect opportunities—and the need for decisive action in our sin-sick world is too pressing—to delay taking up our calling with every ounce of faith and commitment that we can muster, whether the prospects of success are superficially hopeful or not, always bearing in mind that every believer's principal aim is to glorify God. It is true that Christians are yoked with Christ and must therefore move at his pace, but when the trumpet sounds in our lives, we must respond wholeheartedly. As with all aspects of life, every action and decision must be built on a solid base of integrity, love and obedience if it is to endure and fulfil God's purpose.

The cost of following Jesus will almost certainly demand sacrifice on our part but the rewards are great if we are willing to persevere and finish the race that he has set before us, as Paul emphasises in his letter to Christians in Philippi: 'I run towards the goal, so that I can win the prize of being called to heaven. This is the prize that God offers because of what Christ Jesus has done' (3:14, CEV)

Holding on or letting go

When young children feel anxious or fearful, they cling tightly to a parent or trusted adult for reassurance. Many a child has let go of a string and watched sadly as the cherished balloon soars into the sky before bursting into fragments or sailing out of sight. As adults, turbulent experiences can make it feel that we are being swept away like that renegade balloon, or tossed and twisted like an unwieldy kite, as the situation veers out of control and we scarcely know where to turn or how to act.

A film of young naval recruits in the 1920s showed them trying to secure a giant passenger balloon (commonly referred to as a 'blimp') as it threatened to break loose from its moorings. The balloon had twenty or more ropes dangling from it, each one held by a recruit to aid stability. Unfortunately, a powerful gust of wind ripped the airship from its anchorage and sent it speeding into the atmosphere, whereupon most of the boys let go of the ropes and dropped safely to the ground; two boys, however, clung on. The balloon continued to rise high into the air and one young man fell to his death after his strength gave way and his grip failed. A second boy managed to clutch the main rigging and was eventually saved.

From time to time, and usually without warning, our lives reflect that tragic event, as external forces threaten to tear us from our moorings and sweep us into the air. Uncertainty about the right course of action can introduce a period of disorientation that ends in either a jarring or a gentle landing. It is during these unsettled times when faith is tested that we need to take seriously the reassuring promises of God that He is present through all the vagaries of life.

The question often arises in Christian service as to whether someone should persevere in a sphere of service ('holding on') or step back from the present undertaking and take a different direction ('letting go'). Making the right choice leads to satisfaction and an inner sense of peace. Making the wrong decision can lead to confusion and unease. If we are abiding in Christ—that is, walking close to him and trusting him absolutely—decisions should never have to be 'forced' or contrived or rushed, as the Spirit will teach us all things. God is never in a hurry.

It is sometimes the case that a faithful worker will hold on to a position in a church or Christian organisation because there does not appear to be an obvious successor; relinquishing the responsibility will create a void and create practical problems for other team members. The tension between, on the one hand, perseverance and commitment, and on the other hand, responding to what we believe to be the Spirit's leading to lay down the role, is always a difficult and delicate one. Ideally, a potential successor should be identified well in advance of the incumbent's decision; in reality, the situation is usually less straightforward.

When situations are perplexing and the way ahead is shrouded in uncertainty, the solution lies in exercising wisdom (either individually or with the help of mature Christians) and trusting that God will not allow us to rush ahead recklessly or endlessly dither. The promise expressed in Psalm 94:18: 'When I said, "My foot is slipping," your love, O Lord, supported me' (NIVUK) is that even when—perhaps *especially* when—we feel that situations are sliding out of control, we can claim and receive and believe God's promise that His love is ever-present to fortify and preserve us. God will bring us through a period of uncertainty to a secure place if we allow Him to exercise His will in our lives, though it may not be in the way we expect. Isaiah powerfully expresses the Lord's promise in the matter: 'I will go before you and make the crooked places straight; I will break in pieces the gates of bronze and cut the bars of iron. I will give you the treasures of darkness and hidden riches of secret places that you may know that I, the Lord, who call you by your name, am the God of Israel' (45:2–4, NKJV).

Insight

Though going through 'dark places' in our lives is never a pleasant experience, God often reveals more of His will and purpose during these difficult times than when life is smooth and unhindered. Someone has made the astute observation that although 'mountain top experiences' are delightful and evoke praise and thankfulness, it is down in the valley that the richest fruit is found: the 'treasures of darkness', as Isaiah described them (45:3, NKJV).

Even in our darkest moments, when nothing makes sense and we lose our bearings, we have a God who rescues us and carries us back into the sheepfold with great rejoicing (John Chapter 10). But it would be disingenuous to pretend that life is always straightforward or that decisions made in good faith invariably lead to a satisfactory outcome. God never takes us over or around our troubles and periods of disorientation, but promises that He will accompany us *through* them to the far side and a brighter tomorrow.

From start to finish

Perseverance seems to have become a less desirable attribute in our 'instant gratification' generation. By contrast to this tentative level of commitment, persevering through times of doubt, fear and disappointment is an essential test of faith and provides the impetus for spiritual growth for those who take seriously the claims of Christ upon their lives. Isaiah expresses God's declaration on the benefit of being purified by Him through a period of testing: 'See, I have refined you, though not as silver; I have tested you in the furnace of affliction' (48:10, NIVUK). Being a disciple means that we have to persist and be faithful to the end and not surrender to circumstances and attacks from satanic influences during a time of discouraging setbacks. There are many instances of Christians who strive and refuse to give way to despair, despite enduring heartache, physical suffering and misrepresentation. The testimony of these saints is that their faithful God supported them along each step of the journey, offering solace and strength.

Juxtaposed with the determination shown by true saints of God, we read of Old Testament kings who began well but, as they grew older, fell prey to self-indulgence, arrogance and the lust for power. Examples of kings that succumbed to ungodly desires include Saul, Solomon, Joash (Jehoash) and Amaziah, all who reigned wisely in the early period of monarchy but ended miserably. The common factor in each case was the king's increasing reliance their own influence and a failure to trust God as they once did. Their loss of focus and trust in God should act as a warning to each of us, as Paul expressed his disappointment about the Galatian Christians' fickleness: 'You were running a good race. Who cut in on you to keep you from obeying the truth?' (5:7 NIVUK).

Supremely, the example set by the Lord Jesus Christ is one that should inspire and challenge every Christian, as he set his face towards Jerusalem and, despite having the power and authority to save himself, endured the shame and anguish of the cross. As the sinless 'Lamb of God', he was made sin for us, bearing in his body the transgressions of the world to achieve salvation. Jesus could have called twelve legions (thousands) of angels to protect both him and his disciples but chose to take the path of suffering instead (see Matthew Chapter 26) and finish the job for which he was sent (Luke 4:43).

Insight

After reading about how Jesus could have called legions of heaven's angels to save him but chose the road of suffering, Ray Overholt wrote a song that included the lyrics: 'He could have called ten thousand angels to destroy the world and set him free... but he died alone for you and me'. From living a godless life, Ray Overholt became a travelling singer and preacher, and wrote over 200 songs. He served Christ until the end of his life and is a modern example of 'finishing well'.

Summary

In this chapter, I have reiterated the importance of inner transformation to produce godliness, as opposed to maintaining the outward appearance of goodness and exhibiting shallow behaviour to impress others. In doing so, I have shown the many and various ways in which Jesus is our supreme example, as revealed through the extensive evidence that validate his claims about his status, and explored his submission to the Father's will that resulted life-transforming ministry and deeds. Christ's life and subsequent death is also a powerful revelation of his humility and obedience in pursuing the principle purpose for which he came to live on earth as a man.

The challenge for followers of Jesus is to glorify God by allowing the Spirit of Christ to indwell their minds, hearts, eyes, voices, feet and hands, such that they become his true ambassadors and impact the community they inhabit with the Gospel. Faithful endurance will reap a rich spiritual reward, providing we are walking in step with the Spirit and allowing Him to direct our paths. God is the instigator and the sustainer through the ups and downs of life. He only asks that we trust Him and persevere to live responsible, devoted lives for His glory.

A checklist for would-be imitators of Jesus

'And whatever you do in word or deed, do all in the name of the Lord Jesus, giving thanks to God the Father through Him' (Colossians 3:17, NKJV)

1. *Which of the following statements most accurately describe you?*
   - I pray when I need help but otherwise I tend to make my own decisions.
   - I worked actively for Christ years ago but my enthusiasm seems to have faded recently.

- I have been steadfast as his disciple, persevered to walk in union with the Spirit and invited him to have his way in my life.

2. *Which of the following statements reflect your priorities?*
   - I enjoy myself and squeeze all I can from life in the belief that 'you only live once'.
   - I see to my own needs first but gladly give God what is left.
   - I look after my health and live carefully to ensure that I am better able to serve God faithfully and care for others.

3. *Which of the following statements best describes how you treat other people?*
   - I give as good as I get!
   - I am friendly towards most people but avoid those I find difficult.
   - I seek to see others as Jesus sees them and do my best to show his unconditional love in every situation.

4. *Which of the following statements describes the work of the Spirit in your life?*
   - I try to be kind and good but struggle with people that I naturally dislike.
   - I display the fruit of the Spirit when life is smooth but I am less godly when placed under pressure.
   - I make every effort to submit myself to the Lordship of Christ and allow his spirit to work in and through me.

5. *Which of the following statements best describes how you use your gifts and talents?*
   - I tend to use them to gain success in my career and gain prestige.
   - I use them to make money and enhance my lifestyle, as well as in direct service for the Lord.
   - I strive to use them in every area of my life—employment, church and leisure—to benefit other people and bring glory to God.

Chapter 12
Going Deeper with Jesus

Introduction

In the process of learning to swim, young children initially dip one toe in the water and jump back onto the bank. When accompanied and advised by a reliable guide, however, repeated attempts to venture into deeper water leads to increased confidence and, over time, the ability to swim independently. The experience of Christians in exercising faith follows a similar pattern of taking 'small steps' then becoming increasingly bold, as they begin to realise the certainty of Jesus's promise that he would always be with them through the abiding presence of the Spirit. Ezekiel's vision (47:1–12) depicted the prophet wading into a river until the water covered his ankles then his knees and his waist, before the volume of water allowed him to swim in the fresh ('sanctified') water.

The prophet perfectly captured the process of increasing faith and trust in God, as unbelief is swept away by the cleansing flood of righteousness that only Christ can impart. The manifestation given to the prophet is a model of how God gradually leads us into greater depths of faith-driven experience until we are fully liberated from the trappings of sinful pride. He then reveals the blessings that await us, and the godly effect we will experience on those we seek to influence. If we are content to paddle in the shallows, we shall never enjoy the fullness of God's grace and power that comes with trusting him fully, such that we are able to flourish in the anointed waters of worship and service.

Growing More Like Jesus

Fact not fantasy

As noted earlier, we do not have any contemporary images of Jesus, though various claims have been made down the years purporting to resemble him. In the numerous books published with illustrations of Jesus, he is frequently pictured as a tall man with a pale complexion, wearing a white flowing robe. In reality, it is likely that he was darker skinned than commonly depicted, owing to his outdoor life as an itinerant preacher and teacher. It is also possible that Jesus had short hair and was clean-shaven, as only wealthy men of high status wore long tunics, flowing robes and magnificent beards. It is also fairly certain that he would have worn a rough tunic for everyday use, which for men of that time finished just below the knees. Jesus was scathing about the ostentatious attire worn by religious leaders in an attempt to impress onlookers and promote their high societal status; it is therefore unlikely that he would be similarly dressed during most of his ministry.

In truth, we don't know the nature of Jesus's raiment, though a clue is found at the time of his crucifixion when the soldiers gambled to see who would inherit his 'seamless' robe, which was probably a cloak used to repel the chilly night air. It was common practice for Jewish mothers to provide such a garment for their sons. The need for Jesus to wear such attire is confirmed by the fact that when Simon Peter gingerly approached to observe what was taking place, there was a fire burning in the nearby courtyard due to the chilly conditions (Luke 22:55). What we can be certain about is that Jesus was extremely fit as he walked the hot, dusty trails of the Holy Land, doubtless spending some nights 'under the stars', as budget hotels were few and far between!

Despite the fact that it has become quite fashionable in recent years to wear a bracelet on which the initials WWJD are printed ('What Would Jesus Do?'), the idea of formulating the way in which we conduct ourselves in accordance with how we imagine Jesus would react and behave, though well-intended, needs to recognise that mere imitation is destined to fall well short of what becoming more like Jesus Christ entails (see Chapter 11). Perhaps the WWJD bracelets would be more accurate, though less snappy, by being printed with WWTHSHM2D, standing for: *What Would The Holy Spirit Have Me To Do?*

Such worthy sentiments to 'follow in the footsteps of the Master' must be underpinned by acknowledging that we cannot achieve anything worthwhile by relying solely on our own instinct, strength of character, good intentions or perseverance, though all of these are important attributes. It is only by the power of God through the transforming work of the Spirit that we grow to be more like Jesus.

The unique Jesus

Jesus Christ is no longer a man on earth. He is seated at the right hand of the Father, interceding for us, as the Apostle Paul explained in his letter to Christians in Rome: 'Who then is the one who condemns? No one. Christ Jesus who died—more than that, who was raised to life—is at the right hand of God and is also interceding for us' (8:34, NIVUK). The Jesus that we are encouraged to represent is the person who was conceived of the Virgin Mary; born in abject conditions in Bethlehem; grew up in the degenerate town of Nazareth; did not possess a home or property; walked countless miles along the dusty streets and rocky terrain of Galilee; preached, taught and healed in Jerusalem, Capernaum, Perea, Samaria and other local areas. The Jesus we seek to emulate was one who spoke words of comfort; condemned hypocrisy; healed the sick; showed the way to eternal life; freely gave his life upon a cross; rose from the grave and ascended into heaven.

Prior to his ascension to rejoin his Father, Jesus told his disciples that they were to wait and receive power for their ministry when the Holy Spirit came upon them (Acts 1:8). Jesus refused to answer the disciples' questions about future events, stressing the need for patience, submissive obedience and sharing the good news of the Gospel. To become more like Jesus does not, therefore, involve replicating the pattern of his earthly life, which is obviously impossible, but rather being totally submissive to the Father's will and purpose, as he was, such that the power of the Spirit can work through us to achieve what He desires for God's Kingdom on earth today. Only our obedience to the Father's will brings blessing for ourselves and for others. There are no short cuts or alternative pathways.

True likeness

Although the Christian life involves making numerous decisions about the way in which we act and speak, everything must be rooted in 'having the mind of Christ' which, coupled with the submission of our will, spontaneously generates the likeness of Christ in such a way that our thoughts, reactions, words and deeds reflect his attitude, priorities and character. The ideal situation is to be so closely allied to the will of God through abiding in Christ that we scarcely have to ask Him for guidance, as we are wholly 'at one' with Him and what appear to be spontaneous decisions are in reality reflecting His will and purpose.

Furthermore, the path to becoming more like Jesus must include learning to pray as Jesus did through intimate connection with the Father; working hard like Jesus did, as he trod the highways and byways, yet recognising the need for rest and refreshment; and suffering like Jesus did by facing the mockery and insults of those who considered themselves morally superior. To be the 'face of Jesus' in the world, we must expect to receive similar treatment to him, namely, hostility from a few people, polite disinterest from the majority and a positive reaction from the rest.

We must accept the fact that the more we resemble the Saviour, the more likely we are to invite opposition, scorn and attacks from the enemy, Satan. King David had first-hand experience of being insulted and threatened, as he described in Psalm 64: 'They sharpen their tongues like swords and aim their deadly arrows' (3–4, NIVUK). Nevertheless, in verses 7–8, he goes on to express his confidence in how God will deal with those who exhibit such offensive behaviour: 'But God will shoot them with his arrows; they will suddenly be struck down. He will turn their own tongues against them and bring them to ruin; all who see them will shake their heads in scorn'. Such is the certainty that we can enjoy when confronted by evildoers.

As described in Chapter 9, if we genuinely want to become more like Jesus, we must ask ourselves if we are willing to pay the price involved, as well as receiving the considerable benefits of sins forgiven, guidance from the Spirit, courage to face adversity and a clear purpose for living. It is, of course, perfectly possible that despite our sincere resolve, when prompted by God's Spirit to behave or respond in a certain way or give priority to a particular form of service, we may find that the price of obedience is too high. If so, we might 'close our minds' to His promptings and carry on as normal or enquire meekly of Him if there is a less costly alternative (by contrast with Jesus's wholeheartedly positive attitude). While God doubtless appreciates our transparency in the matter, He must surely be disappointed if our fine intentions evaporate when exposed to the reality of serving in the way that He desires.

Foot-Washing

The challenge

There is something about dealing with other people's feet that most of us find to be rather disagreeable. Feet get smelly after physical activity, toes can become deformed and some people have swollen areas of thick skin that needs skilful treatment to correct. Chiropodists have to cope with these challenging issues as part of their responsibilities; most of us are happy to let them deal with such matters! It is stating the obvious to say that few people would choose to exhibit their feet in the way they might show off their hairstyles, muscles or slender figures.

In this connection, John records a remarkable event that preceded the Passover Ceremony in advance of Jesus's final hours before he faced the Cross of Calvary and gave his life for the sins of the world: 'After washing their feet, Jesus put on his robe again and sat down and asked, "Do you understand what I was doing? You call me 'Teacher' and 'Lord,' and you are right, because that's what I am. And since I, your Lord and Teacher, have washed your feet, you ought to wash each other's feet. I have given you an example to follow. Do as I have done to you"' (13:12–15, NLT).

It is difficult for us to appreciate the impact that Jesus's actions must have had had on the disciples, who would never consider that their Lord and Master should undertake such a menial task. Washing feet was not a job for important guests but was normally ascribed to one of the household servants. In this case, we must assume that there wasn't a servant present to perform the courteous act; Jesus took charge and broke the chains of tradition and status that had become entrenched in the culture of that time.

Resistance to washing feet

From the three Gospel accounts of Jesus's foot-washing, the disciples appear to have remained silent (perhaps from shock!) as Jesus moved around until he reached Peter, who asked in a horrified tone: 'Lord, are you going to wash *my* feet?' Peter appears to have been thinking something along these lines: *This isn't the way we do things around here! Don't ask me to change the way I've always accepted as normal, Jesus. Let the others receive this blessing from you but count me out because it doesn't fit my idea of who you are, Lord. I want to keep you safe and secure on a pedestal, not fulfilling the role of a servant.* The tension in Peter had built up to bursting point, as he exclaims: 'No, Lord! You shall never wash my feet!' It seems that Peter had a great deal to learn about allowing the Holy Spirit to reveal fresh truth to him and not to place human traditions in the way of God's power to renew and reconstruct lives. Doubtless, some of us are similarly inclined to overlook the transforming work of the Spirit, due to our insistence on placing manmade conventions ahead of His desire to fill us with a loving compassion and the incentive to serve others.

Peter's protest triggered a vigorous exchange between him and his Lord. Jesus might have paused after hearing Peter's objection then uttered words that must have chilled Peter to his core: 'Unless I wash you, you have no part with me'. In resisting Jesus's teaching and demonstrating his desire to serve rather than be served, we can have 'no part' with him unless we identify with him. Until we die to self as he did, we will never be fully effective in our work and witness. We may be talented, hardworking, faithful and committed, but without embracing genuine humility, we are more likely to hinder than to assist God's purposes. Assuming the role of a servant reflects the character of Jesus, as we display his love in practical ways, after first being renewed by the Spirit.

Here was the Son of God who inhabited eternity—the one who was there at the beginning of creation and who would soon become the Saviour of the world—doing the job of the lowliest servant. The disciples struggled to grasp the implications of the situation, as they watched Jesus take the initiative and provide them with a powerful example of the way in which they were to approach their ministry and attitude towards those they served.

Insight

It is significant that Judas Iscariot was among the disciples whose feet were washed by Jesus, which is a sharp reminder that our service should not exclude certain groups of people (however disreputable) and always be carried out without expectation of reward or reciprocation. As God shows us undeserved kindness in bringing salvation and showing great patience when we fall, so the same characteristic should be embedded within every believer's attitude towards others.

True greatness

Jesus was the supreme example of someone who challenged manmade social structures when they interfered with Kingdom principles and the Holy Spirit's intentions. He kneels before us and soothes our aching feet. He refreshes our weary souls and helps us to understand that by acts of graciousness, we can find deep satisfaction and fulfilment in life. Even when we are in a position of seemingly low status, starved of human admiration and populist renown, the angels of heaven celebrate our unconditional love for people. Although our Christ-like attitude, care and compassion may not always be recognised or acknowledged by the world, we are amply compensated by the Spirit's approving touch, which produces soul-refreshing restoration and renewal.

Jesus, our Servant King, is not too proud to humble himself, to heal the broken-hearted and set captives free; to give hope to the hopeless and peace to the troubled mind. As his followers, we have the same opportunity to emulate the precedent he has established. Though the world views eminence in terms of the greater are people's standing in society, the more others serve them, Jesus defines status in the opposite way, namely, the greater you are, the more you are willing to serve others.

In seeking to go deeper with Jesus, Paul places great emphasis on performing acts of kindness: 'So then, whenever we have an opportunity, let us work for the good of all, and especially for those of the family [household] of faith' (Galatians 6:10, NRSV). Although Paul's instruction includes the phrase 'for the good of all', it is still necessary for us to be wise and discerning about use of time and resources. While a compassionate, loving heart should be a key characteristic of every believer, serving others is not a case of becoming a 'doormat' to be exploited by unscrupulous people, who prefer to rely on charity instead of making an effort to earn their way and become independent. Rather, it is to do good works: first and foremost to our family and fellow believers, then to the wider community. Attempts to respond to each and every human need leads to exhaustion and stress, as many pastors and church leaders will readily confirm.

There were a number of other occasions when Jesus reinforced the priority of serving our neighbours (people with whom we have contact) before considering our own needs, notably when the disciples argued among themselves about who would be greatest in the Kingdom of Heaven. Jesus made it clear that God's priorities for achieving high status depend upon our willingness to take the humblest position and not to seek grandeur. In his Gospel account, Matthew records that Jesus even used small children to reinforce the need for humility. The Amplified Bible offers a helpful expanded translation: 'I assure you and most solemnly say to you [I tell you the truth], unless you repent [that is, change your inner self—your old way of thinking, live changed lives] and become like children [trusting, humble and forgiving], you will never enter the Kingdom of Heaven. Therefore, whoever humbles himself [i.e., turns his back on self-righteous pride] like this child is greatest in the Kingdom of Heaven. Whoever receives and welcomes one child [new, childlike believer] like this in my name receives me' (14:3–4, AMP).

It must have been a sobering moment for some of the disciples, who fondly imagined that by following Jesus, they were destined for prominence and privilege. In the same way, each believer must resist the desire to be acknowledged as 'someone significant' in the church, an attitude that can lead to pride and resentment from fellow believers, a predicament that can largely be avoided through allowing the Spirit to take control and choose whom He will for whatever role or task is needful. Genuine humility and thankfulness to God is of crucial importance.

It is never easy to let a fellow believer be credited with an idea or initiative that you initiated; nevertheless, an essential element for growing in grace is to accept the situation without complaining or 'setting the record straight'. The only essential factor is that God is glorified. Maintaining such a humble attitude is a sign of deep, selfless Christian maturity.

Embracing Fresh Revelation

The revitalising Spirit

It is easy to criticise Peter's objection to Jesus washing his feet (see earlier) but Christians may show a similar reaction to his indignant response if they close their minds to a new direction that God is prompting them to pursue. Procedures and traditions are useful if they are Spirit-initiated and have proved to be an effective channel for teaching, preaching and edifying the saints of God. Similarly, good habits, such as regular prayer, meditation on the Bible and church attendance, are important factors in moulding us to live pure and holy lives. Unfortunately, traditions can also become repetitive and narrow our perspectives; habits can become stale and lifeless; repeated statements of basic truths (however accurate) can become unhelpful if not applied to real-life situations. Jesus described the danger of 'vain repetitions' when praying (Matthew 6:7, NKJV); the NLT translates the verse using a more modern idiom: 'When you pray, don't babble on and on as the Gentiles do. They think their prayers are answered merely by repeating their words again and again'.

James's much quoted and greatly debated statement: 'So you see, faith by itself isn't enough. Unless it produces good deeds, it is dead and useless' (2:17, NLT) exposes the fundamental truth that any claims to possessing faith are of little value unless accompanied by action that reveals the revitalising work of the Spirit, both in individual lives and the life of a fellowship. As God revealed to John, recorded in the Book of Revelation: 'Look, I am making everything new! And then he said to me: Write this down, for what I tell you is trustworthy and true' (21:5, NLT). The continuous present tense used in this verse establishes that God *goes on* making all things new. It is for each believing Christian to ask what 'new thing' God is showing him or her and the church to adopt, both when worshipping together and also engaging with people who are living in the darkness of sin.

Openness to a fresh move of the Spirit is sometimes discussed in terms of those who (a) are resisting change and (b) those who are willing to embrace it. Such a polarisation of viewpoints is unhelpful and may cause a damaging rift if pursued relentlessly within a fellowship. As some changes will inevitably occur naturally over time, the key issue is the *direction* of change and how it is controlled. If the Holy Spirit is in control, the direction will be positive and honouring to God. If change is random—subject only to the vagaries of time and personal preference—change is almost certainly going to be ruinous to a fellowship. See Chapter 6 for further exposition of this topic.

Regular cleansing

After Jesus explained the importance of 'being washed' during the feet-washing episode described earlier, Peter went to the other extreme and demanded that he was washed all over. Jesus retorted, rather mysteriously, that 'People who have bathed and are clean all over need to wash just their feet. And you, my disciples, are clean, except for one of you' (John 13:10, CEV). The spiritual explanation of Jesus's words is that a person is made clean when he or she is washed in the blood of Christ, which sounds rather gruesome until we realise that Jesus was speaking metaphorically (i.e., symbolising the process, not describing the practice). The Bible makes it clear that nothing can deal with the sin in our lives except the blood of Jesus Christ (see, for example, Hebrews 13:12; 1 Peter 1:2; 1 John 1:7). Even when we have been 'immersed' in the blood and thereby sanctified (made right with God), the Spirit of Jesus needs repeatedly to 'wash our feet', which represents cleansing the recurring sins from our lives and empowering us for service.

Insight

Tragically, Judas Iscariot was not included as one who was 'clean', despite having served alongside Jesus for several years. We are reminded of Jesus's sombre warning that not everyone who calls him 'Lord' will enter the Kingdom of Heaven.

The relationship between being cleansed by the blood of Christ, yet still needing to be cleansed through 'having our feet washed' can be further explained as follows. Total cleansing through the shed blood of Christ that ensures our righteousness in God's sight is our *status* before God. By contrast, even after being totally cleansed, our tendency to fall short of God's requirement to live a holy and blameless life is indicative of our human *condition*. Our *status* before God, in which we are seen as wholly righteous, is secure because Christ died according to the Scriptures and rose again, thereby redeeming us from the penalty of original sin. By contrast, our human *condition* means that we are prone to sin and fail to meet God's holy standard; thus the need to regularly confess and repent to fully restore our relationship with Him. If we know the life-transforming experience of being born anew (from above) then our status before God is secure, but because of our earthly weaknesses and imperfect condition, the Holy Spirit has to create the likeness of Christ in us by working in four ways:

1. Taking control of areas of our life where we have formerly refused Him access.
2. Showing us how to return to the right path after we have strayed.
3. Helping us to forgive and show mercy to those who have wronged us.
4. Persuading us to accept that God's will is best, even when our human instincts suggest otherwise.

As the Spirit of Jesus comes and washes our feet, so we, as Christ's representatives on earth, must follow his example in learning to identify and respond to the needs of those around us. The more that we accept the foot-cleansing in our own lives, the more we are able to speak wisely, learn to be patient with the failings of others, and have the grace to be considerate, courteous and kind at every opportunity, even when the recipient is ungrateful or attempts to take advantage of our loving actions.

As Paul reminds the Christians in the Galatian churches: 'But the Holy Spirit produces this kind of fruit in our lives: love, joy, peace, patience, kindness, goodness, faithfulness, gentleness and self-control. There is no law against these things!' (5:22–23, NLT). Paul contrasts these characteristics of 'cleansed' godly living with the anger, immorality, hostility, envy, drunkenness, wild parties and associated behaviour that characterised the conduct of large numbers of the ungodly; sadly, these descriptions apply as much to contemporary society as they did in the first century.

Spiritual progress

For people who select the wide road that leads to a morally damaged life and eternal destruction (see Matthew Chapter 7 and Luke Chapter 13) there is everything to be gained from having a big head (prideful) and a small heart (unloving). Jesus, however, commanded that we have a small head (representing humility) and a big heart (representing loving kindness) by choosing his narrow way that leads to eternal life. The 'big head and small heart' approach to life may lead to popularity, climbing the ladder of success in business and a healthy bank balance, but can also lead to separation from God, loss of His special blessing in our endeavours, and an eternity without hope.

Followers of Jesus Christ can never and must never remain spiritually passive; instead, they must be vigilant to understand God's intentions for humankind more fully. To facilitate this active mind-set, every sincere believer must be in intimate touch with Father God through prayer, earnestly seeking the truth revealed in the Scriptures, and gaining wisdom and insight through all available means, including Bible-based sermons, wholesome teaching (light in tone but with serious intent and free from seducing rhetoric), use of background information from the Internet and reading scholarly books written by people of deep faith and insight.

It is important to issue a 'doctrine warning' at this point because the fact that the Holy Spirit is continuously refreshing believers does not mean that we should become obsessed by the latest trendy ideas and thereby fail to give proper attention to established beliefs and commitments. Nor does it mean that we jettison well-established doctrines in our desire to keep up to date with the Spirit (as might be claimed), as there is an ever-present danger that false teaching, whether virtuous or mischievous, will penetrate the church and damage its witness. It *does* validate the dictum concerning the Christian life that you move forward or drift backwards in your relationship with God, but can never stand still.

Just as the early church wrestled with the problem of teachers that seemed to be genuine but were preaching a 'false Gospel', so similar challenges exist today. Perhaps the most pervasive example is the prevalence of what has been described as 'prosperity preaching', which is founded on the principle that God invariably rewards faith and financial commitment with significant improvements in health and wealth. In essence, proponents of this doctrine insist that the atoning work of Christ is not only to deal with human sin but also to procure the removal of sickness and poverty.

Insight

Whatever the validity or error attached to 'health and wealth' preaching, it has created considerable division in the church and must therefore be subjected to intense scrutiny in the light of biblical revelation that emphasises the grace of God and His undeserved favour.

Hunger for God

The occasion when Jesus washed the disciples' feet exposed Simon Peter's failure to grasp the implications of being a servant but also revealed his subsequent change of heart and hunger for more of God that led to his desperate plea to be 'washed all over'. Oh, that we might be similarly desperate for God's glory: hungry enough to let go of the things that hinder the work of the Holy Spirit in our lives; hungry enough to say to Jesus, 'not only my feet but my whole body'; hungry enough to say with Job of old, 'though He slay me, yet will I trust Him' (13:15, KJV). Yearning to allow the Holy Spirit to reign in our lives is not to be equated with weakness or servility or neglect of family and regular commitments; rather, it begins with a decision to serve Christ as our priority, which is cashed out in living a holy life and serving others through the warp and woof of everyday experiences.

There will be occasions when in attempting to be obedient and faithful to the Lord, the task proves difficult and discouraging, but the words of Isaiah provide encouragement: 'Don't be afraid, for I am with you. Don't be discouraged, for I am your God. I will strengthen you and help you. I will hold you up with my victorious right hand' (Isaiah 41:10, NLT). Although suffering and fear may be a consequence of our actions, we must continue to worship Christ throughout the ordeal, a sentiment beautifully expressed in the words of the chorus in Helen

Lemmels' delightful hymn: 'Turn your eyes upon Jesus; look full in his wonderful face; and the things of earth will grow strangely dim in the light of his glory and grace'.

Moses' words to Joshua prior to the change of leadership and entry into the Promised Land can be a source of strength for everybody who seeks to serve the Lord but hesitates in the face of the challenges ahead: 'Do not be afraid or discouraged, for the Lord will personally go ahead of you. He will be with you; he will neither fail you nor abandon you' (Deuteronomy 31:8, NLT). The inclusion of the word 'personally' in the NLT is significant, for it conveys the essential truth that the God is interested in the *individual*. For believers, the constant presence of the Holy Spirit provides both reassurance and challenge, as nothing we think, do or say is hidden from His sight (Hebrews 4:13).

A prime example of a sacrificial attitude and willingness to expose himself to extreme dangers is found in Paul's commendation of Epaphroditus: 'Meanwhile, I thought I should send Epaphroditus back to you. He is a true brother, co-worker, and fellow soldier. And he was your messenger to help me in my need… Welcome him in the Lord's love and with great joy and give him the honour that people like him deserve. For he risked his life for the work of Christ; and he was at the point of death while doing for me what you couldn't do from far away' (Philippians 2:25, 29–30, NLT). Key phrases in Paul's description include 'risked his life' and 'at the point of death'. We are not given details about how Epaphroditus risked his life for Paul but from the context of Philippians Chapter 2 it clearly involved being closely associated with Paul and Silas while they were in prison (see Acts 16). His ill-health is not specified but it was clearly serious, as Paul writes that Epaphroditus almost died but God spared his life—a valuable reminder that God's eye is ever on us when we are serving Him faithfully. It has been rightly said that God does not want to purify us and make us righteous in Christ to display us like a trophy in a glass case, but rather to send us out as His witnesses in a sinful world that needs the light of Christ to shine in the darkness.

Power surge

Although we are cleansed by the blood of Christ to free us from the penalty of sin and renewed by the Spirit through repenting and asking for God's forgiveness, there are times when we need His special enabling to be adequately equipped for a specific and demanding call upon our lives. Examples include performing an exceptionally challenging task; having supernatural wisdom and discernment in offering advice or guidance; resolving a seemingly impossible personal situation; and being used as a channel for preaching the Gospel in a hostile environment. On such occasions, God provides us with an extra 'in-filling' of power to perform the duty or discern the wisest approach or cope with the opposition to our message.

Examples of the 'release of power' in the lives of individuals can be found throughout the Bible (e.g., Samson, King Saul and the Apostle Peter were so-enabled) but the events at Pentecost described in Acts Chapter 2 illustrate most clearly the way in which the Holy Spirit provides what every follower of Jesus or group of believers requires for a specific and sometimes unique situation.

Some people refer to this renewed experience as being refreshed or drenched or soaked in the Spirit; others speak of receiving the fullness of the Spirit or the second blessing. Yet others describe the episode as allowing the Spirit of Jesus to take total control; some believers think in terms of wholly yielding our lives to God; other believers refer to a 'topping up' of the Spirit. The *way* we describe the encounter is far less important than the *effect* it has on our life and witness. God will always give us everything we need for serving Him in a specific way and release supernatural power into our lives that creates boldness and courage to take us above and beyond what we could ordinarily expect to do. Our role is to invite Him to take control, receive His anointing and move forward with confidence. God offers His enabling power but never obliges us to receive it; as ever, individual choice is involved.

As always, the praise and glory for any outstanding accomplishment and favourable outcome must be given to the Lord, as without the Spirit of the indwelling Christ, our accomplishments will be as seed that falls on stony ground.

The prophet Jeremiah was mocked and derided when he declared God's Word, such that he became what he described as a 'household joke'. Yet the power of the message was such that he could not contain it: 'But if I say I'll never mention the Lord or speak in his name, his word burns in my heart like a fire. It's like a fire in my bones! I am worn out trying to hold it in! I can't do it!' (Jeremiah 20:9, NLT) Oh, that all God's people were so full of unbridled passion in proclaiming His word!

Making disciples

In his first letter to Christians in Corinth, Paul reminded them that all believers have a privilege and a responsibility to be ambassadors of the Gospel of grace to bring about reconciliation between God and mankind: 'For God was in Christ, reconciling the world to himself, no longer counting people's sins against them. And he gave us this wonderful message of reconciliation. So we are Christ's ambassadors; God is making his appeal through us. We speak for Christ when we plead: Come back to God!' (5:19–20, NLT)

I have previously referred to the numerous challenges and opportunities confronting true believers (i.e., those with a sincere faith and trust in Christ's redemptive work on the Cross of Calvary) in sharing the Gospel and obeying the Lord Jesus's instructions to his followers: 'Therefore go and make disciples of all the nations, baptising them in the name of the Father and of the Son and of the Holy Spirit' (Matthew 28:19, NIVUK), which is commonly quoted as the seminal instruction at the heart of evangelical endeavour. The use of the word 'therefore' is significant because Jesus preceded the command with an astounding statement about his status: 'All authority in Heaven and on earth has been given to me' (28:18, NIVUK). Jesus not only had authority on earth as a man but also complete authority in Heaven, which underlines his position as 'fully God and fully human'. By means of his Spirit, he is able to exercise power through every believer who is willing to submit to his will. The Son of God is therefore supremely equipped to provide all the divine energy that each Christian needs to live and witness effectively.

Jesus concluded his instructions by placing the responsibility for the training in righteousness of new believers in the hands of his disciples: 'teaching them to obey everything I have commanded you' (Matthew 28:20a, NIVUK). Jesus's instruction contains the key element of which every Christian should take note when seeking to spread the Good News, notably that the process of making disciples is not merely convincing people of their need of salvation but also building them up in their faith. New followers of Jesus have to be gently taught that allegiance to him involves more than acceptance of the truth and affirming it: there is also a requirement for spiritual growth, much of which is embedded in active obedience.

The process of making disciples requires consistent teaching and encouragement, together with personal determination, as we learn to rely increasingly on God and less on self. Even the 'Twelve', as they were known, had many hard lessons to absorb, and frequently stumbled in implementing Jesus's demands of them. Yet over time, with one notable exception (Judas Iscariot) they became courageous purveyors of the Gospel and were bold in demonstrating their allegiance to Christ, both by what they proclaimed and the way they lived. Their confidence was rooted in an absolute trust in God and His indwelling power. Similarly, through all the ups and downs of the faith-driven life, modern-day disciples have Jesus's words of comfort and reassurance that provide them with the same confidence and courage he offered to the early disciples: 'And be sure of this: *I am with you always, even to the end of the age*' (Matthew 28:20b, NLT).

Handling responses

There have been a large number of books and articles about effective evangelism, including helpful advice about when, how and where to go about reaching people for Christ. The present book is not seeking to replicate these commendable endeavours (though see Chapter 10 for an overview of pertinent issues). Nevertheless, it must be emphasised that one of the primary factors in reaching people for Christ is *the spiritual condition of the person who is witnessing*; it is not principally about finding the most effective strategy that 'works'. Exercising wisdom about use of time and physical resources is important, but if we are led by the Spirit and living obediently, God will touch hearts and convict people of sin, regardless of the clumsiness of our approach or limitations in communicating the truth. People may, of course, choose to resist Him and reject the salvation message, but that is not our problem or responsibility. We have only to be faithful and trust God to do His work. Our role is to be wholesome channels for blessing, ready and available for the Master's use.

The majority of conversations about spiritual matters arise from casual conversations or during specific 'guest services' held on church property or in rented accommodation. Visitors will often feel more comfortable in a non-threatening environment such as a village hall, so location is an important consideration in planning an event with community appeal—notably one that incorporates free food! The purpose of the event should always be transparent, as those who accept the invitation are rightly irritated if they feel they have been hoodwinked to attend what they believed to be a relaxing social evening that turns out to be an overtly evangelistic meeting.

Whatever the circumstances in which the Gospel is presented, it is likely that the people whom we seek to influence reflect one of the following attitudes:

1. They are cynical about Christianity and use any opportunity to scorn and criticise. (This is a small group but extremely vocal and determined.)
2. They rarely give God, church or religion much of a thought.
3. They consider churchgoers to be quaint, harmless, and out of touch with modern thinking.
4. They show a polite interest in Christian things but don't see them as significant for their lives.
5. They will attend church social events, providing they have little or no religious content.
6. They are prepared to attend a few church services and may show genuine interest, but draw the line at making any firm commitment.
7. They embrace the truth about Christ and His saving power but don't respond wholeheartedly and remain on the fringes of church life, aligning with the 'almost persuaded' group (see Chapter 8).
8. They have previously embraced the truth and are, in Jesus's words, 'born again' (John 3:7) but have backslidden over time and need to be assisted in returning to the fold.

Whenever possible, it is important to identify where a person stands in respect of the above list when engaging with him or her. Such awareness is not intended to be used as a means of artificially adjusting the conversation on that basis, but rather to be sensitive to the individual's needs, concerns and possible stumbling blocks to faith in Christ. Genuine concern for a person should not be sullied by being unduly intrusive (expecting to be told personal details) or interrogative (excessive questioning). In every encounter, it is essential to remember that the person is someone for whom Christ died and is precious to God, regardless of how unreasonable he or she may prove to be.

Men and the Church

The changing role of men

In 1935, George F Dempster published a stirring account of his work as a minister of the Gospel in seeking to win men for the Saviour. The book carries the title *Finding Men For Christ* (Hodder & Stoughton, 1935). Dempster's adventurous and courageous efforts to bring men to a saving knowledge of Jesus is both inspiring and, in a few places, quite alarming, as his utter determination to see lives transformed by the Spirit required considerable sacrifice, exposure to danger and a not inconsiderable degree of 'holy guile'.

Down the centuries, men have been at the heart of church life and leadership. In more recent years, changing perceptions of male and female roles in society have been reflected in the increasing number of women in senior positions, including high ranks of office in established churches and an increasing number of opportunities for them to minister to an audience or congregation in various denominational settings. Some Christians rejoice at what they see as a more even-handed approach of involving anyone with anointed 'up-front' competence; others are uneasy that the biblical injunction about male leadership is being undermined by female infiltration. Whatever our view on the matter, it is undeniably the case that a focus on the role of women has dominated discourse, while the changing role of men receives relatively little attention.

Jesus worked with both men and women but reserved leadership roles for men, which should not be confused with 'superiority'. In the culture of first century Israel, as in most other parts of the world, the sexes were expected to fulfil specific functions that were largely accepted without serious question until Jesus exploded on the scene and taught that each person is precious to God and can choose to be the recipient and proclaimer of His love and saving power. As discussed in Chapter 9 under 'Mr Procrastinator', Jesus's attitude to women was both courteous and respectful but never patronising. This fact should not detract from searching the Scriptures, especially the New Testament, to discern God's intentions regarding both the different and the comparable roles men and women are called to fulfil in His Kingdom work.

The Christian church as a whole in the United Kingdom has a larger percentage of women than men. There are a number of reasons for the male/female disparity, but the core of the issue lies in the fact that women seem to be more willing to acknowledge their need of salvation than men, or at least have a greater willingness to be involved with church activities and be exposed to Gospel influences. Both the explanation and possible solutions to the problem are located in a number of elements, as explored below.

Cultural issues

In Western societies, women are likely to have close association with a church through shared interests, such as the care and nurture of young children, attendance at craft groups and membership of a choir. By contrast, a high percentage of men are inclined to stay at home and watch sport, pursue hobbies or join their friends for social drinking, rather than attending church services or Christian meetings. Other than in communities such as those based in former mining areas, such as the Welsh Valleys, the idea of belonging to a communal pursuit such as a church choir is not attractive to a large number of men and may even be considered by them to be exclusively suitable for women and 'fragile' males. In addition, though a large number of women are in paid employment, more of them are likely to have time during the day for attending church-based activities. The disintegration of the conventional family, leading to absent fathers and children being 'shared' between their parents, adds further complication and disruption to patterns of social structure that were once taken for granted.

Due to changing societal expectations, traditional ways of viewing masculinity in terms of physical power, principal wage earner and family leader have become less well defined. Men are all too often depicted in the media, especially comedy shows, as inadequate or inviting ridicule for their supposed failings; less often are they presented as reliable, responsible and wise.

By contrast with negative stereotypes that tend to portray men (especially younger ones) as alcohol fuelled, sexually permissive egotists, they become 'tokens of God's grace' when provided with a new, wholesome identity in Christ, and are capable of living noble, God-honouring lives.

Owing to the fact that some men view commitment to Christ as solely appropriate for meeting the needs of women, children and inadequate or older people, they may not wish to identify too closely with church life. However, these barriers of scepticism can dissolve when we acknowledge that men tend to respond more positively to the Gospel when they are confronted with the *challenges* of following Christ. Presenting men with a strong vision of the courage required to be a disciple and the extraordinary things they can achieve when they commit their lives to God, are more likely to impress them than using delicate imagery of 'letting Jesus into your heart' or similar poetic expressions of dedication. The Holy Spirit can, of course, break through the most belligerent scepticism or inappropriate symbolism, but careful use of language makes the task of persuasion easier to accomplish.

Depending on the age, temperament and background of those concerned, discussions between male work colleagues on Monday morning are likely to centre on sporting events, time spent socialising, or progress on practical tasks. References to church attendance or spiritual experiences are highly unlikely to dominate the discourse. Christians in the workplace have to tread a careful line between introducing such topics in a natural way, and being sensitive to the adverse effect that too much 'religion' may have on co-workers. Sadly, it has become increasingly the case that openly expressing Christian beliefs and ideas can lead to antagonistic responses from supervising staff and managers.

Insight

An emphasis on outreach activities that are considered to be of interest to men, such as barbecues, skittles, snooker (pool) and quiz evenings, while a useful starting point for making relaxed contact with members of the community ('friendship evangelism'), can also be viewed by potential attendees as being less attractive than equivalent secular opportunities that do not have any of the behavioural constraints and expectations attached to churches. To attract interest, the highest quality experience and facilities need to be offered and maintained.

Despite the popular depiction of men being strong, confident and determined, the reality is that many of them struggle in unfamiliar social settings and rarely have more than a small number of close friends. It is also the case that clichéd comments about 'typical man' from some women are not borne out by the fact that as they approach middle age, the majority of men become more mature and serious about life. Older men typically 'mellow' and grow more affable. When discussing the most appropriate way to influence men with the Gospel, it needs to be remembered that despite their physical stature and occasional coarseness, men are capable of showing great tenderness and compassion, especially for children.

Church response

In endeavouring to be more sensitive to the needs of men and their attitudes towards church and organised religion, every fellowship will benefit from taking time to evaluate the effect that existing ways of presenting the Christian message might have on them. For instance, the external and internal fabric of the building will communicate a great deal about the church's priorities. Thus, an emphasis on flowers and delicate craftwork, with an absence of more recognisably male-orientated features, conveys something different from (say) pictures of men at work in a variety of settings, together with objects and paintings that depict 'the sweat of the brow' as much as 'the scent of the rose'. In evaluating these peripheral but significant aspects, consider how a six-foot tall rugby enthusiast might react if he gets the impression that the environment is heavily female-orientated with an absence of any male depictions of Christianity in action.

It is also important to pay close attention to the style of music and terminology of hymns and sacred songs used in meetings. In recent years, there has been a tendency to introduce much slower paced devotional songs or revamped versions of established hymns. The zenith of inspiring sentiments contained in dynamic anthems, such as 'Onward Christian soldiers' and 'Fight the good fight', has largely passed and been replaced by more restrained tones and softer lyrics.

The introduction of modern songs requires an assembly of instruments and a 'worship leader' (often the lead singer), as a means of engaging with younger churchgoers. Whether the strategy appeals to younger men as much as to their female peers is inconclusive, though the presence of younger ladies is certainly an incentive for single males to attend. We must bear in mind that while lyrics such as 'falling in love with Jesus' may appeal to committed believers and sentimental minds, they will probably leave our visiting rugby enthusiast feeling distinctly uncomfortable.

Men meeting Jesus

There are a number of instances in the Bible of men inviting other men to meet Jesus, including the disciple Andrew, who went to find his brother Simon and told him: 'We have found the Messiah (which means 'Christ'). Then Andrew brought Simon [Peter] to meet Jesus' (John 1:41–42a, NLT). One of the more compelling instances of bringing men to Jesus involved a Samaritan woman who, after listening to what he told her, ran into the town excitedly to tell people that Jesus had told her everything about her life. On hearing the woman's dramatic testimony, people came streaming towards the well. Subsequently, John records that many Samaritans believed in Jesus; presumably, the group included a number of men. In practice, nothing substitutes for a personal invitation, especially from one man to another.

Statistically, the large majority of people (men and women) make a serious commitment to Christ when they are in their teenage years or twenties. Men in their middle years (30–60) who admit their need of a Saviour tend to do so after being positively influenced by a spouse or close friend. Conversions among older men are quite rare, not least because leaving their former way of life requires them to admit that they had been on the wrong pathway for all of their adult years. Instances of 'deathbed conversions' driven by fear of the unknown or as a 'safety first policy' seem to be more prevalent among men than women, though a degree of scepticism must be attached to the genuineness of such occurrences. Certainly, a last-minute acknowledgement of the need for salvation, while an encouraging sign for Christian loved ones, is hardly an event to be relied on!

Publicity and evangelical literature (newspapers, tracts, leaflets) are commonly used as a means of outreach, specifically aimed at nonchurchgoers and those without faith in Christ. Unfortunately, some of these well-intended pamphlets and invitations are poorly presented or too wordy to appeal to the majority of the population and end up being discarded.

If written forms of communication are used, three considerations are relevant: First, the content should be easily understood by poor readers, as many men are less literate than women and may be unwilling to spend time in assimilating detailed printed material. Second, the publication should contain basic doctrinal information and testimonies but also invite a response from the reader to its contents. Third, there should be a contact name and number or email address, as anonymous literature is likely to raise suspicion about the source more than it generates interest in the message.

On-line material (short messages, testimonies, descriptions of God at work today, etc.) capture a wider potential audience but has to compete with a proliferation of other Internet contributors and may get overlooked in favour of more professional and engaging productions.

Some churches organise 'seeker services' designed to be of non-threatening interest to people who are not regular church attenders. It is one thing to advertise and promote the event, it is quite another to attract an audience. Men are more likely to attend if the main speaker is a well-known, confident and admired Christian sportsman or personality. Assuming that men can be coaxed into attending the meeting, careful attention must be paid to ensuring that the layout is informal, background music is generally uplifting, rather than subliminal and sedate, and food is plain, plentiful and nourishing. The tone and structure of the event depends on the purpose for which the meeting is being held but should take account of the factors described above.

Prayer and wisdom are an irreplaceable combination in reaching any person with the Gospel. Prayer should underpin everything that we do to reach the lost. Wisdom is needed to discern the best ways of (a) showing people that they need Christ in their lives; (b) offering them a scriptural explanation of how to proceed and ensure that they have accepted the free gift of eternal life that Christ offers; (c) establishing a line of communication for follow-up support with a guarantee that the content of discussion will not be stored or shared without the individual's permission. These three principles apply, regardless of the method used in evangelism, which almost invariably requires face-to-face interaction at several points in the process.

The zeal with which we approach the task will depend in the main on the extent of our motivation, which will be greater if we feel that God has placed a responsibility on us to 'seek and save the lost'. If we are uncertain or wavering in that belief, it is unlikely that any amount of persuasion or well-considered technique we use will result in a positive outcome.

Prepared to Give an Answer

In Chapter 2, I described the areas of dispute that both sceptics and genuine enquirers might raise when confronted with the claims of Christ upon their lives and the need for them to respond through repentance and faith. Our conviction that Jesus's statements about himself are verifiably true provides a solid foundation for Christians to speak with confidence about their Saviour. In addition, believers are given clear instructions about their conduct when interacting with non-believers: 'Always be prepared to give an answer to everyone who asks you to give the reason for the hope that you have. But do this with gentleness and respect' (1 Peter 3:15, NIVUK). The civility and graciousness of our behaviour will carry as much (if not more) conviction than our words, as we correctly handle the word of truth (2 Timothy 2:15).

Thorough preparation

As well as familiarity with Bible content and fundamental doctrine, it is incumbent upon every Christian to gain as much knowledge as possible about areas of controversy and likely questions posed by seekers and sceptics alike. Repetitively quoting a narrow range of favourite verses without giving close attention to their implications for living and their place in the wider biblical context can lead to staleness and lack of spiritual growth. It is a sad fact that on venturing outside their familiar home environment, some young people from a Christian background are flummoxed by questions, assertions and objections from their peers. As a result, the young believers may begin to doubt the teaching they have received and turn away from the truth or compromise their beliefs or otherwise confine themselves socially to a knot of like-minded believers, akin to the brave but ultimately doomed General Custer in his 'last stand'.

Although familiarity with doctrine provides the bedrock for witnessing, it offers only limited defence against the rigours of active debate or incisive questioning about moral issues from sceptics and seekers, who are either seriously considering the claims of Christ on their lives or seeking to undermine the Christian faith. The groundwork for always being prepared to give an answer to everyone for the hope that lies within us must consist of addressing and interrogating potential areas of contention in a supportive church environment under the supervision of experienced Christian teachers. Ideally, this form of preparation should take place *before* the issues arise in general conversation with unbelievers.

While it is unreasonable to expect all Christians to have researched every nuance of doctrine and the numerous facets of controversial issues, an inability to respond to basic questions leaves believers exposed to accusations that their faith is shallow and founded on wishful thinking rather than on matters of substance. Without having a grasp of issues that non-Christians deem important (see below for examples and suggested initial responses), individual testimony about the transforming impact from believing in the crucified and risen Christ may be viewed by those outside the church as being unworthy of serious consideration.

Challenging questions asked of Christians

1. How can you be so sure there is a God when you can't see him? *No one can prove the existence of God because no one has seen Him face to face, so we must rely on circumstantial evidence. Look around at the beauty of nature, which reveals the work of a Creator. Think about the*

words of Jesus, who not only total confidence in God but also taught that our belief in Him was fundamental to finding fulfilment in this life and assurance about what happens when we die. Consider the countless millions who are utterly convinced about God's existence; they can't all be deluded! You can't see electricity or air but their presence is easily demonstrable in practice. If you are still sceptical, why not ask God to show you whether He truly exists? If you ask with a genuine desire to find out, He will reveal Himself to you, so prepare to be amazed!

2. If God is a God of love, as you claim, why is there so much hatred in the world? *Hatred is caused by sin. Jesus gave his life so that we can be free from its power. If people choose to ignore Jesus's offer of a life infused with love, it is not surprising if wickedness abounds. You will not find true followers of Christ expressing hatred; they strive to love their enemies, as Jesus commanded, even if they totally disagree with them about an issue or their behaviour. God has given us freewill to exercise for the good of others or for selfish means; the choice is ours.*

3. If God is a God of love, why does he allow so much suffering? *The issue of suffering is a challenging one and there are no simple answers, except to say that human moral weakness is frequently a key factor. If God intervened constantly to impose His will on everyone, He would be a tyrant, not a loving Heavenly Father. If suffering did not exist, would you then believe that there is a God? (Probably not!) Though no one enjoys suffering, it is fair to add that someone coping with a similar condition to another person may view the situation as a challenge more than as a misfortune. We can take comfort in the fact that God has stated that all suffering will eventually cease; but until that day comes, He promises to be with us as we journey through the pain and anguish. We may never 'get over it' but if we ask Him, we can 'get through it' with His help, supported by the loving care of friends.*

4. My mother (father, son, brother, sister, close friend) was a lovely person, yet 'your' God allowed her (him) to die prematurely when other people who lead bad lives seem to go on forever! Why?

The premature death of a loved one is one of the most distressing situations that any of us can face. I can't give you an easy answer about why some people live long lives and others, shorter ones. I can only tell you that God knows the end from the beginning. Nothing surprises Him! Unless a person sacrifices his or her life through foolish behaviour, God is well aware of how long a person will live and promises that despite the human loss, He is waiting to receive that loved one to live with Him eternally if the person is genuinely sorry about neglecting Him. As for wicked people, they must face God's judgement when they die and I wouldn't like to be in their place when they do!

5. Aren't all religions basically the same?

A quick fact check will show you that they are fundamentally different. Christianity is based upon faith in a loving God and salvation from sin found in Jesus Christ. God is like a loving earthly father, who prescribes moral boundaries to safeguard His children, not to frustrate them. Other religious beliefs emphasise the wrath of their 'god' and punishment for disobeying strictly imposed rules. Jesus offers a guarantee of eternal life through God's goodness alone, though our good deeds are important if done through a loving motive, as Jesus frequently reminded people. Christianity emphasises Jesus's invitation to enjoy a close relationship with God and refer to Him as 'Father'; such intimacy is wholly unknown in all other religious beliefs.

6. Aren't you being arrogant to claim that Jesus Christ is the only way to God?

Jesus said that he was the only way, so either he was a liar or telling the truth. I believe that he was being truthful. You must decide for yourself. Jesus said that 'staying neutral' is not an option. He said that he is the narrow door that leads to eternal life and we must seek to find it. The door is always open if we choose to go his way.

7. Someone I know claims he is a Christian and attends church regularly but isn't a very likeable person. It's hardly a confirmation of your claim that Jesus changes lives for the better, is it?

I don't know this man, so can't comment specifically, but I feel sad that he behaves badly in the way you describe. I can promise you that God is even sadder that someone claiming to be a Christian is giving a strong impression that he or she is a charlatan. Jesus said that not everyone who calls him Lord is truly his follower. I can only add that the vast majority of committed Christians that I meet are lovely, kind people but not faultless, of course. Merely attending church does not automatically make you a Christian but it would be unusual for someone claiming to be a Christian not to do so.

8. If we are only saved through faith in Christ, what of the millions who have never heard of him?

You will need to ask God that question. He is completely fair and will not penalise people for their ignorance. He knows those who would respond positively to His offer of freedom from sin if they had the choice. God has given everyone a conscience, so each person is responsible for his or her behaviour and will be judged accordingly. Ultimately, however, Jesus Christ provides the only certain way to be free from the penalty of sin and find joy in Heaven.

9. What happens to the unborn, those who die very young or are mentally deficient?

They are safe with God because they have never knowingly sinned. Jesus died to take away the (original) sins of the world. Those who are sufficiently mature can decide how they behave. They can choose to ignore or reject God's offer of salvation and must bear the consequences of their decision. The unborn, infants and mentally impaired are unable to make such choices, so are covered by the substitutionary death of Christ when he died for the world. We can be reasonably confident that they are safe in Heaven, though it is fair to add that God also knows how they would have responded to Him if they had been able to live a normal and full life.

10. Isn't Hell just a figment of a fertile imagination or a strategy to keep people fearful?

Jesus spoke repeatedly about Heaven and Hell as real places. Hell wasn't an illusion, as far as he was concerned. Either there is a Heaven and a Hell, or neither exists. People should be fearful if they live without acknowledging God and the salvation that Christ offers. Fear is sometimes the catalyst to spur a hesitant person into taking action, which is ultimately for that person's benefit.

These initial responses are merely to set the scene for further discussion and not intended to be a 'silver bullet' to end the conversation, stifle additional questions or discredit the questioner. If the person is serious about discovering the truth, it is inevitable that supplementary points will emerge. If the respondent is deliberately obstructive, the conversation won't prove to be worthwhile, regardless of what we say or how we handle the person's objections. We must leave God to deal with such people as He chooses.

As with every situation, it is essential that we allow the Holy Spirit to speak through us, including being willing to admit our uncertainty about how to answer a question. Once the exchange with the enquirer is over, he or she will continue to think about the issues and God can use those thoughts to prompt the person to seek Him or discover more about salvation. God is able to use what we have said to penetrate a sceptic's resistance, even if his or her initial response is discouraging.

An example of how a troubled conscience can result in a positive outcome is found in Daniel Chapter 6 when much against his better judgement, King Darius ordered godly Daniel to be thrown into the lions' cage. However, we read about the impact it has on the King: 'Then the king returned to his palace and spent the night fasting. He refused his usual entertainment and couldn't sleep at all that night. Very early the next morning, the king got up and hurried out to the lions' den. When he got there, he called out in anguish: Daniel, servant of the living God! Was your God, whom you serve so faithfully, able to rescue you from the lions?' The remainder of the story about Daniel's miraculous escape is one of the widely familiar Bible events and yields many lessons, including Daniel's steadfast courage; the way that even a pagan king has an active conscience; and the reassuring certainty that God is always at work and does not sleep or slumber (Psalm 121:3).

Questions asked by Christians

In responding to enquirers, committed Christians are likely to have unresolved questions in their own minds about appropriate behaviour, lifestyle, priorities and effective use of time. Typically, the following issues invoke a variety of opinions from believers:

11. Should Christians undertake paid employment, play organised sport or go shopping on Sundays?

Societal use of Sundays has changed considerably over the past fifty years, strongly influenced by government policies that relaxed limitations on trading. Self-imposed restrictions by Christians on use of the day have eased significantly; many people now view Sundays as a 'family day' to be used for relaxation and leisure pursuits. Some forms of employment demand Sunday working, so the individuals concerned do not have any choice in the matter.

If leisure or playing organised games interferes with opportunities for sharing fellowship with the Lord's people, serious questions must be raised about its appropriateness. The issue is most keenly felt when parents have to judge whether or not to allow their children to pursue a Sunday morning sporting event, perhaps at the expense of attending church. Shopping has now become a seven-day-a-week activity; so avoiding the use of Sunday for buying goods should not prove difficult with a little pre-planning.

It is undoubtedly true that the issue of strict Sunday observance is no longer considered to be of central importance to the majority of people in Western society, especially among the younger generation. Many of those who were once insistent on making church attendance a priority, and setting aside the day for worship, quiet reflection and contemplation, seem to have accepted the need to adopt a more balanced view of how to spend Sundays. Churches that organise only one formal service each Sunday may have contributed to the decline in attendance.

It can be reasonably argued that there is a danger of allowing Sunday's unique benefits that God intended for us all, to be so compromised that it has a seriously detrimental impact upon church life, witness and wellbeing. From a different perspective, release from the strict traditions that were once held to be sacrosanct offer Christians greater flexibility in balancing their various responsibilities to family, church and community. Key verse: And [Jesus] said to them, 'Come aside by yourselves to a deserted place and rest a while' (Mark 6:31, NKJV).

12. Should Christians belong to secular clubs, groups or societies? *Commitment to Christ is expressed principally through adopting a sanctified lifestyle, attendance at organised church meetings, practical assistance for the needy, and caring for believers (Galatians 6:10). Involvement in other groups allow for Christians to be 'salt' in society but have the potential to distract from holy living (separation from the world). If activities with non-believers begin to dominate time and absorb resources that would otherwise have been directed towards Kingdom work, there is certainly a need for a re-evaluation of priorities.*

The argument is often put forward that unless Christians associate with unbelievers, there will be few opportunities to share their faith. In truth, spending time with people pursuing worldly activities is unlikely to offer the chance to witness and may have an adverse effect on the believer. Some Christian parents have rued the day that their son or daughter was drawn into companionship with unsuitable friends and gradually absorbed their values and culture, rather than positively influencing them for the Lord Jesus.

Key verses: 'Don't become so well adjusted to your culture that you fit into it without even thinking. Instead, fix your attention on God. You'll be changed from the inside out. Readily recognise what he wants from you and quickly respond to it. Unlike the culture around you, always dragging you down to its level of immaturity, God brings the best out of you, develops well-formed maturity in you' (Romans 12:1–2, MSG).

13. Should Christians drink alcohol or use 'social drugs'?

Total abstinence is rare in society, even among Christians, who argue that the occasional drink or having wine with a meal is acceptable because 'Jesus drank', so should not be the subject of dispute. In fact, the wine referred to in the Bible was normally of very low alcohol content or the alcohol was boiled off completely or simply used to purify water. Drunkenness and drug abuse are serious social problems and an increasing number of people consider being teetotal (i.e., eschewing alcoholic drink completely) to be a responsible position to take. It is estimated that around seventy per cent of crimes are due the adverse influence of alcohol. The Bible denounces being intoxicated ('drunk') and the associated lewd conduct that often follows. The use of so-called social drugs to induce feelings of pleasure and temporary elation has been shown to be a dangerous deceit that can lead to excessive forms of behaviour and further experimentation with more addictive substances.

Key verse: 'Don't be drunk with wine, because that will ruin your life. Instead, be filled with the Holy Spirit' (Ephesians 5:18, NLT).

14. Should younger Christians visit nightclubs and attend 'pop' concerts?
    Young people enjoy having fun with their friends and spending time together. Music plays an important role in their lives, as witnessed by the large number of them wearing headphones to listen to their favourite songs. Unfortunately, nightclubs and music 'pop' concerts and so-called 'raves' are often associated with illicit and godless behaviour, and may be the breeding ground for the introduction of damaging habits. In response to secular attractions, many churches attempt to make alternative youth activities appealing and entertaining, without discarding the spiritual content entirely. In doing so, however, many organisers of church activities struggle to compete with the secular world's glamorous and well-funded events.

Key verse: 'Therefore, come out from among unbelievers and separate yourselves from them, says the Lord. Don't touch their filthy things and I will welcome you' (2 Corinthians 6:17, NLT).

15. Should Christian women have abortions?

Destruction of the unborn is one of the most contentious issues of recent years. Increasingly, people are divided into two opposing factions: either for or against abortion, with little middle ground. The biblical view of the sanctity of life from conception to final death is challenged by some activists, who claim that it is a woman's right to choose whether or not to keep an unborn child. Slogans such as "a woman's right to choose" and "my body, my choice" have been central to the pro-abortion camp's public utterances. Pro-life groups have adjusted their stance on the subject by rightly stressing that both preborn children and their mothers are precious to God and need protection and support. It is regrettable that many pastors in Protestant churches appear uneasy about mentioning the subject for fear of offending any women who may have had an abortion, while the Catholic church is more forthright about protecting unborn life and campaigning for an end to the widespread destruction.

Key verse: 'For you created my inmost being; you knit me together in my mother's womb. I praise you because I am fearfully and wonderfully made' (Psalm 139:13–14a).

16. Should Christians support assisted suicide and euthanasia? *In more recent years, there has been a growth of organisations and pressure groups insisting that it is inhumane to allow a seriously ill person's life to be extended when it could be terminated safely and relatively painlessly. Others argue that improvement in end-of-life (palliative) care is a far better option. In countries where euthanasia (deliberately ending life by medical practitioners) and assisted suicide (facilitating a person to end his or her own life) have been enacted in law, the rate of such deaths has increased dramatically, raising serious questions raised about the pressure on elderly people in particular, and the procedures undertaken to euthanise. Inevitably, the original 'strict safeguards' have been manipulated and legally challenged by supporters of these practices to ease the pathway to ending lives prematurely.*

The Bible is clear that God alone is the author of life; therefore seeking His will in this delicate matter is of fundamental importance. Unfortunately, medical practitioners and large sections of the population rely solely on secular arguments. For example, a common statement is something to the effect: "We wouldn't let a dog suffer unduly, so why do we let people do so when they can be released from pain and misery?" However, this particular argument is invalid because people (not animals) are uniquely made in God's image. While we feel a deep compassion for those who suffer, especially our loved ones, a process that takes God out of the equation will inevitably leave decisions to those who consider Him to be of marginal importance or an irrelevance.

Key verse: 'Just as people are destined to die once, and after that to face judgement' (Hebrews 9:27).

17. Should Christians tell young children the truth about Christmas, the 'Tooth Fairy' and other fantasies?

Fantasy is important for children, as they gradually come to terms with life's complexities. Playing with toys, inventing games and responding to stories all help them to shape thinking and make sense of the world. Gradually, 'imaginary friends' and play-acting are replaced by concrete ideas, as they progress from these early experiences and engage with enduring realities. Reference to fantasy figures, such as Santa Claus (Father Christmas) and the Tooth Fairy may assist the developmental process in much the same way as fairy tales and 'action heroes' do. However, a fundamental difference between telling fantasy stories, as opposed to promoting Santa and fairies, is that the fantasy is detached from the here-and-now, while parents and relatives, whom children trust above anyone else, promote Santa and fairies as a present reality. When the truth about these mythical beings is exposed or admitted, it can cause disappointment and confusion in children's mind as to why they were deceived. Some parents have adopted a middle position by saying that dad becomes Santa for one night, while mum is the Tooth Fairy, but these fabrications may create further confusion.

Key verse: 'Start children off on the way they should go and even when they are old, they will not turn from it' (Proverbs 22:6, NIVUK).

18. Should Christians marry non-Christians or members of other faiths?

There are more women than men who are committed to following Christ. This being the case, a young woman seeking a life partner has limited choice in finding a suitable Christian husband. It is inevitable that love will sometimes blossom between two people, regardless of their commitment to Jesus. Four points are relevant: First, regular mixing in church-based activities with believers of similar age will increase the likelihood of meeting that 'special committed Christian someone', whereas spending too much time socialising with non-Christians will significantly reduce the possibility. Second, although mixed marriages (believer and non-believer) can be fulfilling, they can also create areas of tension, as the wife feels that church life is a priority, while the husband does not share that conviction, though he may not object to her involvement. Third, the husband will have his own social priorities that may clash with the woman's beliefs about appropriate use of time. Fourth, if sons are born, they are more likely to follow in the father's ways and thereby resist being committed to Christ. Although these issues can be resolved, both before and during marriage, they need to be discussed honestly and openly to minimise the possibility of becoming a stumbling block to the relationship or to the woman's faith or both.

Key verse: 'Can two walk together, except they be agreed?' (Amos 3:3, KJV)

19. Should Christians gamble and enter lotteries?

Gambling has become a serious problem in affluent nations and caused considerable grief and despair among those who become addicted. Christians' primary financial commitments (outside of basic commodities and regular expenditure) should be, in order of priority: (a) to their dependents; (b) to the church in which they share regular fellowship; (c) to Christian organisations that espouse biblical principles. While the argument is propounded that spending a small amount of money ('having a flutter') does not do any harm, the principle of being satisfied with God's provision should supersede all other desires. However much believers—especially those who are struggling on low incomes— may be tempted to indulge in gambling occasionally, the determining factor must be if the action is undermining or enhancing their trust in God as Provider.

Key verse: 'People who want to be rich bring temptations to themselves. They are caught in a trap. They begin to want many foolish things that will hurt them. These things ruin and destroy people' (I Timothy 6:8, ERV).

20. Should Christians fight in wars?

Thankfully, the likelihood of becoming involved in serious physical combat has receded in Western nations, though the threat has grown in recent years. In other areas of the world, however, conflict has produced misery and economic collapse, usually caused by an ungodly lust for power, seizure of financial assets or a desire for religious domination. When conflicts occur, the combatants are normally younger males, but the casualties often include large numbers of civilians. Those who insist that war is regrettably necessary to protect cherished freedom and resist tyranny will point to the fact that God sanctioned attacks by Israel on godless nations, and permitted wicked nations to attack and conquer Israel. Pacifists point out that Jesus was the Prince of Peace and encouraged us to love even our enemies. In resolving these differences, it is helpful to distinguish between wars between nations, in which the defence of a country is at stake, and small-scale 'incursions' that can often be remedied through compromise and negotiation.

Key verse: 'If it is possible, so far as it depends on you, live peaceably with all' (Romans 12:18, NRSV).

Insight

It is estimated that as well as responding to questions from his disciples, religious leaders and the general public, the Gospels record that Jesus also posed around one hundred questions. The use of careful questions to make people think or elicit a positive response from them—not to catch them out or embarrass—is a scriptural practice, both to counteract a deliberately difficult question from an enquirer and to direct their thoughts heavenward.

The Prospect of Heaven

Jesus told his disciples: 'In my Father's house are many dwelling places. If it were not so, I would have told you, because I am going there to prepare a place for you. And if I go and prepare a place for you, I will come back again and I will take you to myself, so that where I am you may be also' (John 14:2–3, AMP). It is clear the house to which Jesus referred was a heavenly one not an earthly one. The argument that the promise was only intended for the twelve disciples is shallow, as in that case, heaven would be almost empty! In the revelation given to John, he refers to 'a great multitude which no one could number, of all nations, tribes, peoples and tongues, standing before the throne and before the lamb, clothed with white robes, with palm branches in their hands' (Revelation 7:9, NKJV). The prophecy states that the souls of men and women from every corner of the earth will one day be assembled in the presence of Christ. It should be noted that in John's vision, he refers to bodily presence (wearing white robes and holding branches), not disembodied spirits.

Heaven's whereabouts

On numerous occasions, Jesus referred to God as 'Heavenly Father' or as 'my Father in heaven'. One of the problems associated with the single English word 'heaven' is that it has three possible meanings in the Bible. The common use of the word refers to the physical area of sky above the surface of the earth; for example, reference to 'the heavens' in Psalm 19.

A second use refers to outer space, as introduced in the Book of Genesis at the dawn of time: 'Let there be lights in the firmament of the heavens to divide the day from the night' (1:14, NKJV). In the New Testament, Paul associates heaven with the omnipresent Christ inhabiting the universe: 'And the same one who descended is the one who ascended higher than all the heavens, so that he might fill the entire universe with himself' (Ephesians 4:10, NLT).

The third use of 'heaven' is to describe the place where God dwells. For example, Isaiah had a vision of God on His heavenly throne and described what he saw: 'He was sitting on a lofty throne and the train of his robe filled the temple' (Isaiah 6:1b, NLT).

The different meanings of heaven as (1) the earth's atmosphere; (2) space; and (3) God's abode, has led to the erroneous idea of God's dwelling being 'up in the sky', a misconception reinforced by the ascension of Jesus when he rose into the air until hidden by a cloud (Acts Chapter 1). The concept of God being in a fixed location is questionable, as God inhabits eternity (past, present and future) so He cannot be pinned down to a single identifiable location, despite the plain way in which it is described in the Bible for the sake of our finite minds. Even so, in the revelation given to John, he describes the place of God's abode in graphic detail: 'Then as I looked, I saw a door standing open in heaven, and the same voice I had heard before spoke to me like a trumpet blast. The voice said, "Come up here, and I will show you what must happen after this." And instantly I was in the Spirit; and I saw a throne in heaven and someone sitting on it' (Revelation 4:1–2, NLT).

It seems that God has His *seat of power* in Heaven (capital 'H') but occupies every sphere, including, by His Spirit, the innermost being of a believer. King Solomon expressed his sense of bewilderment, as he attempted to explain where God dwells, first by asking a question that unbeknown to him had prophetic insight about the coming of Jesus: 'But will God really dwell on earth?' (I Kings 8:27, NIVUK). In the same verse, Solomon goes on to express the awesome truth that 'the heavens, even the highest heaven, cannot contain you'. God responds graphically to the question of his whereabouts by speaking through Isaiah: 'Heaven is my throne and the earth is my footstool' (66:1).

To add to the fascination of Heaven, Paul refers to a remarkable experience in which he was given a privileged glimpse of Paradise or the 'third heaven', as he describes the setting. As might be expected, the experience was overwhelming for Paul, who struggled to describe what he had seen: 'And I know that this man [i.e., Paul] was taken up to Paradise. I don't know if he was in his body or away from his body, but he heard things that he is not able to explain. He heard things that no one is allowed to tell' (2 Corinthians 12:3–4, ERV). Paul's revelation indicates that 'Paradise' presently exists and is not merely a future creation or prospect. Jesus referred to the Kingdom of Heaven (Kingdom of God) as being a *present* reality for believers that is inextricably linked with their *future* following death or when Christ returns. In other words, being part of God's Kingdom on earth through faith in Jesus Christ is a necessary prerequisite for our eternal destiny with Him in the heavenly abode.

As a precursor to Heaven, Jesus explained how the end of the world would come about: 'And I assure you that the time is coming, indeed it's here now, when the dead will hear my voice—the voice of the Son of God. And those who listen will live. ... Indeed, the time is coming when all the dead in their graves will hear the voice of God's Son, and they will rise again. Those who have done good will rise to experience eternal life, and those who have continued in evil will rise to experience judgment' (John 5:25–29, selected verses, NLT). It should be noted that Jesus explained that: (a) the dead will hear his voice; (b) only those souls those who listen will live; (c) every person will rise, not just believers; and (d) there is a vital distinction between, and eternal implications for, those who 'do good' and those *continuing* to do evil.

The emphasis on 'continued in evil' is significant, as Jesus's promises would be a fabrication if the occupants of Heaven were those who had never been sinful—the 'many mansions' of which Jesus spoke would remain unoccupied! There is also a suggestion in Jesus's words that there might be a 'second chance' for souls if they are willing to listen and repent, even at this final moment in time.

Death and Heaven

Death may be defined in three ways, all of which involve some form of severance:

(1) Spiritual death in which people choose to separate themselves from God by rejecting Him and His provision of salvation through the Son, described by Paul as being 'dead in trespasses and sins' (Ephesians 2:1, NKJV).

(2) Physical death when the soul is uncoupled from the body: 'It is appointed for men to die once, but after this the judgement' (Hebrews 9:27, NKJV).

(3) Eternal death in which the soul is parted from God for all time: 'But the cowardly, unbelieving, abominable, murderers, sexually immoral, sorcerers, idolaters, and all liars shall have their part in the lake which burns with fire and brimstone, which is the second death' (Revelation 21:18, NKJV).

The key message of *Totally Christian* is to ensure that we address (1) above, such that when (2) takes place, as it will for everyone, we avoid the horror of (3). The importance of being found 'in Christ' becomes sharply defined when these realities are squarely faced.

Paul dwells in some depth on the way in which the present era will end after the second appearance of Christ ('Second Coming/Second Advent'). For instance in the first letter to Christians in Corinth: 'It will happen in a moment, in the blink of an eye, when the last trumpet is blown. For when the trumpet sounds, those who have died will be raised to live forever. And we who are living will also be transformed' (15:52, NLT). We can only imagine what the 'last trumpet' will sound like, but it will doubtless exceed in volume anything that humans can produce and penetrate every corner of the globe. Paul highlights three aspects of this monumental event: (1) It will be sudden. (2) The dead will be raised to live eternally. (3) Those still living will also be transformed. Paul does not describe the transformation in detail but in the following verse goes on to explain: 'For our dying bodies must be transformed into bodies that will never die; our mortal bodies must be transformed into immortal bodies'.

The question is often raised about what happens to believers in the instant that their physical body dies. Do deceased Christians immediately find themselves 'in Heaven' or 'in Paradise' or 'asleep' until the last trumpet sounds and Christ returns to make all things new? Jesus's words to the dying thief on the cross (Luke 23:43) are frequently quoted as proof that there is an immediate state after death called Paradise that exists for those who repent of sin and trust him for their future. Significantly, John records Jesus's reference to Paradise as a place of reward: 'To everyone who is victorious, I will give fruit from the tree of life in the paradise of God' (Revelation 2:7, NLT), though whether Paradise should begin with a capital letter to indicate a specific location or a small case letter ('paradise') to indicate a descriptive term is difficult to determine, as some translations (e.g., NKJV) employ a capital and others do not.

Despite the uncertainty, it is reasonable to surmise that Paradise is the abiding-place for the spirits of believers prior to the time when Christ returns to create a new heaven and earth, at which time they will be raised with new spiritual bodies. Whether Paradise and Heaven are one and the same place remains something of a mystery. The only certainty is that believers can be confident that they will be in God's secure keeping when this life ends, for which we should give Christ all the thanks and praise.

A further question concerns the physical appearance and consciousness of those who reside in Heaven. Will we recognise one another? Will we have physical bodies? Will we remember events that took place on earth? Scriptural passages that help us to answer these questions include this section from Paul's letter to the Philippians: 'But our citizenship is in heaven. And we eagerly await a Saviour from there, the Lord Jesus Christ who, by the power that enables him to bring everything under his control, will transform our lowly bodies so that they will be like his glorious body' (3:20–21, NIVUK). Paul's divinely inspired message clearly states four certainties:

(1) Believers' natural habitat is with Christ in Heaven.
(2) Christ will return to earth from Heaven.
(3) The chaotic earth will be brought under divine control.
(4) Our bodies will be transformed to resemble Jesus's body.

The fourth point reveals that we will not be 'spirits' floating about in a nebulous state but will ultimately take a recognisable, immortalised form.

Jesus's reference to a deceased rich man named Lazarus and to the Old Testament character, Abraham, who lived some 2000 years before Jesus came to earth (Luke 16:19–31), together with the event on the 'Mount of Transfiguration' in which Moses and Elijah appear (Luke 9:28–36), all point to the fact that physical recognition is possible beyond the grave, despite the fact that our earthly bodies have 'seen corruption'. As Jesus promised to prepare a heavenly home for believers, it is difficult to conceive of a situation where people did not know one another or were unable to share fellowship. Although none of these references are specific in confirming that we will be able to recognise others, the scriptural evidence strongly supports such a truth.

Whether there will be memories of time on earth is a more perplexing issue. On the one hand, the deceased man, referred to as Dives in some translations, asked if his brothers back on earth could be warned, so he was clearly able to remember them and their attitude towards the poor and needy. It must be noted, however, that Dives was in torment, so regrets and painful thoughts of life on earth would form part of his soulful agony. By contrast, Lazarus, in his blissful state, would have no such emotional turmoil. Even here on earth in its 'fallen' condition, time tends to soften and heal unhappy memories. Heaven is described as a place without pain or suffering, so if it is true that saints *can* remember events and people from their earthly sojourn, the memories will be free from anguish and regret.

Insight

Those whose names are written in the Lamb's Book of Life (Revelation Chapter 20) do not need to fear the future or be concerned about precisely what will happen to them. Through faith in Christ and his blood shed on the cross for their sins, they are destined to live eternally in God's presence.

Heavenly minded

It is sometimes alleged that some Christians are too heavenly minded to be of much earthly use, the implication of which is that a fascination—even an obsession—with what is promised beyond this life can create an apathy about grappling with present realities. While there may be an element of truth attached to this assertion, it is based on the false premise that a focus on what follows our time on earth has a detrimental effect on the way we behave and engage with the issues and challenges during this life. In fact, acknowledging that one day we will have to face Almighty God, where our time on earth will be fully revealed, should be a spur to wholehearted commitment and submission to His will and purpose, not sanctioning indifference or a 'head-in-the-clouds' mentality.

It is reasonable to surmise that two groups of people are likely to dwell obsessively on the prospect of Heaven. The first group consists of people whose lives are permanently miserable and offer little prospect of improvement. The second group are non-Christians who hold a fanciful view of Heaven as the ultimate destiny for everyone except the most perverse and wicked. In effect, they anticipate Heaven as being a place reserved for those who have lived generally decent lives without serious misdemeanours, which contrasts sharply with Jesus's description of the narrow road that leads to life and the need for repentance and righteousness.

No one was more rooted in the realities of this world than Jesus, yet his ministry was abounding with references to the Kingdom of Heaven (used solely in Matthew's Gospel account) and the Kingdom of God (used by all the Gospel writers, notably in parables). The distinction between the two uses of 'Kingdom' is not the main subject of this discourse, other than to note that in Matthew's Gospel (19:23–24), he records that Jesus uses both expressions when speaking on the same occasion. Similarly, in parallel accounts of the same event, while Matthew uses 'Kingdom of Heaven', Mark and Luke use 'Kingdom of God'. It may be the case that Matthew preferred using 'Heaven' rather than 'God' to avoid upsetting his largely Jewish audience, who would consider it inappropriate to refer to the name of God directly in this way. The important point is to emphasise that Jesus constantly cited Heaven when teaching about repentance, prayer, spiritual growth, wisdom, rewards, thankfulness and the starting point for his future return to earth. The mutual use of Heaven and God with reference to the Kingdom underlines the fact that the two are inseparably linked.

End and beginning

From a human perspective, Heaven marks the end of a Christian's earthly existence and the beginning of eternal life. As noted above, Paul refers to believers in the Philippian Church as 'citizens in heaven' where the Lord Jesus Christ lives, so it could be argued that heavenly existence begins the moment a person is born from above by the Spirit of God. Whatever the validity of this explanation, we can be certain that our citizenship is secured when we accept the offer of salvation, much as holding a ticket to a concert is a guarantee for eventual entry into the arena when it is presented at the door.

The writer of Hebrews encourages his principally Jewish Christian readers to have confidence in Jesus, who has returned to the heavenly abode: 'So then, since we have a Great High Priest who has entered heaven—Jesus, the Son of God—let us hold firmly to what we believe' (4:14, NLT). Jesus was in every sense Son of Man and Son of God, whose mission was in essence to 'bridge the gap' between earth and heaven, such that the desire conveyed through the prayer that he taught his disciples: 'Thy Kingdom come, Thy will be done on earth, as it is in heaven', is presently being fulfilled and one day will be consummated.

Jesus died so that when he comes again, he will come 'on the clouds of heaven with power and great glory' (Matthew 24:30, 26:64, various translations) to judge the living and the dead but crucially to take to be with him in Heaven those who have trusted him as Saviour and long for his appearing. Believers can take great encouragement from Paul, as he quotes from Isaiah 64:4: 'No one has ever seen, no one has ever heard, no one has ever imagined what God has prepared for those who love Him' (I Corinthians 2:9, ERV). What a mighty promise!

Focusing on Heaven becomes highly significant when we acknowledge that there will be a day of reckoning for every person in the world, including the person you sit next to in the office, work alongside in the factory, chat to at the school gate, and watch stacking the shelves in the local supermarket. To grow deeper with Jesus, we need to be passionate about saving souls by helping our family, friends and neighbours to love God and obey His commandments. As children of the King, believers have a responsibility to encourage those with whom we have contact to make Jesus the priority in their lives and place their trust in the One who is the only guarantee of life everlasting. Such is the responsibility and privilege of every child of God.

Summary

In this concluding chapter of *Totally Christian*, I have offered a variety of perspectives on ways in which believers can grow in their knowledge and understanding of wholehearted commitment to Christ, including the need for regular cleansing through confession, maturing in faith, witnessing, confronting unbelief, and responding to difficult questions. In seeking to discern the narrow path and walk in the righteousness of Christ, I stressed that his followers should be eagerly awaiting his reappearance at the end of time (the 'Second Advent').

As we wait for his appearing, a believer's life must show genuine humility; a willingness to embrace fresh revelation from God; seeking His guidance every step of the way; abiding in Christ; and delving deep into His revealed word, the

Bible, in order to stand firm against secular and ungodly influences. I have placed special emphasis on the importance of encouraging men to commit their lives to Christ, and ways in which church leaders and members may need to adjust their thinking and approach to facilitate a positive, God-glorifying outcome to evangelism.

I concluded the chapter and the whole book by focusing on the anticipation of heaven and eternal glory, which is the privilege and unmerited prospect for every true believer in Jesus as Saviour and Lord. So we can say confidently with Paul: 'I have fought the good fight, I have finished the race. I have kept the faith. From now on, there is reserved for me the crown of righteousness, which the Lord, the righteous judge, will give me on that day, and not only to me but also to all who have longed for his appearing' (2 Timothy 4:7–8, NRSV).

What do you believe?

1. I believe in serving Christ but endeavour to balance my commitment with opportunities to enjoy other pleasures and experiences outside church life.
2. I believe that Christians either grow in grace and love for God or experience spiritual decline.
3. I believe it is possible to emulate Jesus's earthly existence if we ask for the help of his Spirit and obey what he commands.
4. I believe that our life and witness should be principally directed towards serving others.
5. I believe that if you are asked a difficult question, you should refer it to a leader or elder, rather than stumble over answering it.
6. I believe that church leadership (preaching and teaching) is largely the responsibility of men.
7. I believe it should be a priority to further your knowledge and understanding of what the Bible says about difficult human issues.
8. I believe that there is a place reserved in Heaven for all those who acknowledge and love God by trusting in Jesus Christ.

Appendix

Doctrinal synopsis

1. The sin nature ('original sin') is present in everyone from conception to the grave.

2. Jesus Christ came from his place alongside God the Father, voluntarily lived as a man on earth and freely gave his life upon a Roman cross. He suffered the sort of death reserved for the worst type of criminal, sacrificing his life as a perfect offering to atone (pay the price) for the sins committed by every person: past, present and future.

3. Even the most morally pure person cannot claim to be worthy to receive the free gift of eternal life through Jesus Christ's death because no one fully acknowledges or loves God in the way that He demands and deserves. Thus, the Old Testament prophet, Isaiah, describes the way in which people's sinful condition taints even the right things they do: 'We are all infected and impure with sin. When we display our righteous 'deeds, they are nothing but filthy rags' (64:6a, NLT).

4. The offer of salvation is a gift from God to all mankind but it requires a positive response from every person through repentance and turning to Christ to make salvation a reality and not merely an interesting proposition.

5. People who respond in faith to God's gracious offer of salvation by listening to godly preaching, personal testimony, reading about or hearing the truth spoken, or through supernatural means, such as dreams and other Holy Spirit instigated manifestations, will be saved from sin.

6. Christ invites our allegiance to Him but does not coerce us to respond to his offer.

7. Actively rejecting God's way of salvation through the death of His Son has serious present and future consequences. The Gospel writer, John, records Jesus's words: 'And anyone who believes in God's Son has eternal life. Anyone who doesn't obey the Son will never experience eternal life but remains under God's angry judgement' (3:36, NLT).

8. No one can be saved by undertaking good deeds (works) but doing so in obedience to Christ and for God's glory impacts on his or her eternal reward.

The sort of people that Satan wants in the church

- *Academic* Christians, who know the Bible of God but don't know the God of the Bible.
- *Scrooge* Christians, who only submit a small proportion of their time and resources to God.
- *Nominal* Christians, who do not make the effort to seek God's will and purpose through prayer, study of the Bible and interaction with believers.
- *Stunted* Christians, who are prepared to settle for minimal commitment to Christ.
- *Stagnant* Christians, who are resistant to any revitalising work of the Holy Spirit.
- *Historic* Christians, who prefer to reminisce than to look ahead.
- *Confrontational* Christians, who prefer to challenge people abruptly, including fellow believers.
- *Self-centred* Christians, who focus on their own feelings, needs and concerns, rather than being attentive to those of other people.
- *Temperamental* Christians, who are unpredictable and lacking in grace.
- *Spectator* Christians, who are content to sit back and watch other people working and taking responsibility.
- *Critical* Christians, who are eager to find fault and reluctant to commend fellow believers.
- *Envious* Christians, who are resentful when God chooses to bless others.

The sort of people God wants in the church

- Those who desire to know Him intimately.
- Those who are wholeheartedly submissive to Him.
- Those who genuinely desire to discover His will for their lives.
- Those whose hearts are open to a fresh anointing of the Holy Spirit.
- Those who pray before they act rather than act first and pray afterwards.
- Those who seek to walk in step with the Spirit along new pathways of faith.
- Those who are prayerfully and practically interested in the needs of others.

- Those who, in deep humility, seek to love others as God loves them.
- Those who are consistently approachable, caring and compassionate.
- Those who encourage and support others in their endeavour.
- Those who share other people's joys and sorrows.
- Those who celebrate the talents and spiritual victories of others.
- Those who radiate the love of Christ.
- Those who live and work and persevere in the light of Jesus's imminent return.